THE ALAND ISLANDS QUESTION:

ITS SETTLEMENT BY THE LEAGUE OF NATIONS

The Aland Islands Question:

Its Settlement by the League of Nations

by James Barros

New Haven and London, Yale University Press, 1968

Library of Congress catalog card number: 68–27746

Designed by John O. C. McCrillis,
set in Baskerville type,
and printed in the United States of America by
The Colonial Press Inc., Clinton, Massachusetts.
Distributed in Great Britain, Europe, Asia, and
Africa by Yale University Press Ltd., London; in
Canada by McGill University Press, Montreal; and
in Latin America by Centro Interamericano de Libros
Académicos, Mexico City.

To A and A

Contents

Maps

Preface

Prior to the First German War, if one may borrow a phrase from Sir Harold Nicolson, the process of international conciliation was generally ad hoc in nature and buttressed by few permanently established organs dedicated to achieving peaceful settlement under the auspices of an international organization. Indeed, it was only as late as The Hague Peace Conferences in 1899 and 1907 that it was decided that unilateral moves by a state offering its good offices or its mediation in a dispute were not to be considered an unfriendly act. The establishment of the League of Nations and its successor, the United Nations, has of course helped to fill the gap. In what manner and to what extent the labors of these organizations have been able to accomplish this will be examined in the pages that follow by an investigation in time and space of one of the League's earliest attempts—a successful one—at political conciliation and mediation.

Fortunately, inaccessibility of Finnish and Swedish materials has been more than offset by the rich information that is to be culled from the reports of the British diplomatic missions and especially from those of the British peace delegation at Paris in 1919, a richness of information repeated on the American side and including the meetings of the Paris Peace Conference's Baltic Commission. To these are added the League's Geneva archives, which help appreciably. All of these materials, supplemented by private papers, clearly show how the Aland Islands dispute was settled and how the new world organization was used or manipulated by all parties to assist them in attaining their domestic and international policy goals. The role played by the League Secretariat and the actions of its Secretary-General are also discussed.

The belief in 1919 that the League had opened a new era in international relations and that new standards and new impulses would influence states in their relations one with the other was strengthened by the peaceful settlement achieved in the Aland question. Whether the Aland settlement was due to the League's presence or to considerations more fundamental in nature will, it is hoped, become obvious. That the League and, for that matter, the United Nations have had a role to play in international relations cannot be denied except by the most cynical or the most blind. The possibilities of the role, however, and the limitations that burden it become quite obvious in an examination of the events leading to the settlement of the Aland Islands question.

Acknowledgments

I would like to thank the American Philosophical Society of Philadelphia, the Barnard College and the Dartmouth College Research Committees, and the Comparative Studies Center of Dartmouth College, whose support made it possible to examine the widely scattered materials that comprise this study.

Access to the papers of Herbert A. L. Fisher and quotation from these papers was kindly made possible by his daughter, Mrs. Mary Bennett, Principal, St. Hilda's College, Oxford; to the papers of Frank L. Polk by the Sterling Library, Yale University; and to the papers of Henry White by his family. Special thanks are due Mr. Norman Field, Deputy Librarian of the United Nations Library, Palais des Nations, Geneva, who though understaffed and overworked assisted me in my endeavors especially with access to the unpublished archives of the League of Nations. The same also goes to the institutions, both public and private, which assisted me, including the National Archives of the United States and the Library of Congress, both in Washington, D.C., and to the Public Record Office and The British Museum, both in London. I am deeply obligated to the ladies in the Reference Department of Baker Library, Dartmouth College, and especially to Miss Virginia Close and Mrs. Valerie Mullen, as well as to Mrs. Nadezhda Koroton and Mrs. Vera Vance, Thomas Bertleman, and Ivor Holmqvist for assistance in Russian and Swedish materials. A special note of thanks is due my Dartmouth College researchers, Peter Baumbusch and Gerhard Oswald.

James Barros

Barnard College
Columbia University
New York
December 1967

Abbreviations

Balfour Papers	Lord Balfour, Personal papers and letters, Department of Manuscripts, The British Museum, London.
BrDOW, 1898–1914	Great Britain, Foreign Office, *British Documents on the Origins of the War, 1898–1914,* ed. G. P. Gooch and Harold Temperley (London, H. M. Stationery Office, 1926–1938), 11 vols.
Bulletin périodique de la presse scandinave	France, Ministère des Affaires Étrangères, *Bulletin périodique de la presse scandinave.*
DBrFP, 1919–1939	Great Britain, Foreign Office, *Documents on British Foreign Policy, 1919–1939,* ed. E. L. Woodward, Rohan Butler, and J. P. T. Bury (London, H. M. Stationery Office, 1947—), 1st ser., 13 vols.
Fisher Papers	Herbert A. L. Fisher, Diary, personal papers, and letters, Bodleian Library, Oxford University.
Die internationalen Beziehungen	Russia, Komissiia po Izdaniiu Dokumentov Epokhi Imperializma, *Die internationalen Beziehungen im Zeitalter des Imperialismus; Dokumente aus den Archiven der zarischen und der provisorischen Regierung,* ed. Otto Hoetzsch (Berlin, R. Hobbing, 1931–1943), 1st ser., 5 vols.; 2d ser., 3 vols.; 3rd ser., 4 vols.
Krasnyi arkhiv	Dnevnik Ministerstva Inostrannykh del za 1915–1916 gg (The journal of the Ministry of Foreign Affairs for 1915–1916 [The journal of Baron Mavriky Fabianovich von Shilling], *Krasnyi arkhiv* (Red Archives), *32* (1929).

Lansing Papers	Robert Lansing, Diary, personal papers and letters, Manuscripts Division, Library of Congress, Washington, D.C.
LNA	League of Nations Archives, United Nations Library, Palais des Nations, Geneva, Switzerland.
NA	National Archives of the United States, Washington, D.C.
Polk Papers	Frank L. Polk, Diary, personal papers and letters, Sterling Library, Yale University.
PRFRUS	U.S. Department of State, *Papers Relating to the Foreign Relations of the United States . . .* (Washington, D.C., Government Printing Office).
PRFRUS 1919. PPC	U.S. Department of State, *Papers Relating to the Foreign Relations of the United States 1919. The Paris Peace Conference* (Washington, D.C., Government Printing Office, 1942–1947), 13 vols.
PRO	Public Record Office, London.
White Papers	Henry White, Personal papers and letters, Manuscripts Division, Library of Congress, Washington, D.C.
Wilson Papers	Woodrow Wilson, Personal papers and letters, Manuscripts Division, Library of Congress, Washington, D.C.

CHAPTER 1

The Aland Islands' Servitude

The Treaty of Frederikshamn

The modern history of the Aland Islands (Ahuenanmaa) falls into three distinct periods: Swedish occupation from 1157 to 1809; Russian occupation from 1809 to 1917; and Finnish control from 1917 to the present. These varying occupations make it clear that the key factors determining possession of the Aland Islands have been geography and the struggle for control of the Baltic. During the seventeenth century a vigorous foreign policy, especially under Gustavus Adolphus (1594–1632) and his successors, had achieved for Sweden almost complete domination of the Baltic. By the early eighteenth century the continual clash between Sweden and Russia had intensified over whether the Baltic was to be a Swedish or a Russian lake. Exhausted by its wars and faced by a resurgent Russia under Peter the Great, Sweden found herself unable to resist the increasing Russian pressure.

In the struggles that followed, the strategic importance of the Aland Islands was underlined. In 1714 they were occupied for the first time by Russia under Peter the Great and were quickly converted into a naval station from which attacks were mounted on the Swedish coast.[1] This Russian occupation, however, was short-lived, for, under Article 5 of the 1721 Peace Treaty of Nystad (Uusikaupunki), Finland, along with the Aland Islands —not specifically mentioned in the treaty—was restored to Sweden.[2]

Further Swedish defeats followed in the wars of 1741–43 and

1. Carl Hallendorff and Adolf Schück, *History of Sweden,* trans. Lajla Yapp (London, Cassell, 1929), pp. 207–305; Great Britain, Foreign Office Historical Section Handbooks, *The Åland Islands* (London, H. M. Stationery Office, 1920), pp. 14–15.

2. Jean Dumont, *Corps universel diplomatique* (Amsterdam, 1731), *8,* Pt. II, 36–37; Hallendorff and Schück, p. 317.

1788–90; and in the 1743 Peace Treaty of Åbo (Turku), Sweden yielded considerable Finnish territory. It was, however, the campaign of 1808–09 that finally led to Russian acquisition of the Aland Islands. This war was sparked by the refusal of Sweden to join Napoleon's Continental System. Rebuffed by the Swedes, Napoleon at the Congress of Erfurt (1808) consented to the complete incorporation of Finland into the Czarist Empire. Assured of French support, the Russians attacked. The Swedes, lacking British support, could offer little resistance and succumbed; all of Finland as well as the Aland Islands was occupied.[3] Undoubtedly aware of Napoleon's remark that "Aland is the key to Stockholm,"[4] the instructions given the Swedish commissioners in the peace negotiations "laid stress on the fact that they might, if the worst came to worst, agree to the cession of Finland, but *not* to that of the Aaland Islands; the frontier was to be traced to the east of Aaland, so that Aaland should remain Swedish 'as it had been since ancient times.' "[5] True to their instructions, the Swedish negotiators vainly "insisted upon the fact that the Åland [Islands] has never been anything other than a Swedish province and that loss of Finland should not entail that of the archipelago."

Fully aware that the islands were important for the defense of Finland, the Russian commissioners were not moved by the Swedish appeal and curtly replied: "We are not concerned with old Swedish frontiers, but with new Russian frontiers."[6] An attempt to obtain assurances that the islands would not be fortified was likewise dismissed as a humiliating restriction on Russia.[7] Thus under the Treaty of Frederikshamn both Finland and the Aland Islands were ceded to the Czar.[8]

3. Hallendorff and Schück, pp. 329, 350–53, 359–62; Great Britain, Foreign Office Historical Section Handbooks, *The Åland Islands,* pp. 15–16.

4. As quoted in J. Hampden Jackson, *Finland* (New York, Macmillan, 1940), p. 119.

5. League of Nations, *Official Journal,* spec. suppl. no. 1 (Aug. 1920), p. 16.

6. *PRFRUS 1919. PPC,* 7, 521.

7. J. O. Söderhjelm, *Démilitarisation et neutralisation des îles d'Aland en 1856 et 1921* (Helsingfors, 1928), pp. 87–88; League of Nations, *Official Journal,* spec. suppl. no. 3 (Oct. 1920), p. 17.

8. G. F. de Martens, *Nouveau recueil de traités* (Gottingue, Librairie de Dieterich, 1817), *1,* 23; Great Britain, Foreign Office, *British and Foreign State Papers* (London, Ridgway, 1841), *1,* 341.

Though the Russian–Swedish struggle for control of the Baltic had ended, the desire of the Swedes for security coincided with the interests of other nations—especially Great Britain—to maintain a balance of power in the Baltic and to prevent the area from being turned into a Russian lake.

Having used the Aland Islands as a military base against the Swedes, the Russians were well aware of their strategic importance, not only for the defense of Finland but also for control of the Baltic, especially domination of the Gulf of Bothnia. Thus, not too long after the islands were ceded the Russians began to plan and build fortifications. Sensitive to this development, "representations" were made by the British government about the "undesirability of such fortifications," and the Russians "undertook to discontinue them." [9]

But by 1834 the Russians were again building fortifications on the Aland Islands. Rising British–Russian tension during this period and the fear that war might bring an English fleet into the Baltic compelled the Russians to fortify Bomarsund on Aland, the largest island in the group, commanding the great bay of Aland. The British, for their part, in November of 1833 alerted the Swedes to the danger that arose from any Russian fortifications in the Aland Islands. Whatever the British hoped to gain by this warning never materialized. Fearful of its great neighbor and undoubtedly wishing to remain neutral in any British–Russian clash, Sweden expressed "its full confidence in the honesty of Russia." [10]

The Paris Treaty of 1856

Though no war commenced in 1834 Russia maintained her fortifications on Aland. By the 1850's a "formidable fortress" built of granite stood at Bomarsund.[11] Understandably, these Russian in-

9. Hugo Vallentin, "Sweden and the Åland Islands," *The New Europe*, 6(21 Feb. 1918), 185.

10. Erik Sjoestedt, *La question des îles d'Aland* (Paris, Grasset, 1919), p. 14. See the dispatch of January 8, 1834, from Count Gustavus Wetterstedt, the Swedish Foreign Minister, to Baron Nils Palmstierna, the Swedish minister in Russia in ibid., pp. 14–15n.

11. Vallentin, "Sweden and the Åland Islands," 185; Léouzon le Duc, *Les îles d'Aland* (Paris, Hachette, 1854), pp. 88–89.

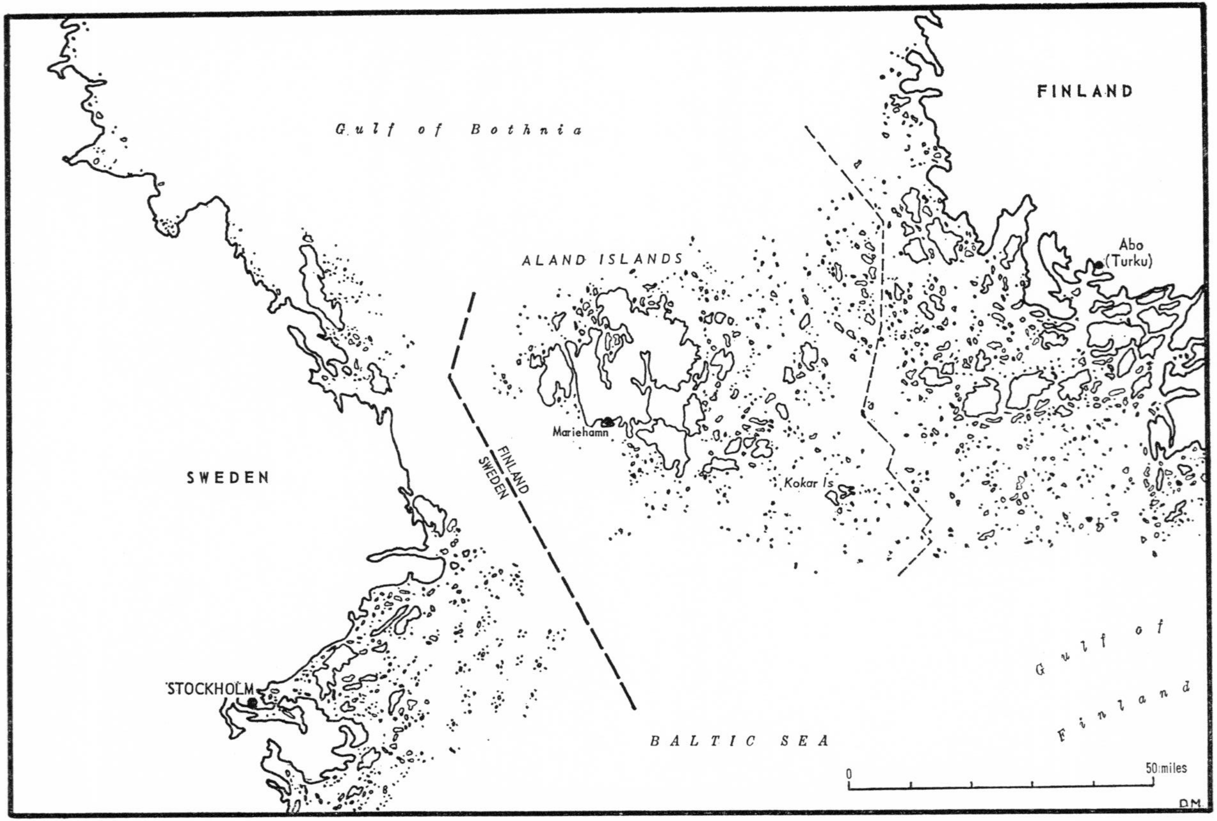

Map 1. The Aland Islands

stallations "were eyed with fear" by the Swedish government.[12] Such fears, however, were premature. The fort at Bomarsund proved rather weak and was easily destroyed in August of 1854 during the Crimean War by an Anglo-French force assisted by Admiral Sir Charles Napier's Baltic squadron.[13]

The British government hoped that with the conquest of Bomarsund, Sweden would commit herself against Russia.[14] However, King Oscar had no intentions of supporting the Anglo-French forces "without clearly expressed guarantees." [15] He desired first Anglo-French military support, restoration of Finland to Sweden, an Anglo-French guarantee after its incorporation into the Swedish kingdom, and Austria's adherence to the treaty. After extended negotiations these conditions were rejected by the Allies.[16] King Oscar insisted on these conditions in spite of the strong pro-British and pro-French lean of Swedish public opinion. As the King made it clear in an interview with Admiral Napier, "neither he nor his people required conquest, even of the Aland Islands, whilst the neutrality of Sweden was secured. His position was delicate, and he would remain as he was." [17] Regardless of the King's attitude, constant pressure was applied on Sweden to enter the war against Russia.

The Swedes, sensitive to the Russian menace and to their isolated position in the Baltic, would consider entering the war only after Austria had declared herself. This was a clever Swedish attempt to skirt the issue, for Stockholm was undoubtedly aware that Austria had no intentions of committing herself against

12. Franklin D. Scott, *The United States and Scandinavia* (Cambridge, Mass., Harvard University Press, 1960), p. 212; Hallendorff and Schück, p. 376.

13. Elers Napier, *The Life and Correspondence of Admiral Sir Charles Napier* (London, Hurst & Blackett, 1862), *2*, 276–90; H. Noel Williams, *The Life and Letters of Admiral Sir Charles Napier* (London, Hutchinson, 1917), pp. 321–29.

14. Williams, p. 316.

15. Söderhjelm, p. 93.

16. *BrDOW, 1898–1914, 8,* 81; E. Tarlé, "La diplomatie pendant la guerre de Crimée et le congrès de Paris (1853–1856)," in Vladimir P. Potemkin, ed., *Histoire de la diplomatie,* trans. Xenia Pamphilova and Michel Eristov (Paris, Librairie de Médicis, 1946), *I,* p. 450.

17. Napier, *2,* 242. The last phrase in the first sentence on "neutrality" does not appear in Williams, p. 290.

Russia at this time, except in conjunction with Prussia, who in turn had every intention of staying out of the conflict.[18]

When she was asked, Sweden refused to occupy the islands after they had been cleared of Russian troops. To take the islands, she correctly replied to the British minister, Arthur Magenis, would be a hostile act toward Russia.[19] A similar proposal by the French received the same answer.[20] In the end, Sweden's fear of Russia and strong desire to remain neutral thwarted all attempts to draw her into the struggle during this period.[21]

Though the Swedes had refused to occupy the islands, their interest in them continued. On June 3 of the following year, 1855, the Swedish minister in London pointed out to the Prime Minister, Lord Palmerston, that it would be important in the peace negotiations, not only for Sweden but also for Europe, to restore the islands to Sweden. If this proved impossible, then guarantees were to be given against reconstruction of the fortifications destroyed during the war.[22] But Palmerston was only willing to promise Sweden defensive support.[23] Spurred by the fall of Sevastopol in September and desirous of protecting themselves against future Russian designs, King Oscar and his ministers accepted Lord Palmerston's proposal. Thus there was concluded with the Allies in November of 1855, during the course of the Crimean War, a treaty which, as the preamble so nicely put it, was undertaken "with a view to secure the integrity of the United Kingdoms of Sweden and Norway." For Sweden it ensured British and French support in case of a Russian attack, though it created for her no corresponding obligation if Britain and France were attacked by Russia. Therefore, it was in no way a treaty of alliance. The treaty restricted Sweden only by denying her the

18. Williams, p. 313; Napier, *2*, 266, 272; A. W. Ward and G. P. Gooch, eds., *The Cambridge History of British Foreign Policy, 1783–1919* (Cambridge, Eng., The University Press, 1922), *2*, 377–79.

19. Williams, p. 334.

20. Söderhjelm, p. 93.

21. Albin Cullberg, *La politique du roi Oscar I pendant la guerre de Crimée* (Stockholm, Författarens, 1912), *1*, 58–100.

22. Söderhjelm, p. 93.

23. *BrDOW, 1898–1914, 8,* 81–82.

right to make territorial cessions or to confer any right of pasturage or fishery to Russia in Sweden and Norway.[24]

The conclusion of the treaty coincided with increasing Allied successes and with Austria's decision to take a more active role in mediating the conflict. With the war running strongly against Russia, King Oscar was more than willing to abandon his cautious policy and exploit the opportunity presented by an Allied victory, thus recovering Finland and increasing Sweden's security vis-à-vis Russia. But he was too late. Negotiations to end the conflict began before Oscar could join the Allied coalition. Even though unsuccessful in joining the winning side, Sweden because of her treaty arrangements with the Allies was in a strong position to press for protection of what she considered her vital interests.

Upon hearing of the cessation of hostilities, Oscar wrote immediately to Napoleon III a personal letter in which Swedish desires over the Baltic were presented. According to the King, Stockholm desired a limitation of Russian naval forces in the Baltic and White Seas, restitution of the Aland Islands to Sweden or their neutralization under the collective guarantee of France, England, and Sweden, and prohibition of Russian fortifications along the Finnish coast west and north of Sveaborg (Suomenlinna).

It became more and more evident, as the preliminary discussions progressed, that the Aland Islands would be a topic for discussion at the forthcoming peace negotiations. Near the end of January 1856 the Danish minister in London reported that the Foreign Secretary, Lord Clarendon, considered as absolutely necessary, if a peace were to be concluded, a promise by Russia not to reconstruct the fortress of Bomarsund. Weakened by the struggle and in no position to resist, the Russians did not consider this prospective prohibition an impossible demand.

To present their case the Swedes selected their most accomplished diplomat, Baron Ludwig Manderström, as delegate for the Paris Peace Conference, scheduled to open on February 25,

24. Edward Hertslet, *The Map of Europe by Treaty* (London, Butterworths, 1875), 2, 1241–42. For negotiations leading to the treaty see Cullberg, 2, 33–80.

1856. Upon his arrival in Paris, Manderström found that though the English were warm to Swedish desires, the French were not.[25] Indeed, the English probably viewed Swedish designs for protection against Russia as a useful tool to be manipulated in furthering Palmerston's policy of denying Russia, as much as possible, any use of the Baltic. As to the French, they were now committed to a policy of rapprochement with Russia.[26] This policy isolated the British at the conference, divided Allied councils, and weakened the possibility that Sweden would achieve her demands at Paris.

Faced by a break in Allied ranks, Manderström was compelled to drop Sweden's various claims and to concentrate solely on the issue of the Aland Islands. According to Manderström, Sweden wanted restitution of the islands, their neutralization as an independent state under the protection of France, England, and Sweden, but failing this solely under the protection of Sweden, or military neutralization of the islands.[27] In the course of a private conversation with his Russian counterpart, Count Alexis Orlov, Lord Clarendon supported the Swedish position and proposed the restitution of Finland and the Aland Islands to Sweden, a suggestion that Orlov immediately dismissed.[28]

Without active French support the British were in a weak position to press for the restitution of the islands to Sweden. The negotiations that followed helped to merge Swedish and English interests toward the Aland Islands specifically and the Baltic in general. The dangers that would accrue for London and Stockholm by insisting on restitution of the islands to Sweden were undoubtedly considered far heavier liabilities than any assets acquisition of the islands might bring. For it was obvious that Russia, unless coerced, would neither surrender Finland nor resign herself to seeing the islands in foreign hands, since they were considered essential for the defense of Finland. On the other hand, the British navy during this period still depended on large-

25. Söderhjelm, pp. 94–97.

26. Agatha Ramm, "The Crimean War," in J. P. T. Bury, ed., *The New Cambridge Modern History* (Cambridge, Eng., The University Press, 1960), *10*, 484, 487.

27. Söderhjelm, p. 97.

28. Ibid.; Sweden, Utrikesdepartementet, *Ålandsfrågan inför Nationernas Förbund* (Stockholm, Norstedt & Söner, 1920), p. 216.

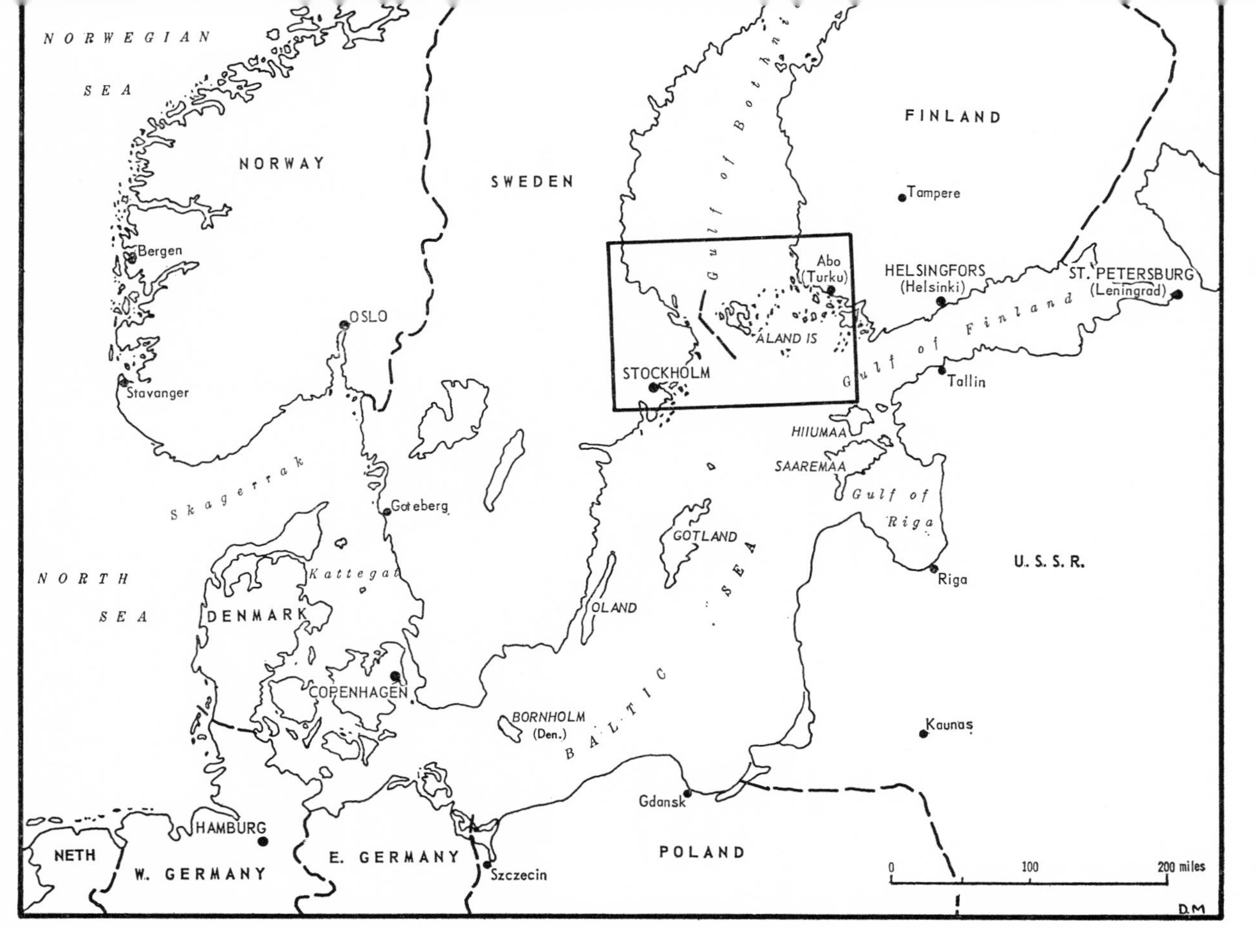

Map 2. Approaches to the Aland Islands

scale importation of timber for the construction and repair of ships. Indeed, free access to Baltic timber had always been an important consideration in British foreign policy, and this attitude in large measure explains British policy shifts in the area.[29] During the decade 1830–40 "the importation of Swedish timber had begun to acquire importance," and consequently freedom of communication between Britain and Swedish ports on the Gulf of Bothnia was of the highest interests to both states. Control of the Aland Islands by the Russians and with it entrance and exit from the Gulf of Bothnia was undoubtedly, from the British point of view, an unsatisfactory situation, while continued fortification of the islands was intolerable.[30] This consideration and Lord Palmerston's desire not to abandon the Baltic to Russian domination explains British support of Swedish desires to demilitarize the islands. By agreeing to this, Britain also acquired Sweden as a friend and potential ally who in seeking protection had found it. Although memories are notoriously short in interstate relations, Stockholm's knowledge that Britain had given support in the past and, most important, could give it again in the future, established a relationship that did not weaken with time. Ultimately, caution and prudence rather than expediency carried the day. Faced by the choice between what was possible and what was desirable, London and Stockholm limited their demands to demilitarization and nonfortification of the islands.

This limitation was accepted by Orlov at the third meeting of the Conference on March 1, 1856.[31] With the acceptance of the restriction the second phase of consideration of the question began. This concerned the desire of the British and Austrians that the convention on the demilitarization and nonfortification of the Aland Islands be annexed to the peace treaty ending the Crimean War. The proposal, it appears, did not receive the active support of Count Alexander Walewski, the French Foreign Min-

29. For an excellent discussion on this point see Robert G. Albion, *Forests and Sea Power,* (Harvard Economic Studies, *29;* Cambridge, Mass., Harvard University Press, 1926), pp. 139–99.

30. Sjoestedt, pp. 15–16.

31. G. F. de Martens, *Nouveau recueil général de traités* (Gottingue, Librairie de Dieterich, 1857), *15,* 707–08.

ister,[32] "dubbed by Clarendon the third Russian plenipotentiary." [33] As was to be expected, Orlov and his colleague, Baron Philip von Brunnow, strenuously resisted this condition. In the end, however, faced by a combined Austro-British front, Orlov gave in.[34] Russia's failure to block this Austro-British move and the inclusion of the convention within the larger European settlement gave the restriction greater force[35] and fixed the attention of Europe on the whole question.[36]

The convention embodying the restriction was signed on March 30, 1856, in Paris and was annexed as Article 33 to the treaty of peace, concluded that same day, terminating the Crimean War.[37] It should be noted that the servitude imposed upon Russia was not unusual or onerous and that restrictions of this type had been imposed in the past as they were to be imposed in the future.[38]

An important aspect of the convention was that it did not include Sweden as one of the signatories. Technically, the three signatories, Britain, France, and Russia, could at any time have

32. Joseph Alexander von Hübner, *Neuf ans de souvenirs d'un ambassadeur d'Autriche à Paris sous le second empire 1851–1859* (Paris, Plon-Nourrit, 1904), *1*, 406, 407.

33. Ramm, "The Crimean War," in Bury, 487.

34. Hübner, *1*, 405, 410.

35. All realized, during the Paris negotiations, that the convention would gain force by being annexed to the treaty of peace. Therefore, that the Russians attempted to divorce the convention from the treaty of peace in order to remove "son caractère européen" is understandable. Conversely, Count Charles Buol, the Austrian Foreign Minister, supported by Lord Clarendon, wished the convention annexed "au point de vue européen." Hübner, *1*, 410.

This point was subsequently confirmed by Lord Clarendon in the House of Lords when he explained that the convention by being annexed to the treaty of peace was "therefore part of the national law of Europe," guaranteeing the possessions of Sweden from Russian attack. Great Britain, *Hansard's Parliamentary Debates*, 3d ser., vol. 141 (1856), col. 2001.

36. Regarding Europe's attention being drawn to the question of the islands, see the conversation with Napoleon III reported on April 5, 1856, by Manderström to the Swedish Foreign Ministry. Sjoestedt, p. 19.

37. Hertslet, *2*, 1268, 1272–73.

38. Helen D. Reid, *International Servitudes in Law and Practice* (Chicago, University of Chicago Press, 1932), pp. 189–203; Ferenc A. Váli, *Servitudes of International Law* (2d ed. London, Stevens, 1958), pp. 263–72; Sjoestedt, pp. 19–20; Söderhjelm, pp. 1–79.

abrogated the agreement without Sweden's consent if they so wished, an important point that would be raised in the years to come. Nevertheless, the Swedes could only have been pleased with the results, for they had achieved in 1856 what the Russians had denied them in 1809. For the next fifty years this situation continued undisturbed. Inevitably the continual execution of the convention by all parties and its respect by others made it, as Lord Clarendon had stated, part of the public law of Europe.

The Negotiations of 1906–08

The issue of the Aland Islands did not attract attention again until 1905 during the dissolution of the Swedish–Norwegian Union established in 1814. The dissolution of the Union necessitated abrogating the Treaty of Guarantee of November 21, 1855. In Copenhagen, the Russian minister, Alexander Isvolsky, viewed the dissolution of the Union as an opportunity for renegotiating the status of the Scandinavian peninsula established by the treaties preceding and following the Crimean War. His advice to St. Petersburg in 1905 was to seize the occasion presented by the dissolution of the Union in order to liquidate the restrictions resulting from the 1856 convention. He felt the propitious moment had arrived and that a precedent existed, since during the Franco-Prussian War of 1870–71 Russia had profited from the disarray in western Europe to liquidate some of the onerous clauses of the Treaty of Paris of 1856 dealing with the Black Sea. It can be questioned whether the conditions of 1870–71 were similar to those of 1905 and whether Isvolsky's analogy was correct.

At any rate, his advice to St. Petersburg went unheeded. With Russia losing disastrously to the Japanese in Manchuria and on the edge of a revolution at home, her Foreign Ministry was in no mood for diplomatic adventures in the Baltic. It was not until Isvolsky himself was appointed Foreign Minister in April of 1906 that the idea could again be pursued.[39]

Almost simultaneously with Isvolsky's appointment as Foreign Minister, Russian troops were dispatched to the Aland Islands, a

39. Isvolsky, when he was ambassador in Paris during the First World War, related the above to F. de Jessen. *Le Temps,* Feb. 10, 1918, pp. 1–2.

wireless station established there, and naval units sent to patrol the waters of the archipelago. These actions were justified on the ground that internal disorders in Russia necessitated the surveillance of the archipelago to prevent the smuggling of arms.[40] With the events of the day in mind, this seems a perfectly cogent argument.[41] In London, St. Petersburg's actions provoked repeated questions in the House of Commons. In reply, Sir Edward Grey, the Foreign Secretary, pointed out that the British government had no information showing that the Russian government contemplated "any breach of the provisions of the Treaty of Paris by fortifying the Aland islands, or maintaining or creating military or naval establishments there." By October 1906, the Russian garrison, originally 750 men, was reduced to two officers and fifteen men, and these too were subsequently withdrawn.[42] In the end, neither London nor Paris lodged any protests. The lack of any official protest could only have encouraged Isvolsky to believe that he would be successful if he opened the question of the islands. Yet, he failed to learn from this experience that any alteration of the islands' status could not occur without serious questions being raised, especially by the British Parliament and public opinion.

However, almost a year after his appointment on April 21, 1907, Isvolsky again broached the issue during negotiations leading to a new treaty guaranteeing the independence and integrity of Norway. According to the German ambassador in St. Petersburg, Wilhelm von Schoen, Isvolsky intended to abrogate the Aland Islands convention of 1856 and desired Berlin's "moral support" in the question, since the convention had placed an intolerable limitation on Russia's sovereign rights, thus injuring her interests.[43]

40. Söderhjelm, p. 119.

41. In the period 1905–06 there was gun running by Finnish nationalists, some of the arms and ammunition paid for by the Japanese. John H. Wuorinen, *A History of Finland* (New York, Columbia University Press, 1965), pp. 207–08.

42. Great Britain, *Parliamentary Debates,* 4th ser., vol. 159 (1906), cols. 1132, 1415; vol. 160 (1906), col. 512; vol. 161 (1906), cols. 1190–91; vol. 163 (1906), col. 411; vol. 164 (1906), col. 532; vol. 179 (1907), cols. 765–66; Söderhjelm, p. 123.

43. Germany, Auswärtiges Amt, *Die grosse Politik der europäischen Kabinette, 1871–1914,* ed. Johannes Lepsius, Albrecht M. Bartholdy, and Friedrich Thimme (Berlin, Deutsche Verlagsgesellschaft für Politik, 1925), *23,* Pt. II, 433–34.

The reply of the German Secretary of State, Heinrich von Tschirschky, was that Germany would offer no objection to the abrogation of the Aland Islands convention. On the other hand, he pointed out that raising the question might produce a dangerous situation jeopardizing the negotiations then in progress.[44]

Actually, Isvolsky's approach to Berlin had been inept, for Germany was not a signatory to the 1856 convention. Thus there was no legal significance to the subsequent secret protocol signed on October 29, 1907, in St. Petersburg between Russia and Germany in which the latter promised not to object to the eventual abrogation of the convention of 1856. To abrogate the convention legally the permissions of the other two signatories were needed.[45] The key to the problem lay not with Germany but with France and Britain, and especially with the British Foreign Office.

On June 25, 1907, disregarding Tschirschky's advice, Isvolsky officially asked the British Foreign Office for abrogation of the 1856 convention. The French and German governments were willing to acquiesce to this request and the Norwegian government urged the British to accept it also.[46] Norway's actions were undoubtedly motivated by the fear that complications over abrogation of the 1856 convention might delay the treaty guaranteeing its independence and integrity. France's acquiescence was probably made to assuage the feelings of an ally in an area of the world where Paris had no vital interests, while Germany saw it as an action which might frighten Stockholm into closer relations with Berlin. This last was not so remote, for upon hearing of the Russian proposal the Swedish Foreign Minister, Eric de Trolle, frankly admitted in a conversation with the British minister in Stockholm that closer relations with Germany were a possibility.[47]

Faced by this totally unexpected proposal, the British government raised no objection in principle. Though Sir Edward Grey was willing to admit that the convention of 1856 no longer corresponded to the political situation of the day, he felt that abrogation of the convention would be painful to Sweden and leave

44. Ibid., p. 435.
45. Ibid., pp. 484–85.
46. *BrDOW, 1898–1914, 8,* 115–16.
47. Ibid., p. 117.

her in an isolated and delicate situation. Furthermore, he was not interested in handling Baltic questions piecemeal. On the contrary, Sir Edward believed that any discussion of the islands should be undertaken in connection with negotiations of the whole Baltic question at a conference of the interested states, Germany included. Not until England had seen the terms of the proposed arrangements could she consent to the abrogation of the 1856 convention. However, Grey made it quite clear to the Swedes that if England was strongly pressed by Russia, she might abrogate the convention, merely consulting Sweden before coming to a final decision. This would be done in the hope that some sort of a satisfactory arrangement could be made.[48]

Grey's tack spurred Isvolsky to see if Sweden's disquietude could perhaps be allayed by an arrangement between the three Baltic states: Germany, Russia, and Sweden. He hoped in this manner to bring about an abrogation of the convention. But no arrangement that he offered appeared to quiet Stockholm's anxieties.[49]

Disclosure of Russia's proposal in February of 1908 unleashed both in England and in Sweden a public outcry. Questions were asked of Grey in the House of Commons,[50] while in Sweden there was an interpellation of the government in the Riksdag and outcries in the Swedish press.[51]

Pressing the Aland Islands question at this time, coming as it did on the heels of a determined parliamentary attack against the Anglo-Russian Convention of August 31, 1907, could perhaps have jeopardized Russian gains achieved by the convention,[52] an

48. Ibid., pp. 116, 139, 141–42, 147, 149, 154–55, 168, 171. On this issue see also Sir Edward Grey, *Twenty-five Years, 1892–1916* (New York, Frederick A. Stokes, 1925), *1*, 138–44.

49. *BrDOW, 1898–1914, 8,* 159. For the negotiations as they appeared from the German side see Germany, Auswärtiges Amt, *Die grosse Politik, 23,* Pt. II, and *24* passim.

50. Great Britain, *Parliamentary Debates,* 4th ser., vol. 184 (1908), cols. 1020–21; vol. 185 (1908), col. 1749; vol. 187 (1908), cols. 1089, 1395.

51. Sjoestedt, pp. 24–28; *The Times* (London), Feb. 24, 1908, p. 6; Feb. 26, 1908, p. 7.

52. On this point see the letters from the Permanent Under-Secretary of the Foreign Office, Lord Hardinge of Penshurst, on February 19 and March 3, 1908, to Sir Arthur Nicolson, the ambassador in St. Petersburg, as well as Sir Edward

agreement covering outstanding questions in Persia, Afghanistan, and Tibet, and constituting the first step toward a rapprochement between the two countries.

Thwarted in his attempt to remove the restrictions of the 1856 convention, Isvolsky was forced to settle for something less. The something less was the Baltic Declaration of April 23, 1908, by Germany, Denmark, Russia, and Sweden which merely confirmed the territorial status quo of the contracting states. At the same time, attached to the agreement was a memorandum explaining that the principles of the status quo confirmed by the declaration only referred to the "territorial integrity of all the present continental and insular possessions" of the contracting powers in the Baltic, and that, consequently, the declaration could in no way be "invoked, should any question arise as to the free exercise of the sovereign rights" of the contracting powers over their respective Baltic possessions.[53]

As the League of Nations Commission of Jurists subsequently pointed out, this statement in no way implied that Russia had been released from her 1856 servitude. Indeed, Grey and his Swedish counterpart, Eric de Trolle, denied that any such release was intended, denials not contradicted by any other state, Russia included. Merely from a legal point of view the Baltic Declaration of April 23, 1908 could never affect the 1856 convention, since England and France, signatories of that convention, were not signatories of the 1908 declaration.[54]

In the end, the agreement of 1908 solved nothing, and the problem of the Aland Islands was reserved for the future. Isvolsky's attempt to abrogate the 1856 convention had produced in Swedish–Russian relations a coolness which was not removed by the Czar's visit to Stockholm in the summer of 1909. Indeed, the hostility provoked on this occasion, especially by the Socialists, was controlled only by appealing to every Swede's politeness, hospitality, and patriotism.[55] During this visit, Isvolsky, who had

---

Grey's communication on February 29, 1908, to Sir Frank Lascelles, the ambassador in Berlin. *BrDOW, 1898–1914, 8,* 165, 171, 169.

53. *BrDOW, 1898–1914, 8,* 184.

54. League of Nations, *Official Journal,* spec. suppl. no. 3 (Oct. 1920), p. 15.

55. *The Times* (London), June 16, 1909, p. 5; June 19, 1909, p. 5.

accompanied the Czar, broached the issue of the islands, promising not to do anything without first informing the Swedish government.[56] His removal shortly after as Foreign Minister can only have sent a sigh of relief through the Swedish Foreign Ministry.

Though the personal feelings of the Swedish populace could be expressed, the government in Stockholm could ill afford this luxury. On the contrary, official circles strove to normalize relations with their great neighbor to the east. Especially notable were the efforts of the liberal ministry of Karl Staaf (1911–14), who in July of 1912 succeeded in arranging a meeting between King Gustaf and Czar Nicholas at Pitkäpaasi in Finnish waters.

At this meeting, the new Russian Foreign Minister, Serge Sazonov, hoped to reassure the Swedes that Russia had no hostile intentions toward her. His task was even more difficult than he realized because of continuing reports from the Swedish Legation in St. Petersburg of Russian activity in the archipelago whose ultimate purpose was seen as fortification of the islands.[57]

Sazonov's own feelings were that the question of abrogating the 1856 convention was really of "no practical importance" for Russia, and he regretted that Isvolsky had ever raised the question. He thought that during times of peace no fortifications on the islands were necessary and were in fact politically undesirable, since they frightened the Swedes and threw them into the arms of Germany. On the other hand, during times of war the archipelago could be easily defended to prevent the entrance and exit of enemy forces from the Gulf of Bothnia.

On his appointment as Foreign Minister, Sazonov immediately ordered the negotiations started by Isvolsky on the question of the Aland Islands to be terminated in order to avoid complications with the Swedes. Thus, the Pitkäpaasi meeting offered Sazonov the opportunity to reassure the Swedes on this point, which, as was to be expected, also influenced the Swedish Foreign Minister. In the conversations that followed, Sazonov sincerely assured the Swedes "in the name of the Russian Government,

56. Pontus Reuterswärd, *Generallöjtnanten och envoyén Edvard Brändström svenskt sändebud i Ryssland 1906–1920* (Stockholm, Norstedt & Söners, 1947), p. 118.

57. Ibid., pp. 119–20.

that Russia had no intention whatever of undertaking measures of any kind for converting these islands into an advanced base against Sweden." The friendly relations between Russia and Sweden since 1809 "gave special value to the peaceful assurances of the Russian Government." He earnestly hoped that the Swedes "would repose equal confidence" in Russia.[58]

In spite of the friendly communiqué that terminated this meeting[59] the Aland Islands question and the events of 1906–08 remained vivid in the minds of the Swedish people. These events inspired a fear and mistrust of Russia that was aggravated by the knowledge that any Russian fortification of the Aland Islands was a direct threat to the safety of Stockholm. Similarly, current espionage cases implicating the Russian Legation did little to assuage Swedish fears about their eastern neighbor's good intentions.[60] The situation prevailing hastened the tendency in certain Swedish circles to look toward a possible German alliance. Needless to state, Germany whenever possible sowed seeds of mistrust to widen the Swedish–Russian breach.[61]

By January of 1914, Sweden was busily engaged in reorganizing its military establishment in order to defend its neutrality more effectively in the event of a European war. As the Swedish Foreign Minister warned Émile Thiébaut, the French minister, the only thing that could throw Sweden into the arms of Germany was "la fortification des îles d'Aland qui mettrait Stockholm sous le canon russe." [62] This warning was far more specific than the one Thiébaut had received some time earlier when he was told that Russian fortifications three hours from Stockholm would be so "intolerable" for Sweden that if Russia persisted in her

58. Serge Sazonov, *Fateful Years 1909–1916* (London, Jonathan Cape, 1928), pp. 66–67.

59. Reuterswärd, p. 123; Sjoestedt, pp. 31–32; *The Times* (London), July 22, 1912, p. 5; July 24, 1912, p. 5; July 25, 1912, p. 5.

60. France, Ministère des Affaires Étrangères, Commission de publication des documents relatifs aux origines de la guerre de 1914, *Documents diplomatiques français* (Paris, Imprimerie Nationale, 1936), 3d ser., *11,* 193–94.

61. Luigi Albertini, *The Origins of the War of 1914,* trans. and ed. Isabella M. Massey (London, Oxford University Press, 1957), *3,* 662–64.

62. France, Ministère des Affaires Étrangères, Commission de publication des documents relatifs aux origines de la guerre de 1914, *Documents diplomatiques français,* 3d ser., *9,* 63.

demand, it would "drive Sweden into the arms of any other power." [63]

At the outbreak of the war, however, this did not seem to be the intention—at least of the Russian ambassador in London. On the contrary, Count Alexander Benckendorff, in an obvious analogy toward German actions in Belgium, in a conversation with Sir Edward Grey pointed out that Russia had no intentions of violating her Aland Islands treaty commitments. Undoubtedly pleased by Benckendorff's remark, Sir Edward answered he would on the first opportunity inform the Swedish minister, Count Herman Wrangel, that he had proof that the Aland Islands "were not fortified against Sweden." [64]

Within six months the very action that Benckendorff promised would never occur and which the Swedish Foreign Minister threatened would throw Sweden into Germany's arms had come to fruition. But in spite of this, Sweden maintained her neutrality. It is to these events that we now turn.

63. *Die internationalen Beziehungen,* 3d ser., *2,* Pt. II, 879.

64. Ibid., 1st ser., *5,* 315; Alfred von Wegerer, ed., *Das russische Orangebuch von 1914* (Berlin, Deutsche Verlagsgesellschaft für Politik und Geschichte m.b.h., 1925), p. 211; Friedrich Stieve, ed., *Iswolski im Weltkriege; der diplomatische Schriftwechsel Iswolskis aus den Jahren 1914–1917; neue Dokumente aus den Geheimakten der russischen Staatsarchiven* (Berlin, Deutsche Verlagsgesellschaft für Politik und Geschichte m.b.h., 1925), pp. 19–20.

CHAPTER 2

The First World War

The Fortification of the Aland Islands

In Stockholm, the momentous events of July through August 1914 were faced by a conservative government that had in February of that same year replaced the pacifist Staaf. During the summer crisis the Prime Minister, Kunt Hjalmar Hammarskjöld, and the Foreign Minister, Knut Wallenberg, showed a marked proclivity for the Triple Alliance. Warnings, instigated by Sir Edward Grey, from London, Paris, and St. Petersburg, informed Sweden that if she took Germany's side the Triple Entente would be "freed from all obligations toward her." In the end, these threats helped cool whatever feelings might have existed for Germany. Hammarskjöld and Wallenberg must also have realized that victory for the Central Powers, after Britain's entry into the war, could not be assured. That Norway and Denmark had no intentions of being involved was another factor in forcing Sweden to proclaim its strict neutrality in the struggle that commenced.[1]

For the next five months, as the tide of war ebbed and flowed across the western front, Sweden maintained her perilous position. The government was not even moved to intervene after assurances that the Aland Islands would be returned to Sweden if she joined Germany's side were given to a member of the opposition in mid-October by the German minister in Stockholm.[2] Indeed, to keep the conflict as far from Sweden's shores as possible, Stockholm in January of 1915 suggested to Berlin that the Aland Islands be neutralized for the duration of the war on the supposition that Russia would agree to it. This proposal, how-

1. Luigi Albertini, *The Origins of the War of 1914,* trans. and ed. Isabella M. Massey (London, Oxford University Press, 1957), *3,* 664–72.

2. Erik Kule Palmstierna, *Orostid; politiska dagboksanteckningar* (Stockholm, Tidens, 1952), *1,* 69.

ever, was not to Germany's advantage, for her Baltic fleet was far stronger than Russia's, and Stockholm's overture was rejected.[3]

In fact, increasing German naval activity in the Gulf of Bothnia by December of 1914, prompted the Commander of the Russian Baltic fleet to direct the government's attention to the necessity of fortifying the Aland Islands. As the Minister of Marine, Vice-Admiral Ivan K. Grigorovich, pointed out in a letter to the Foreign Minister, Sazonov, on January 1, 1915, the whole area was of "great strategic importance" and consequently the navy's task was to keep the area firmly in Russia's possession. He thought that German attempts to occupy the islands were likely to occur in the course of the winter or by the early spring of 1915. By occupying the islands the Germans would establish a base for the operation of U-boats, torpedo boats, and other naval vessels. This would allow the Germans to command the approaches to the Gulf of Bothnia and by their use of U-boats create for the Russian Baltic fleet an "extremely unfavorable situation" at the mouth of the Gulf of Finland. These reasons, Grigorovich noted, compelled an immediate fortification of the area in order to have the defenses finished by spring. The fortification of the archipelago would include the positioning of batteries covering the sea approaches, the establishment of wireless stations, and the landing of troops, as well as the concentration of gunboats, torpedo boats, and U-boats in the area. The execution of these measures would permit the Imperial government to keep a firm grip on the archipelago and thus thwart the Germans in "conducting undisturbed operations in the Gulf of Bothnia and at the mouth of the Gulf of Finland."

The problems, however, were Sweden's sensitivity to all measures of a military nature in the Aland archipelago and her position as a neutral, as well as Germany's ability to alarm her by pointing to Russia's alleged "aggressive intentions." Therefore, it was important to obstruct German agitation of the Swedish government and Swedish public opinion by giving the Swedes advance notice of Russia's actions.

Grigorovich's own desire was that Sazonov notify the Swedish

3. Howard (Stockholm) to Grey, No. 672, Feb. 22, 1917 (File 3184 in FO/371/3021, PRO); *Krasnyi arkhiv, 32* (1929), 35–36n.; Palmstierna, *Orostid, 2,* 20.

government of the military measures to be taken, along with the reasons that made this action necessary, thus avoiding from the very beginning undesirable interpretations by the Swedish government.[4] Grigorovich ended the letter with a postscript in his own hand requesting to speak to Sazonov personally.[5]

Faced by a situation of this nature Sazonov had no real choice. Within four days after receipt of this letter he instructed the Russian minister in Stockholm, Anatole Nekludov, to inform the Swedish government of the military measures contemplated by the Russian Imperial government. In his communication to the Swedish government, Nekludov was to emphasize the "exclusively defensive character" of these measures and was to express the hope that when they became public they would not be interpreted to Swedish public opinion in a manner injurious to Russia's relations with Sweden.[6] Three days after the communication of these instructions on January 8, Nekludov called on Wallenberg and informed him of the Russian fears that the Germans were intending to occupy the Aland Islands to use them for military operations against Finland and to disrupt commerce between Sweden and Russia. In order to prevent this German move the Russian government was forced to take special defensive measures in the island group. Nevertheless, the Russian Imperial government considered it its duty to warn the Swedish government confidentially of this intended Russian action, stressing the exclusively defensive character of the measures, which were meant only for the present hostilities. Nekludov then repeated Sazonov's wish that, in the case these moves became public knowledge, the Swedish government would attempt to calm public opinion in Sweden concerning the character of the Russian moves which as he had already stated were strictly defensive in character.[7]

Wallenberg informed Nekludov, after reporting the Russian intentions to King Gustaf and the Swedish Cabinet, that Sweden would not protest the military measures envisaged for the Aland

4. *Die internationalen Beziehungen,* 2d ser., *6,* Pt. II, 616–17.

5. Ibid., p. 617n. 2.

6. Ibid., p. 617n. 1.

7. *Krasnyi arkhiv, 32* (1929), 44–45n.

Islands. He added that the Swedish government was pleased at any measures that could contribute to the safeguarding of maritime commerce between the two countries. Moreover, his government would keep the Russian moves secret, but should the measures taken on the Aland Islands become known, it agreed to calm Swedish public opinion. In ending, Wallenberg observed that he personally viewed the Russian note as proof of Russia's trust in the Swedish government.

The arrival of this news in St. Petersburg moved Sazonov to inform the military and Grigorovich in particular that he saw no obstacle to the realization of the military measures intended for the defense of the Aland archipelago.[8] The Swedes, like Sazonov, had had no real choice. To appeal to Britain and France, the other signatories of the 1856 convention and Russia's allies, would have been fruitless. Conversely, to declare war against Russia and join the Central Powers not only would have been politically dangerous but would have been an action strongly resisted by almost all sectors of Swedish public opinion intent upon remaining neutral in the great struggle being waged across Europe.

While these events were unfolding between Stockholm and St. Petersburg, other discussions involving the Aland Islands were taking place in Berlin. During the winter of 1914–15 there appeared on the scene Swedish and Finnish groups and individuals intent on drawing Sweden into the war on the side of the Central Powers. For want of a better word all of these groups have been labeled "activists." A close examination of their programs will show, however, that, while they were moved by a mutual hostility toward and fear of Russia, wide divergencies existed on a number of issues especially on what connection there should be, if any, after the war between Sweden and the independent Finland that most of the Finnish activists desired.

One such activist with a strong pro-German orientation was Fredrik Wetterhoff, a Finnish judge, who was especially enterprising in Berlin during this early period. In conversations with the Swedish minister in Berlin, Count Arvid Taube, Wetterhoff pointed out that Sweden should intervene on Germany's side and

8. *Die internationalen Beziehungen,* 2d ser., *7,* Pt. I, p. 29; *Krasnyi arkhiv, 32* (1929), 36n.

Germany should support a Finnish insurrection, for in any separation of Finland and Russia which would follow, the Aland Islands and perhaps other Finnish territory might be transferred to Sweden. These proposals when conveyed to Stockholm personally by Taube were firmly rejected by Hammarskjöld who had no intentions of compromising Sweden's neutrality on any such nebulous scheme.

Undismayed, Wetterhoff continued his endeavors. In subsequent discussions within his group it was thought that the best means of forcing Sweden to Germany's side would be an occupation of the islands. It was envisaged that Germany would press Sweden to occupy the islands—an obvious *casus belli* with Russia—and, if Sweden refused, threaten to occupy them herself. Though nothing developed from Wetterhoff's activities, the problem that constantly had to be faced was how Sweden was to be forced to join the camp of the Central Powers. The scheme perpetually visualized was an "occupation by Germany of the Aland Islands." [9]

In the end the islands were to be occupied by German troops, but this led to no Swedish involvement in the war. Wetterhoff's activities, though almost amusing in retrospect, were nevertheless indicative of an underlying conflict which was moving through the Baltic during this early period and which would strongly manifest itself in the coming years: the desire of the Finnish nationalists to use the war to advance the cause of Finnish independence and the Swedish desire to use this same war to acquire for Sweden greater security in the Baltic. These desires were not necessarily compatible. Wetterhoff would, in October of 1915, once again assume an important though transient role in this conflict.

No sooner had Wetterhoff's activities come to an impasse than the issue of the islands was raised publicly on the side of the Triple Entente. On August 11, 1915, there appeared in the Parisian daily, *Le Figaro,* a front-page article entitled "Sweden and the War." The article was signed by Eric Sjoestedt, a Swedish writer resident in Paris and well known for his French and Entente sympathies.

In Sjoestedt's article, which was friendly to Russia in tone, the thought was expressed that in any Russo-Swedish rapprochement

9. *Bulletin périodique de la presse scandinave,* No. 242, p. 7.

it would be useful to sell or cede the Aland Islands to Sweden for some sort of compensation. The analogy drawn was Russia's sale of Alaska to the United States for the price of seven million dollars in 1867. That Alaska, unlike the Aland Islands, had no strategic importance to Russia during this period was of course ignored. On the matter of compensation, Sjoestedt envisaged some sort of commercial or transit arrangements. The latter point was crucial at this juncture by reason of Russia's relative isolation from her western allies. Certainly, the article continued, so small an archipelago would not be missed in so immense an empire. For Sweden it was not a question of the acquisition of territory but a matter of security and international balance. Of course, it went without saying that if the islands were acquired by Sweden their servitude would remain.[10]

Almost immediately, Sjoestedt's article was picked up by the influential Swedish newspaper, *Göteborg Handelstidning,* the liberal organ of the former Prime Minister, Karl Staaf. This newspaper assured its readers that the article had been written by a person in close communication with French government circles. It stated, moreover, that it was possible that these French circles, not disagreeing with the proposals broached in the article, allowed them to be published and passed on to the public.[11]

Whatever the reasons behind Sjoestedt's article, it did not go unnoticed by the Russian Embassy in Paris. More sensitive to the issue of the islands than most of his colleagues, Isvolsky, now Russian ambassador to France, immediately contacted Sazonov. He undoubtedly felt the article was some sort of political trial balloon, for he pointed out that Sjoestedt enjoyed the confidence of the Swedish Foreign Minister, Wallenberg, and that he was in communication with the Swedish Legation in Paris. Nevertheless, until the Russian government would express an opinion on the matter, Isvolsky stated that he would "endeavor to hinder the discussion of this topic in the local press."[12] Official support

10. *Le Figaro,* Aug. 11, 1915, pp. 1–2.

11. *Die internationalen Beziehungen,* 2d ser., *8,* Pt. II, 476n. 2.

12. Ibid.; Friedrich Stieve, ed., *Iswolski im Weltkriege; der diplomatische Schriftwechsel Iswolskis aus den Jahren 1914–1917; neue Dokumente aus den Geheimakten der russischen Staatsarchiven* (Berlin, Deutsche Verlagsgesellschaft für Politik und Geschichte m.b.h., 1925), pp. 200–01.

followed. "I consider all discussion in the press of the topic of the Aland Islands as completely inopportune, and request you to take appropriate measures to prevent it," Sazonov quickly replied.[13]

In the meantime events occurring in the Aland Islands would bring to Sazonov's desk news of a more disturbing nature from the Russian minister in Stockholm. On August 10, the day before Sjoestedt's article appeared in *Le Figaro,* a German attack was made on the island of Utö, one of the smaller islands in the Aland archipelago. Naturally the question of the islands became a topic of conversation in the Swedish press. A host of articles followed—unleashing a literary war—over what Sweden was to expect if the Germans did occupy the area, whether it was possible for Sweden to take possession of the islands again, or whether it was not better to maintain the old political division, with Russia merely confirming the promise it had made in 1856 never to fortify the archipelago.

These exchanges in the Swedish press, Nekludov revealed to Sazonov, prompted Wallenberg "on his own initiative" to enter into a discussion with him over the topic of the Aland Islands. Wallenberg began the conversation by pointing out that he clearly understood that the Russian government was in no position either to give promises in regard to the islands, or to occupy itself with the question at the present time. On the other hand, Sweden would be pleased and heartened if it had assurances that immediately at the end of the war Russia would repeat to Sweden its promise of 1856 not to militarize the islands. Wallenberg begged Nekludov not to misunderstand his present request, for it was repugnant to his government to take advantage of Russia's present military difficulties in order to stipulate any sort of changes in Swedish–Russian border arrangements. The only thing that Sweden desired was the "moral assurance" that after the war St. Petersburg would fulfill Stockholm's wishes in regard to the demilitarization and nonfortification of the Aland archipelago.

Nekludov made no reply to Wallenberg except to state that he would pass the request on to Sazonov. In conversation with the British minister, Sir Esme Howard, Nekludov, while making no

13. *Die internationalen Beziehungen,* 2d ser., *8,* Pt. II, 484.

mention of his interview with Wallenberg, stated that he had suggested to Sazonov the possibility of "giving [to the Swedes] . . . some such assurances [which] might . . . be hinted at in [the] Russian press." In fact, it would appear that Nekludov made no such suggestion. On the contrary, he felt that despite the mildness and restraint of the communication it was to a certain extent blackmail. Wallenberg had, Nekludov noted to Sazonov, obviously commenced the discussion very reluctantly. Nekludov thought that he had made the request only to take the wind out of the sails of his critics, who accused him of not using the war to further Sweden's interests.

In ending, Nekludov asked what answer he was to give Wallenberg. His own feelings were that any answer would depend upon the outcome of the present war. If Germany were no longer a danger to Russia in the Baltic, all fortifications and military installations in the Aland Islands would be superfluous, since Russia had nothing to fear from Sweden. On the other hand, if Germany were not destroyed by the war, then Russia would have to reserve her rights to the islands for defensive and offensive purposes.

Though Nekludov was not to receive a reply to this report for close to a month, a decision on the question he posed was made on September 2 at Czarist headquarters when an unknown hand scribbled on Nekludov's dispatch, "*such a promise may not be given.*" [14]

Official word was flashed to Nekludov on September 23. In his reply the Foreign Minister, Sazonov, in large measure concurred with his minister in Stockholm. He observed that the present war had clearly shown the importance of the islands for Russia's self-defense. If Russia did not hold the Aland Islands she could not defend the Gulf of Bothnia; thus ties with Sweden across the Baltic would be endangered. If the archipelago were to be in the hands of a neutral state, defense of Finland would be made more difficult, for the Russian Baltic fleet would not be in a position to

14. Ibid., pp. 527–29; Howard (Stockholm) to Grey, No. 944, Aug. 18, 1915 (File 115138 in FO/371/2455, PRO). The discussion of the Aland Islands in the Swedish press during this period indicated that the question would "become current," wrote Palmstierna, *Orostid, 1,* 116.

take measures in the territorial waters of the islands, measures indispensable for defending Russia's interests. In the matter of fortifying the islands, Russia—who sincerely desired friendly relations with Sweden—would obviously not wish in the future, as in the past, to create without reason fortifications in the vicinity of Stockholm which would threaten the capital and which would in turn impair Russo-Swedish relations.

Concerning Wallenberg's desire for some sort of promise not to militarize the islands after the war, Sazonov thought this was impossible especially at the present moment. The answer to this question largely depended on what Germany's position would be after the present struggle had ended. Obviously a strong Germany would make it necessary for Russia to take measures on the islands to protect Russian possessions against any future German attack.

On the basis of these considerations Sazonov was of the opinion that Nekludov could—if he deemed it necessary—give Wallenberg an evasive answer on the subject. Above all he was to express Sazonov's satisfaction with the Swedish Foreign Minister's realization that it was impossible for the Russian Imperial government at the present juncture to deal with the question of the Aland Islands. Nekludov could also add that Russia had the greatest desire to establish friendly relations with Sweden, and naturally did not intend to create anything on the islands which would be directed against Sweden. If it made any use of the islands it would be for the purpose of self-defense against Germany.[15]

It was this last point which was the crux of the problem. For no informal assurance by the Russian government, no matter how well intentioned, could assuage Swedish fears. To Stockholm, fortifications on the Aland Islands, even if meant against Germany, could also be used against Sweden and were thus a potential threat to Sweden's freedom of action. But before Nekludov could contact Wallenberg to convey Sazonov's reply the situation changed markedly.

Increasing discussion by the Swedish press of the Aland Islands was capped by the disclosure in early October by the Norwegian newspaper *Tidens tegn* that the archipelago had been fortified by the Russians in January. This forced the Swedish govern-

15. *Die internationalen Beziehungen*, 2d ser., *8*, Pt. II, 690–91.

ment, in the face of an anxious if not aroused public opinion, to issue a statement affirming the report and recounting Nekludov's communication requesting that the Swedish government, if the Russian moves became known, "reassure the public as to the character and purpose of the military measures."

Who informed *Tidens tegn* of Nekludov's overtures to the Swedish government is unclear, though by late September the fortification of the islands had become known to the opposition. It is conceivable that the opposition or elements in the government or even in the Foreign Ministry, restless at the government's cautious policy toward Russia, may have leaked the news. In doing so, interestingly enough, they avoided the Swedish press and divulged the information to the newspaper of another state "neutral" in this Russo-Swedish question.

Significantly, *Tidens tegn* incorrectly reported that Russia had assured Sweden that the fortifications would not be maintained after the conclusion of peace, which was a point the official Russian statement had not made but which was an assurance, as we have seen, that the Swedes were trying to extract from the Russians.[16] It is possible that this incorrect leakage to the Norwegians was a *ruse diplomatique* exposing Swedish desires publicly but unofficially in an attempt to commit Russia to the Swedish point of view. Since only a few selected individuals could have known that this point was being pressed by the Swedish government, credence is lent to the possibility that the news leak was officially inspired. The fact that *Le Figaro* had perhaps been used by Stockholm some months earlier for a somewhat similar purpose helps to support this thesis.

At any rate, the issue of how *Tidens tegn* acquired the information was of secondary importance in October of 1915. Of primary importance was the public outcry that was raised throughout Sweden and the use that the activists made of the disclosure.

Word of what had transpired in Stockholm prompted Sazonov to request an interview with the Swedish minister, General Ed-

16. Morris (Stockholm) to the Department of State, Oct. 9, 1915 (File 763.72/2223, Record Group 59, NA); Palmstierna, *Orostid, I*, 125–26, 129, 132; *Le Temps*, Oct. 5, 1915, p. 2; Erik Sjoestedt, *La question des îles d'Aland* (Paris, Grasset, 1919), pp. 38–40.

vard Brändström. Upon Brändström's arrival at the Foreign Ministry, Sazonov expressed his astonishment over the public announcement made in Stockholm by the government. Without even trying to defend his government's actions, Brändström pointed out the importance for Sweden of receiving calming assurances concerning future Russian intentions on the Aland Islands. Sazonov responded that the present fortification of the islands was dictated by wartime necessity. As to the future, Sweden could judge Russia by her past actions, for during the whole period that the islands were in Russian hands they had never been turned into a threat against Sweden. He added that he was using the present opportunity to confirm personally to Brändström everything said repeatedly by Nekludov in Stockholm about Russia's friendly inclinations toward Sweden.[17]

Nekludov's subsequent aide-mémoire to Wallenberg on October 14 merely reflected what was expressed by Sazonov during this interview with Brändström. He repeated Sazonov's satisfaction with the fact that Wallenberg understood that it was impossible for the Russian government under present conditions to satisfy Sweden on the question of the Aland Islands. Desirous of strengthening its relations with Sweden, Russia had no intentions on the islands which might be aimed against Sweden, except to use them as a defensive base against a German attack. As for future assurances, Sweden had only to look at the experience of over a century during which time the islands had never been used by Russia in a manner that could be regarded as a threat to Sweden.[18]

By this note it was made obvious that the initial reaction of Swedish public opinion had not caused Sazonov to modify his prior position. Yet, if Sazonov had been aware of certain other events in Stockholm during this period, his complacency might have been shaken and perhaps greater attention might have been paid to General Brändström's words.

The prolongation of the war had inspired Finnish nationalists to hope and plot for the removal of Russian control and the in-

17. *Krasnyi arkhiv, 32* (1929), 37n. 1.

18. *Die internationalen Beziehungen,* 2d ser., *8,* Pt. II, 801.

dependence of Finland. To this end there was formed in the autumn of 1915 a committee including one representative from each of the political parties in the Finnish Diet. This committee, which arrived in Stockholm in October without the knowledge of the Russian authorities, was composed of Professor Rafael W. Erich of the University of Helsingfors (Helsinki), subsequently Prime Minister and Finnish minister at Stockholm; Kuopio Saastamoinen, a wealthy merchant, subsequently Finnish minister at London; Samuli Sario, director of an insurance company at Tampmerfors (Tampere); Otto Stenroth, President of the Bank of Finland, subsequently Finnish Foreign Minister; and lastly, a Dr. Lille. Their mission to Stockholm: "to try to conclude an agreement [with the Swedish authorities] on the liberation of Finland in the course of the World War." Their middle man in establishing contact with the Swedish General Staff was the ubiquitous Wetterhoff, but their relations with him went no further. The committee believed it could "offer to Sweden the Aland Islands in payment of its aid in liberating Finland from Russia," though other territorial concessions were also envisaged. Unsuccessful with the Swedish General Staff, the committee then turned and cautiously established indirect contacts with Wallenberg, whom they did not trust, as they considered him to be Entente-oriented. Here also it would appear that nothing concrete developed.[19]

These endeavors are to be contrasted with a September proclamation of Finnish nationalists in Stockholm directed against any cession of the Aland Islands to Sweden as demanded by the activists. These Finns felt that the islands belonged to Finland and not to Russia and that the annexationist desires of the activists aimed at a dismemberment of Finland and the acquisition of the islands in payment for Swedish assistance to Finland. No

19. Otto Stenroth, *Ett halvt år som Finlands första utrikesminister* (Helsingfors, Söderström, 1931), p. 10; *Bulletin périodique de la presse scandinave,* No. 242, p. 8. The proposal that Sweden enter the war on Germany's side and assist Finland's independence had been made by Finnish nationalists to one of the leaders of the opposition as early as January of 1915. It was pointed out at that time that in declaring her neutrality Sweden should have extracted concessions from Russia on the question of the Aland Islands and Finland. Palmstierna, *Orostid, 1,* 89.

such assistance was needed, they explained. Above all, the Finns wished to help themselves without foreign support.[20]

The only bond between these two Finnish camps was their desire for Finland's independence and their natural hostility to Russia. Of the two, the committee of the Finnish Diet was more realistic. The possibilities of a successful armed rebellion, without outside assistance, against the forces of Czarist Russia were nil. Independence, if it were to be achieved at all, had to be achieved with some sort of outside aid. Thus from necessity rather than choice, they were forced to make overtures to the Swedes and later to the Germans. Since altruism is not an abundant commodity in interstate relations, their only inducement to Stockholm to aid their cause was some sort of territorial concessions in which at the very least the Aland Islands would be included. When Finnish fortunes subsequently changed, what was offered in 1915 as an inducement for Swedish aid would be withdrawn.

Admission that the Aland Islands had been fortified immensely strengthened activist agitation, a situation of which Sir Edward Grey was quite aware.[21] By January of 1916, Nekludov's mission was further complicated by a rising displeasure in Swedish government circles over the British blockade and British interference with Swedish merchant shipping. The recrudescence of pro-German feelings did little to ease his task. Receipt of these reports could only have produced uneasiness in the Russian High Command, for at this juncture, with Russia heavily engaged on the eastern front, war with Sweden would have been foolish and was to be avoided. Reassuring statements by Sazonov near the end of January, in an attempt to allay Swedish fears,[22] generally made a "good impression," though the Swedish press accepted them "with certain reservations." [23]

Nekludov's fears were that fresh efforts would be made by the activists in the spring of 1916 to create discord between Sweden and the Entente, thus drawing Sweden to Germany's side. The

20. *Die internationalen Beziehungen,* 2d ser., *8,* Pt. II, 528n. 1.

21. Palmstierna, *Orostid, 1,* 174.

22. *Le Temps,* Jan. 21, 1916, p. 4; *New York Times,* Jan. 31, 1916, p. 1.

23. *Bulletin périodique de la presse scandinave,* No. 2, p. 3.

ammunition for this activist compaign would be furnished by the Entente's economic blockade and chiefly by the question of the Aland Islands. To thwart this action the Russian minister thought it would be wiser to support with "just concessions" the more moderate elements in government circles and Swedish public opinion. Feeling that he could overcome the difficulties by direct and personal contact with the Foreign Ministry and War Ministry, Nekludov asked and received permission to return to St. Petersburg. So as not to arouse suspicions in Stockholm, he explained that he was returning because of family considerations.

In the discussions that ensued in St. Petersburg in February of 1916, Sazonov concurred completely with Nekludov's point of view on the question of the Aland Islands as well as on the actions of the Swedish activists. It was agreed, however, that "there was no immediate or very grave danger." Nevertheless, it would be "necessary to make reasonable concessions to the Swedes." [24] Promises more concrete in nature were received from the Czar, who commanded Nekludov upon his return to Stockholm to inform King Gustaf that he would be pleased to do everything possible to strengthen Russo-Swedish relations and that he hoped that King Gustaf on his part would likewise try his very best to do the same.[25] He was also to "assure" King Gustaf "thoroughly" on Russia's intentions in the Aland Islands, pointing out that the fortifications erected on the islands were necessitated by the war, and "would disappear as soon as the war was over." [26] Silence and the lack of any assurances on the part of the Russian military were significant.

Concurrent with Nekludov's visit to St. Petersburg, Sazonov again tried to reassure the Swedes publicly, this time during an address to the Duma reviewing the war situation. The Foreign Minister said he thought it unfortunate that across the Gulf of Bothnia there were people who, because of deep-seated prejudices —an obvious allusion to the activists—and German influence,

24. Anatole Nekludoff, *Diplomatic Reminiscences,* trans. Alexandra Paget (London, John Murray, 1920), pp. 385–87.

25. *Krasnyi arkhiv, 32* (1929), 12–13.

26. Nekludoff, pp. 399–400.

cherished toward Russia a "feeling of mistrust." Russia, he insisted, had no aspirations to the "territories of our neighbors in the North." Of what use, he asked, in an oblique reference to the Aland Islands, would an icebound port on the Scandinavian peninsula, in icebound waters, be to Russia? His country's history did not impel it toward the Scandinavian coast. Russia had to "obtain an outlet in a free sea in quite another direction." [27]

Yet, shortly after the above declaration, Sazonov was instructing Isvolsky in Paris that the Allies should endeavor to divert Sweden from a hostile Russian policy and simultaneously to consider the means and steps of drawing Norway into the Entente camp, in case war with Sweden could not be averted.[28] Mutual mistrust and fear persisted in the Baltic.

One man who was honestly striving to reduce this fear and mistrust was Nekludov. Immediately upon his return to Stockholm, he requested an audience with King Gustaf to transmit the Czar's words. The King's initial reaction was to ask Nekludov if this information had also been conveyed to Wallenberg. Assured that it had, the King was moved to state that it was "with sincere pleasure and gratitude" that he received the Czar's message. He could not hide from Nekludov, the King continued, that the question of the islands had seriously preoccupied the Swedish government. Public opinion had been repeatedly aroused over the issue. Within a few weeks a new session of the Riksdag would open, and his ministers thought they would be closely questioned on the subject. King Gustaf then alluded to the events of 1908 and the Russian attempt to revise the 1856 convention. He pointed out that the war had revealed "possibilities and dangers" which had not existed before—an obvious reference to the fortification of the islands during a period when the other signatories of the 1856 convention were Russia's allies and unwilling to protest this action. Therefore his government had a "legitimate desire" to settle the question of the islands in a "definitive manner" which would not allow for "any ambiguity." The only way this could be done was by "direct and formal" discussions between Stockholm and St. Petersburg.

27. *The Times* (London), Feb. 24, 1916, p. 7; *New York Times,* Feb. 24, 1916, p. 1.
28. *Krasnyi arkhiv, 32* (1929), 24n.

Nekludov replied that Wallenberg had already indicated to him Sweden's desire for a new and special convention between Stockholm and St. Petersburg covering the question of the Aland Islands. He admitted that on his recent visit to St. Petersburg he had transmitted this proposal to Sazonov and that as far as the Russian Foreign Ministry was concerned there was no objection to beginning negotiations on this point, on the understanding that any negotiations would only deal with the postwar period and not with the present hostilities.

In subsequent meetings after the question had been examined more carefully by Nekludov and Wallenberg, the Russian minister asked Sazonov to authorize him to address an official note to the Swedish Foreign Minister in which the assurances he had conveyed to King Gustaf from the Czar would be recorded: that the fortifications "would disappear" with the end of hostilities. Nekludov felt that Russia should take into consideration the fears manifested in Sweden over the fortification of the islands, fears cultivated by the activists and German propaganda. He thought that if Russia refused to explain itself "explicitly" on the question of the islands and to give Sweden formal assurances, Stockholm would consider it proof that St. Petersburg was only intent on gaining time and contemplated eventual use of the islands as a military base which would, of course, constitute a menace to Sweden. On the other hand, if Russia entered into negotiations with Sweden over the question of the islands, it would prove that there existed no ulterior motives or schemes injurious to Sweden's safety.

While he did not commit himself on the matter of Wallenberg's proposed negotiations, Sazonov did authorize Nekludov, at the proper moment, to record in a formal note to the Swedish government the verbal assurances which he had conveyed to King Gustaf on behalf of the Czar concerning the fortifications.[29]

Between further antagonizing the Swedes, thus throwing them into German arms, and retreating somewhat from his earlier position, Sazonov chose the second alternative.

As these negotiations were proceeding between Stockholm and

29. Nekludoff, pp. 411–12, 415.

St. Petersburg the campaign of the activists, as foreseen by Nekludov and expected by the Swedish government, began to increase in volume and intensity, reaching its peak by April and May.[30] Its coda was an interpellation in the Riksdag on May 2 by Professor Gustaf Steffen, a former member of the Social Democratic party dismissed from the party the previous autumn for "activism." [31] Steffen's interpellation, wrote a member of the opposition, was both "challenging in its form and insinuating in its contents." [32]

Wallenberg's reaction was to point out that the activists who were so agitated over the question of the islands represented only a small fraction of the Swedish people, so small, in fact, that they could not exercise any influence on the decisions of the Swedish government. He did not see any likelihood of Sweden's being dragged into the war, though he was willing to admit that the government did have, at this juncture, a number of foreign policy difficulties to resolve. Personally he saw no cause for fear. One had simply to keep calm.[33]

Regardless of Wallenberg's assurances, the campaign unleashed by the activists unnerved the Russian Foreign Ministry and military establishment. Where previously Nekludov had had to warn them about being too complacent in their attitude toward the Swedes, he now had to restrain them from moving too far in the opposite direction. But Nekludov's sang-froid was not a quality found among the Entente ministers in Norway, who "uttered loud cries of alarm," [34] nor was it found, at least at this point, in Sir Esme Howard, his British colleague in Stockholm. The latter had from the beginning of hostilities been assigned by Whitehall two tasks: keep Sweden out of the war, and prevent her from assisting Germany economically.[35] The agitation of the activists he found a threat and his dispatches recorded this feeling.

30. Palmstierna, *Orostid, 1,* 229; Nekludoff, pp. 415–16; *Bulletin périodique de la presse scandinave,* No. 1, pp. 3–4; No. 2, p. 3; No. 3, p. 4; No. 4, p. 3; No. 5, pp. 1–3; No. 6, pp. 1–3.

31. *Bulletin périodique de la presse scandinave,* No. 5, p. 2; *Le Temps,* Nov. 16, 1915, p. 2.

32. Palmstierna, *Orostid, 1,* 230.

33. *Bulletin périodique de la presse scandinave,* No. 7, pp. 2–3.

34. Nekludoff, p. 416.

35. Sir Esme Howard, *Theatre of Life* (Boston, Little, Brown, 1936), 2, 218.

Russian and Anglo-French Assurances

On May 9, a week after Steffen's interpellation had been posed in the Riksdag, Sir George W. Buchanan, the British ambassador in St. Petersburg, paid a visit to the Russian Foreign Ministry. He was inquiring, he explained, about events in Sweden, since the dispatches he had received from his associate in Stockholm, Sir Esme Howard, were rather alarming. He then informed Baron Mavriky Fabianovich von Shilling, the Under-Secretary of State for Foreign Affairs, the contents of several telegrams that he had received from Sir Esme. In the conversation that ensued Sir George stressed that he was expressing only his personal views and not those of his government, meaning in diplomatic parlance that he had been instructed by his government not to present his remarks as officially inspired.

He understood, he explained, that fortification of the Aland Islands could not be avoided regardless of whether this action were in keeping with the 1856 convention. Yet, this Russian move had proved a useful weapon in the hands of the Swedish activists. He asked, therefore, if measures could not be taken as quickly as possible to prevent agitation of the question which could lead to a war with Sweden. It was in the interests of the Entente to do everything possible to avoid hostilities with Sweden. Sir George feared that if the Entente did not liquidate this activist agitation by timely and reassuring statements to the Swedish government and if the problem were further aggravated, Entente assurances would still have to be given to Sweden and would be too late to stop the course of events.

Sir George believed that the assurances desired by Sweden from Russia could be covered by a statement that at the end of the war the fortifications constructed on the Aland Islands would be destroyed, and this statement would be confirmed by England and France. The desired statement might read that Great Britain and France confirm that the Aland fortifications are of a temporary character and that Russia was forced to erect them to protect herself against a German attack, intending, as soon as the war ended, to conform again with the servitude imposed by the 1856 convention.

In reply, Baron Shilling pointed out to Buchanan that the latest information received by the Russian Foreign Ministry from Nekludov in Stockholm was of a calming character. As to Buchanan's proposed draft statement, Baron Shilling believed that Foreign Minister Sazonov could accept it only in agreement with the Russian military. The latter in all probability would hardly decide to bind themselves for the future on this question. The present war had shown the importance of the Aland archipelago. Without possession and fortification of the islands, Russia would not be able to repulse German attacks on the Finnish coast. At the time it was not known if it would be necessary at the end of the war to take new measures to protect Russia from danger in this direction. In any case, the draft statement proposed by Sir George, referring to the 1856 convention, seemed to Baron Shilling unacceptable mainly because the wording of the 1856 convention permitted wide interpretation. Indeed, under the 1856 convention even the erection of a radio station, which was absolutely necessary, could be considered as prohibited by the convention. Buchanan noted with a smile that at the present moment the main thing was to avoid a war with Sweden. Later if the necessity were to arise it would undoubtedly be possible to find not one but a host of excuses to justify new fortifications in the island group. On this cynical note the interview ended.

Informed later that same day of Shilling's conversation with the British ambassador, Sazonov thought that it would be difficult to accept Buchanan's proposed draft statement in the form suggested. Instead, he expressed the opinion that the statement he had made to the Swedish minister, Brändström, in October of the previous year was enough for Russia—the statement that Sweden had to judge the future by the past, since Russia had never in her possession of the Aland Islands used them, nor was she intending to use them in the future, for hostile actions against Sweden. This statement, as we have seen, had been included in the aide-mémoire of October 14, 1915, conveyed by Nekludov to Wallenberg. Sazonov's proposal was that, if the English and French considered it appropriate, they could transmit officially and confidentially to Stockholm the statement: "The Allied Governments are able to assert that Russia had been compelled to fortify the Aland Islands only in order to prevent Germany from possessing them and has not the slightest intention of using these islands as a base for any hostile acts against Sweden." The divergency between this declaration and the one proffered by Ambassador Buchanan was obvious; Russia had no intention of committing herself to future arrangements at this time.

When Buchanan called at the Foreign Ministry the next day Sazonov gave him his proposed draft statement. Sazonov explained to Sir George that, though he was sympathetic and in complete agreement with the idea of a declaration to be made to the Swedish government, he preferred to substitute his own draft for the one tendered by Buchanan the previous day.[36] Buchanan remarked that he feared that, since this proposed formula said nothing about the future fortification of the islands, it was not likely to satisfy the Swedish government. Sazonov replied that Russia's past conduct should assure the Swedes for the future. It was through the Dardanelles, the Russian Foreign Minister commented, and not through Sweden that Russia hoped for access to the sea. Sazonov added that he had no objection to Wallenberg's stating that he had received satisfactory assurances from the Russian government and that these assurances had in turn been confirmed by the British and French governments.[37] Buchanan's fear that the Russian formula would be insufficient for the Swedes, since it contained "no engagement for the future," was also voiced by the British and French ministers in Stockholm. Their recommendation was that there be added to Sazonov's formula the sentence: "The Allied Governments can further affirm from assurances received from the Russian Government that in regard to fortifications the status of the islands established by the treaty of 1856 will be restored as before the war." [38] It would be several days, however, before Buchanan could discuss this proposed addition with Sazonov.

While the Shilling–Buchanan interview was going on in St.

36. *Krasnyi arkhiv, 32* (1929), 35–38.

37. Buchanan (Petrograd) to Grey, No. 672, May 10, 1916 (File 5562 in FO/371/2753, PRO).

38. Howard (Stockholm) to Grey, No. 1122, May 11, 1916 (File 5562 in FO/371/2753, PRO).

Petersburg, Nekludov was also holding an interview with Wallenberg in Stockholm in view of the growing agitation concerning the Aland Islands. Following this interview he sent to Wallenberg that same evening a private letter, friendly and calm, in which he expressed the desire that, in replying to Steffen's interpellation, the Swedish government stigmatize the unappeasable agitation of the activists and do justice to Russia's correct and friendly behavior, at the same time expressing trust in his country's unequivocal and repeated assurances. In short, he was asking that they renounce the activists in the clearest way.[39] Nekludov subsequently wrote that this letter, which was approved by his Entente colleagues, was worded so that Wallenberg "could submit it to the King and to the political personages in view—which Wallenberg made a point of doing." [40] The next day, at the time Sazonov's draft statement was being given to Buchanan, Nekludov, in line with a previous request that he had made, had an interview with the Prime Minister, Hammarskjöld, with Wallenberg present. The results of this interview he found displeasing. Hammarskjöld throughout the discussion defended the activists and pointed out to Nekludov that the problem of the fortification of the Aland Islands was the source of the understandable and excusable agitation to be found not only among activists but throughout Sweden. He twice repeated the Latin maxim, *"ablata causa cedit effectus"* (when the cause has been removed the effect gives way). In ending the interview, Hammarskjöld and Wallenberg expressed the desire that Russia agree to continue to exchange ideas on the Aland question. Nekludov replied that his government had no reason to avoid such discussions under normal conditions, but the Swedes themselves had to create the atmosphere in which such discussions could take place. He feared that, in the present agitated and threatening atmosphere directed against Russia, any kind of concessions from the Russian side would appear as surrender to extortion, and no Russian would sponsor such concessions.

Reporting to Sazonov, Nekludov wrote that he thought the situation was still not dangerous but could become more com-

39. *Krasnyi arkhiv, 32* (1929), 39n.
40. Nekludoff, p. 417.

plicated. The real danger, as far as he was concerned, was a possible conflict between the government and the Riksdag majority over foreign policy. In this situation, the Swedish Royal Court might attempt to establish an activist cabinet and mobilize the armed forces with the intent of controlling the Social Democratic party. This party, though Nekludov did not mention it, was partial to the Entente cause. Nekludov therefore believed that a "more positive declaration" from Russia concerning the Aland question after the war could do a great deal to calm public opinion and assist the Hammarskjöld government. But if this was to be done Russia would have to have as a necessary precondition a cessation of the agitation. Likewise, the government would have to disclose to the Riksdag the prior assurances given by the Russian government. Time for this, he informed Sazonov, was to be had since the scheduled reply to Steffen's interpellation had been postponed. He closed with the request that he be instructed: first, to permit Wallenberg to use the information that he had given him on January 8, 1915, when he first announced to him Russian intentions to fortify the islands as well as the information contained in his aide-mémoire of October 14, 1915; second, to declare that Russia had no objections to further talks but only with the preconditions mentioned above.

The nature of the reply sent to Nekludov was determined by the necessity to receive instructions from the Czar himself before a decision on the Aland question could be made. Especially necessary was the Czar's permission as to whether a promise should be given to the Swedish government concerning nonfortification of the island group after the war. Sazonov's reply, therefore, merely instructed Nekludov to remind Wallenberg of his January 1915 promise to attempt to calm Swedish public opinion if it became agitated on learning of the Russian fortification of the archipelago. He was also to ask him to disclose in the Riksdag the explanations given by Nekludov on the necessity of the Russian action and the reassurances given him concerning Russian intentions toward Sweden. On the question of further talks with the Swedish government, Nekludov was to inform Wallenberg that Russia did not avoid such talks, but that they would be fruitful only if they were carried on in a calm atmosphere. Thus Sazonov hoped that the Swedish government would find a way to influence the present agitation by moderating the Swedish press and public opinion.

On May 12, the day following this dispatch to Nekludov, Sazonov reported to the Czar the situation as it had developed up to that point. He pointed out to the Czar that the question of the Aland Islands, which was an irritant in Russo-Swedish relations, naturally gave Germany and her supporters in Sweden a weapon for exciting Swedish public opinion against Russia, especially after it became known that the islands had been fortified. He recalled that Nekludov had reassured the Swedes when the news was given to them of Russia's intention to fortify the islands, and the Swedes had understood the necessity of Russia's defensive measures. Though they did not object to this action, they did express the desire to receive assurances from Russia that after the war the islands would not be fortified. Since he did not wish to commit himself to any future arrangements, Sazonov, as instructed by the Czar, entrusted Nekludov to limit himself to stating that Russia, intent on maintaining good relations with Sweden, was not interested in using the islands to create any threat against her but was merely using them in self-defense against Germany. He then repeated to the Czar the comments that he had made to the Swedish minister in October of 1915, that Sweden had nothing to fear from Russia as was to be assumed from Russia's past behavior in the islands.

However, the intense agitation in Sweden threatened to aggravate severely Russo-Swedish relations. Since the Russian military, Sazonov continued, had repeatedly stated that every effort should be made to avoid war with Sweden, he asked if the Swedish desire for some sort of assurances on the nonfortification of the islands should not be met. To gain time and simultaneously help calm Swedish public opinion he had instructed Nekludov in Stockholm to inform Wallenberg that Russia would not avoid any talks with the Swedes over the Aland question, but these talks to be fruitful could only take place quietly and removed from the present agitation. If discussions with the Swedish government could be opened and maintained, the next question that had to be faced was how to satisfy the Swedish desire for assurances on the nonfortification of the Aland Islands. He recalled to the Czar that the British ambassador, Buchanan, had objected to any fortification of the Aland Islands for the future in order to avoid Swedish hostility. Sazonov believed that if Sweden were unsatisfied by a Russian declaration that the fortification of the Aland Islands would not be directed against her, then Russia would have to decide whether to risk war with Sweden or agree to promise that at the end of the war the islands would not be fortified. By nonfortification of the islands Russia would also receive as a quid pro quo a Swedish promise to remain neutral during the present war. After posing this Russo-Swedish problem, Sazonov closed his report to the Czar and awaited his instructions. Later that same afternoon at a Cabinet meeting Sazonov was assured that no obstacle would be raised to any Russo-Swedish understanding by the naval authorities. At this meeting the Minister of Marine, Vice-Admiral Grigorovich, confirmed that from the navy's point of view demolition of the fortifications after the war would cause no damage to Russia's defenses in the Baltic.

On this same day Nekludov was also cabling from Stockholm his own views on what Russian policy should be toward Sweden as well as reporting disturbing developments in German–Swedish–Russian relations. According to information that had been given to him, Berlin had suggested to King Gustaf that the Swedish government propose to Russia that Russia declare the Aland archipelago neutral under a guarantee to be given both by Russia and Germany. If this were agreed, strict neutralization of the island group would then be entrusted to units of the Swedish army and navy. This proposal, Nekludov warned, would be communicated in a few days, though Wallenberg, he added, would resign if it were. Thus, for the purpose of bringing the Swedes in on their side, the Germans were willing to promise neutralization of the islands in 1916, an action they had rejected when it was proposed by the Swedes in early 1915. But for the Germans a new and daring move was needed—like bringing Sweden in on Germany's side—to change the tide of war, which on the western front by 1916 had bogged down to a war of attrition. The marginal annotation on this report written by the Czar several days later was that he would never forgive Sweden for this action. In the end he never had to, since the demand was never made, thanks to timely Russian concessions and to English and French assurances to the Swedes.

This disturbing information was mirrored in the recommendations Nekludov offered in his second report. After examining the whole situation he had come to the conclusion that Russia should declare to the Swedish government that at the end of the war Russia would demilitarize the Aland Islands. Likewise, Russia would promise not to have on the islands during peacetime any military or naval bases. This declaration, thought Nekludov, should be immediately given before Sweden presented impossible demands of her own after which any Russian declaration would be a concession to extortion. If any declaration were to be made it had to be given publicity so that in Sweden it would be public knowledge the very next day. At the same time it should be pointed out that this Russian declaration was only a more definite and solemn repetition of the assurances given to Wallenberg in January and October of 1915. In this way the voluntary character of the declaration would be stressed even more.

The advantage of such a step was that as a result all the present agitation and fears existing in Sweden would disappear, and reasonable men would be convinced of the artificiality of the present agitation and of the sincerity and goodwill of Russia. Looking toward the future, Nekludov believed that Germany could become stronger in the Baltic only if she was victorious in the present war. In such a situation she would demand from Sweden neutralization of the islands. In case of her defeat Germany would no longer be a danger in the Baltic and it would be absolutely unnecessary for Russia to maintain military bases on the Aland Islands against Sweden.[41]

Aside from Nekludov, the other Entente ministers were also sending disturbing reports out of Stockholm. Reception of similar information in St. Petersburg on the following day, May 13, as well as the desire to pressure the Russians to promise Stockholm that they would demilitarize the Aland Islands after the war and thus calm Swedish public opinion, propelled Buchanan and his French colleague, Maurice Paléologue, to call on Sazonov. Dur-

41. *Krasnyi arkhiv, 32* (1929), 38–41 and ns.

ing that morning Sazonov had been preoccupied with the report communicated by Nekludov that the Swedes contemplated neutralizing the islands under a joint German–Russian guarantee to be exercised by the Swedish fleet. Any demand of this nature, Sazonov warned Buchanan, "would be tantamount to an ultimatum and lead to war." On the question of a statement to be made to the Swedes, Buchanan repeated his fears that Sazonov's proposed formula would fail to impress the Swedes and disclosed to the Russian Foreign Minister that this attitude was also shared by his associate in Stockholm, Sir Esme Howard. He then read to Sazonov the sentence that the British and French ministers in Stockholm thought should be added to Sazonov's draft formula: "The Allied Governments can further affirm from assurances received from the Russian Government that in regard to fortifications the status of the islands established by the treaty of 1856 will be restored as before the war." Sazonov had no objection to this proposed addition provided the words "established by the treaty of 1856" were omitted. Sazonov refused to have any reference to the 1856 treaty mentioned in the statement. Though he was in favor of a statement to the Swedes, he wanted it to be the more indefinite draft declaration submitted by him to Buchanan and Paléologue on May 10. Thus including the section that he had accepted from Buchanan, Sazonov's statement was to read: "The Government of the [French] Republic and the British Government are moreover in a position to declare, according to the assurances they have received from the [Russian] Imperial Government concerning the fortifications, that the status of the islands will be re-established as before the present war." This communication was to be made verbally to Wallenberg, and its terms were not to be published, though Sazonov had no objection if Wallenberg wanted to publish some sort of statement.

Sir George then turned Sazonov's attention to the fact that the influential Swedish newspapers *Dagens Nyheter* and *Handelbalded* had asked the Foreign Secretary, Grey, to express his opinion on the Aland question. Since it was desirable to calm Swedish public opinion Grey wished to reply and asked Sazonov's permission to state that "The recent agitation in Sweden with regard to the question of the Aland Islands seems to us here to be of an unfair and somewhat fictitious character. This is shown by the fact that, as far as we are aware, the Swedish Government have not, since the agitation began, approached the Russian Government on the subject. If they did we feel certain that the Russian Government, who have every desire for good relations with Sweden, would evince a friendly disposition with regard to Swedish wishes." On the whole, Sazonov thought the proposed statement very useful and gave his consent. However, ever alert to protecting Russia's position his only objection was to the concluding word, "wishes," which he felt could be interpreted too widely and which again in his opinion should be replaced by the word "interests." With this the interview terminated.[42]

The arrival of Nekludov's disturbing cables as well as those of the Entente ministers in Stockholm and the visit of Buchanan and Paléologue moved Sazonov early that afternoon to contact the Czar again. After reporting the disturbing information received from Stockholm he asked the Czar for a reply to his report submitted to him the previous day. Under pressure from all sides, the Czar had no real choice. Thus late that evening the Czar empowered Sazonov to make a statement to the Swedish government that after the war the Aland archipelago would not be fortified during peacetime on the understanding that the Swedes would promise to remain neutral during the present hostilities. The necessary instructions were urgently cabled to Nekludov on the understanding that this proposal was not to be made to the Swedes unless he considered the situation dangerous, and it would be desirable to solemnize this understanding in a bilateral treaty.

No sooner had these instructions been dispatched to Stockholm than there arrived from Nekludov a reply to Sazonov's instructions of May 11 dealing with the dilatory response he was to give to Wallenberg on the Aland question. Nekludov, however, continued to press Sazonov for authority to permit Wallenberg to communicate to the Riksdag the verbal and written assurances that Nekludov had given to him on January 8 and Oc-

42. Buchanan (Petrograd) to Grey, No. 695, May 13, 1916 (File 5562 in FO/371/2753, PRO); *Krasnyi arkhiv, 32* (1929), 42–43.

tober 14, 1915. Nekludov considered this communication absolutely necessary. To show that the time factor at this point was becoming more and more important, he pointed out to Sazonov that Wallenberg was scheduled to answer Steffen's interpellation on Tuesday, May 16. He then took the opportunity to confirm his prior cable about the German suggestion to King Gustaf that Sweden ask for neutralization of the islands from Russia and their occupation by Swedish military forces. In ending, Nekludov reported that he had been informed by a "reliable source" that Wallenberg was ready to reassure the Riksdag provided Sazonov would permit him to transmit to the Swedish Foreign Minister in written form the two statements that he had made to him in January and October of 1915.

This news from Stockholm caused the Foreign Ministry to reexamine the whole situation. If Nekludov's report were correct, Wallenberg was willing to settle for much less than Sazonov was prepared to give him. Therefore, it was in Russia's interest to agree to Wallenberg's request. The pressure of the activists and the fear that Sweden might be dragged into the war had caused Wallenberg to scale down his demands for a declaration sufficient to stem the agitation in Sweden and especially in the Riksdag, yet anodyne enough so it could be granted by the Russians. Thus, it was proposed that Nekludov be permitted to transmit to Wallenberg a written statement in line with the declarations he had made to him on January 8 and October 14, 1915. But cables reaching the Foreign Ministry the next day, May 14, showed that Wallenberg was willing to accept even less than this. According to Nekludov, Wallenberg asked that Sazonov facilitate his task in calming the present agitation and also the sincere fears of reasonable Swedes by putting at his disposal a communication which would be "an obvious justification of his actions and would help the [Swedish] policy of absolute neutrality." The communication that Wallenberg had in mind was a written declaration based on Nekludov's verbal comments made to him on Sazonov's instructions in January of 1915. In conjunction with Wallenberg, Nekludov had then drawn up the written statement which he submitted to Sazonov for his consent. The statement merely explained the reasons for the Russian occupation of the islands and stressed that the Russian measures were of a defensive character and meant only for the present hostilities.

In exchange for this declaration Nekludov reserved the right to draft, in cooperation with Wallenberg, the reply to Steffen's question concerning the Aland Islands. Taking into serious consideration the general situation and the necessity to support the Hammarskjöld–Wallenberg government, Nekludov thought that without any doubt Russia had to agree to this arrangement and give Wallenberg the declaration he desired. To strengthen his position he informed Sazonov that his Entente colleagues completely shared his opinion. Nekludov's last comments were that he was waiting for Sazonov's immediate instructions and that Wallenberg's reply to Steffen's interpellation had been postponed until Wednesday, May 17.

Since the written declaration Sazonov was being asked to give to the Swedes by Wallenberg and Nekludov was far less than what the Czar had empowered him to make, the Foreign Minister agreed. He pointed out to Nekludov that if war with Sweden could be avoided without any Russian promise not to fortify the Aland Islands in the future, so much the better. Thus he also instructed Nekludov, if there was no great urgency, to refrain from making the declaration approved by the Czar and cabled to him the previous day. Despite this hopeful situation Sazonov thought it necessary to warn the Russian military staff of the developing situation so precautionary measures could be taken in the northern areas. Further disturbing reports from Nekludov could only have reinforced his caution.[43] Though Sazonov's caution was commendable it was also superfluous, for the crisis had passed.

Not forgetting his allies, Sazonov also informed Buchanan that Nekludov had been instructed to give to Wallenberg in writing the assurances that he had already given to him verbally in January of 1915. At the same time he asked that the British and French ministers in Stockholm refrain from making the communication they had agreed upon. Instead, they were to confine themselves to confirming the written assurances being given by

43. *Krasnyi arkhiv, 32* (1929), 43–46 and ns.

Nekludov. Sazonov thought it unnecessary at present to go beyond the assurances requested by Wallenberg.[44]

As agreed with the Swedish Foreign Minister and acting on Sazonov's instructions, Nekludov "drew up a thoroughly explicit statement" on the Aland question in line with the verbal assurances that he had given Wallenberg in January of 1915 and gave it to him. It was understood that Wallenberg was to communicate the statement to the Riksdag. If for some reason he failed to do so he was to return the statement to Nekludov and "look on it as a verbal communication." [45] However, Nekludov made it clear to Wallenberg that he would only sign the statement after he had seen the "terms of [the] reply" that Wallenberg would make to Steffen's interpellation in the Riksdag. Wallenberg was then shown by Howard the intended Anglo-French text, which Nekludov had agreed to, confirming the Russian declaration, to be given to the Swedes after the Russian declaration was signed by Nekludov. Wallenberg was also told that he could inform the Swedish Cabinet that Britain and France were prepared to make this statement. Though Wallenberg appeared "very satisfied" with the intended Anglo-French statement, he asked if it would be verbal or written. Since Sir Esme Howard had no instructions on this point he turned immediately to London for guidance.[46] Because the situation had become critical, Grey wanted no last-minute complications and instructed Howard in Stockholm to give his confirmation in writing,[47] a procedure to which Sazonov readily agreed.[48]

On May 16, the day before Wallenberg's scheduled reply to Steffen's interpellation in the Riksdag, Howard reported from Stockholm that Nekludov had finally signed the Russian statement after Wallenberg had shown him his intended reply to the

44. Buchanan (Petrograd) to Grey, No. 698, May 14, 1916 (File 5562 in FO/371/2753, PRO).

45. Nekludoff, p. 417. For the Russian statement see Appendix A.

46. Howard (Stockholm) to Grey, No. 1160, May 15, 1916 (File 5562 in FO/371/2753, PRO). For the Anglo-French statement see Appendix B.

47. Grey (London) to Buchanan, No. 1024, May 16, 1916 (File 5562 in FO/371/2753, PRO).

48. Buchanan (Petrograd) to Grey, No. 712, May 16, 1916 (File 5562 in FO/371/2753, PRO). On this point see also *Krasnyi arkhiv, 32* (1929), 48.

interpellation. Wallenberg confirmed that he would read the Russian declaration to the Riksdag and asked Howard if the Anglo-French statement would be in writing. Not yet informed that there was no objection on this point, Sir Esme could only reply that it was preferred that the Anglo-French statement not be read to the Riksdag; Wallenberg agreed, promising that he would only refer to it.[49] On the following day, May 17, the day scheduled for Wallenberg's address to the Riksdag, Nekludov informed Howard that he thought it necessary that Wallenberg be allowed to publish also the Anglo-French statement confirming the Russian declaration. Nekludov rightly thought there would be no Russian objection to this move. Since events were moving rapidly Howard informed London that unless he heard to the contrary before Friday morning, May 19, he proposed to give Wallenberg the permission that Nekludov was requesting.[50]

Everyone had done his work well. Wallenberg was of course satisfied with the contents of the declaration which Nekludov had given him, which he showed—as Nekludov later heard—to all the influential members of the Riksdag. However, he did not "communicate it officially" to the Riksdag as he had initially promised. This action, which perplexed Nekludov and his Entente colleagues, was made necessary by Hammarskjöld's and Wallenberg's desire to avoid establishing a precedent by virtue of which the Riksdag might be able to demand communication to it of certain German statements. Communication of the latter, they felt, might antagonize Berlin, and Stockholm did not feel sure enough of an Entente victory to risk subsequent retaliation.[51]

In spite of this, by showing Nekludov's statement to the influential members of the Riksdag, Wallenberg had prepared the ground for answering Steffen's interpellation. Thus the support that the activists thought they would get in the Riksdag if the

49. Howard (Stockholm) to Grey, No. 1180, May 16, 1916 (File 5562 in FO/371/2753, PRO).

50. Howard (Stockholm) to Grey, No. 1190, May 17, 1916 (File 5562 in FO/371/2753, PRO). That Sazonov had no objections to this was cabled to Howard the following day. Buchanan (Petrograd) to Howard, No. 729, May 18, 1916 (File 5562 in FO/371/2753, PRO). On this point see also *Krasnyi arkhiv*, 32 (1929), 48–49.

51. Nekludoff, p. 417.

government were interpellated on the question of the Aland Islands melted away even in the ranks of the conservatives who had been their warmest parliamentary supporters.

Defending his policies in the Riksdag on May 17, Wallenberg reaffirmed the government's desire to remain neutral. On the matter of the Aland Islands he observed that anyone who had followed the historical development of the question recognized its vital importance to Sweden. "This was the opinion of the Riksdag in 1908," he continued, "and is the opinion of the Government in 1916, and I believe the Riksdag shares that opinion in 1916." He assured the chamber that the government thought it to be its duty to follow the question with the greatest attention, neglecting nothing to "preserve the rights and interests of Sweden in this, as in other fields." The conclusion of Wallenberg's speech brought cries of "bravo" from the crowded chamber, and words of support from the opposition leaders.[52] The activists had shot their bolt.

The following day Wallenberg informed Nekludov by note that his written declaration of May 16 dated January 8, 1915, would not be communicated to the Riksdag nor be released to the public—for reasons which have already been explained but were unknown to Nekludov at that time. The Russian minister was asked not to press for publication of the note in the interests of both Sweden and Russia. Furthermore, he was asked to authorize Wallenberg to postpone publication of the note to a more favorable date in the future.[53] On that same day Howard and his French colleague delivered to Wallenberg two identical written statements confirming the Russian declaration. Wallenberg assured the British and French ministers that he would show their statements to the Secret Committee of the Riksdag that afternoon. As to publication, he asked if this might be left to his discretion, a request to which both ministers agreed.[54] Nekludov's reaction to Wallenberg's note was immediate. He called on Wal-

52. *New York Times,* May 18, 1916, p. 2; *The Times* (London), May 19, 1916, p. 7.

53. Howard (Stockholm) to Grey, No. 1216, May 20, 1916 (File 5562 in FO/371/2753, PRO).

54. Howard (Stockholm) to Grey, No. 1201, May 18, 1916 (File 5562 in FO/371/2753, PRO).

lenberg the next day and asked for a return of the Russian declaration on the grounds that the Swedes had not executed their half of the agreement, i.e. publication and release of the Russian declaration. Without any protest Wallenberg returned the declaration, and Nekludov said that he would ask Sazonov for new instructions in light of the unexpected events that had occurred. These events moved Howard to propose to London, provided the French agreed, to have their statements returned to them since they confirmed a now nonexisting Russian declaration.[55] However, the Russian minister's overzealous action was soon countermanded by Sazonov, who informed Nekludov that no condition had been attached to the Russian note and that it should therefore be returned to Wallenberg.[56] Instructions that no return of the English and French statements was to be made were also communicated to Howard in Stockholm.[57]

Even if Nekludov had been correct in his belief that a condition had been tied to the Russian statement, to have insisted on its return would have thwarted the very situation Sazonov had hoped to achieve: Swedish confidence in Russia's future actions and an undermining of the activist position in Sweden. The Russian statement, though it had not been officially communicated to the Riksdag nor released to the public, appeared to have achieved all this and more. For the moment, the situation had returned to normal.

Subsequent Negotiations

Though private assurances had been given to the Swedes, Sazonov tried, as he had in the past, to assure them publicly of Russian friendship. Chosen for this task was the correspondent of *The Times* of London, who was granted a special interview. Russia, Sazonov claimed, was not a "menace to Norway and Sweden, or to our other European neighbours." He hoped that the Swedes in particular would "now realize the falsity of the vicious

55. Howard (Stockholm) to Grey, No. 1216, May 20, 1916 (File 5562 in FO/371/2753, PRO).

56. Buchanan (Petrograd) to Grey, No. 750, May 21, 1916 (File 5562 in FO/371/2753, PRO); *Krasnyi arkhiv, 32* (1929), 50.

57. Grey (London) to Howard, No. 1514, May 23, 1916 (File 5562 in FO/371/2753, PRO).

idea circulated among them" by Russia's enemies that his country had any aspirations that infringed upon Sweden or its national life. He also hoped and believed that the recent agitation over the Aland Islands, which he was happy to say had been removed as Wallenberg himself announced in the Riksdag, would "prove [to be] the last error or suspicion of the Swedes in regard to Russia that this century will live to see." [58]

But the desire to maximize one's security in interstate relations cannot be ignored by any nation. In a unique position in 1916, Sweden had not the slightest compunction in pressing Russia on the Aland question in a way that, at another time and under different conditions, would have been impossible. The first move by the Swedes was a letter from King Gustaf to the Czar on May 29 several days after Sazonov's interview with the correspondent of *The Times*. Writing in English and addressing the Czar as "Nickie," Gustaf reminded the Czar of all the Russians that he had once told Gustaf that he could always write to him frankly if he were troubled at any time. Gustaf then thanked the Czar and told him how much he appreciated the assurances of friendship and good neighborly relations conveyed to him by Nekludov, expressions which he also shared. He recalled that because of the Czar's intervention the Aland question in 1908 was solved satisfactorily. At that time as well as now, the Swedish Riksdag had unanimously expressed the opinion that the Aland question was of "vital importance" for Sweden. It was for this reason he hoped that at present the Czar's friendly intervention would make "easier the negotiations" intended for dealing with the Aland question. These negotiations, as we have seen, the Russian government was willing to commence as Nekludov had admitted to both King Gustaf and Wallenberg after his visit to St. Petersburg in February. King Gustaf wished that these negotiations could begin as quickly as possible and expressed the hope to the Czar that they would bring mutual understanding and a strengthening of Russo-Swedish relations. King Gustaf would in time be disappointed on all three counts.

The reception of the King's letter provoked a discussion between the Czar and Sazonov as to whether a promise should not

58. *The Times* (London), May 29, 1916, p. 9.

be extracted from the Swedes to remain neutral during the course of the present conflict and to dismantle the Swedish forts along the Russian border. Since any demands of this nature would again have strained Russo-Swedish relations, the reply, drafted by Sazonov but handwritten by the Czar in English, contained no such requests. After explaining Russian actions leading to the fortification of the islands, and the assurances recently given, the Czar thought that Gustaf's worries concerning the Aland question were "absolutely unfounded." But if Gustaf thought it necessary that new negotiations dealing with the Aland question commence, he gave his consent. He warned, however, that it was of "vital importance" that these negotiations be carried on by both sides in a "conciliatory manner"—a hint that Russia would not negotiate under an atmosphere of renewed activist agitation. It was only through "true reciprocity," the Czar wrote, that they could "keep intact the community of aspirations for the strengthening of our good neighborly relations." [59] To agree to negotiations was no great concession on the Czar's part. To arrange them, to conduct them, and to conclude an agreement acceptable to both sides was another matter.

The Czar's June reply of consent moved Wallenberg in July officially to request the Russian Imperial government to commence negotiations for the purpose of coming to an agreement on Russian liquidation after the war of the fortifications constructed on the Aland Islands.[60] Unfortunately, for the Swedes, however, their request was delivered at a most inopportune time, for in late July, the Prime Minister, Boris V. Stürmer, also assumed the post of Foreign Minister replacing Sazonov. In early August Brändström, having received no reply, visited Stürmer and reminded him of the note he had delivered the previous month to Anatole A. Neratov, the Secretary-General of the Foreign Ministry, in which his government expressed its desire to commence negotiations on the Aland question.[61]

59. *Krasnyi arkhiv, 32* (1929), 56–57 and ns.

60. Johannes Hellner, *Memorandum rörande sveriges politik i förhållande till Finland under tiden från Finlands självständighetsförklaring till det finska inbördeskrigets slut* (Stockholm, Norstedt & Söner, 1936), p. 22; Johannes Hellner, *Minnen och dagböcker* (Stockholm, Norstedt & Söners, 1960), p. 392.

61. *Krasnyi arkhiv, 32* (1929), 69.

The question was then raised in Stockholm in September, when Nekludov was asked by Wallenberg if he considered it an "opportune moment for formal negotiations between the Russian and Swedish Governments concerning the Aland Islands." "Most decidedly not," Nekludov unhesitatingly replied. He believed that nothing could be accomplished because the fall of Sazonov and his replacement by Stürmer, whom he heartily detested, had thrown the Foreign Ministry into great confusion. At any rate, it would be hardly worth while to begin negotiations with the new Foreign Minister, for he felt that Stürmer would be replaced within two or three months.[62] Though Nekludov was right—Stürmer was removed in November—Brändström again raised the issue with Neratov near the end of September before departing for Stockholm on a leave of absence. At this meeting with Neratov he inquired if he could report to King Gustaf anything about the Aland question. Brändström added that he understood how difficult it was for a new minister like Stürmer to immediately assume the reins of office, and it was for this reason that he had, during the last two months, avoided raising the question. But he hoped that by this point he could be given some kind of information. Neratov's evasive reply was that the Czar's decision to open negotiations was for the government a binding decision. At the moment, however, the question was being studied by the Foreign Ministry and by all the departments concerned.[63]

In London in early November, the Russian ambassador, Count Benckendorff, expressed the fear that any discussions might oblige St. Petersburg "to make it clear to Sweden that Russia can consider herself no longer bound by the restrictive clause of the Convention of 1856 relating to [the] Aland Islands." It was explained to Buchanan in St. Petersburg that Benckendorff had been told that it was the opinion of the Foreign Secretary that unless Sweden was pressing for a reopening of the question "it would be far better to leave well enough alone." If there was a desire for discussion it would probably be sufficient for St. Petersburg to "renew and emphasize the assurances given last May." It was feared that any reopening of discussions of the islands' future

62. Nekludoff, p. 444.

63. *Krasnyi arkhiv, 32* (1929), 84.

with a view to modifying the assurances given to Sweden in May would assist the activists and cause misgivings to the elements friendly to the Entente cause; "the consequences might be disastrous," Buchanan was warned.[64] Russia had no intention of raising the question, Buchanan quickly responded, but there was reason to believe that Sweden was about to press for some assurances regarding the islands' fortifications after the war. If this were done, "it would be very difficult" for the Russians "to avoid stating that they considered themselves (no longer?) bound by the restrictions of 1856." [65]

Finally on December 27, under heavy Swedish pressure, Russia agreed to convene a conference in Stockholm and requested that the conference should consider "une réciprocité réelle" in the matter of the Aland Islands.[66] That same day, to sound out British opinion, Count Benckendorff again called at the Foreign Office. He was told, Buchanan was informed, that if the negotiations went smoothly to proceed but if "no agreement was likely to be arrived at" it seemed to the Foreign Secretary (now Lord Balfour) "a great pity to embitter international relations at a moment when so many difficult and critical questions were under discussion between Sweden and the Allies." [67] A written note to Benckendorff several days later recommended that "a dilatory reply" be given to King Gustaf on this issue.[68] But Buchanan's disclosure on January 10, 1917, was that the Russian Foreign Minister had "accepted in principle [the] proposed resumption of negotiations for fear of offending [the] Swedes." However, the Russian Foreign Minister had "no wish to commence them earlier than necessary," and would "therefore do all he can to procrastinate." [69] The note which was finally sent to the Swedes

64. Grey (London) to Buchanan, No. 2566, Nov. 4, 1916 (File 148328 in FO/371/2754, PRO).

65. Buchanan (Petrograd) to Grey, Nov. 6, 1916 (File 148328 in FO/371/2754, PRO).

66. Palmstierna, *Orostid*, 2, 20.

67. Balfour (London) to Buchanan, No. 2, Jan. 3, 1917 (File 3184 in FO/371/3021, PRO).

68. Note from Balfour to Benckendorff, Jan. 5, 1917 (File 148328 in FO/371/2754, PRO).

69. Buchanan (Petrograd) to Balfour, No. 41, Jan. 10, 1917 (File 3184 in FO/371/3021, PRO).

expressed the hope that these negotiations would be conducted in a "friendly spirit on both sides by which means only an arrangement satisfactory to both parties can be reached."[70] The Russians, however, fixed no specific date for convening the conference.

Satisfied, the Swedes waited, but the Russians, keeping the British advice in mind, became "dilatory" and began to "procrastinate." In February, the Swedes were informed that negotiations among the Allies would cause a delay in convening the conference, though the names of the Russian delegates would shortly be announced.[71] By the spring Brändström attempted, though in vain, to hasten the projected Stockholm discussions. In April he was forced to report to Stockholm that the solution of the question was being delayed and made difficult by the revolutionary changes wracking Russia—the fall of the Czar and the establishment of the Provisional government. Receipt of these reports prompted Stockholm in May of 1917 to instruct Brändström to press the Russian government on the issue, prevailing on it to be faithful to its decision to choose negotiators as soon as possible (Sweden already had chosen hers). In Stockholm it was feared—rightly in light of the events that would follow—that if Finland obtained her freedom from the Russian state in one form or another, the question would become even more complicated. Pressed by Brändström, the Russians promised that the question would be discussed as soon as the new Russian minister assigned to Stockholm arrived at his post; Nekludov had been transferred to Madrid.

The new Russian minister, Constantin N. Goulkevitch, former Counsellor of the Russian Embassy in Constantinople, did not arrive until late June. Almost immediately upon his arrival Goulkevitch was pressed on the Aland question and asked when his government would begin discussions on the question in order to come to some sort of settlement. Goulkevitch observed that Sweden had all the assurances possible from his own country, as well as from Britain and France. He thought it would be difficult

70. Howard (Stockholm) to Balfour, No. 126, Jan. 12, 1917 (File 3184 in FO/371/3021, PRO).

71. Palmstierna, *Orostid*, 2, 21.

during the course of the war to do any more. However, in an attempt to appease the Swedes he stated that his government had no objections to starting "conversations" on the question—no great concession since this had been promised months before. Needless to state, Goulkevitch's arrival in no way hastened a solution of the question. Though Russian negotiators were finally appointed in the autumn of 1917 these, citing one obstacle after another, never arrived in Stockholm.[72] As Goulkevitch subsequently admitted, he came with instructions to Stockholm to "discuss the Aland question with the [Swedish] Government but not to come to any definite agreement." [73]

These delays and obstructionist tactics raised doubts and suspicions in the minds of the Swedes that Russia might have other intentions. Though they had no concrete proof at the time, their doubts and suspicions were well taken, for Russia was endeavoring during this same period to obtain from her allies a release from the restrictions placed upon her under the 1856 convention.

The opportune moment to press her demands came in February of 1917. At this point France's desire to come to an agreement with Russia over postwar boundaries made it possible for St. Petersburg to ask for parallel concessions. France naturally desired the return of Alsace-Lorraine, a special arrangement for the Saar, and the political division of Germany, the latter step to protect her from any future German invasion. On her side, Russia wanted complete freedom of action in determining her western frontiers. In addition, St. Petersburg considered it necessary to make a proviso that France agree to the abrogation after the war of the Aland Islands' servitude of 1856. Isvolsky in Paris was instructed to draw up the necessary agreement covering these points with Aristide Briand, the French Foreign Minister.[74] Of course, abrogation of the convention of 1856 without England's

72. Pontus Reuterswärd, *Generallöjtnanten och envoyén Edvard Brändström svenskt sändebud i Ryssland 1906–1920* (Stockholm, Norstedt & Söners, 1947), pp. 131–34; Hellner, *Memorandum,* p. 22; Hellner, *Minnen,* p. 392; Howard (Stockholm) to Balfour, No. 1893, June 21, 1917 (File 3184 in FO/371/3021, PRO).

73. Milmore (Stockholm) to the Department of State, June 29, 1918 (File 758.6114A1/32, Record Group 59, NA).

74. Stieve, pp. 211–12; *Pravda,* Nov. 23, 1917, p. 1; *Isvestia,* Nov. 23, 1917, p. 1; *Bulletin périodique de la presse scandinave,* No. 35, p. 6; No. 36, p. 4.

consent would not have been legal, but with France in agreement England's ability to resist Russia's request would have been greatly weakened.

In his note to the Quai d'Orsay on Russia's wish to have a free hand in regulating its borders with Germany, Isvolsky, as instructed, also pointed out: "Le gouvernement impérial croit devoir demander le consentement de la France à la suppression des servitudes, qui pêsent sur les îles d'Aoland." [75]

Though the French agreed to give Russia "toute liberté pour la fixation de ses limites occidentales," they avoided committing themselves on abrogating the 1856 convention. Nevertheless, Isvolsky, who when he drew up the original note must have thought that his ten-year-old dream was near fruition, pointed out to St. Petersburg that the French reply did not exclude regulation of the question by means of a separate agreement.[76]

Paris' caution was undoubtedly motivated by the fear that Stockholm might be pushed into the German camp if she became aware that France had released Russia from her 1856 obligation and had also gone back on her assurances given during the crisis of May 1916. In 1917, Allied arms were not so successful that they could hazard so great a risk for an ally militarily and politically exhausted.

Thus, it is quite clear that there really had been no change in Russian policy in regard to the Aland Islands either under the Czarist or Provisional governments. Both had wished to remove the 1856 servitude at the first favorable opportunity regardless of prior promises, and both had geared their efforts in that direction.

75. Hellner, *Minnen,* p. 397.

76. René Marchand, ed., *Un livre noir, diplomatie d'avant-guerre d'après les documents des archives russes* (Paris, Librairie du Travail, 1934), *3,* Pt. IV, 186–88.

CHAPTER 3

Finnish Independence

German Overtures to Sweden

Isvolsky's messages had arrived at the moment Russia was beginning her long descent into the abyss of revolution. In the ensuing months neither the Provisional government under Alexander Kerensky nor the Bolsheviks under Lenin, struggling to maintain their power, were in a position to pursue the question of the Aland Islands.

In Sweden also, governmental changes were occurring, though in no way as cataclysmic as those in Russia. In late March, the Hammarskjöld–Wallenberg government, in power since the beginning of the war, was forced to resign by the Riksdag and was replaced by another conservative government under Carl Swartz as Prime Minister, with Admiral Arvid Lindman as Foreign Minister. This government in turn was replaced in October of 1917 by a Liberal–Socialist coalition with Nils Edén as Prime Minister and Johannes Hellner as Foreign Minister.

The internal chaos in Russia, however, made it easier for the Germans to approach the Swedes on this question. On November 11, 1917, four days after the Bolshevik seizure of power, King Gustaf was contacted and given a secret and personal message dealing with the islands from the Kaiser and the German Foreign Minister, Baron Richard von Kühlmann, by a Swedish go-between, Count Archibald Douglas,[1] an avid Germanophile, activist, and son of the former Grand Marshal of the Swedish Court.[2]

1. Johannes Hellner, *Memorandum rörande sveriges politik i förhållande till Finland under tiden från Finlands självständighetsförklaring till det finska inbördeskrigets slut* (Stockholm, Norstedt & Söner, 1936), p. 22; Johannes Hellner, *Minnen och dagböcker* (Stockholm, Norstedt & Söners, 1960), p. 388; Erik Kule Palmstierna, *Orostid; politiska dagboksanteckningar* (Stockholm, Tidens, 1953), *2*, 103.

2. *Bulletin périodique de la presse scandinave,* No. 242, p. 7; Palmstierna, *Orostid, 2,* 104. The Russians had complained about the activist activities of Count Douglas' father as early as June of 1916. *Krasnyi arkhiv, 32* (1929), 59–60.

Immediately, the King informed his new Prime Minister, Nils Edén, and new Foreign Minister, Johannes Hellner, of the German overtures. On November 13, this time with his ministers present, the King again received Douglas. According to Douglas, Kühlmann proposed that Germany occupy the Aland Islands. Once this was done, they would be handed over to Sweden on the understanding that they would be occupied by Swedish troops and not turned over to any other power. Kühlmann had added that Germany in no way desired to pressure Sweden, and that it was not Germany's intention to recommend an action which might be injurious to her neutrality. This proposal was so secret, Douglas explained, that not even the German minister in Stockholm knew of it.

The offer was irreconcilable with Sweden's neutrality—any occupation of the islands would have been a *casus belli* with Russia and the Entente—and was so patent an attempt to entrap her in the war that it envoked no real discussion in Swedish government circles. At the same time, cautious as ever, the answer imparted by King Gustaf was no outright rejection of the offer. The King began by expressing his gratitude for the message, in which he noted with joy that there was an opinion in Germany that realized the importance of the question for Sweden and was favorably disposed to Swedish interests. The King emphasized that the question, as pointed out by Sweden so often in the past, was one of the greatest importance to her. Yet at the same time, to take up the issue with Russia and her allies during the present hostilities was impossible. Sweden could only examine the question when all the parties concerned wished to do so—an allusion to any future peace conference. Hence, King Gustaf concluded, he found himself unable to say anything on the question.[3]

Undismayed, the Germans made a second offer, again with Count Douglas as the go-between, about five weeks later on December 17, 1917.[4] At this juncture any offer to the Swedes of the islands, or so the Germans must have thought, would look even more inviting than their November offer. Russia under the

3. Hellner, *Memorandum,* p. 22; Hellner, *Minnen,* pp. 388–89; Palmstierna, *Orostid,* 2, 103–06.

4. Hellner, *Memorandum,* p. 23; Hellner, *Minnen,* p. 389; Palmstierna, *Orostid,* 2, 111.

Bolsheviks had concluded an armistice with the Central Powers and had commenced negotiations toward a peace treaty. The publication by the Bolshevik press of the secret correspondence between Russia and France to liquidate the convention of 1856 after the war had aroused Swedish public opinion.[5] On December 4, the Finnish Diet had proclaimed the independence of Finland. In Sweden itself, pressure had increased for union with the island group.[6] Finally, the Alanders made themselves heard. On August 20, 1917, several months before the fall of the Kerensky government and the Bolshevik seizure of power, an assembly was held in the islands to consider reunion with Sweden. After some discussion, a four-man delegation was chosen, with instructions to bring to the Swedish government and Parliament the knowledge that for special reasons the "population of Aland deeply desired the reincorporation of its islands with the Kingdom of Sweden." Though no representations were made by the islanders at this time, the resolution became known in Sweden.[7]

Yet it was the action of the Aland Islanders which supplied the Germans with the excuse they needed for a new offer. According to Douglas, Germany had become aware of the fact that the population of the Aland Islands desired a union with Sweden. Therefore, if Sweden were to contact Germany officially on this point, the issue could then be brought up with Russia at the peace negotiations which would shortly commence, and the Bolsheviks could be forced to hand the islands over to Sweden. Germany would be willing to do this provided Sweden promised: to allow the islanders to decide the issue in a plebiscite; to construct no fortifications on the islands; not to hand over the islands to any other power; and, lastly, to begin negotiations for an increase of iron ore exports to Germany after the war.

Unlike the first offer, this second offer invoked greater Swedish interest, primarily because of the changing nature of relations in

5. *Bulletin périodique de la presse scandinave,* No. 35, p. 6; No. 36, p. 4.

6. Palmstierna, *Orostid,* 2, 109; Herbert Tingsten, *The Debate on the Foreign Policy of Sweden 1918–1939,* trans. Joan Bulman (London, Oxford University Press, 1949), pp. 86–87.

7. League of Nations, *Official Journal,* spec. suppl. no. 1 (Aug. 1920), p. 27; Sweden, Utrikesdepartementet, *Ålandsfrågan inför Nationernas Förbund* (Stockholm, Norstedt & Söner, 1920), p. 46; Tingsten, p. 84.

the Baltic sparked by the military and political collapse of Russia. Nevertheless, still cautious, Edén decided to decline the German offer, for he felt, as in the case of the first offer in November, that acceptance of the islands from Germany's hands was irreconcilable with Sweden's neutrality and would be interpreted by the Entente as an unfriendly act. It would bind Sweden to Germany and its allies with a concurrent loss of freedom. Furthermore, in any decision on the question the interests of Russia and Finland had to be considered. The collapse of Russia had for the moment removed any threats from that direction. But if Sweden took this occasion to force Russia off the islands, Russia would remember this in the future and good relations between the two powers would be impossible. Then there was the problem of Finland to be considered. All indications were that Finland, which in the meantime had declared its independence from Russia, wanted to keep the Aland Islands. Thus, were Sweden to go behind Finland's back and force Russia to surrender the islands to her, it would strain future Finno-Swedish relations. This would be unfortunate, for it was far more important to have Finland as a "trustworthy friend and good neighbor," if Finland were to maintain her freedom, than to attempt to acquire the islands in the manner now suggested. The value of a Finnish buffer between Sweden and Russia was thus clearly seen by Edén's government, but its geopolitical value would, of course, be further enhanced if Finland were also friendly. Though Edén felt that the islands in Swedish hands could prove an advantage, it would be an advantage in large measure negated by their nonfortification—a condition that would undoubtedly continue into the future. The Prime Minister also believed that the last German stipulation—an increase of iron ore exports to Germany after the war—was unacceptable to Sweden.

Though prior Swedish opinion had been that the issue of the islands should be discussed at a future peace conference, Russia's collapse and its pending peace negotiations with the Central Powers had modified this stand. Edén thought that the best way to protect Sweden's interests was to address a *note verbale* to Germany as well as to Austria and Turkey—all signatories of the Paris Peace Treaty of 1856, in which the Aland Islands Convention had been included—requesting that the legal relationship established, i.e. the Aland Islands servitude, violated by Russia in the course of the war, be reestablished by these powers in their peace negotiations with Russia. Lastly, another solution to be emphasized to these powers would be the complete neutralization of the archipelago.

Both offers left Hellner distrustful of Germany, and especially of Kühlmann. He saw in these proposals a crude attempt to entrap Sweden, perhaps to lure Sweden into actions that would force her into the war. At any rate, Edén's point that Sweden desired a free Finland as a friend and good neighbor, as opposed to acquisition of the islands and the loss of Finnish friendship, was the delicate scale on which all future Swedish decisions touching on the question of the Aland Islands would have to be weighed.

In his reply to Count Douglas, the King pointed out that though no official appeal had been received by the Swedish government from the Aland Islanders, he thought the issue should be brought up with Russia at the coming peace negotiations. Furthermore, it had come to the attention of the Swedish government that Finland would feel offended by Swedish acquisition of the islands, since she was unwilling to let them go voluntarily. Therefore, King Gustaf explained, in a few days the German government would be officially informed of the desires of his government for the solution of this question in a manner considered satisfactory by Sweden.[8]

Sweden's Note of December 1918

During this period, the action of the Aland Islanders was also the topic of discussion between Hellner and the French minister, Émile Thiébaut. Informed that a delegation of islanders was coming to Stockholm to petition him for a restoration of the islands to Sweden, Hellner, seemingly "embarrassed" as to how to reply to them, asked the French minister for "his views on the subject." Though he may have been genuinely interested in Thiébaut's comments, it also provided an excellent opportunity to sound

8. Hellner, *Memorandum,* pp. 23–25; Hellner, *Minnen,* pp. 389–91; Palmstierna, *Orostid,* 2, 111–12.

out French views. Thiébaut replied that his personal opinion was that the Swedish government "should avoid all acts or promises which might not be considered strictly neutral." In spite of the political uncertainty in Russia, he did not think it impossible that the future Constituent Assembly might choose a federal system of government like that of the United States, which Finland might then decide to enter. Thus, the Swedish government should avoid compromising its relations with a nation that under its new Bolshevik masters might once again become a great power in world affairs. Conversely, if Finland were to remain independent, it should be the policy of Sweden to attract her into the Scandinavian grouping of states in order to have a continuous Finno-Swedish shore on the Baltic in opposition to the southern shore of the Baltic, which might become Germanized. In this case, it would be unfortunate to commence a policy of such a nature by depriving Finland of an island grouping considered by the Finns as a natural protection. Thiébaut believed that the Swedes would be safe in replying to the petitioners that the future of the islands could be decided only "by the peace conference and with the consent of the Entente powers." [9]

This conversation by Thiébaut was repeated to Howard.[10] His remarks were approved by the Quai d'Orsay and confirmed to Hellner. Since they closely coincided with the position held by Edén and Hellner, the American minister, Ira Nelson Morris, to whom the conversation was also described, was on firm ground when he reported to Washington that he had reason to believe Hellner completely shared Thiébaut's views on the matter.[11] To make sure that on this issue there would be a united Anglo-French front, Paul Cambon, the French ambassador in London, contacted the Foreign Office, stating that the French government would be happy to see the British minister in Stockholm "s'exprimer au sujet des îles d'Aland dans le même sens que M.

9. Morris (Stockholm) to the Department of State, Dec. 19, 1917 (File 758.6114A1/—, Record Group 59, NA).

10. Howard (Stockholm) to Balfour, No. 3516, Dec. 22, 1917 (File 3184 in FO/371/3021, PRO).

11. Morris (Stockholm) to the Department of State, Dec. 19, 1917 (File 758.6114A1/—, Record Group 59, NA).

Thiébaut."[12] Instructions to Howard from London soon followed: if approached by Hellner he was to "use similar language to that held by your French colleague."[13] As to the proposed delegation, they never arrived. Morris credited their absence from Stockholm to Thiébaut's discouraging comments.[14]

Nevertheless, on December 23, despite Thiébaut's comments but in line with the government's decision and the promise of King Gustaf, a note was addressed to Germany, Austria, and Turkey requesting that the Aland question be considered during the peace negotiations with the Russians at Brest-Litovsk "in order to safeguard [the] vital interests of Sweden in those islands." Though the note did not raise the question of the islands' sovereignty, it asked that Russia promise to destroy the fortifications constructed during the war. Since the convention of 1856 was unsatisfactory, at least as far as Sweden was concerned, it was suggested that the Aland Islands be "neutralized completely." It ended with a statement that Sweden would see in the recognition of the independence of Finland a new guarantee for Swedish security.[15] The latter comment reflected clearly the Edén–Hellner thesis that a Finnish buffer between Sweden and Russia was in Sweden's interests. Inasmuch as Sweden did not recognize the Bolshevik government, no similar request was made to Russia, an action that in a few days time would be criticized by the Entente ministers. When the note was received in Berlin, according to the Swedish chargé d'affaires, it was forwarded to Kühlmann at Brest-Litovsk "with instructions to bring the matter up."[16]

12. Letter from Cambon to Balfour, Dec. 17, 1917 (File 3184 in FO/371/3021, PRO).

13. Balfour (London) to Howard, No. 3317, Dec. 25, 1917 (File 3184 in FO/371/3021, PRO).

14. Ira Nelson Morris, *From an American Legation* (New York, Alfred A. Knopf, 1923), p. 257.

15. Morris (Stockholm) to the Department of State, Jan. 3, 1917 [sic] (File 758.6114A1/1, Record Group 59, NA); Howard (Stockholm) to Balfour, No. 3563, Dec. 29, 1917 (File 3184 in FO/371/3021, PRO); Great Britain, Foreign Office Historical Section Handbooks, *The Åland Islands* (London, H. M. Stationery Office, 1920), p. 22; Hellner, *Minnen*, p. 393; Hellner, *Memorandum*, p. 25.

16. Morris (Stockholm) to the Department of State, Jan. 3, 1917 [sic] (File 758.6114A1/1, Record Group 59, NA).

Six days after the dispatch of the note, Hellner summoned the Entente ministers, informed them of the step taken by the Swedish government, and gave them a copy of the note addressed to the powers at Brest-Litovsk. Thiébaut and his Italian colleague, Francesco Tommasini, were visibly angered. Thiébaut remarked that the Entente had already guaranteed that the Aland fortifications would be demolished at the end of the war. Hellner agreed that this was so, but Swedish opinion was anxious over the matter, especially because of Russia's prior attitude. Sweden, he explained, wanted the subject discussed particularly at this juncture when it appeared that Russia would sign a separate peace treaty.

Tommasini then queried when the note had been handed to the powers at Brest-Litovsk, and if a similar request had been made to Russia, an allusion that Russia, at least in theory, was still a member of the Entente coalition in spite of its control by the Bolsheviks. Legally, because of prior agreements she was prohibited from signing a separate peace treaty with the Central Powers without the consent of her allies. The Foreign Minister replied that the note had been sent a few days before, and, though no note had been sent to Russia, the Swedish Legation in St. Petersburg had informed the Russians of the step which the Swedes were taking. To this answer, Tommasini reflected "sourly" that the Swedish action had only been taken "à nos ennemis." Significantly, throughout this obviously painful interview, Sir Esme Howard made no comments and posed no questions. The ministers, in closing the interview, stated that they would inform their governments of Hellner's statements, and at this point they could say nothing more on the question.[17]

If Sir Esme had remained silent throughout this interview, it was because he saw in the Swedish action, as precipitate as it may have been viewed by his Entente colleagues, certain advantages for the Entente in general and for Britain in particular. He argued in a long report to the Foreign Office that it was not Great

17. Hellner, *Minnen*, pp. 393–94; Howard (Stockholm) to Balfour, No. 3563, Dec. 29, 1917 (File 3184 in FO/371/3021, PRO). Writing in 1936, Hellner, in *Memorandum*, p. 25, states that his interview with the Entente ministers took place on December 20, 1917. Since the note to the powers was sent on December 23, this would appear to be a typographical error for December 29.

Britain's desire to see the islands in Germany's possession. Yet at the moment Finland and Russia were less likely to keep them out of Germany's hands than Sweden. Acquisition of the islands by Sweden would force her to defend them, and thus she would be inclined to support any combination that struggled against the power controlling the Baltic. Swedish possession of the island group would produce a conflict of interests between Stockholm and Berlin and "tend to divorce Sweden politically from Germany." Since Russia was no longer of any assistance in the war, British policy should be to have Scandinavia on the Entente side. All these reasons and goodwill in the Aland question would tend to swing Sweden in Britain's direction. Sweden's anxiety to preserve the Aland archipelago once she acquired it would "create an identity of interests between Sweden, with her control of the entrance to the Baltic, and ourselves in combatting the powers having naval domination in that sea." On the other hand, if Britain were to oppose Swedish union with the archipelago she would "alienate Sweden's sympathies and leave the islands at the mercy of Germany." [18] Within six weeks Swedish occupation of the Aland Islands, followed by a German landing and occupation, would help produce the very Swedish reaction that Howard prophesied.

The answer of the Entente to the Swedish action was not delivered until February 25, 1918. By this point, as we shall see, Swedish occupation of the Aland archipelago had again altered the situation, and, as Howard wrote, it was thought "inadvisable" for the Entente ministers "to make any joint and formal protest on the subject," for fear of antagonizing the Swedes. But they agreed that, in order not to allow the Swedish action to pass completely without notice, it would be useful for Thiébaut as their doyen to make verbal representations to Hellner and at the same time hand him an aide-mémoire containing what he said.[19] In his conversation with the Swedish Foreign Minister, Thiébaut maintained that instead of contacting merely some of the signa-

18. Howard (Stockholm) to Balfour, No. 21, Jan. 11, 1918 (File 2371 in FO/371/3352, PRO).

19. Howard (Stockholm) to Balfour, No. 80, March 6, 1918 (File 2371 in FO/371/3352, PRO).

tories of the Paris Treaty of 1856 "it might have been preferable for Sweden to have addressed in the same manner all the Powers" who were signatories of that treaty. The Allies were ready to take into consideration, as they had always done, Sweden's "special interests" in preserving the 1856 servitude. However, they found it difficult to admit the Swedish thesis that a state which was not a signatory of a treaty should have a right to intervene in the regulation of questions covered by the treaty. If it were true that the Russian government had asked France to give its support with a view to abolishing the 1856 servitude—a point that the Swedes had raised in the December note to the Central Powers—it was no less true that France and Britain had remained faithful to their assurances given to Sweden in May of 1916. While Thiébaut did not wish to enter into a discussion of the solution suggested by Sweden, the Allies, well disposed to her "special interests," reserved the option "to take them into consideration at the opportune moment." [20]

Brest-Litovsk

While the Swedes had been busy contacting the Central Powers, the Alanders were also affecting the flow of events. From December 25 to 29 a sort of plebiscite was held in the islands in which over seven thousand adult men and women signed a petition addressed to King Gustaf and the people of Sweden expressing their intense desire to see the "reunion of the archipelago to Sweden." [21] Though the petitioners' delegation would not arrive in Stockholm to see the King until February 1918, the plebiscite lent support to those elements that desired an immediate occupation of the area.

20. *Aide-mémoire* presented to the Swedish Minister for Foreign Affairs by the French minister re Swedish government note to the Central Powers on the Aland Islands, Feb. 25, 1918. Attached to Howard's (Stockholm) to Balfour, No. 80, March 6, 1918 (File 2371 in FO/371/3352, PRO).

21. League of Nations, *Official Journal*, spec. suppl. no. 1 (Aug. 1920), pp. 27–29; Sweden, Utrikesdepartementet, *Ålandsfrågan*, pp. 48–52. There is no evidence to support the subsequent allegation by the Finnish Foreign Minister, Rudolf Holsti, that the separatist movement in the Aland Islands in December 1917 was begun by Germany as compensation to Sweden for a German monarchy in Finland. Rudolph Holsti, Memoirs and recollections of Rudolf Holsti: abridgment of the author's memoirs (MS), p. 18.

With the coming of the new year, the need to normalize relations with Finland moved the Swedish government, after consultation with Russia and the Entente powers on one side and Germany and the Central Powers on the other, to recognize Finland on January 4, 1918, exactly one month after it had proclaimed its independence.[22] Its recognition, however, was, like that of England, France, and Russia, unconditional and without any reservations,[23] an action that weakened Sweden's case, at least legally, for Finland would later argue that Sweden and the other powers had, by their unconditional recognition, accepted the Aland Islands as part of the sovereign Finnish state.

Nevertheless, during this same period Finnish elements in Berlin indicated a willingness to cede the Aland Islands to Sweden in return for Eastern Karelia,[24] though authoritative statements emanating from Helsingfors, including one from Pehr Svinhufvud, the President of Finland, indicated quite the opposite.[25] With the islanders firm in their demands and supported in Sweden especially by elements within the Conservative party pressing for a return of the archipelago, the Swedish government's position would become increasingly difficult.[26] What had once been solely a Russo-Swedish problem would change and become a Finno-Swedish one because of the pressure of events, and against the will of the Edén–Hellner government.

One of the events ushering in this problem was the negotiations between the Central Powers and the Bolsheviks at Brest-Litovsk. As instructed by Berlin Kühlmann first broached the issue of the Aland Islands to Leon Trotsky and the Russian delegation on January 18, during deliberations on political and territorial questions. He wished to know, he told Trotsky, if the Aland question was to be dealt with by the Soviets or by the new Republic of Finland. Trotsky retorted that a proclamation of Finnish independence had not changed the question of the Aland Islands. Kühlmann observed that on any agreement covering the

22. Hellner, *Memorandum*, pp. 5–7.

23. Finland, Ministeriet för Utrikesärendena, *La question des îles d'Aland (Octobre 1920)* (Helsingfors, Imprimerie du Gouvernement, 1920), pp. 31–35.

24. Clarence J. Smith, *Finland and the Russian Revolution 1917–1922* (Athens, Universty of Georgia Press, 1958), p. 98.

25. Tingsten, p. 89.

26. Palmstierna, *Orostid, 2,* 122, 124, 127.

islands "Sweden—which, owing to her geographical position, was greatly interested in this question—would be requested to give their advice and signature." He admitted that Sweden "was not represented at the present negotiations, but he had good reason to suppose that the wishes of the Swedish people lay in this direction." [27] On this score Kühlmann was quite correct.

Arrival of this news in Stockholm[28] moved the Swedish Foreign Ministry to telegraph to Germany asking for more details about the "attitude of the German Government" on the sending of a Swedish delegate to Brest-Litovsk. The thought that Sweden would send delegates to Brest-Litovsk to defend Swedish interests caused "great enthusiasm" among Hellner's Cabinet colleagues. But because of his own recent experiences with the Entente ministers, Hellner was more doubtful and anticipated trouble with them. Edén, on the other hand, felt that Hellner was overly pessimistic. He thought that the Entente would have no reason to be annoyed.[29] Hellner was correct. The first to complain was the Italian minister, Tommasini. When informed by Hellner that Sweden had not yet been invited to Brest-Litovsk, Tommasini warned him that the acceptance of the invitation "would certainly cause [an] unfavourable impression in Allied countries as it was difficult to understand how Sweden could engage in negotiations concerning modifications" of the Paris Treaty of 1856 with only some of the signatories of the treaty. Tommasini also thought it strange that Sweden, having recognized Finland's independence, should negotiate at Brest-Litovsk with Germany and the Bolsheviks on a matter which concerned Finland more than any other country. Throughout the whole conversation Hellner appeared embarrassed, and Howard, to whom this conversation was reported, informed London that when he saw Hellner he would speak to him in the same sense as Tommasini.[30] Hellner's apprehensions had now been further aroused and were obvious

27. U. S. Department of State, *Proceedings of the Brest-Litovsk Peace Conference* (Washington, D.C., Government Printing Office, 1918), p. 114; Judah L. Magnes, ed., *Russia and Germany at Brest-Litovsk* (New York, The Rand School of Social Science, 1919), p. 93.

28. *PRFRUS, 1918, Russia, 1,* 427–28.

29. Hellner, *Minnen,* pp. 394–95.

30. Howard (Stockholm) to Balfour, No. 171, Jan. 22, 1918 (File 2371 in FO/371/3352, PRO).

when queried on the subject by the American minister on January 23. Asked by Morris whether it was true as reported in the press that the Swedish government "might send delegates" to the negotiations at Brest-Litovsk, Hellner replied that this was so, though he realized it "might create a bad impression" if Stockholm joined in the talks. He added, however, that the question might be handled through the German Legation in Stockholm or through the Swedish Legation in Berlin.[31]

Following this meeting with Morris, Hellner was repeatedly contacted by Sir Esme Howard requesting an interview. When he informed Edén that he suspected Howard wanted to warn him against sending delegates to Brest-Litovsk, Edén replied that it was absurd for England and the Entente to be against such a step, especially if Sweden emphasized that it was interested only in the Aland question. He felt that the Entente should understand that the Swedish government could not allow the Aland question to be excluded from Brest-Litovsk, and Sweden had to be there to defend its interests if the question arose during the negotiations. As cogent as Edén's arguments may have been, Hellner's suspicions and his apprehensions about the reaction of the Entente to any such step were not exaggerated.

In this meeting with Hellner, Sir Esme Howard, as the Foreign Minister had expected, immediately broached the issue of Swedish representation at Brest-Litovsk. Howard stated that though he was speaking personally and without instructions, he thought that the dispatch of Swedish delegates "would create [an] unfavourable impression in Allied countries which might prejudice a settlement of the Aland Islands [question] at a general peace [conference] against Swedish interests." It seemed to the British minister "extraordinary" that the Stockholm government would participate in talks on an international treaty when only a few of the countries which had originally signed the document would be present. Then there was the legal side of the question to consider. How, he asked, could the Swedish authorities negotiate with the Russians at Brest-Litovsk when they did not recognize the Bolshevik government sitting at St. Petersburg? The Bolshe-

31. Morris (Stockholm) to the Department of State, Jan. 23, 1918 (File 763.72119/1163, Record Group 59, NA).

viks, Sir Esme noted optimistically, might fall, and any agreement would prove worthless. He believed that the question could only be solved with the agreement of all the signatories of the 1856 treaty and only at the end of the war, and he insisted that Sweden's present plans would "land them in serious embarrassment." Sir Esme thought that any Swedish participation at Brest-Litovsk with the enemies of the Entente and one of its allies—for Bolshevik Russia, regardless of its denials, was legally still a member of the Entente coalition—would not be compatible with her neutrality.

Hellner denied this assertion. Swedish participation, he maintained, was perfectly natural, for Sweden had important interests to guard in the question of the Aland Islands. Sweden could not regard passively a question of great importance to her and permit it to be decided by other powers, perhaps in a manner harmful to Sweden. It was necessary for Sweden now, while Russia was engaged in peace negotiations, to get from her and the Central Powers a formal declaration, as signatories of the 1856 convention, in favor of the neutralization of the islands. This act would, of course, have to be ratified by all the signatories of the Paris Treaty when a general peace conference took place. Hellner explained that Swedish public opinion was agitated over the Aland fortifications. These fortifications, Howard interrupted, were no threat. The Finns could arrange with the Russians for withdrawal of their troops from the islands and the Swedes could then negotiate with the Finns for destruction of the fortifications. The fortifications were only dangerous to Sweden if they fell into German hands. Hellner observed that an agitated public opinion like that in Sweden did not understand the intricacies of the international situation. Howard retorted that it was the duty of a government to educate the public in another direction if the agitation of public opinion would lead to a serious embarrassment of the government.

As the conversation progressed Sir Esme "insisted more and more" that any participation in the negotiations at Brest-Litovsk was incompatible with Sweden's neutrality. His tone "got more and more determined." The British minister's "countenance got stiffer and his eyes got a cold and stubborn expression." Seeing that they were getting nowhere, Hellner remarked that though he did not share Howard's opinion, he would of course consider his protests if the matter were to develop further. The interview closed on this note, no doubt much to Hellner's relief.

Aside from Sir Esme Howard's *démarche,* indirect pressure on the Swedes by the British was also attempted through the Norwegians and the Danes. In the end the anticipated German invitation to send Swedish delegates to Brest-Litovsk never materialized—an omission that annoyed the Swedes exceedingly—and the question was not pursued further by the Entente. Yet it showed Hellner quite clearly how extremely sensitive the Entente coalition was to any agreement by Sweden with Germany and the Central Powers over political questions.[32]

Though Sweden did not go to Brest-Litovsk to defend her interests, Germany in pursuing her own also furthered those of Sweden. On February 9 the issue of the islands was again brought up in the final session of the Committee on Political and Territorial Questions. In this meeting Kühlmann pointed out to Trotsky that the maximum demand that Germany could make over the islands would be their "neutralization," with the consent of the peoples bordering the Baltic shores.[33]

Neutralization of the islands, however, with the Russian threat removed but with the war continuing, would not have been in Berlin's interests. Therefore, rather than neutralize the islands as desired by the Swedes, Article 6 of the Treaty of Brest-Litovsk of March 3, 1918, merely stipulated that the islands were to be cleared of Russian troops and the Russian Red Guard. Furthermore, the military installations built during the war were to be "removed as soon as possible." On the question of the permanent nonfortification of the islands, as well as their future use for military and navigational purposes, a special treaty was to be con-

32. Howard (Stockholm) to Balfour, No. 195, Jan. 24, 1918 (File 2371 in FO/371/3352, PRO); Hellner, *Memorandum,* pp. 14–15; Hellner, *Minnen,* pp. 395–96. In the first book cited above Hellner states that the interview took place on January 24, and in the second he states that it took place on January 25. The interview, according to Howard's report to the Foreign Office, took place on January 23.

33. U. S. Department of State, *Proceedings of the Brest-Litovsk Peace Conference* (Washington, D. C., Government Printing Office, 1918), pp. 168–69; Magnes, pp. 130–31.

cluded between Germany, Finland, Russia, and Sweden. However, it was understood that upon Germany's wish, other countries also bordering on the Baltic would be consulted on the matter.[34] An article similar to this was likewise included in the Finno-German Treaty signed four days after Brest-Litovsk on March 7, 1918.[35]

Almost two months after the signature of the Finno-German Treaty it was announced that Finland, Germany, and Sweden, but not Russia, had agreed to commence negotiations immediately for the demolition of the Aland Islands' fortifications built during the war.[36] Commencement of these negotiations was delayed until August 21, 1918. A treaty was finally negotiated in November and signed on December 30, 1918.[37] By this time, however, the political configuration in the Baltic had changed once again, and the victorious Germany of Brest-Litovsk was a defeated Germany preparing for peace negotiations with the Allies at Versailles. In the interim, Finno-Swedish relations had also changed markedly, primarily because of the Swedish occupation of the Aland Islands, an action justified by the Swedes on humanitarian grounds but viewed by the Finns as an attempt to acquire the islands militarily at a time when they were struggling against a Russian invasion from without and a Bolshevik insurrection from within. It is to this event that we now turn.

Swedish Occupation of the Aland Islands

In his speech from the throne convening the Riksdag on January 16, 1918, King Gustaf pointed out that Sweden had endeavored in every way to favor the Finnish cause and had recognized Finland as soon as circumstances had permitted. He hoped that a free Finland would join the other Scandinavian

34. Jane Degras, ed., *Soviet Documents on Foreign Policy* (London, Oxford University Press, 1951), *1*, 54.

35. U. S. Department of State, *Texts of the Finland "Peace"* (Washington, D. C., Government Printing Office, 1918), p. 26.

36. Morris (Stockholm) to the Department of State, May 8, 1918 (File 758.6114A1/31, Record Group 59, NA).

37. Great Britain, Foreign Office, *British and Foreign State Papers* (London, H. M. Stationery Office, 1923), *113*, 993–99. The negotiations leading to the demolition of the Aland fortifications are handled in the latter half of this chapter.

countries in their endeavors to promote peace and progress, and that Finnish independence would facilitate for Sweden a satisfactory settlement of the Aland question.[38]

In the debate that followed on January 23, the position of the government was attacked by the opposition Conservative party led by Ernst Trygger. It was Trygger's feeling that the convention of 1856 was an inadequate means for safeguarding Sweden's safety, as the war had clearly shown it had no real value. Therefore only occupation of the islands could give Sweden the required security. The Aland Islands occupied by Sweden were a threat to no one but constituted real protection for Sweden. With the Aland Islanders pressing for reunion with Sweden, the Swedish people should regard it as their patriotic duty to bring a reunion of the islands with the mother country. Trygger did not touch upon the attitude of Finland on this question except to point out that Finland had achieved her freedom through the same principle now being invoked by the Alanders. The inference that one could draw from the speech was that, if a friendly agreement on the archipelago could not be reached after negotiations with Finland, Sweden should strive to acquire the islands without Finnish consent.

In his reply Edén expressed the view that Sweden's policy had to be flexible, that it could not insist obstinately on one solution and one solution only. He felt that the strategic aspects of the Aland problem had been greatly altered by recent events, especially the independence of Finland—here he was probably also alluding to the Bolshevik Revolution. In making any decision the government had to keep in mind the attitude Finland would adopt toward Sweden and Scandinavia in the future, which was a consideration of primary importance. His government, Edén maintained, regarded it as imperative to ensure by all means at its disposal that any solution reached would be one which would not impair Finno-Swedish friendship. Finland's friendship, he continued, was far more important for Sweden's future well-being than any considerations advanced by Trygger. Edén's speech had been a clear exposition of the Cabinet's position on

38. *Bulletin périodique de la presse scandinave*, No. 38, pp. 1–2; *The Times* (London), Jan. 25, 1918, p. 5; Tingsten, pp. 89–93.

the whole question of the islands. Though his statement received support especially from the Swedish left, which felt that exceptions to the principle of nationality had to be made, it was criticized by the Swedish right on the grounds that by placing so great an emphasis on Finnish friendship he had weakened Sweden's chances of acquiring the islands.[39]

By the end of January the results of the December plebiscite held in the archipelago had been received by the Swedish government but were kept secret, and the Finnish minister was informed that Stockholm intended to begin discussions on the question.[40] On February 2, a delegation of Alanders presented King Gustaf with a petition asking for a reunion of the islands with Sweden and expressing the hope that the Swedish government in agreement with Finland would find a means of satisfying their desires.

The King, in his noncommittal reply, merely noted the warm feelings of the islanders for union with Sweden. He expressed the hope that the Swedish government in agreement with Finland would be able to find a way of realizing the desires of the Alanders.[41]

In the interim, between Edén's explanation in the Riksdag of the government's policy on the Aland question and the King's audience with the Aland deputation, the long-awaited Finnish civil war erupted.

From the beginning, the question facing Stockholm was that of the extent and manner of help to be given to the anti-Bolshevist forces under the command of General Carl Mannerheim.

To the Finnish request for arms objections were raised not only by the Minister of War but also by the left-wing supporters of the coalition government. The former felt that any shipment of arms to the Finns would be dangerous, since it had been clearly shown that in a modern war the consumption of weapons and ammunition was far greater than ever before. The latter's objections were on ideological grounds, namely, that the shipment of arms to General Mannerheim and his forces would be

39. *Bulletin périodique de la presse scandinave,* No. 38, pp. 1–2; *The Times* (London), Jan. 25, 1918, p. 5; Tingsten, pp. 89–93.

40. Palmstierna, *Orostid, 2,* 127.

41. *Bulletin périodique de la presse scandinave,* No. 38, p. 6; Palmstierna, *Orostid, 2,* 129; Tingsten, p. 93; *The Times* (London), Feb. 4, 1918, p. 8.

used by the bourgeoisie against the working class. To this argument Hellner, who was obviously less ideologically oriented than some of his coalition colleagues, replied that he would in no way hinder the Finns if they wished to buy weapons from private Swedish suppliers, which was perfectly permissible under international law and therefore in keeping with Sweden's strict neutrality.

On the other hand, Hellner was strongly against any open Swedish intervention in the civil war. An action of this sort, he felt, could lead to war with Russia. Intervention in conjunction with the Germans was also out of the question, since it would be a breach of Sweden's neutrality. Moreover, any cooperation between Sweden and Germany on a political matter, as Hellner had already discovered in his conversations with the Entente ministers, particularly with Sir Esme Howard, was a point on which the Entente was extremely sensitive.

Placed in this impossible situation and wanting to end the fighting in Finland, the only plan that the Cabinet could devise was to request Russia to withdraw its troops from Finland and to offer its services to the Finnish government in mediating the conflict.[42] Though the Cabinet based its policy on the necessity of maintaining good relations with the new Finnish buffer, feeling that the Aland question should be solved by peaceful negotiations between the two countries, events developing on the Aland Islands because of the Finnish civil war would go a long way in negating this policy.

About a week after the King's audience with the Aland deputation, Hellner received reports of the anarchic behavior of the Russian garrison on the islands and pleas from the Alanders for Swedish help and protection. The reaction of the government was to dispatch ships to the islands on February 13, with instructions to remove all persons whether Swedish or Finnish who wished to be transferred to Sweden. Since it was not known what the reaction of the Russian garrison might be, a naval vessel was also dispatched to support the expedition. The expedition, however, was quite inadequate to handle a situation of this type. Consequently on the following day, Hellner at the suggestion of the

42. Hellner, *Memorandum*, pp. 8–21.

Minister of Marine, Baron Erik Kule Palmstierna, called in the Bolshevik agent, V. V. Vorovsky, and described the situation to him. To Hellner's and Palmstierna's request for assistance Vorovsky proposed that he go personally to the islands to talk to the Russian garrison. This was immediately agreed to, and a Swedish destroyer was put at Vorovsky's disposal to convey him to the archipelago. It was also agreed that if Vorovsky could persuade the garrison to depart, the Swedish government would transfer them to Sweden and from there to Russia.[43]

In conjunction with the officers of the Swedish naval expedition, Vorovsky was able to draw up an agreement for the evacuation of the Russian garrison.[44] At this juncture, however, the situation was complicated by the arrival of the Nystad Corps, a Finnish detachment of about six hundred men which had retreated from the mainland and crossed the ice to the islands. The corps was warmly greeted by the islanders, who looked upon them as deliverers from Bolshevik anarchy.[45] Fighting which broke out between the Russian garrison and the Nystad Corps was brought to an end only on February 20 through the mediatory efforts of the Swedes. It was agreed by all the parties that the Nystad Corps would be immediately transferred to Sweden with the Russians to follow as soon as possible. The Finns and the Alanders stipulated, however, that upon the evacuation of the Nystad Corps Swedish troops were to be landed to guarantee the safety of the Alanders during the period that the Russian garrison remained. This condition was agreed to by the Swedish Minister of Marine, Palmstierna, and the first Swedish troops landed on Aland several days later.[46]

The whole operation, at least according to the American minister, Morris, indicated that the Swedish government in-

43. Hellner, *Memorandum*, pp. 26–27; Palmstierna, *Orostid*, *2*, 134; *PRFRUS, 1918, Russia, 2*, 751–52; *The Times* (London), Feb. 16, 1918, p. 5.

44. Hellner, *Memorandum*, p. 28; Palmstierna, *Orostid*, *2*, 134.

45. Joose O. Hannula, *Finland's War of Independence* (London, Faber & Faber, 1939), pp. 85–86; Smith, p. 53.

46. Hellner, *Memorandum*, p. 28; *PRFRUS, 1918, Russia, 2*, 751–54; *The Times* (London), Feb. 20, 1918, p. 5. See also the Swedish blue book dealing with Swedish mediation in the Aland archipelago during February of 1918. Sweden, Sjöförsvarsdepartementet, *Ålandsuppgörelsen* (Stockholm, Norstedt & Söner, 1918).

tended to acquire the Aland Islands "eventually in accordance with the desires of the population as expressed by the confederations [deputations] sent here some weeks ago." [47] This initial impression of Morris was refuted by Hellner, who insisted that the landing of Swedish troops "was not to be considered as the beginning of a permanent occupation as the Swedish government was still of the opinion that the Aland Islands question should be solved by negotiations between England, France, and Finland and if these negotiations led to no result, then at the peace conference." [48] It was a position that the Swedes maintained without qualification. Indeed, somewhat similar words were spoken to Howard that same day. In this interview Hellner assured the British minister, in order to avoid any misunderstanding, and in the name of the Swedish government, that this "was not [a] regular occupation of [the Aland] Islands but merely taken to protect [the] inhabitants until peace was re-established." The question of the islands' sovereignty, he remarked, was one to be settled between Sweden and Finland—an exclusion of Britain and France which he had mentioned to Morris. As for the matter of the nonfortification or neutralization of the archipelago, the Swedish Foreign Minister thought that this could be settled at the general peace conference ending the war with the consent of the signatories of the 1856 Paris Treaty. A like communication, Howard reported to London, had also been made to the French and German ministers in which Hellner had "expressed to the latter [the] hope that temporary Swedish occupation of the Islands would be respected by Germany during the war." Sir Esme's observation was that Sweden's occupation would "at least guarantee [the] Aland Islands from falling into the hands of Germany." [49] His joy here, however, was to be short-lived, for the

47. *PRFRUS, 1918, Russia, 2,* 753.

48. Ibid., p. 754.

49. Howard (Stockholm) to Balfour, No. 487, Feb. 20, 1918 (File 2371 in FO/371/3352, PRO). See also Hellner, *Memorandum,* pp. 28–29. The Swedish minister, appearing at the State Department on February 28, pointed out that the Swedish occupation of the Aland Islands was the "first time troops had left Swedish territory in 110 years." He explained that the Swedish "action was taken to protect the inhabitants of the Aaland Islands but that his Government probably would not claim ownership to the Islands as reported in the newspapers but would simply hold the Islands during such time as it was necessary to protect

Swedish occupation would soon be followed by a German one. These words were repeated by Hellner when he requested the Riksdag to appropriate money to cover the costs of stationing troops on the islands. He assured it that "no political aims" were intended by the occupation, that Sweden desired only the pacification of the islands in accordance with the settlement reached by the parties concerned.[50]

In acknowledging this information and the assurances given to Howard, the British Foreign Office observed that any settlement of the Aland question, insofar as it concerned the British government as a signatory of the 1856 convention, could "only be made after agreement with and with the concurrence of the British Government." This latter point was also stressed in a similar note dispatched by the French government.[51] The reaction of the Soviets was less understanding. In a note handed to Hellner by Vorovsky the Russians protested against the military measures taken on the islands and warned that unless the Swedish troops were withdrawn the Russian government would "be forced to look upon these operations as a hostile action against the Russian Republic." [52] As Russia was exhausted by war and revolution and on the verge of signing a peace treaty with Germany, these threats could be ignored.

The Finnish minister, Alexis Gripenberg, was also uneasy. In a note to Hellner on February 23, he revealed that he had read in the local Swedish press of the government's decision to send troops to the Aland Islands. He thought the Finnish government would greet this action "with satisfaction and gratitude," viewing it as Sweden's first assistance to Finland in her struggle for freedom. Yet at the same time he had to express his surprise that the Swedish government had taken the step without first consulting the Finnish government. He knew, from his conversations with Hellner and his colleagues, that the Swedish

---

the Aalanders." Memorandum from the Office of the Third Assistant Secretary, Feb. 28, 1918 (File 758.6114A1/–, Record Group 59, NA).

50. Morris (Stockholm) to the Department of State, Feb. 23, 1918 (File 758.6114A1/5, Record Group 59, NA).

51. Hellner, *Memorandum*, p. 30.

52. Russia, Komissiia po Izdaniiu Diplomaticheskikh Dokumentov, *Dokumenty vneshnei politiki SSSR* (Moscow, State Publishing House, 1959), *1*, 207.

government planned to send troops to the archipelago, but he did not believe that a definitive decision would be made before the opinion of his government was ascertained. However, since the sending of Swedish troops to the islands had already taken place, Gripenberg emphasized that he put the greatest confidence in Edén's statement given to the Riksdag the previous day, as well as Hellner's verbal assurances given to him several times in the past, that in this action no permanent occupation of the islands was intended. He naturally assumed that the Swedish troops would be recalled as soon as the Finnish government found itself in a position to ensure the safety of the Alanders. In closing his note he asked Hellner to "verify in writing" not only Edén's statement to the Riksdag but also the verbal assurances he had given to him previously. The occupation had sown seeds of mistrust that would be reaped in subsequent events.

In his reply, Hellner pointed out that under the agreements negotiated by the Swedish expedition, both the Finnish Nystad Corps and the Alanders had requested the presence of Swedish troops during the period the Russian garrison remained on the islands. His government thought it was obliged to land troops as had been requested. However, in order to assuage whatever anxieties Gripenberg might have, he confirmed, on behalf of the Swedish government, the prior verbal assurances that he had given to him: that the dispatch of Swedish troops to the islands was necessitated by the insistence of the Alanders and the Nystad Corps and thus had "no political purpose whatsoever." Finally, he requested that the Finns do everything possible to remove the islands from the theater of operations.[53]

It would appear that Gripenberg's anxieties were in large measure due to the activities of the Minister of Marine, Palmstierna. Upon the dispatch of the original Swedish expedition to the Aland Islands, Gripenberg, without Hellner's knowledge, established contact with Palmstierna. Palmstierna agreed that Gripenberg could communicate with the Nystad Corps by way of the Ministry of Marine and the ships of the Swedish expedition. Hellner felt that direction of the expedition was Palmstierna's responsibility, but once the officers of the expedition began to

53. Hellner, *Memorandum,* pp. 30–32.

mediate the dispute, the prerogatives of the Foreign Ministry were usurped.

The Finns subsequently objected to this mediatory endeavor on the ground that the participation of Swedish officers in the negotiations was an intrusion upon Finnish sovereignty over the islands, a charge Hellner denied.[54] The more serious charge was that Palmstierna had given Gripenberg "misleading" information, influencing him to urge the Nystad Corps to consent to the agreements negotiated by the Swedes. Allegedly Palmstierna dispatched a message stating that General Mannerheim had requested Swedish help in transferring the Nystad Corps to Sweden and from there back to Finland. Believing that it was acting on Mannerheim's instructions, the Finns agreed to surrender their weapons and be transported to Sweden. It is pointed out that no corresponding limitation was placed on the Russian garrison, who kept their weapons and were given a month to evacuate the area.[55] At the time, Gripenberg charged publicly that his legation had not been in a position "freely to communicate" with the Nystad Corps, that it had not been in a position to receive information during "several phases" of the events on the islands, and that the agreement concluded on the islands had not been submitted to him beforehand, nor had he recognized it.[56] All these charges, as might be expected, were denied by Palmstierna.[57]

Whether the Finnish charges against Palmstierna were correct or whether the whole episode was due to some misunderstanding is unclear.[58] At any rate, Palmstierna had decided views on the

54. Hellner, *Minnen,* p. 494.

55. Hannula, pp. 85–88; Hellner, *Minnen,* p. 494.

56. Morris (Stockholm) to the Department of State, Feb. 27, 1918 (File 758.6114A1/7, Record Group 59, NA); Finland, Ministeriet för Utrikesärendena, *La question des îles d'Aland,* pp. 62–63.

57. Morris (Stockholm) to the Department of State, Feb. 27, 1918 (File 758.6114A1/7, Record Group 59, NA); Morris (Stockholm) to the Department of State, March 1, 1918 (File 758.6114A1/8, Record Group 59, NA); Hellner, *Minnen,* p. 495.

58. For the Finnish side of the case see Carl Gustaf Mannerheim, *Minnen* (Stockholm, Norstedt & Söners, 1951), *1,* 231–35; Finland, Ministeriet för Utrikesärendena, *La question des îles d'Aland,* pp. 60–64; Finland, Ministeriet för Utrikesärendena, *La garde civique de Nystad à Aland et l'expédition suédoise à Aland en 1918* (Helsinki, Imprimerie du Gouvernement, 1921); Willem van der

whole question which would manifest themselves in the future. As for the Finns, the whole experience left them doubtful of the repeated expressions of friendship and goodwill given by the Edén–Hellner government, as well as of their desire to solve the Aland question amicably.

German Occupation of the Aland Islands

While these events were going on in Stockholm, Helsingfors, and the islands, other decisions taken at Brest-Litovsk and Berlin were further confusing the situation.

Trotsky's decision to break off negotiations with the Central Powers at Brest-Litovsk on February 10 to 11 moved the Germans to seize the rest of the Baltic coast still under Russian control: Estonia, Latvia, and Finland. This was to be done to force the Russians to a peace settlement and to push the Bolshevik infection as far to the east as possible. Thus on February 14, several days after Trotsky broke off negotiations, the Finnish minister in Berlin, Edvard Hjelt, was urged by the German military to request again the dispatch of German troops to Finland as he had done in early December of 1917. No doubt thankful that at last someone was coming to Finland's assistance, Hjelt and Professor Rafael W. Erich drew up the pertinent memorandum that same day. A week later, on February 21, Hjelt discussed the memorandum with Generals Hindenburg and Ludendorff and was informed that German operations would begin with the landing of troops on the Aland Islands.[59] This meeting, it will be

Vlugt, *La question des îles d'Aland considérations suggérées par le rapport des juristes* (Paris, Dumoulin, 1920), pp. 60–64. Palmstierna's *Orostid,* (*2,* 135–38) throws a great deal of light on everyone's actions during this period, as does his memorandum on Finno-Swedish relations in 1917–20 written in 1931 (ibid., pp. 407–13). When he was subsequently Foreign Minister, Palmstierna published his own defense in an official blue book: *L'expédition suédoise de secours aux îles d'Aland en 1918. Exposé redigé d'après les documents officiels en réponse aux observations du gouvernement finlandais et M. W. van der Vlugt, professeur de droit à l'université de Leyde* (Stockholm, 1921). For the rejoinder see Willem van der Vlugt, *Réponse au livre bleu du gouvernement de Suède* (Leyde, E. J. Brill, 1921). See also Herman Gummerus, *Sverige och Finland 1917–1918* (Stockholm, Holger Schildt, 1936).

59. Edvard Hjelt, *Från händelserika år. Upplevelser och minnen* (Helsingfors, Söderström, 1920), *2,* 87–91; Mannerheim, *Minnen, 1,* 258; Hannula, pp. 169–71; Smith, p. 61.

noted, took place on the day following the agreements negotiated by the Swedish expedition between the Russian garrison, the Alanders, and the Nystad Corps.

On the very day Hjelt was having his conversation with Generals Hindenburg and Ludendorf, Hellner in Stockholm was informing the German minister, Baron Hellmuth von Lucius von Stoedten, of the government's decision to dispatch troops to the islands in line with the agreements negotiated. Later that afternoon Lucius returned to the Foreign Ministry and read a telegram from Kühlmann which informed Sweden that Germany had decided to comply with Finland's request for assistance against the Bolsheviks and that the Aland Islands would be used as a base of operations. Because of this, Kühlmann's note continued, the German government requested the Swedish government to recall all its ships and vessels from the archipelago, in order to avoid complications and accidents. The communication ended with an assurance that Germany would regulate the future of the islands in concert with Sweden, at the same time denying any territorial designs on the islands.

Hellner was very surprised at this request, an action he obviously had not expected, and especially over the blunt request that Sweden "recall its ships and vessels from the area of the Aland Islands." Unaware, of course, of what had transpired that same day in Berlin between Hjelt and the German military, Hellner said his own impression was that Kühlmann believed Sweden's decision to send troops to the islands was a preliminary to full Swedish occupation, an action that he would not consent to. Hellner asked Lucius the reason for this blunt request and pointed out that Germany's sudden decision to intervene in the Finnish civil war was taken before it was in a position to dispatch its troops. Furthermore, he noted that the Finnish port of Hangö (Hanko) was a much more appropriate base for German operations in Finland than the Aland Islands. He thought that because of this there had to be a special reason for the request that Sweden immediately recall its ships from the area. Lucius, evidently as surprised as Hellner over what had happened, was at a loss for an explanation. Hellner reminded Lucius of what he had told him earlier that day: that Sweden would evacuate both the Nystad Corps and the Russian garrison from the islands and that during the evacuation it would maintain order on the islands and prevent excesses by the Russian garrison against the population. Sweden was doing this in the hope that the islands would be removed from war operations. If this could not be done "it would cause great gloom" in Sweden. He also feared that in spite of the assurances given by Kühlmann that Germany had no territorial desires on the Aland Islands, Swedish opinion would become anxious over the matter. This last comment was prompted no doubt by the knowledge that the islands had in the past been offered by the Finns to Germany as an inducement to intervene in the Finnish civil war. In Stockholm a German Aland was as unattractive a proposition as was a Russian one.

Lucius responded that he wanted to contact Berlin and transmit the objections raised by Hellner and asked that no steps be taken until he had received a reply. Immediately upon termination of the interview Hellner informed King Gustaf of what had occurred. The King became agitated and declared that he could not consent to Germany's conduct. He wished to talk to Lucius personally and that evening he emphasized to the German minister everything that Hellner had told him. This was followed by a sharply worded personal communication from Gustaf to Kaiser Wilhelm requesting that the Aland Islands not be involved in the German operations in Finland. In his reply on February 25, the Kaiser explained to Gustaf that he had decided to support the Finns, since they could no longer hold out against the Bolsheviks without outside support. Moreover, the Finns had requested assistance from Germany. His country, the Kaiser explained, would have preferred to have given support in concert with Sweden, but because of the position of the Swedish government this approach had to be abandoned. The islands had to be used, he continued, because of military necessity, since the expedition could not be executed without their use. He denied any German territorial desires on the islands. The request that the Swedes retire from the islands had been made to avoid incidents which might arise if the Russian garrison were to resist a German landing. However, he was prepared to drop this request if the Germans could arrange to use the islands merely as a staging area. The Kaiser ended his message with the hope that a satisfactory solution could be found. This was followed by comments from Lucius that he was commissioned by Kühlmann to state that Germany wanted to support Sweden's desire for possession of the islands, and Germany was willing to negotiate this with Sweden as soon as the war ended. If need be, Germany was willing to negotiate this matter immediately, if Sweden so desired.

After further negotiations, Germany declared that it had no desire to hinder Sweden's humanitarian actions in the Aland Islands and consequently would not demand the recall of Swedish troops. Germany reduced her request to the occupation of a region on the islands as a staging area. The limits of the Swedish and German areas would be settled by an agreement between the two commanders on the islands.[60]

It was obvious from the concessions given by the Germans that the Swedish objections had had their effect in Berlin. To antagonize Sweden and push her into the Entente camp over an issue that could be compromised would have been very foolish for Germany in the winter of 1918.

The whole episode left Hellner insecure. He felt that Kühlmann's actions had been hostile and an attempt to humiliate Sweden, and the placing of German troops on the islands beside Swedish troops increased the possibility of future trouble. All this furthered Hellner's desire that the work of the Swedish expedition be ended as soon as possible, a desire strengthened when he found that the intended purposes of the expedition, both in Sweden and abroad but especially in Finland, were misunderstood. To add to this, words of disquiet were heard from the Entente over the continuing occupation of the islands. Tommasini, the Italian minister urged Hellner to terminate the expedition as soon as its humanitarian work was accomplished, since in his opinion the situation was dangerous for Sweden and could easily develop in a manner prejudicial to Sweden's neutrality.

All this was conveyed by Hellner to his Cabinet colleagues and

60. Hellner, *Memorandum,* pp. 32–34; Hellner, *Minnen,* pp. 416–17; Palmstierna, *Orostid,* 2, 138–47; Morris (Stockholm) to the Department of State, March 3, 1918 (File 758.6114A1/10, Record Group 59, NA).

to King Gustaf. The government's decision on March 8 was to affirm its prior announcement repeated so often in the past that the evacuation of the Russian garrison would lead to a Swedish withdrawal from the islands. It was also agreed to press the Finns for the immediate demolition of the Russian fortifications, while a small contingent of Swedish troops remained and assisted in the work. Though the King consented to this, it was Hellner's impression that Gustaf would have liked Sweden to remain in occupation of the islands, a point about which the King appears to have been ambivalent. Hellner thought that Gustaf's subsequent dissatisfaction with him was due to his insistence that the occupation cease once the expedition's task had been completed. He suspected that Palmstierna had influenced the King's attitude, though Hellner could offer no real evidence on this point.[61]

Immediately after the government's decision was taken Hellner summoned Lucius and assured him that once the Russian evacuation had been completed Sweden would recall its expedition. Furthermore, the Swedish government felt that the question of sovereignty over the Aland Islands should remain in abeyance until peace had been restored to Finland. With the Brest-Litovsk and Finno-German treaties in mind he then mentioned that the government desired demolition of the islands' fortifications as quickly as possible, and suggested to Lucius that Germany complete arrangements with Sweden and Finland so that the demolition of the fortifications could be carried out by the three countries together. Finally, the servitude of 1856 should continue into the future, since it would please Swedish public opinion. That a continuance of the servitude would please the Swedish government even more was not mentioned by Hellner.

Lucius promised to pass Hellner's information along to Berlin. At the same time he declared that Germany fully agreed with Sweden that this was not the propitious moment to discuss the question of the islands' sovereignty. The Wilhelmstrasse's reply, conveyed by Lucius on March 13, was that Germany was pre-

61. Hellner, *Memorandum,* pp. 34–35; Hellner, *Minnen,* pp. 493–94; Palmstierna, *Orostid,* 2, 148–50. Subsequently Palmstierna, when he was Foreign Minister, arranged to have the Aland question taken to the League of Nations. The King expressed great satisfaction with his minister's action and remarked to Hellner that the latter would never have taken such a step. Hellner, *Minnen,* p. 494.

pared to come to an agreement with Sweden and Finland on the demolition of the Aland fortifications. But, in order to avoid misunderstandings and complications, the demolition of the Aland fortifications would take place only after the Russian ratification of the Treaty of Brest-Litovsk. Germany could not promise execution of the treaty until it was ratified. Because of this, Swedish troops should remain in occupation of the Aland Islands until further notice. If there were any need, appropriate German pressure would be applied on the Finns to accept this situation. Finally, an agreement regarding the islands' servitude could only be accomplished in concert with Russia as stipulated in the Treaty of Brest-Litovsk.

Whatever the German motive in recommending a continuation of the Swedish occupation of the Aland Islands, it had not the slightest chance of success, for on the previous day Hellner had already communicated to the Finnish minister, Gripenberg, as he had to Lucius, his government's decision to recall the Swedish detachment. This was to be done once its task was ended and its request for the demolition of the Aland fortifications was executed as stipulated in the Treaty of Brest-Litovsk and the Finno-German Treaty which followed it. The note ended with the comment that Sweden reserved the right to return to the question of the disposition of the islands at a later date. In handing the note to Gripenberg, Hellner observed that the assurances he had given Gripenberg in the past and those the Prime Minister had given in the name of the government in the Riksdag had been sincerely meant. He also thought it would be desirable for the anti-Swedish campaign in Finland to cease, as this could only damage good relations between the two countries. After touching on Sweden's decision not to intervene in the Finnish civil war, he again emphasized that it was desirable to avoid any strains in order to have good relations between the two nations. According to Hellner, Gripenberg declared that he shared his views and promised to convey them to his government.[62]

Rising Finno-Swedish Tension

The events that unfolded in the period between the dispatch of this note and the arrival of the Finnish reply in large measure

62. Hellner, *Memorandum,* pp. 35–37.

decided the tenor of the Finnish note and led to the very situation that Hellner and Gripenberg both wished to avoid. The move that triggered this situation was the simultaneous appeal by the Alanders to the Finnish Diet, the Kaiser, and King Gustaf renewing their request that the island group be united with Sweden. They invoked the right of national self-determination, demanding that their desire for freedom be recognized as Finland's had. If this could not be done they wanted the question to be considered at the peace conference terminating the war. They declared further that if any of the powers to whom they now appealed deemed it necessary, a new and conclusive plebiscite should be held in the presence of the Swedish and German troops on the islands.[63]

The Finns have asserted that the Alanders' appeals for self-determination were inspired and supported by the Swedish government.[64] Though it cannot be denied that the islanders were in contact with Stockholm during this period, their desire for union with Sweden appears sincere, and the Finnish criticism loses sight of the fact that national self-determination, an idea unleashed by an American President, had captured the imagination of everyone.

The reply of the Finnish Diet to the Alanders' appeal was in no way encouraging. They would avoid, they stated in their reply, touching upon the events which had propelled the islanders to appeal to Sweden, an action which resulted in the Swedish government's landing troops on the islands. On this action the Finnish government would shortly give its views to the Swedish government. In the meantime, the Finnish government wanted to inform the islanders that they undertook to guarantee "full security" for the islands and urgently requested them "to avoid all acts which would injure Finland's integrity, as this would not be tolerated." [65]

63. Otto Andersson, *Les origines de la question d'Aland; l'Aland en 1917–1918* (Helsingfors, Imprimerie du Gouvernement, 1920), pp. 56–57; Morris (Stockholm) to the Department of State, March 13, 1918 (File 758.6114A1/22, Record Group 59, NA); *The Times* (London), March 14, 1918, p. 5.

64. Johan R. Danielson-Kalmari, *La question des îles d'Aland de 1914 à 1920* (Helsinki, Imprimerie du Gouvernement, 1921); Andersson, passim.

65. Andersson, p. 58; Morris (Stockholm) to the Department of State, March 16, 1918 (File 758.6114A1/24, Record Group 59, NA).

In conveying the Diet's message, the islands' governor, Colonel Hjalmar Bonsdorff, was of the personal opinion that the Alanders should be loyal and wait. Anyone seeking to make trouble for Finland now would place himself on the same level as the "rebel reds." Settlement of the question could be reached either through "force or agreement." He did not think the population would resort to force. Consequently, they should not take a position that would "incite" the Finnish people and government against them, since in the last analysis the question would be decided by Finland. The rejoinder of the Alanders was that they did not believe they had caused difficulties for the Finnish authorities. On the contrary, they had expressed their desires in a most loyal way and the governor's personal remarks, as far as they were concerned, were therefore uncalled for. The words "red and rebels" used by Bonsdorff, cabled the American Legation in Stockholm, had produced an "outburst [of] rage" from the islands' population.[66]

Bonsdorff also wrote in *The Aland* on March 13 that some persons were attempting to take advantage of the Alanders' "natural sympathies" for Sweden with a view toward a political union. Most Finns have had "analogous sympathies" and therefore understand this desire. But there was another side to the question. No one could ignore that at this very moment all Finland, whether Finnish-speaking or Swedish-speaking, was desperately battling the worst elements of the population allied with the Russians. Was this the moment for intrigues? he asked. Will it be said that only the Alanders deserted the country in its hour of danger? All Alanders with a heart had to consider this question and act according to their consciences. Everyone knew that "history condemned without mercy traitors and cowards." Be loyal "to our common free fatherland," Bonsdorff concluded, and "see what time will bring." [67] A notice of this type with its appeals to loyalty and hints of reprisals could have assured very few Alanders about the Finnish government and could only have strengthened their resolve to achieve union with Sweden. Reports

66. Morris (Stockholm) to the Department of State, March 22, 1918 (File 758.6114A1/28, Record Group 59, NA); Andersson, p. 58.

67. Andersson, pp. 60–61; Morris (Stockholm) to the Department of State, March 15, 1918 (File 758.6114A1/23, Record Group 59, NA).

at about the same time that the islanders were planning to form their own government and had held meetings for the appointment of representatives for the elections[68] could only have added to Finnish suspicions and anxieties in the same way that the Alanders' appeal had done. All these suspicions and anxieties in turn were probably heightened when the visit to Stockholm, on March 19, of the President of the Finnish Diet, Svinhufvud, failed to produce an agreement with Sweden over the question even after a meeting with King Gustaf.[69]

The Finnish reply, written on March 22, did not arrive in Stockholm until April 3. It commenced with an accusation—understandable in light of the events that had occurred—that Sweden had interfered in Finland's internal affairs contrary to international law. This interference had begun when the Swedes, without the consent of the Finns, had sent ships to the Aland Islands to evacuate the population and then followed with the landing of a detachment of Swedish troops. Criticized also was Swedish participation in the negotiations leading to the evacuation agreements with the Alanders, the Nystad Corp, and the Russian garrison. In this action the Swedish government was accused of having given misleading information to the Finnish Legation in Stockholm and of hindering transmission of telegrams between the legation and the Nystad Corps on the islands. Because of this Finland could not recognize any of the agreements made at the time and especially the one between the Russian garrison and the Alanders. For it was obvious, the Finnish note continued, that the islanders by their deputations and petitions to a foreign government had acted in a manner which could not be regarded as loyal. The note then asked for Swedish verification that it would immediately recall its military forces still on the islands. To speed up this process the Finns maintained that any consideration of the islands' fortifications and their regulation would have to wait until Sweden had recalled its troops. Moreover, Finland wanted to emphasize that a happy solution of the

68. Morris (Stockholm) to the Department of State, March 17, 1918 (File 758.6114A1/25, Record Group 59, NA).

69. Erkki Räikkönen, *Svinhufvud the Builder of Finland: An Adventure in Statecraft* (London, Alan Wilmer, 1938), p. 227.

Aland question could only be promoted if Sweden made a categorical assurance that it had under no circumstances any demands on the islands or on any other part of the Finnish state.[70] The arrival of this note only annoyed the Swedish government. "Our answer will be sharp," Palmstierna wrote in his diary, since he felt the Swedish government was claiming a right to which it was entitled by treaty and custom.[71]

Two days after the receipt of this note, pressure to demolish the fortifications was also applied from the German side. In a letter from Stockholm, Gripenberg reported that he had been informed by Lucius that the German and Swedish governments wanted to have a Finnish decision on the demolition of the Aland fortifications as quickly as possible. According to Lucius it was extremely important that this action occur under the Edén–Hellner coalition government which he felt would not remain long in power. He thought that it would fall within several months and Finland "would not find a ministry more favorable to its views." Moreover, the Edén–Hellner government would not ask for a cession of the islands but would finally content itself with some Finnish concession aside from the demolition of the fortifications. What this concession might be, Lucius did not elaborate. On the other hand, he continued, any ministry that replaced it would probably be more chauvinistic and cause Finland a great deal of difficulty. Therefore he expressed the opinion that Finland should take advantage of the present situation in order to conclude an agreement on Aland. In fact, it was in Germany's and Finland's interests to have good relations with Sweden—and here was the crucial point—and thus indirectly bring Sweden into the camp of the Central Powers. He warned Gripenberg that if Finland wanted to have Germany's support in its Aland negotiations it should not delay final settlement of the question.[72] Later, on April 11, the German Legation made this view clear to the Swedes when it informed them that Germany would pressure Finland for demolition of the fortifications.[73]

70. Hellner, *Memorandum*, pp. 37–38.

71. Palmstierna, *Orostid*, 2, 158.

72. Otto Stenroth, *Ett halvt år som Finlands första utrikesminister* (Helsingfors, Söderström, 1931), pp. 200–02.

73. Palmstierna, *Orostid*, 2, 159.

In his reply on April 17 to the Finnish note of March 22, Hellner pointed out that the demolition of the Aland fortifications was in no way connected with either recall of the Swedish detachment or with the question of the islands' reunion with Sweden. After recounting the Russian fortification of the islands contrary to the 1856 convention, Sweden's protests at the time, and Russia's assurances, Hellner asserted that in this question Sweden had rights based on the Treaty of Paris of 1856. But, Hellner continued, it was not solely a question of Swedish rights because of an international agreement "but also of an interest of vital importance for her." The note reminded the Finns of the views held on this question by prior Swedish governments, the Swedish public, and the Riksdag and expressed the hope that the Finnish government would be willing to agree immediately to the demolition of the fortifications, especially since the Finns had signed a treaty with the Germans covering this point. Indeed, this condition had also been agreed to by the Russian government under Article 6 of the Treaty of Brest-Litovsk. Hellner, moreover, rejected the point in the Finnish note that demolition of the fortifications would be contingent on the approval of the Finnish Diet. He insisted that the prohibition against fortification of the islands was an international servitude, and it did not devolve upon Finland's Diet to decide whether or not this servitude should be respected.[74] On this score Hellner was on firm ground, strengthened by the fact that demolition of the fortifications had been stipulated in both the Treaty of Brest-Litovsk and the Finno-German Treaty that followed it.

Five days later, on April 22, Hellner followed with another note to the Finnish government. It was a long and critical rejoinder to the charges that Sweden had interfered in Finland's internal affairs and that the Finnish minister in Stockholm had been given misleading information during the negotiations leading to the evacuation agreements with the Alanders, the Nystad Corps, and the Russian garrison.[75]

Events had come full circle. The cordial relations that the Edén–Hellner government had hoped to establish with the new

74. Hellner, *Memorandum,* pp. 38–40; Stenroth, p. 202.

75. Hellner, *Memorandum,* pp. 40–44.

Finnish buffer had eluded them. But this had been inevitable almost from the start. For the government had attempted to reconcile two irreconcilables: the desire to maintain friendly relations with Finland and the desire to achieve some sort of solution of the Aland question in conjunction with Finland, a solution that in Finnish eyes demanded a cession of the islands to Sweden. The whole situation had been further complicated by the subsequent landing of Swedish troops for humanitarian purposes meant to be only temporary, at least in the minds of Edén and Hellner. Nevertheless this action only fed the fires of Finnish suspicion. Understandably they looked upon the whole operation as a not-too-well-disguised Swedish attempt to occupy the islands permanently.

Negotiations to Destroy the Aland Fortifications

The same day this note was dispatched to the Finns, the Swedish minister in Helsingfors, Claës Gustaf Westman, concluded an agreement with the Finnish Foreign Minister, Heikki Renvall, in the first step toward an eventual demolition of the Aland fortifications. According to the Renvall–Westman agreement, the Finnish government acknowledged the rights assured to Sweden under the 1856 convention and was willing to sign a treaty with Sweden and Germany for the immediate demolition of the fortifications. The parallel concession demanded of the Swedes—as would be expected—was the complete evacuation of the Swedish detachment from the Aland Islands. When Finland was informed that this had been done, a time would then be agreed upon for initiating the discussions covering the destruction of the fortifications. It was Renvall's opinion that it was politically necessary for Finland to have the closest possible relations with Sweden and the other Scandinavian states, and it was for this reason that he was pleased to have the Aland question removed as a cause of disunity. Four days after this agreement, on April 26, Westman in a note to the Finnish government expressed Stockholm's desire that any demolition of the fortifications be executed "under Swedish military supervision." This stipulation, which was to cause problems in the future, evoked no response from the Finns. However, the news that the Swedish detachment had been evacuated from the island group moved the Finns to state that they were ready to begin negotiations about destruction of the fortifications and were looking forward to an agreement on the question.[76]

Despite these developments there was absolutely no support in Finland for the sweeping recommendation tendered about this same time by the Finnish minister in Berlin, Hjelt, that the Aland Islands be ceded to Sweden in exchange for Swedish support in the question of Eastern Karelia. Hjelt reasoned that it was necessary to have good relations with Sweden, that the Alanders would be a constant bother to Finland, and that Finland needed a Scandinavian counterweight against too strong a German influence. The last, Hjelt felt, could only be obtained, despite the difficulties involved, by trying to come to an agreement with Sweden and the rest of the Nordic states. To be associated only with Germany—here Hjelt was reflecting a growing Finnish fear—had its dangers. Finland needed a counterweight to which Germany would pay attention, and this could be obtained by a joint orientation of Finnish and Swedish foreign policies. Sweden's foreign policy in the end would also attract Norway's. Hjelt thought that the first step in this direction should be a note by the Finnish government to Sweden and perhaps Norway reviving the question of a commission to discuss frontier questions. Then if hints were made about the Aland Islands and frontier regulation in the north, Sweden and Norway might be prevailed upon to take up the question of Eastern Karelia with Russia.[77] The question that could have been asked of Hjelt was whether Germany would have been impressed by this collaboration unsupported by a great power. In the power relationships of the day the combined strength of all these states was nowhere nearly as great as that of Germany.

The disruption caused by the Finnish civil war interrupted the Westman–Renvall exchanges until May. On May 24, Westman recommenced the talks with a request that there be appointed German, Finnish, and Swedish representatives to meet without delay to conclude a treaty concerning the destruction of the

76. Stenroth, pp. 203–04, 214.

77. Ibid., pp. 75–76.

Aland fortifications and "other military establishments" to be found in the archipelago. The last phrase, "other military establishments," which was to cause trouble in the future, went unchallenged at the time. It was also Sweden's suggestion that the representatives at the inception of the negotiations meet at Mariehamn in the Aland Islands in order to inspect the fortifications and military establishments locally, with the writing and signature of the treaty taking place in Stockholm. Renvall's reply three days later was one of complete agreement.

In Stockholm, Gripenberg was appointed the Finnish representative to the Commission. To show that they considered this work of the highest importance, Sweden appointed as its representatives, Eric de Trolle, the former Foreign Minister, and Carl Sandgren, the King's secretary. At this point the first of many delays ensued when the Finnish Defense Minister sent the Foreign Ministry a note from the General Staff expressing the view that the Aland fortifications should not be destroyed because of the "general political situation" and suggested instead their preservation. With this view the Defense Minister had concurred.

Because of this view by the Finnish General Staff the question was again taken up by the Finnish government. The new Foreign Minister, Otto Stenroth, was opposed to the position of the General Staff. Stenroth's arguments were legal as well as political. His legal argument was based on the peace treaty with Germany, in which it had been agreed that the fortifications would be destroyed as soon as possible, as well as on the exchange of notes between Westman and Renvall on May 24 and 27. Politically, he argued, the respective governments had already appointed their representatives for the forthcoming negotiations and to suspend them would disturb relations with Sweden, who, as everyone knew, was especially desirous of destroying the Aland fortifications. There were many good reasons, he cautioned, that called for the preservation of good relations with Sweden. In the end, Stenroth had his way, and the government's decision was to continue with the scheduled talks.

German unpreparedness caused further delays, and though the date for convening the Commission was finally set for July

15 at Mariehamn, this meeting also had to be cancelled again because of the Germans. Whereas before the Germans had been the Swedes' greatest supporters on the question of demolishing the fortifications, they now had changed their minds and wished the fortifications preserved at least for the time being. This change of heart can be traced to the German design to drive all Entente troops out of Russian territory and their plans for a military alliance with Finland.

In early August, Edén summoned Gripenberg and demanded that the Aland Commission be immediately convened so that the fortifications could be removed, a step, according to Edén, supported by the Swedish press regardless of party affiliation. In order to ascertain Germany's attitude on the question, Gripenberg called on the German naval attaché previously appointed as his country's representative on the Commission. The latter declared to Gripenberg that he also thought it wise to convene the Commission in order to calm Swedish public opinion, but he added that the "destruction of the fortifications at present was impossible."

Within two weeks after Edén's demand, on August 21, the Commission was convened at Mariehamn and the discussions began, punctured by Russian protests to be allowed to participate, a right they claimed under the Brest-Litovsk Treaty. The first question faced was the extent of the demolition to be carried out. Since the Swedish note of May 24 that had been accepted by the Finns had spoken of the fortifications and "other military establishments," it was the Swedish desire to include not only the fortifications but also the barracks, roads, bridges, various buildings, telephone and telegraph lines etc., put up by the Russians during the war. Supported to some extent by the Germans, the Finns in the end managed to save a good number of useful establishments from destruction. What should be demolished, however, had been easy to decide in comparison with the question of who should do the actual demolition work and how this work was to be executed.

In this question the Swedes contended that the demolition of the fortifications had to be done with the assistance of the Swedish military forces. Though it was true that Westman's note of

April 26 had stated that this work should be executed "under Swedish military supervision" it had been specifically neither accepted nor rejected by the Finns. The fortifications could just as easily be destroyed, wrote one of the Finnish representatives to Gripenberg, by Finnish workmen with several Swedish officers supervising the work. Stockholm's insistence on this point naturally raised Finnish suspicions and was looked upon as a Swedish attempt to meddle once again in the affairs of the island group. Another question that complicated the picture was that of who should pay for the demolition of the fortifications. The Finns insisted that destruction of the fortifications was not in her interest and would increase her defense costs, while the Swedes and Germans maintained that each country should pay for its own costs. The last question that contributed to the protraction of the negotiations was that of the time for the actual demolition of fortifications. The negotiations dragged on from September through November. The Finns were finally forced to compromise all the issues and especially the landing of Swedish troops to demolish the fortifications. With Germany losing the war, Finland had been forced to give concessions. Her need for a friendly Sweden had increased rather than diminished by the late autumn of 1918.[78] Thus the treaty finally agreed upon on December 30, 1918, devised a plan whereby the demolition of the fortifications would be effectuated by German, Finnish, and Swedish military personnel according to a prearranged plan.[79] By this time, of course, the war in Europe had ended.

Swedish Desires for a Plebiscite

Though the war had ended and the demolition of the islands' fortifications had been resolved in a manner satisfactory to Sweden, the main question of the disposition of the islands was still unresolved. Yet the Swedes had made clear in the past that they would present this question to the peace conference that would

78. Ibid., pp. 205–27; Palmstierna, *Orostid, 2,* 166, 169–73, 176, 182, 184–85, 195, 198, 204, 207, 209–10, 217, 219, 222, 226, 230. For the Russian protests of July and August 1918 see Russia, Komissiia po Izdaniiu Diplomaticheskikh Dokumentov, *Dokumenty, 1,* 411, 434, 436, 537.

79. Great Britain, Foreign Office, *British and Foreign State Papers* (London, H. M. Stationery Office, 1923), *113,* 993–99.

terminate the war. When Germany's defeat was fast approaching, a warning that this would be Sweden's tack was given to the Finns on October 19, when Westman divulged to Stenroth that his government was inclined to propose a settlement of the question by a plebiscite of the Alanders. Stenroth's reaction was to request Westman for a written communication on the subject, but at the same time he pointed out that a plebiscite would be unjustified, since the Alanders composed only a very small part of the Swedish-speaking population of Finland. In a letter several days later Stenroth informed Gripenberg about this talk and added that he had also informed Rudolf Holsti, who was representing Finnish interests in London, so that the Entente position toward the Aland question could be ascertained.[80] The dispatch of these instructions to Holsti perceptibly widened the international scope of what had until this point been solely a Baltic affair.

In the days that followed, the pressure on the Finns increased. At this point the Alanders again entered the picture. They had been advised by Stockholm as early as the spring of 1918 that independence could only be acquired by developing their own self-governing institutions, by an act of will of the Alanders themselves, as well as by organizing public opinion for a union of the islands with Sweden and for a plebiscite at the proper moment which the Swedish government would request from Finland.[81] Now in October of 1918 they were influenced by Palmstierna's advice to contact the Entente directly before victory over the Central Powers was assured.[82] Thus on November 9, two days before the armistice, a request that the question of the islands' ownership be examined at the forthcoming peace conference and a desire for a plebiscite invoking President Wilson's principle of national self-determination was transmitted by the Aland Diet to the Allied governments through their diplomatic missions in Stockholm.[83]

The question was not raised officially by the Swedes with the

80. Stenroth, p. 228.

81. Palmstierna, *Orostid, 2,* 162, 167–68, 195.

82. Ibid., p. 225.

83. Sweden, Utrikesdepartementet, *Ålandsfrågan,* p. 54; *PRFRUS 1919. PPC, 2,* 447; League of Nations, *Official Journal,* spec. suppl. no. 1 (Aug. 1920), pp. 29–30.

Finns until ten days later on November 19, 1918, when Westman—as Stenroth had requested—expressed in an official *démarche* the Swedish government's "desire that the question of the future regulation of the Aland archipelago be resolved by a plebiscite," the results to be obligatory on both Finland and Sweden. A favorable Finnish response to this suggestion, the Swedes maintained, would more than anything else contribute to strengthening the ties between the two countries.[84]

That same day in Stockholm Hellner revealed to the Italian minister, Tommasini, that his government had posed to the Finns that the question of the islands be solved by a plebiscite. Hellner expected that the Finnish government would reject this proposal which had been made to the Finns merely to raise the issue formally from the diplomatic point of view. The Swedish Foreign Minister wanted his Italian counterpart to be aware of the step taken by the Swedish government and asked that Italy support the Swedish point of view with the Finnish government and also at the peace conference. An analogous communication, Tommasini reported, would also be sent to the other Allied governments. In requesting instructions, Tommasini pointed out that the great majority of the islanders wanted union with Sweden.[85] At about the same time news of the Swedish proposal for a plebiscite was also received in Rome from the Marchese Imperiali di Francavilla, the Italian ambassador in London.[86] Stockholm had wasted no time in making its desire known.

For Stockholm the hope that a solution of the problem could be found at the Paris Peace Conference rested in her belief that the principle of national self-determination applied to the question of the islands and her belief that her neutrality during the war put her in a far stronger position than Finland, whose past cooperation and dependence on Germany had made her suspect in the eyes of the Allies. In this hope the Swedes would be disappointed.

84. Sweden, Utrikesdepartementet, *Ålandsfrågan*, pp. 70, 78–80.

85. Italy, Ministero degli Affari Esteri, Commissione per la Pubblicazione dei Documenti Diplomatici, *I documenti diplomatici italiani* (Roma, Libreria dello Stato, 1956), 6th ser., *1*, 118.

86. Ibid., p. 107 n.

CHAPTER 4

The Paris Peace Conference

Initial Reactions

Strong support for the Swedes was lacking in almost all the Allied capitals. In the British Foreign Office opinion was mixed on the request of the Swedish minister, Count Wrangel, that the Allies obtain Finland's agreement to have a plebiscite held in the islands and to abide by the result of the Alanders' vote. However, the Permanent Under-Secretary, Lord Hardinge of Penshurst, minuted: "I do not think we should tie ourselves up in this question at present. The Finns will probably be opposed to a plebiscite, and how can we enforce one? It will probably come before the Peace Conference in connection with the Finnish question and, if necessary, a plebiscite could then be taken." To this minute the Foreign Secretary, Lord Balfour, scribbled his agreement.[1] The reaction of the Italian Foreign Minister, Baron Sidney Sonnino, to Hellner's request for support was to caution his missions in London, Paris, and Stockholm to maintain the greatest reserve in the question of the Aland Islands.[2]

An approach on November 25 was also made to President Wilson by King Gustaf. The King, according to the American minister, requested "that at the proper time, when the question of the Aland Islands was brought up either at the Peace Conference or otherwise, he hoped [that] President [Wilson] would help in the settlement of the question so that these islands might become part of Sweden." He felt that this was in keeping with the desires of the islanders, and he hoped that this could be "brought about in accordance with the President's views on self-determination."[3]

1. Minute by [Lord] H[ardinge], Nov. 20, 1918? (File 2371 in FO/371/3352, PRO).

2. Italy, Ministero degli Affari Esteri, Commissione per la Pubblicazione dei Documenti Diplomatici, *I documenti diplomatici italiani* (Roma, Libreria dello Stato, 1956), 6th ser., *1*, 140.

3. *PRFRUS 1919. PPC, 2,* 447–48.

Five days later the Swedish minister in Washington, W. A. F. Ekengren, delivered a memorandum to the Department of State disclosing that, by reason of the Alanders' appeal of November 9 to the Allied governments, Stockholm had informed Helsingfors that it shared completely the desire of the islanders to have the future disposition of the islands decided through a plebiscite. Moreover, Stockholm desired that the plebiscite be made "under satisfactory precautions," no doubt to lessen the chances of coercion and "with the obligation for both Finland and Sweden to submit themselves to its results." However, the minister's memorandum continued, his government did not desire the "solution of the question without the concurrence of the powers interested" but just wished that the "desire of the Aland population should be expressed, and constitute a basis for the solution." His government hoped, the minister concluded, that the Entente powers could induce the government at Helsingfors to meet the population's desire for a plebiscite and "eventually agree to a solution in accordance with the vote."

When he was handed the memorandum, Frank L. Polk, the Department's Counselor, informed Ekengren that the United States Government had not yet stated its position on the matter and "would reserve all these questions until later." [4]

Several days later in London, Count Wrangel called on Lord Hardinge at the Foreign Office to inform him that the French Foreign Minister, Stephen Pichon, had signified his approval of the Swedish proposal. Lord Hardinge replied that the British government felt diffident in approving a plebiscite proposal which was a foregone conclusion in Sweden's favor, as opposed to Finland's, especially as a reconstituted Russian government might presumably and with justification lay claim to the archipelago. Lord Hardinge remarked that it seemed to the British government that, if Sweden attached so great an importance to acquiring the islands, she would have to offer something to Finland in return. He asked whether it would not be possible for the Swedes to cede a part of their territory in northern Sweden now inhabited by Finns. Count Wrangel replied that the Finnish in-

4. Memorandum of the Legation of Sweden at Washington, D. C., Nov. 30, 1918 (File 758.6114A1/35, Record Group 59, NA).

habitants had no desire to associate themselves with Finland and that there was also a large river which formed a natural boundary between the two countries which Sweden did not care to surrender. Lord Hardinge observed that if no territorial compensation were feasible, it might be possible that a poor country like Finland would welcome some sort of financial compensation for the archipelago—an idea that would be repeated many times in the future. This, Wrangel replied, was a possibility. The Swedish minister then asked if the Aland question was likely to be discussed during the London visits of the French Prime Minister, Georges Clemenceau, and the Italian Foreign Minister, Sonnino. Hardinge replied "that there was not the slightest chance of it unless it were initiated by either of these two statesmen." [5]

Lord Hardinge's proposition that Sweden buy the island group from Finland was developed further by a high official of the Foreign Office in an interview with the Swedish diplomat, Jonas M. Alströmer. It was proposed to Alströmer that Sweden purchase the islands for 25 to 30 million kronor (about $7,500,000 to $9,000,000 in 1918). The official pointed out to Alströmer that the purchase of territory was common and that Denmark had only recently sold the Virgin Islands to the United States. The official thought that Finland, because it was hard pressed financially, might accept the offer. To Alströmer, it appeared that the unofficial desire of the British government was to have the problem solved in a friendly manner and so forwarded the proposal to the Foreign Ministry in Stockholm.[6] Alströmer's message—and Wrangel's report of his conversation with Lord Hardinge and the latter's proposal—could only have fallen upon receptive ears, for Finland's bankrupt position and Sweden's financial resources had been used as early as July 1918 to pressure the Finns on the Aland question. At that time Hellner had made it clear to Helsingfors that agreement to a plebiscite in the islands

5. Hardinge to Balfour, Dec. 2, 1918 (File 2371 in FO/371/3352, PRO); Balfour (London) to Clive, No. 113, Dec. 17, 1918 (File 2371 in FO/371/3352, PRO).

6. Jonas M. Alströmer, *Diplomatminnen från tio huvudstäder, 1908–1933* (Stockholm, Hökerbergs, 1951), p. 101. It was proposed in June of 1919 that if Finland were forced to sell the islands to Sweden it should ask for a sum of 40 million British pounds (about $194,000,000 in 1919). Carl Enckell, *Politiska minnen* (Helsingfors, Söderström, 1956), 2, 9 n.

would lead to a Swedish loan to Finland.[7] Though Hellner would subsequently deny that the Swedish government could "for a moment entertain the idea," since the question was one of principle,[8] nevertheless, as we shall see, the Swedish minister in Helsingfors verbally and perhaps without instructions did make such an offer—which was rejected by the Finns.

Some days after his interview with Lord Hardinge, Wrangel again called at the Foreign Office, this time to speak to Lord Balfour. He hoped, he explained to the Foreign Secretary, that the Aland question might be dealt with either by the signatories of the 1856 convention or by the Paris Peace Conference. If it was to be dealt with by the latter, Wrangel hoped his country would be given an opportunity to state her case. He reminded Lord Balfour that from the island group Stockholm could easily be shelled and that the islands were inhabited by Swedes who had by an overwhelming vote expressed their desire for union with Sweden. Count Wrangel was willing to admit that General Mannerheim disapproved of this, but only because loss of the Alanders would decrease and hence weaken the Swedish element in Finland. This element, which was more advanced than the Finnish majority, was the one to which General Mannerheim belonged. Lord Balfour restricted himself to saying that he thought the question of the archipelago "would not improbably come before the [Peace] Conference." If this occurred he was "confident that the Swedish Government would be given a full opportunity of expressing their views." [9]

A noncommittal attitude was also found in Rome by the Swedish minister, Baron Carl Bildt, when he called on Sonnino and related his government's proposal to Finland for a plebiscite. Bildt admitted that his government recognized that the states who were signatories of the 1856 convention might decide to determine the fate of the islands, perhaps during the forthcoming peace conference. Thus he asked the disposition of the Italian

7. Erik Kule Palmstierna, *Orostid; politiska dagboksanteckningar* (Stockholm, Tidens, 1953), 2, 182.

8. Clive (Stockholm) to Curzon, No. 23, Jan. 16, 1919 (File 591/2/1 in FO/608/179, PRO).

9. Balfour (London) to Clive, No. 112, Dec. 13, 1918 (File 2371 in FO/371/3352, PRO).

government on this matter, which he hoped would be favorable to Sweden. Sonnino replied that in the Aland question, which was a special case in that it entailed the detachment of a piece of one state and its annexation by another, he could not foretell what would be the conference's decision. Hence Sonnino reserved his opinion on the question, wishing first to ascertain the views of Italy's allies. Indeed, he observed, the same would be necessary in the Danish–German question of Schleswig-Holstein. Special questions of this kind, he thought, had to be presented to the peace conference for action by those nations which "might be more directly interested," an allusion that in the Aland question Italy had no direct interests.[10]

However, the attitude of the Italian minister in Stockholm, Tommasini, was that since the Swedish case on the Aland Islands rested on historic and ethnic grounds, it appeared to him impossible for Italy, which had based its whole policy since the war on these same grounds, to refuse Sweden at least some "manifestation of platonic sympathy." This manifestation could be accompanied by reservations justified by the wish to proceed in concert with Italy's allies in order to resolve the question of the islands without offending Finland, all this being done to maintain good relations between Finland and Sweden. Such an approach, Tommasini continued, did not appear to him to be in any way inconvenient and could produce in Stockholm a good impression, since Swedish public opinion was in favor of Sweden's annexing the islands.[11]

What Tommasini failed to see was that the Baltic was not an area of Italian interest—a point Sonnino had alluded to in his conversation with the Swedish minister. Nor did he see that Italy would shortly be pressing for areas in the southern Tyrol and along the Istrian coast, where, as Sonnino well knew, even if Tommasini did not, Italians were not always in the majority, and hence they were questionable acquisitions for Italy under the principle of national self-determination. To deny the principle of self-determination in the Tyrol and the Adriatic and espouse

10. Italy, Ministero degli Affari Esteri, Commissione per la Pubblicazione dei Documenti Diplomatici, *I documenti diplomatici italiani,* 6th ser., *1,* 381.

11. Ibid., p. 404.

it in the Baltic would not have been in Italy's interest. Though unknown to them, the Swedes had during these days suffered their first setbacks.

Mannerheim's Visits to London, Paris, and Stockholm

At the time these attitudes were being formed, General Mannerheim was visiting London, Paris, and Stockholm. On his arrival in London in November, Mannerheim discovered to his "amazement" that the view held in the British Foreign Office was that "Finland should surrender [the] Åland [Islands] to Sweden and be compensated for this in Eastern Karelia"—an idea which, like the proposed Swedish financial compensation to Finland, would be repeated many times in the future. In discussing the problem with Mannerheim, Count Wrangel, the Swedish minister in London, maintained that any solution of the question required the incorporation of the islands into Sweden. Mannerheim's reply was that the islands had always belonged to Finland. However, since the islands controlled exit and entrance from the Gulf of Bothnia they had strategic importance for Sweden and Finland, and "a solution satisfactory to both countries should therefore be sought." [12]

In Paris, where the Prime Minister, Georges Clemenceau, appeared to be favorably disposed toward the Finns,[13] Mannerheim broached the question with Philippe Berthelot, the Director of Political Affairs of the Quai d'Orsay, and Stephen Pichon, the Foreign Minister. The latter felt that France "was under no obligation to Sweden," though he did attach a certain importance to the desire of the Alanders for union with her. Subsequently, the Swedish minister in Paris was to report that Pichon had advised Mannerheim to yield to Swedish demands on the Aland question, and that France supported Sweden's position, advice

12. Carl Gustaf Mannerheim, *The Memoirs of Marshal Mannerheim,* trans. Eric Lewenhaupt (New York, E. P. Dutton, 1954), pp. 193–94; Carl Gustaf Mannerheim, *Minnen* (Stockholm, Norstedt & Söners, 1951), *1,* 312.

13. Gripenberg in Stockholm had written to Svinhufvud in early December of 1918 that, according to a French savant, Clemenceau had remarked that one had to "respect the Finns in spite of their German orientation because they had the courage to openly join the Germans while the Swedes had not dared to embrace one side or the other." Enckell, *2,* 9 n.

no doubt given with Alsace-Lorraine in mind. In addition, Mannerheim also met, during his stay in Paris, Henry Franklin-Bouillon, the powerful chairman of the Chamber of Deputies' Foreign Affairs Committee. Queried by Franklin-Bouillon on the possibilities of a Baltic alliance in which Finland would be included, Mannerheim replied that for historical and cultural reasons he would rather see Finland joined to a Scandinavian bloc, though Swedish policy on the question of the Aland Islands at the moment prevented such cooperation. Nevertheless, Franklin-Bouillon's seemingly innocent question suggested that French views on Finland might change if Finland could play an important role for France in the Baltic, not only against Germany but also especially against Bolshevik Russia.

Returning to London, Mannerheim opened the question of the islands "for a new discussion" with Lord Hardinge. At this meeting Mannerheim made it a point to refute all prior arguments offered Lord Hardinge by Count Wrangel. After his visit to both Allied capitals Mannerheim concluded that there was no "immediate danger" of the islands being taken from Finland.[14] The new French minister in Stockholm, Louis Delavaud, informed Palmstierna that Mannerheim had obviously "made a great impression" in London, where the only resistance there was in the Aland question was to be found.[15]

On his way back to Finland, Mannerheim stopped off at Stockholm and had an interview with Edén and Hellner. The day before his arrival, the government, in a patent move to put Mannerheim on the defensive, published their month-old note to Finland requesting a plebiscite on the islands. Both Edén and Hellner made it clear to Mannerheim that Sweden had no annexationist policy in the Aland question, but the principle of national self-determination on which Finland's own independence was founded should also be applied to the island group.[16]

Mannerheim was particularly annoyed during his stay in Stockholm by what he considered the "provocative articles" in the

14. Mannerheim, *The Memoirs of Marshal Mannerheim,* pp. 194–200; Mannerheim, *Minnen, 1,* 318–25; Palmstierna, *Orostid, 2,* 273.

15. Palmstierna, *Orostid, 2,* 249.

16. Ibid., pp. 263–64.

press, to which Karl Hjalmar Branting, leader of the Social Democratic party, had contributed. Mannerheim told the British chargé d'affaires, Robert Clive, that he wished for a friendly settlement of the problem, though in his opinion the Swedes were approaching the question in the wrong way. The island group, he observed, was an "integral part of Finland, and no responsible statesman in Finland could expect the support of the Finnish people if he recommended a concession to the present Swedish demands." Clive replied that he understood that his government had proposed that the Aland question be solved at the Paris Peace Conference, that it had no interest in the question other than for a permanent settlement satisfactory to both states.

Mannerheim was anxious for the Swedes to recognize that the Allied governments "fully admitted the legal right of Finland to keep the Islands." Sweden, he maintained, was attempting to "prejudice public opinion" by evoking the concept of national self-determination, alleging that because the Alanders desired union with Sweden, there was nothing to be heard from the Finnish side. He asked Clive if he could not say something to Hellner to show that the British government "had no parti pris in the matter, but that they considered that the Swedish Government must realise the legal rights of Finland." Mannerheim then divulged to Clive that as soon as he returned to Helsingfors he intended to warn the Finnish press to write calmly on the question and not allow themselves to be provoked by the attacks of the Swedish press.

In a conversation with Branting, Clive recounted his interview with Mannerheim. Branting responded that he was pleased to learn that Mannerheim was moved by "bonne volonté." Branting understood that Mannerheim had suggested dividing the islands, a solution he considered neither possible nor acceptable. Clive admitted that this had been mentioned to him by Mannerheim, but the General "had also suggested a condominium and in fact shewed a very open mind regarding possible solutions." His government, Branting revealed, had expected no agreement from the Finns on their proposal for a plebiscite, "but they thought it well to keep the Aland question in the limelight for fear of it being overlooked in the mass of other questions to be settled at the [Paris] Peace Conference." [17]

Because of the role Mannerheim had played in Finland's internal politics and his rejection of Swedish designs for annexation of the Aland Islands, the attitude toward him in Stockholm's official circles had been one of great reserve. The Aland issue was particularly delicate for him because of his Swedish descent. The annexationist comments of Stockholm's press had irritated him. At the same time Mannerheim was wise enough to recognize, Tommasini reported to Rome, "that to admit [to a] plebiscite means to admit [to] annexation." He did not think that the Alanders understood that it was necessary to eliminate the question as an irritant in Finno-Swedish relations. Therefore, Tommasini observed, General Mannerheim was disposed to accept some sort of compromise arrangement—a point he also made to Clive. Mannerheim thought the Aland Islands could be given a great deal of autonomy under Finnish sovereignty, and, in case of a war in the Baltic with other states, both Sweden and Finland would be obliged to defend the islands in common in order to keep the hostilities from moving into the Gulf of Bothnia. Mannerheim failed to see, however, that this was no solution for Sweden. For it was most unlikely that Stockholm would get itself involved in any Finno-Russian war by defending the islands in conjunction with Helsingfors against a Russian attack.

Regardless of Mannerheim's scheme, the Italian Minister observed, it appeared that Finland was opposed to ceding the Aland Islands to Sweden, though Finnish public opinion could resign itself to this if they obtained in compensation a "considerable rectification" of the Russian border in Eastern Karelia to unite with areas inhabited by Finns. In wishing for this rectification of the frontier there was no desire on the part of the Finns to hinder or imperil communications between Russia and the Arctic Ocean. In Tommasini's opinion, if the Allies wished Mannerheim to remain in power because of his anti-Bolshevik and pro-Entente attitude, it was necessary to caution the Swedes that if they undermined his position in Finland with the hope of ac-

17. Clive (Stockholm) to Balfour, No. 491, Dec. 20, 1918 (File 2371 in FO/371/3352, PRO).

quiring the islands more easily, the Entente would be opposed to the annexation and would endeavor to come to a satisfactory solution of the question "according [to] their policy in the Baltic." [18]

Tommasini's own proposal for a solution of the problem was somewhat similar to Mannerheim's. It called for continued Finnish sovereignty over the Aland Islands and a neutralization of the upper Baltic Sea and the Aland archipelago, with Sweden and Finland being obligated to preserve the neutralization of the island group. Though this scheme had certain attractions for the Swedes, the fact that sovereignty of the islands would remain in Finnish hands was, of course, from their point of view an unsatisfactory solution.[19] But Tommasini's proposal was stillborn, for in a solution of this type greater problems are posed than the one being solved. In London, it was considered conceivable to compromise the question by drawing a line at the straits of Delet (Teili), with all the islands to the east of the straits going to Finland and all the islands to the west going to Sweden.[20] A second compromise solution subsequently advanced by the Political Intelligence Department of the British delegation at the Paris Peace Conference was to draw a line at the Kökar Islands, a smaller grouping of islands within the Aland archipelago, giving the "Kökar group and [all the] other islands east of it to Finland," and everything west of it to Sweden.[21] Though Professor Edward Hallett Carr, who was handling Baltic questions for the British delegation at Paris, wrote that this was the "frontier recommended," [22] these British proposals were of course never acceptable to the Finns, since the most important islands in the Aland archipelago were to the west of both the Delet Straits and the Kökar group.

18. Italy, Ministero degli Affari Esteri, Commissione per la Pubblicazione dei Documenti Diplomatici, *I documenti diplomatici italiani,* 6th ser., *1,* 337–38.

19. Palmstierna, *Orostid, 2,* 271, 273, 277–80.

20. Ibid., p. 273.

21. Memorandum on the Aland Islands by the P[olitical] I[ntelligence] D[epartment] of the British delegation at the Paris Peace Conference, Feb. 4, 1919 (File 591/2/1 in FO/608/179, PRO).

22. Minute by E[dward] H[allett] Carr, Feb. 11, 1919 (File 591/2/1 in FO/608/179, PRO).

The possibility that the Swedes might attempt to undermine Mannerheim's position in Finland, as mentioned by Tommasini, also appears to have been a thought in the mind of the British Foreign Office. For in the following month, January of 1919, Henry Bell, the British Consul in Helsingfors, admitted that he had been queried by London "whether he had the impression that Sweden's Minister in Helsingfors [Westman], was working against Mannerheim in order to bring about a Socialist government which he hoped would prove more flexible in the Aland question." Bell had replied that Westman seemed convinced that no separation of the islands and their reunion with Sweden would be supported by the present government and Diet. Bell also noted that, though the Finnish Social Democratic party approved of the right of national self-determination, it did not approve of its application in the case of the Alanders. The Consul's recommendation to London for a solution of the problem was an agreement between both countries for neutralization of the archipelago under a guarantee of the great powers.[23] His proposed solution, however, did not touch upon the crucial issue: who was to have ultimate sovereignty over the island group?

Finnish and American Decisions

In late November in Helsingfors, the Aland question was also a topic of discussion between Westman and the recently appointed Finnish Foreign Minister, Carl Enckell, who had replaced Otto Stenroth. To Westman it appeared desirable that a meeting of the Finnish and Swedish Foreign Ministers take place to solve the Aland issue. But before this idea could be developed, Westman on December 11 handed a note to Enckell offering Swedish mediation in the question of Eastern Karelia—a proposal that he had already made to Stenroth in July—in turn for Finnish concessions on the Aland issue. On the question of the proposed plebiscite the Swedes thought, if the Finns consented, it would go a long way in strengthening the ties between Sweden and Finland. Finnish consent to a plebiscite, the note continued, would move the Swedes to give their "diplomatic support to facilitate the recognition of Finland on the part of the Allies."

23. Enckell, 2, 17–18.

Orally, Westman added that if no agreement on the question of the islands could be arrived at between the two countries, Sweden would appeal to the Paris Peace Conference. He also dismissed the belief that Finland ought to receive territorial compensation in the predominantly Finnish regions of Swedish Norrland for reunion of the Aland Islands with Sweden—a proposal, as we have seen, broached by Lord Hardinge in his conversation with Count Wrangel some days before. Westman instead suggested the possibility of some sort of financial compensation by Sweden to Finland for its surrender of the archipelago[24]—again an idea, as we have seen, that had its origins in the British Foreign Office.

To all that Westman had said, Enckell replied that the Finnish government could not treat the question immediately, since on the following day, December 12, General Mannerheim was to be elected Regent of Finland, and he would not return from his European visit before the end of the month. The note and Westman's comments had made an "unfavorable impression" on the Finns. It was unimaginable that Finland would release the islands to Sweden for that country's "feeble diplomatic support" in acquiring Entente recognition of Finland's sovereignty. The Finns thought it obvious that Sweden, like other Scandinavian countries, would welcome and assist Finland—without any territorial claims—in her quest for diplomatic recognition and independence. Enckell and his colleagues could in no way visualize Swedish support on the issue of Eastern Karelia, since Sweden's posture during the war had in no way ingratiated her with the Entente powers. They felt that the Swedish threat to appeal to the Paris Conference rested on the assumption that the islands would be given to them on the principle of national self-determination, with Finland being forced to agree to this solution. Enckell also dismissed Westman's offer for some sort of financial arrangement in exchange for the islands as not "worthy of discussion." In Finnish government circles it was thought that agreement on demolition of the Aland fortifications built during the war by

24. Enckell, *2*, 7–9; Mannerheim, *Minnen, 1*, 322; Palmstierna, *Orostid, 2*, 188. Enckell writes that Westman delivered the *note verbale* on December 11. Mannerheim writes it was delivered on December 12.

the Russians had been a considerable concession to Sweden, while her threat to refer the question to the Paris Peace Conference was dismissed as presenting no real danger. As the Finnish Defense Minister, Rudolf Waldén, assured his Cabinet colleagues on December 30, 1918, "England would not agree to a weakening of Finland." On the contrary, he believed that a "strong Finland [in the Baltic] offered greater guarantees [to England] than a politically indecisive Sweden." Thus on the issue of the islands a decision in Paris would probably be more favorable to Finland than any decision that could be arrived at in Stockholm. To this all the members of the government agreed, Mannerheim included. The Cabinet's decision, to which Mannerheim also agreed, was that no immediate reply was to be made to the Swedish note of December 11.[25]

All these events required the United States to establish some sort of authoritative position on the Aland question. This pressure increased when the American minister in Stockholm erroneously reported to the State Department on December 19, 1918, that the Swedish Foreign Ministry had made the whole question an official one by addressing a *note verbale* to the Finns "demanding" a plebiscite by the islanders so they could choose their ultimate nationality, the results of the plebiscite binding both Finland and Sweden.[26]

Though Polk had been correct in his November statement to the Swedish minister, Ekengren, that the United States had not yet stated its position on the matter, the Administration, during the early summer months of 1918, when the defeat of Germany had become more apparent, had undertaken studies of all Scandinavian questions that might emerge at the peace conference. The vehicle for this investigation was "The Inquiry," organized at the request of President Wilson in September of 1917. A preparatory commission, its task was to draw up the United States government's peace plans prior to the armistice and the peace conference to follow. From its inception until the armistice of November 1918, it was directed by Colonel Edward M. House, President Wilson's chief adviser. It was composed mostly of

25. Enckell, 2, 9–10.

26. Morris (Stockholm) to the Department of State, Dec. 19, 1918 (File 758.6114A1/36, Record Group 59, NA).

academic personalities and staffed, for example, by such luminaries as Walter Lippmann, Parker T. Moon, Samuel Eliot Morison, Charles Seymour, and James T. Shotwell.

The Inquiry's studies of Scandinavian problems were not begun until the summer of 1918. In May of that year, its Director, Sidney E. Mezes, formerly President of the City College of New York, suggested that The Inquiry in its work make use of the American–Scandinavian Foundation, a private organization devoted to promoting closer cultural ties between the United States and Scandinavia. Despite objections by Walter Lippmann, Mezes' suggestion was accepted. A report by Edwin Bjorkman of the American–Scandinavian Foundation on November 29, 1918, one day before the Swedish minister's call on Polk at the State Department, touched on the Aland question, though it made no specific recommendations. Bjorkman pointed out that the islands' population was mostly "pure Swedes" and that economically and culturally the archipelago was Swedish, though he recognized that geopolitically the "islands belong to Finland." [27]

A month after Bjorkman's report the question of the islands was again broached on the American side by James Brown Scott and David Hunter Miller. Both of these gentlemen, who were experts in the field of international law and technical advisers to the American delegation at Paris, had been instructed by Secretary of State Robert Lansing to draw up a skeleton draft of the peace treaty. The draft treaty offered to Lansing, they noted, was only suggestive of some of the questions that might arise at the peace conference and of the difficulties connected with them. The question of the Aland Islands appears in subsection seven under section twelve of the draft treaty headed Boundary and Territorial Questions. The difficulty in this issue, Miller and Scott explained, was that though the islands were a part of Finland their cession to Sweden had been raised. Aside from this the servitude of 1856 was also involved and "to some extent, the control of the Baltic." [28]

In the end, on January 21, 1919, the recommendation presented by The Inquiry to President Wilson and the American

27. Lawrence E. Gelfand, *The Inquiry: American Preparations for Peace, 1917–1919* (New Haven, Yale University Press, 1963), pp. 209–10.

28. *PRFRUS 1919. PPC, 1,* 300.

delegation at Paris was that the Aland Islands be transferred to Sweden. This action was justified on the grounds that the population was "almost purely Swedish in race and language" and that the inhabitants of the islands had in the past year repeatedly expressed "a strong desire to be united to Sweden." [29]

A similar recommendation containing explanation in greater detail was also tendered in a paper on Finland prepared by The Inquiry and probably written by Professor Samuel Eliot Morison. Aside from considerations of race, language, culture, and repeated expressions for union with Sweden, the strategic importance of the Aland Islands was such that it seemed desirable that only Sweden or Finland, but certainly not Russia or Germany, should possess them. The paper explained that though the islands were only 15 miles off the Finnish coast and 45 miles from Stockholm and the Swedish coast it was clear "that the latter country has a more vital interest in possessing them than Finland has." [30] In a sense this was the most perceptive comment, for, in the end, interests and strategy, not nationality, language, and culture, would decide the issue.

Finno-Swedish Talks in Stockholm

In Helsingfors on January 24, several days after The Inquiry's secret recommendation that the Aland Islands be given to Sweden, Westman called on Enckell and on behalf of King Gustaf invited General Mannerheim to visit Sweden—a visit that he had proposed to Enckell several times in the hope that it would hasten a solution of the Aland question.[31] However, there were some among the government in Stockholm, especially Palmstierna, who had not been consulted about the invitation and considered the move unwise. They felt the visit was premature and that if it failed it would only increase difficulties between the two countries.[32] Nevertheless, the invitation was quickly accepted in Helsingfors and Westman was informed that Mannerheim, accompanied by Enckell, would arrive sometime between February 10

29. David Hunter Miller, *My Diary at the Conference of Paris* (New York, Appeal Co., 1924), *4,* 221–22; Gelfand, p. 182 and n.

30. Miller, *5,* 483; Gelfand, p. 210.

31. Enckell, *2,* 10.

32. Palmstierna, *Orostid, 2,* 281–83.

and 15.[33] In fact, Mannerheim's initial reaction to the King's invitation was favorable. He took it as an indication of Finno-Swedish solidarity, especially since King Gustaf, in his speech from the throne opening the Riksdag, had spoken of Swedish friendship for Finland and her desire to bring Finland into closer contact with the rest of Scandinavia.[34]

Within a week, on January 31, the Alanders hastened consideration of the issue by appealing directly to the Peace Conference. In their appeal for union with Sweden (they were of course unaware of the American decision to support their cause), they offered, as the Swedish government had, to hold a plebiscite so that the wishes of the population could be ascertained, the plebiscite to be binding on both Finland and Sweden. In ending the appeal they could not help but press the concept of national self-determination by noticing that their problem was no more unusual than that of the French in Alsace-Lorraine, or the Danes in Schleswig-Holstein.[35] Fittingly, one of the persons to whom this appeal was given by the Aland deputation was Sir Esme Howard, temporarily attached as a technical adviser on political and diplomatic questions to the British delegation at Paris.[36] In handing the appeal to Sir Esme, they pointed out that the Finnish government had objected to the deputation's coming to Paris. Yet while the "Finnish Government had themselves received a deputation from the inhabitants of Russian Karelia and they regarded that as [a] perfectly honourable and loyal proceeding," the Alanders were branded "as traitors because they tried to present their case to Sweden which they regard as their mother country, and to the Peace Conference." [37] After reading their appeal Professor Carr, who was to show the greatest sympathy for their cause, minuted: "A good case, moderately put." [38]

33. Enckell, *2*, 10.

34. Mannerheim, *The Memoirs of Marshal Mannerheim*, p. 209; Mannerheim, *Minnen*, *1*, 334–35.

35. Sweden, Utrikesdepartementet, *Ålandsfrågan inför Nationernas Förbund* (Stockholm, Norstedt & Söner, 1920), pp. 55–58; League of Nations, *Official Journal*, spec. suppl. no. 1 (Aug. 1920), pp. 30–31.

36. Sir Esme Howard, *Theatre of Life* (Boston, Little, Brown, 1936), *2*, 305.

37. Minute by E[dward] H[allett] Carr, Feb. 1, 1919 (File 591/2/1 in FO/608/179, PRO).

38. Minute by E[dward] H[allett] Carr, Feb. 11, 1919 (File 591/2/1 in FO/608/179, PRO).

Several days after the deputation's visit he was to write that the Alanders' case was a "strong one" and that "their claim to a plebiscite will be difficult to resist." The Finnish delegate, Adolf Törngren, to whom Carr had spoken that same morning, realized this, but Törngren feared that Helsingfors would "take up an absolutely intransigeant attitude" on the matter. It was Törngren's suggestion that instructions be sent to the British Consul at Helsingfors, Henry Bell, "asking him to impress upon the Finnish Government the desirability in their own interests of seeking a compromise." [39] Mannerheim had spoken to him in the same sense when in London, Sir Esme Howard noted to Lord Balfour, "saying that if the Allies suggested a compromise or decision it would be easier on Finland to yield." [40] A further comment by Professor Carr was that the Swedes appeared "confident of success" and thus did not propose to offer any kind of inducement to Finland to help "arrive at a compromise." As to financial compensation he thought that precedent would be followed so that Sweden would not escape giving the Finns "some financial compensation if she gets the Aland Islands." [41] This belief prompted someone in the Treasury Section of the British delegation to minute that financial compensation and cession of territory did not go together in every case. Would France compensate Germany for Alsace-Lorraine? The question, he pithily noted, "would seem, in the first instance at least to be purely political." [42]

Though these comments are an insight into the thinking of the British delegation during this period, they in no way moved the question any closer to a solution. However, the Alanders' appeal soon after the King's invitation to Mannerheim had ever so subtly increased the pressure and created for the Finns a situation in which the forthcoming Stockholm visit loomed even

39. Minute by E[dward] H[allett] Carr, Feb. 3, 1919 (File 591/2/1 in FO/608/179, PRO).

40. Sir Esme Howard to Lord Balfour, Feb. 3, 1919 (File 591/2/1 in FO/608/179, PRO).

41. Minute by E[dward] H[allett] Carr, Feb. 3, 1919 (File 591/2/1 in FO/608/179, PRO).

42. Minute by someone in the Treasury Section of the British delegation, Feb. 5, 1919 (File 591/2/1 in FO/608/179, PRO).

larger than before. The Swedes, with the assistance of the Aland Islanders, were cleverly alternating the stick with the carrot.

On their journey to Stockholm, Enckell and Mannerheim had the opportunity to discuss thoroughly the Aland question, which would obviously come up for consideration during the course of the visit. They first decided that the editor, Julius Sundblom, leader of the Aland deputation in Paris, should not "for political reasons" be arrested for treason as demanded by members of the Diet and the Finnish press. This decision was rationalized on the grounds that Sundblom's activities, though unpatriotic, had not been carried on with enemies of the Finnish state but with powers that were amicably disposed to Finland, misinterpreting the principle of national self-determination that had become popular. They also agreed not to let the Aland question hinder greater collaboration with other Scandinavian states. Yet, they would reject any demand that was incompatible with Finland's real interest.

Prior to their departure, Gripenberg in Stockholm, impressed by the atmosphere in the Swedish capital and by the pessimistic reports reaching him from London and Paris concerning Finland's ability to keep the archipelago, wrote a letter to Enckell and Mannerheim arguing that the question of the islands could not be settled and peace established between the two countries unless Finland surrendered the archipelago. He explained that the atmosphere in Sweden was so embittered by the question that Finland's warmest friends now avoided her. Indeed, Norway and Denmark had sided with Sweden over the question, and Finland was thus threatened with isolation in the Baltic.

To avoid this situation, Gripenberg proposed that Helsingfors agree to the plebiscite demanded by Stockholm in return for a Swedish promise to support Finland militarily in case of a war with Russia or any of the countries once part of Russia, that had recently come into being (Estonia, Latvia, Lithuania, and Poland). With the acquisition of the islands, Sweden was also to maintain the fortifications and to provide a sufficient garrison and arms to protect entrance and exit from the Gulf of Bothnia and the Baltic approaches to the archipelago. Lastly, Sweden would influence Norway and Denmark to form, along with Finland, a Nordic Union in which all four states would enter as equal members. Enckell and Mannerheim felt Gripenberg's letter raised more problems than it solved, and their reaction to its sweeping proposals was negative, both agreeing that they could not be discussed. Finland, they felt, was morally justified in this question, and no international organ had the right to decide about the reunion of the islands with Sweden. Furthermore, Finland was strong and united after its victory against the Red Guard and the Bolshevists and was unanimous in its desire to resist the separation of the islands. The agitated atmosphere on Aland that the question had produced was considered contrived. Finally, the Danish and Norwegian sovereigns had in private talks with Finnish diplomats shown full understanding of Finland's point of view.[43]

One of King Gustaf's first acts upon their arrival in Stockholm was to present to Mannerheim the Order of Seraphim. In return Mannerheim bestowed on the King Finland's Great Cross of the White Rose with chain. If the King had looked closely at his newly acquired decoration he would have seen that the original eight heraldic roses linked together by old Finnish swastikas representing the eight districts of Finland had been expanded by Mannerheim to nine roses representing the nine medieval provinces of Finland, the ninth rose representing the province of Aland.[44] This was a symbolic but nevertheless subtle way of telling the Swedes that on the issue of the Aland Islands, though Swedish interests would be considered, Finland would insist that ultimate sovereignty of the islands reside in her hands.

Inevitably King Gustaf brought the conversation around to the crucial question aggravating Finno-Swedish relations: the Aland Islands. Mannerheim observed that all Finns regarded the archipelago as part of Finland. However, this in no way altered the fact that Sweden "was entitled to demand security for her capital, including suitable guarantees that an attack could not be launched on Stockholm and Sweden with Åland as a base." He felt that an unfortified Aland was as great a danger to Sweden

43. Enckell, *2*, 11–13.

44. Mannerheim, *The Memoirs of Marshal Mannerheim,* p. 210 and n.; Mannerheim, *Minnen, 1,* 336 and n.

as it was to Finland. Therefore he proposed with slight modification what he had suggested to Tommasini during his Stockholm visit: that Finland and Sweden share between themselves defense of the archipelago. Mannerheim declared to the King his willingness to bring his influence to bear to ensure that Sweden be granted permission to fortify and garrison one or more of the islands in the archipelago as "observation points." Mannerheim ignored the question of how this would be in keeping with the 1856 convention. Seeing no real advantage to Sweden in this proposal, the King replied that Mannerheim's proposed solution was tantamount to a Finno-Swedish military alliance, and Sweden, of course, could never agree to this. Mannerheim retorted that he did not see it that way and had made the proposal on the assumption that such a compromise solution would be in Sweden's interest. He added that he was convinced that the wide powers conferred on the Finnish executive by the 1772 constitution enabled him to get the scheme through. "Our dominating interest," Mannerheim remarked in closing the conversation, "[is] to dispel for ever the bad feeling that had arisen in connection with the Åland question." [45] The conversation then turned to other matters.

In a subsequent conversation with Enckell, King Gustaf mentioned that he had spoken to Mannerheim and appeared impressed with the Regent's powers under the constitution of 1772. He also expressed the hope that in the discussions that would follow some sort of a solution could be found on the Aland question satisfactory to both Sweden and Finland. He emphasized his sincere desire to bring about collaboration between the Nordic countries and pointed out the advantages to an agreement on the Aland question without reference to the Paris Peace Conference, since small nations so often had to submit to the dictates of the great powers. The King's remarks, Enckell felt, were very amiable and showed goodwill, attempting to erase any ill will produced by Sweden's prior actions.[46]

45. Mannerheim, *The Memoirs of Marshal Mannerheim*, p. 211; Mannerheim, *Minnen*, *1*, 337–38; On Mannerheim's offer for a joint Finno-Swedish defense of the Aland archipelago see also Alströmer, p. 102.

46. Enckell, *2*, 13–14.

In the discussions that ensued between Mannerheim, Enckell, and Gripenberg on one side and Edén, Hellner, and Westman on the other, Mannerheim referred to his proposal for a solution of the Aland question that he had suggested to King Gustaf and stressed the advantages he believed the arrangement would have for Sweden. "From the lack of interest" displayed by his Swedish hosts, the Regent realized that they had already been briefed on his prior conversation with the King.[47] Nevertheless, Mannerheim explained Finland's reasons for rejecting Sweden's proposal for a plebiscite made in its note of December 11 but added that Finland was willing to accommodate all possible Swedish demands for protection dictated by her "strategical interests." Edén's rejoinder was that Sweden had no doubts that its "strategical interests" would be covered in accord with the Paris Treaty of 1856. On the other hand, Sweden also had a "political interest" in the archipelago, since the Alanders had clearly made known their desires for union with Sweden. He emphasized the cultural ties that bound Swede and Alander and pointed out to Mannerheim that the archipelago at the moment belonged to Finland only as a consequence of the Russian Revolution. Since the Alanders did not wish to be tied to Finland, Sweden felt obligated, according to Edén, to honor their wishes and to assist them to reunite with Sweden. Mannerheim attempted to point out that it was incongruous to allow the islanders, "a fraction of a people," to make a demand for self-determination. Edén countered that Finland was guilty of inconsistency. In Eastern Karelia she was striving to achieve possession of an area technically part of Russia by invoking the principle of self-determination while simultaneously opposing the application of this same principle in the case of the Alanders. To this incisive comment no reply was offered by the Finnish delegation.

Edén was of the opinion that the Paris Peace Conference must without reservations support the Alanders and regretted that Mannerheim was willing to acknowledge only Sweden's "strategical interests" in the island group. Since agreement could not be reached on the issue, Edén thought that Finland should offi-

47. Mannerheim, *The Memoirs of Marshal Mannerheim,* p. 211; Mannerheim, *Minnen, I,* 338.

cially reply to the Swedish note tendered by Westman to Enckell on December 11. At this point Hellner interjected to ask what action Finland would take in the case of a decision by the Paris Peace Conference favorable to Sweden. This question received no answer from Mannerheim or his colleagues. Edén, trying to assuage the Finns and make their acceptance of any plebiscite easier, proposed a solution formulated by Karl Hjalmar Branting, leader of the Social Democratic party in Sweden. By Branting's formula the results of any plebiscite in the island group would have to be confirmed by a second plebiscite three years later. This formula was rejected by the Finns on the grounds that it would be impossible to obtain the consent of the Finnish Diet for any plebiscite in the archipelago. The talk, which lasted for two hours, was, according to Enckell, of a "painful character." Especially painful was Edén's threat that Finland by its obstruction of Swedish desires would lose any chances for greater collaboration with Sweden and the other Nordic states—a discreet hint that Finland would be isolated in the Baltic if it failed to establish good relations with Sweden and through her with the other Scandinavian states.[48]

It was clear from the talks with Mannerheim and the Finnish delegation that the Finns would not accept the Swedish proposal of December 11, 1918, that a plebiscite be held in the archipelago. Thus, King Gustaf's subsequent visit to Mannerheim, when he proposed that Finland and Sweden submit the question for decision to the Paris Peace Conference, does not appear to have moved the Finnish Regent. At the same time that the King was visiting Mannerheim, Westman was calling on Enckell to enlarge on King Gustaf's proposal. He began by referring to a statement made the previous day by Prime Minister Edén that Mannerheim could—if he wished—through his personal influence reverse Finland's foreign policy and satisfy Sweden's demands on the Aland Islands. Westman believed that there were only two possibilities for Finland: either approval of Branting's proposal of two plebiscites or acceptance of the Swedish government's proposal that Finland and Sweden refer the question for decision by the Paris Peace Conference. Enckell replied that he did not

48. Enckell, 2, 14–15; Palmstierna, *Orostid*, 2, 288–89.

see how the Paris Conference could concern itself with the question after Finland's sovereignty had been recognized by a number of states, and after Finland's clear statements that she opposed the separation of the archipelago and its union with Sweden. He then repeated that the Finnish Diet would never give its consent and promise in advance to submit to a decision of the Paris Peace Conference on whether or not the archipelago should be governed by Finland. To agree to this would be tantamount to a Finnish declaration that it would be content with recognition of all its territory, with the exception of the Aland Islands, by countries like the United States. Though Enckell was speaking from private conviction he reiterated during this talk, as he was to do in subsequent talks with Westman during his stay in Stockholm, that he could not understand what Sweden intended by a joint reference to the Paris Peace Conference. For example, France and other powers by their recognition of Finland also acknowledged Finnish sovereignty over the islands—a point well taken and one the Finns would strenuously press in the future. He could imagine negotiations at Paris on the Aland question in connection with other Finnish problems only if both nations were invited to take part in the Paris discussions. He did not believe that Sweden and Finland could remain in the anteroom to await the great powers' decision on the Aland question, and he assumed that the great powers, pressed by more important matters, would refuse to handle the question. Westman disagreed and insisted that the great powers could not refuse if Sweden and Finland together asked them for a decision. He then repeated the previous Swedish argument of how important it was for Finland to obtain Sweden's diplomatic support to strengthen its international position.

To all this Enckell replied that he would present Westman's arguments to the government in Helsingfors which, after sounding parliamentary circles and the situation in Paris, would give its reply. Enckell's impression was that Edén and Westman hoped that the Diet to be formed after the forthcoming Finnish elections would be more favorably disposed to Sweden's demands, a hope, as we have seen, that had attracted the attention of Tommasini and the British Foreign Office. Though Edén and Westman advised against postponement of a Finnish answer to the Swedish note of December 11, stating they did not want to wait for the decision of the Paris Peace Conference, it was Enckell's firm impression from the Stockholm talks that the Swedes wished to reach some sort of agreement with the Finns for referral of the question to the Conference at Paris. The Swedish hope rested on the belief that the Paris Conference, influenced by Wilson's interest in national self-determination and by the high regard that Branting commanded among European social democrats, would decide in favor of Sweden for the holding of a plebiscite.

Mannerheim and Enckell took advantage of their visit to Stockholm to discuss Finland's foreign policy problems with the British, French, and American diplomatic missions. The French minister, Delavaud, proved to be very friendly and divulged to Mannerheim and Enckell that they both "enjoyed the confidence of the French Government." On the matter of the Aland question, he was of the opinion that the Paris Conference would not be adverse to a plebiscite as proposed by the Swedes, and that in Paris Finland had to overcome two difficulties the Finns were quite aware of: Wilson's interest in national self-determination and Branting's influence among European social democrats. Delavaud also supposed that the Paris Conference would want to show its goodwill toward Sweden by supporting her proposal for a plebiscite. His own advice to Mannerheim and Enckell was for Finland to delay and procrastinate over the issue as long as possible. According to Delavaud, Finland's chances at the end of the Paris Conference would be better, for at that very moment (by this time it was mid-February) the Conference was going through a crisis, and general confusion reigned because of President Wilson's desire not to concern himself with every issue. Although the French minister believed things would be far better when Wilson left Paris, he thought that a decision favorable to Finland would be unlikely.[49] In their interview with Clive at the British Legation, Mannerheim explained that in their talks the Swedes had employed every argument to convince them that the Aland archipelago should be ceded. He revealed that the Swedes had made it clear that Baltic union including Finland was im-

49. Enckell, 2, 16–19.

possible if the Aland question were not solved in a friendly manner—that is to say, as the Swedes wanted it. As to their offer of diplomatic support in the Eastern Karelian question, Mannerheim found this amusing and remarked to Clive that "he had not been aware before that Swedish diplomacy had added to its laurels in the last few years and had in consequence much weight to lend." He explained to the British chargé that cession of the islands was opposed by all Finns. However, he was willing to propose to the Finnish Diet that the Swedes be given military guarantees, namely, in case of war there would be a joint military occupation of the islands to preclude their use as a military base by any belligerent power. The Swedes, however, were not satisfied with this. Mannerheim was anxious that the Finnish viewpoint be understood by the Allies. He believed that the Alanders' desire for union with Sweden was largely due to Swedish propaganda. Indeed, if pressure were applied to cede the islands to Sweden, there would be immense Finnish resentment and bitterness against Sweden which would last for years. Sweden's past attitude, he observed, did not entitle her to special Allied consideration. Mannerheim also stated that with the Aland Islands in Swedish hands the Gulf of Bothnia became a Swedish lake, and for this reason many Finns suggested putting the islands under great power protection, preferably British. Enckell then pointed out to Clive that Mannerheim's prestige and popularity in Finland would disappear if the Finns thought he was prepared to yield on the question—an allusion that if the Allies wanted him to remain they had to be more understanding of the Finnish position. To all this Clive responded that his government's "chief interest in the matter was to see a lasting settlement acceptable to both sides, but the Finns must not give the impression of being utterly intractable," turning down the idea of financial compensation, which he understood had been tentatively offered by Westman in Helsingfors, and the idea that a plebiscite in Eastern Karelia also meant one in the Aland Islands. It was Clive's impression that the whole question was strategic; the Swedes desired to provide for future eventualities, since they were not convinced Finland would survive as an independent state. It was this, Clive insisted, and not kinship with the Alanders that explained and motivated Swedish policy.[50] Clive admitted to Enckell and Mannerheim that he was personally opposed to self-determination for the Alanders and thought that diplomatic recognition of Finland by his country would be a mere formality.

Both Clive and Delavaud commented on the possibilities of an invasion of St. Petersburg with Finnish assistance, though Delavaud thought that if the question were transferred to the Paris Conference, England would probably oppose it, and no decision would be made. Nevertheless, both diplomats showed a live interest in the question of Russia. Mannerheim and Enckell made it clear, however, that it would be extremely dangerous for Finland to restore a popular Russian government to power without first ascertaining how this future government would view the question of Finland's independence. Certainly, the attitude of political circles of Russian émigrés in Paris gave the Finns no ground for optimism. Yet, in spite of Finnish reluctance to commit themselves to an expedition against Russia, it was obvious that Finland, as far as France and England were concerned, was looming as a larger and larger factor in future Baltic policy.

On Mannerheim's urging, Enckell also paid a call on the former Foreign Minister, Knut Wallenberg, as well as on the eminent historian, Harald Hjärne, both of whom were credited with disapproving of the government's policy on the Aland question. Wallenberg personally was of the opinion that the archipelago did not have the strategical importance generally believed, an attitude entirely different from the one he had had several years before. Because of this, the present Stockholm discussions should not stress the islands' importance for the defense of Finland, since the military–political side of the question had to be considered as solved. Wallenberg thought that Swedish opinion on the Aland question was a sick postwar phenomenon that could be eliminated in time. The separatist campaign on Aland, he told Enckell, had been caused by Finnish and Russian mistakes. Though Wallenberg did not approve of the government's position, he asked Enckell not to quote him and advised Finland not

50. Clive (Stockholm) to Curzon, No. 61, Feb. 17, 1919 (File 591/2/1 in FO/608/179, PRO); Clive (Stockholm) to Curzon, No. 340, Feb. 14, 1919 (File 591/2/1 in FO/608/179, PRO).

to "feed" but rather to "quench" the question of the archipelago's union with Sweden, while waiting for a more "sober" view of the question to take hold in both countries. How much Wallenberg's attitude was conditioned by his dislike of the government in power is unclear. His advice, however, was sound and was similar to that tendered by the French minister, Delavaud.

In his discussion with Professor Hjärne on February 20, Enckell heard remarks similar to those expressed by Wallenberg but with greater elaboration. Hjärne also considered the question inflated beyond its value, and could not approve of his government's policy. On the contrary, he believed that Sweden should have viewed Finland's independence as a godsend and a mutual defense pact should have been signed immediately. Sweden, he maintained, could be threatened not only from Aland but also from along the eastern littoral of the Baltic Sea. Instead of dealing with reality Sweden was quarreling with Finland. He disagreed with the argument that Finland's Swedish-speaking population would be weakened by Aland's separation but considered it indifferent to which of the two nations the islands belonged. The most important thing was to achieve Nordic unity, especially between Finland and Sweden. Thus, the nation to whom the Aland Islands belonged in times past was of no importance. Since the two countries had a common history he could not approve of Finnish insistence on talking of a separate Finnish history. He also believed that the archipelago should have been occupied by Finnish and Swedish troops and the fortifications maintained. The whole question, Hjärne explained to Enckell, should be treated as a Nordic one. In the last analysis he could not recommend Aland's union with Sweden.

Though Enckell—as he admitted to Edén—may personally have been willing to submit the Aland question to the Paris Peace Conference, the views expressed by both these gentlemen and especially those by Wallenberg, a former Swedish Foreign Minister, could only have strengthened Finnish resolve to resist all Swedish pressure on the question of the islands. On his return to Finland on February 22, Enckell gave the government a detailed account of what had transpired during the Stockholm visit and discussed the answer to be given to the Swedish note of

December 11. Keeping in mind the advice proffered by Wallenberg and the French minister in Stockholm, Delavaud, that it was in Finland's interest to delay and procrastinate over the issue as long as possible, it was decided to postpone a reply to the note to allow Helsingfors to obtain further information about what was occurring at the Paris Peace Conference, and to give the new Diet time to meet and perhaps form a new government.[51]

Conversations in Paris and London

While these discussions were taking place in Stockholm, other conversations about the Aland Islands were taking place in Paris and London. One of the first men to be contacted by Count Albert Ehrensvärd, the Swedish minister in Paris, was Henry White, one of the most influential members of the American delegation and former ambassador to Italy and France. The Swedish minister explained that he was calling at Secretary of State Lansing's request in order to make a statement on Sweden's position in respect to the Aland question. Ehrensvärd explained that Sweden and the inhabitants of the islands were anxious for union. In the case of Sweden this was for various reasons, the most important being that the present range of heavy guns would make it simple for any unfriendly power in possession of the islands to bombard Stockholm. He hoped that some sort of amiable arrangement might be made between Finland and Sweden. Failing this, Ehrensvärd trusted that the Peace Conference would take note of the situation and assign the islands to his country.

White observed that the business of the Conference was to conclude a peace treaty between the victors and the vanquished. Therefore he could not quite see how the Aland question would necessarily come before it for consideration. Ehrensvärd noted that Russia, prior to the Revolution, had been a member of the Allied coalition. Since the Aland Islands had been part of Finland and the latter part of Russia, he thought it might be possible for the Conference to deal with the situation. The Swedish min-

51. Enckell, 2, 19–25; Palmstierna, *Orostid*, 2, 291–92, 297. Hjärne was later to voice his opposition to the policy of the Swedish government openly in the press. Ramsay (Stockholm) to Curzon, No. 461, Oct. 10, 1919 (File 591/2/1 in FO/608/180, PRO).

ister in closing the interview informed White that he would forward to him an interesting statement prepared by the Swedish government dealing with the subject. White's noncommittal reply was that he would be pleased to report the present conversation to Lansing and to his colleagues in the American delegation.[52]

The following day, February 12, the tune for union with Sweden was repeated by the Alander deputation composed of Julius Sundblom, Johannes Eriksson, and Johan Jansson, who also called on Henry White. Speaking through an interpreter, the Alanders repeated all the prior arguments about language, race, culture, and so on. They noted in an almost fervent way that the moment they had read President Wilson's Fourteen Points their hopes for union with Sweden had risen. Without the Fourteen Points, they declared to White, they never would have undertaken the Paris journey. But the whole population of the archipelago was so moved by the "lofty principles" enumerated in the Fourteen Points that agitation was begun in order to bring their case for union with Sweden before the Peace Conference and to solicit the support of President Wilson. Wilson's support, they explained to White, meant so much more "now in the world than that of any other human being living." The deputation added that they had come to see White, for Secretary of State Lansing was so busy that it did not seem possible to have an interview with him. Therefore, they hoped White would bring the Aland question in Lansing's behalf to President Wilson's attention. During the course of the interview the deputation accentuated, as Ehrensvärd had done, the vulnerability of the Swedish capital to heavy guns installed on the Aland Islands. They were willing to admit that the islands in the possession of Finland were not as great a danger to the Swedes as they would be if they were possessed by Germany or Russia. Nevertheless, the whole situation and Sweden's uneasiness could be easily appreciated.

As noncommittal as he had been with Ehrensvärd, White merely replied that he had been pleased to receive them and hear what they had to say. He reassured them that he would

52. Memorandum by Henry White, Feb. 11, 1919 (Wilson Papers, ser. VIIIA, Feb. 11, 1919).

bring to President Wilson's attention their statement and the memorandum they had given him, which they had also given to the Secretariat of the Peace Conference. The Secretariat, the delegates disclosed to White, had acknowledged its receipt and had assured the deputation that the question of the islands would be placed in its proper order at one of the Conference's meetings.

The Aland deputation stated to White that the annexation of the archipelago by Sweden had now become a matter of very great interest in all of Scandinavia, and both Norway and Denmark appeared to feel almost as strongly about the issue as Sweden herself. They then repeated, as had been repeated so often in the past, the offer to hold a plebiscite on the islands. In departing, the deputation asked White to present their "homage" to President Wilson and to express their thanks in the name of the islands' inhabitants "for the great hope of a new regeneration of the world which has been inspired not only there [in the islands] but in every country by his Fourteen Points and the other principles laid down in certain speeches of his last year." They hoped that it might have been possible to see a man "so illustrious and upon whom the hopes of the world are centered," but they realized how terribly busy he must be and how difficult it was for him to grant them an audience. White had been reserved throughout the interview. The only comment in his memorandum was that his visitors were "all three plain, earnest men, evidently of the people but not, I should say, of the laboring class."[53] Whether the Alanders held the same high opinion of President Wilson after the Peace Conference had ended, and their claim had been gently but deftly sidetracked, is not known.

White's reserve in his discussion with the Aland deputation may have been due to the telegram received that same day from the American Commissioner in Helsingfors, Thornwell Haynes. In replying to an inquiry by Secretary Lansing, Haynes reported that the whole of Finland was bitterly opposed to ceding the Aland Islands to Sweden. He felt that Swedish and Aland proclamations to the Peace Conference that the islands should go to Sweden on the basis of national self-determination was largely

53. Memorandum by Henry White, Feb. 12, 1919 (Wilson Papers, ser. VIIIA, Feb. 12, 1919).

due to "recent[ly] authorized persistent Swedish propaganda" as well as to the argument by Stockholm that a Swedish Aland would "counteract German ascendency in the Baltic." He added that in normal times Aland would not be pro-Swedish, and that the present anti-Finnish feelings in the islands were nothing in comparison to the anti-Russian hatred found among the Finns in Eastern Karelia. Moreover, if the islands were taken from the Finns and transferred to Sweden, would not the Finns be in a position ironically and justly to ask: "Is it because we have suffered in the war a hundred times more than the Swedes?" Also from the standpoint of postwar reconstruction, Haynes continued, Finland had the better of the argument.

By demolishing the fortifications, which wasted good land to the discontent of the islands' inhabitants, guaranteeing the neutrality of the islands by the League of Nations, and by offering compensation in Eastern Karelia and Petchenga, satisfaction might be made to Finland. But loss of the archipelago to Sweden would hardly make the Finns feel compensated if they were to receive only Eastern Karelia. The only exchange that Haynes thought would satisfy the Finns for the loss of the Aland Islands would be Petchenga, a strip in the Arctic, and Eastern Karelia. He reminded Lansing that Finland feared no attack on the islands if they remained in her possession, but this was not the case with possession of Eastern Karelia, which would mean unending Russian hostility.[54] If Secretary of State Lansing and the American delegation had been somewhat doubtful about the Finnish attitude, Haynes' words must have gone a long way toward removing these doubts.

His report to the American delegation was soon followed by a visit to Secretary of State Lansing by Karl Hjalmar Branting, leader of the Social Democratic party in Sweden, whose pro-Entente sympathies during the war and struggle to keep Sweden neutral gave him entrance into Allied circles at Paris. In this meeting with Lansing, Branting discussed the question of the League of Nations and the Aland Islands.[55] The next morning, February 14, Branting called on President Wilson. Not finding the

54. Miller, 5, 481–82.

55. Diary entry, Feb. 13, 1919 (Lansing Papers).

President at home, Branting left a note in which he stressed the necessity of representation at the Peace Conference for those countries—like Sweden—who had remained neutral during the war. He thought that these countries "could not be expected to accept willingly the views of a League in whose formation they had taken no active part." Branting believed that the neutrals would view the organization in a different light if they were allowed to assist in its formation and establishment.

On the question of the Aland Islands Branting insisted that the population be able "freely to express their desires regarding their future status." His suggestion was an immediate plebiscite allowing the Alanders to decide whether they wanted union with Finland or Sweden, this plebiscite to be taken on the clear understanding that it would be followed by a similar plebiscite a year or so later when passions were cooler—a proposal rejected by Mannerheim and Enckell during their Stockholm visit. The second vote, Branting explained to the President in his note, would be made to appease the Finns, though he was personally of the opinion that the inhabitants of the archipelago would vote solidly for union with Sweden.[56]

Further contact with the American delegation over the Aland question was made several days later when the Swedish minister in London, Count Wrangel, called on Henry White. Like his associate in Paris, Count Ehrensvärd, Wrangel reiterated the Swedish and Alander desires for union of the archipelago with Sweden. Queried by White as to Britain's and France's attitudes on the matter, Wrangel replied that so far as he was aware, they were "both entirely favorable to the project of annexing the Islands to Sweden." He thought the only objection that was likely to be raised would be from Finland, whose agents, Wrangel thought, were actively working against the proposal.[57]

At the time these conversations were going on in Paris, the Aland question was also a topic of discussion in London. On February 13, Crown Prince Gustaf of Sweden called on Lord Curzon, who, because of Lord Balfour's attendance at the Peace

56. Branting's letter to President Wilson, Feb. 14, 1919 (Wilson Papers, ser. VIIIA, Feb. 14, 1919).

57. Memorandum by Henry White, Feb. 17, 1919 (White Papers).

Conference, was the interim Foreign Secretary. It was the Crown Prince's fear that if Russia again acquired Finland and the Aland Islands, Sweden would be endangered. Though he realized that the case was difficult, since the Finns controlled the archipelago and their self-esteem was involved, this was counterbalanced by the concept of self-determination. He frankly admitted that he had no hopes in the Helsingfors–Stockholm talks then in progress, and "was doubtful whether without some external pressure, any such agreement could be concluded." Did Curzon, Gustaf asked, advise the Swedes under these conditions to take it to the Peace Conference? "How should they do it; and what degree of support would they be likely to receive" from the British government? Lord Curzon, hearing all this, said he thought it "would be better if the matter could be amicably settled between the two parties concerned, with proper guarantees for the future safety of the islands." But if this proved impossible, there seemed to Curzon "to be some advantage in obtaining an international decision upon the matter, because this would provide a sanction to the agreement which might otherwise be lacking." The Foreign Secretary thought there was sympathy in England for the Swedish position, and "it seemed desirable that these islands should belong to a stronger rather than weaker Power." He assured the Crown Prince that England welcomed the opportunity of showing its friendly attitude toward Sweden, with whom it hoped "to have close relations in the future in that part of the world." However, Lord Curzon pointed out that the principle of *"beati possidentes"* (blessed are those who have for they shall receive) was very difficult to upset. Therefore, he suggested that Sweden compensate Finland for the islands "in order to soften the pangs of surrender," by ceding, for example, Swedish territory to Finland on the frontier as had been previously suggested. Gustaf replied that this was "for strategical reasons, out of the question." He thought that Finland might be assuaged with territory in Eastern Karelia. This, Curzon observed, was worth considering, but at the same time, he added, the Swedes might "also weigh the idea of pecuniary compensation," since Finland was financially hard pressed. The transaction could be veiled so as not to suggest that it was a direct sale. No matter how high a financial sacrifice it might be, the

Foreign Secretary believed that it had to be considered, if by so doing Sweden could receive a favorable settlement of her claim. In closing this long interview, Lord Curzon promised to contact Lord Balfour "to ask him whether Sweden might rely upon his friendly sympathy; whether [Lord] Balfour would advise Sweden to take steps to bring the case before the Peace Conference; and, if so, in what manner it would be most desirable to proceed." [58]

Twelve days after this interview had taken place, Sir William Tyrrell, Foreign Office Under-Secretary attached to the British delegation at Paris, minuted about this dispatch that it was generally conceded that a solution "out of Court" was "eminently desirable." This might come about if the Swedes were prepared to pay either directly or indirectly for the Aland Islands. He thought that it might be pointed out to Crown Prince Gustaf that, if Sweden obtained the islands, some compensation was due to Finland, who, he noted parenthetically, was giving up territory which had been considered a part of the Grand Duchy of Finland for over one hundred years. Gustaf might also be advised that it would be better for Sweden to attempt to reach some sort of settlement along these lines. Personally, Sir William was pessimistic and feared that the Finns would not surrender the islands unless they were pressured. "They are an obstinate race," he penned, "and have all (Fenomans and Svecomans) set their hearts on the return of the Islands." [59]

By February 28, Curzon was still without instructions and, pressured by the Crown Prince, he again contacted Lord Balfour, asking for replies to the questions that he had previously posed, namely, what were the prospects of the question coming before the Paris Peace Conference, and what did Balfour advise the Swedes? He needed an immediate reply, Curzon explained, to enable him to answer Gustaf before his departure.[60]

Balfour's reply several days later should have alerted the Swedes that appealing to the Peace Conference might not be as productive as they had originally envisaged. In Lord Balfour's opinion it was

58. Curzon (London) to Clive, No. 15, Feb. 14, 1919 (File 591/2/1 in FO/608/179, PRO).

59. Minute by Sir William Tyrrell, Feb. 25, 1919 (File 591/2/1 in FO/608/179, PRO).

60. Curzon (London) to Balfour, Feb. 28, 1919 (Balfour Papers, *49734*, 64).

"questionable whether the settlement regarding the Aland Islands comes within the competence of the Peace Conference." Consequently, he had "no advice to offer on the question of procedure in this connection." While wishing to assure Gustaf of his "friendly sympathy with Swedish aspirations" he suggested—and here he was clearly mirroring the thoughts of Lord Hardinge and Sir William Tyrrell—"that some pecuniary compensation" might be offered by the Swedes to the Finns in order to reconcile Finland to her cession of the archipelago to Sweden and thus obtain a friendly settlement of the matter which was "eminently desirable." [61]

In the interval between Curzon's interview with the Crown Prince and Lord Balfour's reply to the questions posed by Gustaf, the question of the Aland Islands was posed for the first time in the Conference's deliberations. In a discussion of the question of Schleswig-Holstein on February 18 it was pointed out by Lord

61. Balfour (Paris) to Curzon, No. 413, March 3, 1919 (File 591/2/1 in FO/608/179, PRO).

The Finns during this period attempted to place the Swedes in the worst light possible in order to turn the Peace Conference against them. From Bell in Helsingfors, for example, a report was received alleging that the Swedes and Germans had a secret agreement about the Aland Islands in which the Germans were pledged to support the Swedes on the question. Bell (Helsingfors) to Curzon, No. 82, Feb. 27, 1919 (File 591/2/1 in FO/608/179, PRO). This report, Professor Carr wrote, was "a dodge to prejudice" the Peace Conference against ceding the islands to Sweden by pretending what might be true but irrelevant, that this policy had German support. Minute by E[dward] H[allett] C[arr], March 8, 1919 (File 591/2/1 in FO/608/179, PRO). To this Lord Hardinge agreed and observed that the Finns were "disingenuous and crude in their methods." He did not "believe for a moment" that the Swedes had made any bargain with the Germans in this question, since it "would obviously be contrary to their interests" to have German support at this juncture. Minute by [Lord] H[ardinge], March 11, 1919 (File 591/2/1 in FO/608/179, PRO). This was soon followed by another report from Bell in which he wrote that, according to Gripenberg in Stockholm, the Swedes had "firmly decided to acquire the Aland Islands for Sweden at any cost regardless of [the] means it may be necessary to employ." Bell's report moved someone to minute that this news "should be taken with the proverbial grain of salt," since the Finns would do all they could "to prejudice the Swedes in the eyes of the Peace Conference." Bell (Helsingfors) to Curzon, No. 118, March 11, 1919, and the attached minute of March 20, 1919 (File 591/2/1 in FO/608/179, PRO). Disbelief in this report by Clive and the Norwegian minister in Stockholm prompted someone to minute that the "Finns overreach themselves in their desire to blacken Sweden's reputation in our eyes." Clive (Stockholm) to Curzon, No. 536, March 15, 1919, and attached minute of March 31, 1919 (File 591/2/1 in FO/608/179, PRO).

Balfour that this question was different from others in that it concerned a state neutral during the war, namely, Denmark. Pichon thought that before discussing the question he had to ascertain whether the Danes had any representative at the Paris Conference prepared to defend the Danish case. He observed that the same problem applied to the question of the Aland Islands, which would have to be discussed by the Conference.[62]

An indication of what the French attitude might be was soon furnished by Professor Samuel Eliot Morison of the Russian Section of the American delegation a little over a week later, after a long talk on the Finnish situation with Gaillard Lacombe of the French Foreign Ministry and the ministry's expert on Finland. According to Professor Morison, Lacombe thought the Aland Islands "should be ceded to Sweden," and, surprisingly, he was ignorant of the fact that General Mannerheim's visit to Stockholm had resulted in no agreement over the question with the Finns.[63]

The news conveyed by Professor Morison, however, did not fit in with the attitude assumed the following day, February 27, by Pichon when the Aland question was again discussed at some length by the Supreme Council of the Peace Conference. At this meeting Lord Balfour queried his colleagues whether the Aland Islands question "was a matter which the [Peace] Conference had either the right or the competence to determine." Sonnino's view was that, since Italy had not recognized the new Finnish state, the islands, as far as Italy was concerned, were still Russian territory. At this point Henry White interrupted to describe his meeting with the Aland deputation. Sonnino continued his observations by pointing out that it had been previously agreed to reserve all questions relating to Russia, like those of the Baltic peoples and the Ukrainians, until later when the Russian question came up for discussion. To this agreement only one exception had been made, and that was the case of Poland, inasmuch as Russia herself, when a member of the Entente coalition, had recognized the independence of that state. Taking all these facts into consider-

62. *PRFRUS 1919. PPC, 4*, 56.

63. Statement of interview of S[amuel] E[liot] Morison with Gaillard Lacombe of the French Foreign Ministry, Feb. 26, 1919 (File 860D.00/21, Record Group 256, NA).

ation, the Italian Foreign Minister thought it would be better to study the Aland question at the same time the Russian question was studied, especially since in this question the Conference was being asked—a point Sonnino had stressed to the Swedish minister in Rome—to take the territory of one state and give it to another. In answer to Lord Balfour, he thought the whole "question fell outside the competence of the [Peace] Conference, though it might be taken up by the League of Nations."

Sonnino was supported by his French counterpart, Pichon, who admitted that the Aland deputation had also called on him and submitted to him a mémoire, in which they based their request for union with Sweden on the principle of national self-determination enunciated by President Wilson. Pichon disclosed, moreover, that the Swedish government had asked to dispatch representatives to the Peace Conference in order to discuss the Aland question. Despite this, he agreed with Sonnino that the question of the islands should be suspended and considered when a decision was made on the question of Russia. Faced with Sonnino's and Pichon's objections, the Peace Conference agreed to postpone consideration of the Aland question.[64] A perceptive observer could not have but noticed that on the issue of the islands, a French–Italian coalition had emerged, though for different reasons. To Pichon and the French, Finland appeared as a possible collaborator in the Baltic who had to be cultivated and certainly not annoyed. To Sonnino and the Italians, self-determination, though an enviable principle assisting fulfillment of Italy's territorial desires, was at the same time a two-edged sword, which, if thrust to its ideological conclusion, could be dangerous to Italy in areas like the Tyrol and the Adriatic where Italians were not always in the majority. Exceptions to the rule of self-determination, as in the Aland Islands, might therefore be to Italy's advantage.

Sweden Appeals to the Peace Conference

The whole question was soon brought to a head, however, by the announcement that Finland's Foreign Minister would depart

64. *PRFRUS 1919. PPC, 4,* 171–72.

for Paris.[65] This disclosure moved Westman on March 12 to call on Enckell and express his regrets that Finland was delaying its reply to the Swedish note of December 11 and that the government in Helsingfors did not wish to recognize Stockholm's "political interests in the Aland question." According to Westman, the Alanders' appeal had brought Sweden into the question, and she now "had to take steps." During this interview Enckell was supported by Prime Minister Lauri Ingman, Senator Leo Ehrnrooth (who during Enckell's trip to Paris would serve as Foreign Minister ad interim), and Professor Rafael W. Erich, the future Prime Minister.

When queried by Ehrnrooth whether the Alanders' appeal had caused the question to be raised, Westman replied affirmatively. Ehrnrooth remarked that, if this were the case, one must regard as an exaggeration the statement that Finland's alignment with the Nordic nations was impossible without the separation of the island group. Westman observed that this point had not been voiced by official Swedish sources. Ehrnrooth emphasized to Westman that the depression that would be created in Finland by the separation of the Aland Islands and their union with Sweden would far exceed the depression that would be created in Sweden if the archipelago were to remain a part of the Finnish state.

Westman remarked that, since no agreement could be concluded between Finland and Sweden, it remained for the Paris Peace Conference to decide the question. This propelled Prime Minister Ingman to reply that, since Finland had been at war with Russia, the Paris Conference might have an interest in her eastern borders, but since no war had occurred with Sweden—on the contrary Stockholm had recognized the full sovereignty of Finland over all its territory—any regulation of Finland's borders with Sweden could not be handled by the Paris meeting. Westman objected to this and attempted to point out that his country, in recognizing Finland's independence, had not wanted to bring up the Aland question, fearing that it would complicate the whole issue of Finland's recognition. Therefore, there had been no negligence on Sweden's part.

65. Official communiqué issued by the Swedish Foreign Ministry, June 11, 1919 (Attached to File 758.6114A1/41, Record Group 59, NA).

Seemingly unimpressed with Westman's arguments, Ingman expressed the opinion that he would strongly regret the archipelago's separation from Finland. He felt that no "greater disservice" could be made to good relations between the two countries. Finland, he continued, had no reason to look to a court to adjudicate the problem or to the Paris Peace Conference. If the Paris Conference wished to involve itself with the issue, Helsingfors would explain the reasons for its negative attitude.

To this Enckell added that reference to the Paris Conference was at the moment unthinkable, in view of the atmosphere pervading the country following Sundblom's return from Paris. This atmosphere had been produced by Sundblom's actions in the French capital with the assistance of the Swedish government, by his statements on his return that he had been successful in Paris, and by the triumphal welcome of his supporters upon his return to Finland. The Finnish government could not expose itself to the possibility that the great powers at Paris might be willing to recognize Finland's independence on the proviso that the Aland Islands be ceded to Sweden. This was similar to the situation that Finland faced with the Russian émigré groups, who promised recognition of Finnish independence by any future Russian government in exchange for Finnish support of an anti-Bolshevik expedition. In these remarks Enckell was supported by Ingman, who prophesied that the first question that would be posed to the government after the convening of the new Diet would be: "Why isn't Sundblom arrested?"

In summing up the conversation, Westman stated that he understood that no reply could be given to the Swedish note of December 11, because the atmosphere in Finland after Sundblom's return from Paris prevented it; the government was about to be reconstituted; and the Entente powers had not yet recognized Finland's independence. No one present objected to this summary. The talk had ended.

On the day of the Finnish Foreign Minister's departure for Paris, March 13, Westman again called on Enckell and announced that his government had the definitive impression after the Stockholm talks that a Finnish reply would be made to its note of December 11. Thus it was surprised by the delay and the decision to have the Finnish answer given by a new government. Because of this Stockholm felt obliged unilaterally, and not in conjunction with Finland as had been hoped, to refer the Aland question to the Paris Peace Conference. Westman also warned that if any measures were to be taken against Sundblom, as the Finnish press was suggesting, it would only "disturb the good relations between Sweden and Finland." [66] On this last point, Clive's recommendation—after a warning from Palmstierna[67]—was to pressure the Finns, for he felt that "any proceedings taken against Sundblom and his associates will greatly influence Swedish feeling against Finland." [68] Though Lord Hardinge thought that the Finns were "stupid, [and] shortsighted to interfere with the Alanders," [69] the instructions to Clive were that Britain was "reluctant to take any side in this dispute," with Lord Balfour's reply to Crown Prince Gustaf being cited for his information.[70] Though no measures were taken against Sundblom at this time, it was probably due not so much to Westman's words of caution as to Delavaud's warnings to Enckell[71] and a Finnish decision that Sundblom would be a greater liability in prison than out.

Confronted by a Finnish refusal to reply to their note of December 11, the Swedes turned to the Peace Conference. On March 18, on instructions from Stockholm, a memorandum was drafted in the Swedish Legation in Paris for submission to the American, British, French, Italian, and Japanese delegations. As he wished to present it to Lansing personally, Ehrensvärd requested and obtained an appointment to see the Secretary of State.[72] Unable to see Lansing on the appointed day, March 29, the Swedish minister finally communicated it to him under cover of a short personal note.[73]

The memorandum observed that it had been hoped that the

66. Enckell, *2,* 25–27; Palmstierna, *Orostid, 2,* 301, 306–07.

67. Palmstierna, *Orostid, 2,* 304.

68. Clive (Stockholm) to Curzon, No. 531, March 14, 1919 (File 591/2/1 in FO/608/179, PRO).

69. Minute by [Lord] H[ardinge], March 26, 1919 (File 591/2/1 in FO/608/179, PRO).

70. Curzon (London) to Clive, No. 482, March 21, 1919 (File 591/2/1 in FO/608/179, PRO).

71. Palmstierna, *Orostid, 2,* 304.

72. Ehrensvärd to Lansing, March 24, 1919 (Lansing Papers).

73. Ehrensvärd to Lansing, March 29, 1919 (File 860D.014/39, Record Group 256, NA).

Stockholm talks with Mannerheim would lead to an agreement on the Aland question. However, according to information reaching the Swedish government, the Finnish reply had been deferred. Indeed, no reply would be forthcoming in the immediate future. Under these circumstances the Swedish government, "considering that a prolonged delay would present serious inconveniences," expressed the hope that the Peace Conference would wish to consider the Aland question when it considered the question of Finland's recognition.[74] Since the memorandum was not making a request but merely expressing a hope, no reply was drafted.

Within the British delegation Lord Hardinge observed that the question of Finland's frontiers could hardly be decided without discussing the future of Russia. The dispute did not directly affect the peace settlement, but Russia had to be dealt with before long. However, he felt it "would be far better to obtain a settlement outside the [Peace] Conference" and that "an inter-allied Commission might be a way out." [75]

On March 18, the same day that the Swedish memorandum was drafted, the Aland question was also brought up for discussion in London with Lord Curzon by Ossian Donner, the new Finnish representative who had arrived from Sweden the previous month. In discussing the question Curzon noted that both cases were strong—the Swedish argument ethnic and the Finnish argument geographical. To weaken the Swedish ethnic argument Donner observed that the Swedish minority in Finland, which made up a large part of the intelligentsia, wanted Finland to retain the island group. He maintained that public opinion was so agitated over the question that no government could surrender the islands. Curzon asked if the Finns could keep in "contented subjection" the Alanders, who were not Finns and who would continue to agitate for union with Sweden—keeping in mind the attraction of the concept of self-determination. He also asked whether the Finns could afford to have in the west an embittered Sweden who had failed to acquire the islands if Russia recovered and wished

74. Memorandum from the Swedish Legation in Paris, March 18, 1919 (Attached to File 860D.014/39, Record Group 256, NA).

75. Minute by [Lord] H[ardinge], attached to the Swedish memorandum of March 18, 1919 (File 591/2/1 in FO/608/179, PRO).

to resorb Finland. Donner replied that, as to the Alanders, his government was giving them special rights on matters like military service and education in an attempt to reconcile them to the Finnish Republic. Regarding Lord Curzon's query about Sweden, he did not believe in any future Scandinavian combination, especially one in which Sweden could play a military role. He recognized the danger of a resurgent and aggressive Russia but thought that his country "would be just as well able to face such a peril with as without the Islands in her possession." Curzon responded that he himself "rather regretted that the Peace Conference seemed unwilling to discuss or decide the matter, though the reluctance of the Conference to be bothered with so troublesome a question" he thoroughly understood. If the matter had been referred to them they could have settled it in a definitive manner. To the Foreign Secretary it appeared "that the Finns had the best of the position, and the Swedes, on the whole, the best of the argument." As this was the case, to remove the islands as a source of future friction, he asked if the Finns had better not come to a definite understanding with the Swedes about the archipelago. Again, as in the past, Lord Curzon raised the now-familiar British proposal of financial compensation by Sweden to Finland. At any rate, in any arrangement a mutual prohibition on fortifications would be insisted upon. In closing the interview he asked Donner if it was "not worth while for the Finnish Government to approach the Swedish Government in a more serious spirit on the matter and with a longer outlook than hitherto." [76]

Donner thought that the views expressed by Lord Curzon during this interview were typical of those prevailing in England's and France's leading circles. He believed that those supporting the Finnish position were in a minority.[77] Assuming Donner was right and the prevailing opinion at this time was pro-Swedish and anti-Finnish—because of the attraction of the principle of national self-determination—the changing interests of the great

76. Curzon (London) to Bell, No. 50, March 18, 1919 (File 591/2/1 in FO/608/179, PRO); Ossian Donner, *Åtta år. Memoaranteckningar från åren 1918–1926* (Oxford, Eng., Oxford University Press, 1927), pp. 104–05.

77. Donner, p. 105.

powers, especially in the Baltic, would shortly reveal themselves, and the pro-Swedish orientation, if such it was, would reverse itself.

It cannot be denied that some in the American delegation at Paris were pro-Swedish and anti-Finnish on the issue of the Aland Islands. But their attitude was based not so much on pro-Swedish and anti-Finnish sympathies as on their commitment and attraction to the principle of self-determination. One such person was Professor Morison. In a memorandum to Frederic R. Dolbeare of the American delegation on April 4 on the subject of a plebiscite in the island group, Professor Morison pointed out that there was "no practical or other reason why a plebiscite should not be applied in the Aland Islands" except that the Finns refused to accept the results of such a plebiscite. There was no doubt in Professor Morison's mind that the Alanders "would vote almost unanimously for annexation to Sweden." Enckell in conversation with Morison that same morning had admitted it. At the same time he had denied that the Alanders had a right to secede from Finland. Enckell based his argument on several grounds: the island group belonged to Finland historically, geographically, economically, and so on; the Alanders were only a part of the Swedish-speaking population of Finland; the Swedish-speaking population wished to remain Finnish; the Alanders were not a unit by themselves; and finally, the Alanders' desire to join Sweden was not genuine but a reaction to Swedish propaganda.

It was Professor Morison's own opinion that the Alanders had as much right to leave Finland and join Sweden as the Finns had to leave Russia and be independent. He thought that Helsingfors would finally accept this point of view, "but it would be very embarrassing to the Finnish Government to raise the question of a plebiscite now at this critical period in the political situation." [78]

For the next five weeks following their memorandum to the great powers at the Paris Peace Conference the Swedes made no public move. This decision was strengthened by the evasive replies received from Ehrensvärd concerning his conversations with Pichon on whether the Alanders' appeal implied that the ques-

78. Morison to Dolbeare, April 4, 1919 (File 860D.014/40, Record Group 256, NA).

tion would be brought up at the Peace Conference.[79] Thus Swedish silence can only be interpreted as a hope that the threat to act unilaterally would move the Finns to answer the Swedish note of December 11 and, in conjunction with Sweden, appeal the question to the Peace Conference. The realization that their threat to act unilaterally had in no way intimidated the Finns finally forced the Swedish government on April 22 to present its appeal to the Conference.

The appeal, addressed to Clemenceau as President of the Peace Conference, first observed that the Aland question had already been brought to the attention of the Peace Conference by the Alanders themselves. The islands, the note observed, ceded to Russia in 1809 along with Finland, had in the autumn of 1917, simultaneously with the Finnish attempt to establish a free and independent state, expressed their desire for union with Sweden. The wish for union with Sweden was based on the principle of national self-determination. The note then recounted the events that had occurred during the winter, spring, summer, and autumn of 1918 between the island group, Finland, Sweden, and the Allied ministers in Stockholm. It pointed out that, though a solution of the question was a prerequisite for closer Finno-Swedish relations, prior bilateral conversations had been unproductive. Thus the Swedish government had been forced to support the Alanders' request to the Peace Conference. The Swedish government, the note continued, believed that consideration of the issue could take place when the problem of Finland's frontiers was considered at the Paris meeting. It had reason to believe that a solution of the question by the Paris Conference would be accepted by public opinion in both countries. In this way the "inconveniences which might arise" in the relations between the two countries if the issue was to remain "unsolved would be avoided."

These reasons forced the Swedish government to insist that the Paris Peace Conference, as quickly as possible, take up consideration of the Aland question, namely, the right of the Alanders to decide by plebiscite whether the island group belonged to Sweden or Finland. It assumed that, in line with the principles

79. Palmstierna, *Orostid,* 2, 306–07.

proclaimed at Paris, Sweden would be allowed to participate in discussion of the question. In ending the note, the Swedes affirmed that in the event the plebiscite bestowed the islands upon Sweden, Stockholm strongly desired that arrangements be made to continue their former legal status, thus preventing the future establishment of military bases in the archipelago or their attack by another power.[80] The same day that this note was dispatched to Clemenceau, Pichon was officially informed that its signers, Ehrensvärd, Wrangel, Branting, and Baron Marks von Wurtemberg, former Minister and Counsellor of the Supreme Court, had been appointed to represent Sweden's interest at the Paris Conference in regard to the Aland question.[81]

Delivery of the Swedish note requesting that the Peace Conference consider the Aland question provoked a flurry of discussion in the British delegation. Mr. E. Fullerton-Carnegie, who was handling questions dealing with the Scandinavian states, observed that the question of the island group "might well be handed over for settlement to the League of Nations and treated quite apart from the Finnish frontier question"—a prophetic observation in the light of subsequent events.[82] To this Sir Eyre Crowe, Under-Secretary of the Foreign Office attached to the delegation, penned his agreement, adding that referral to the new world organization by the Peace Conference, the Finns, the Swedes, or the Alanders was "probably the best way out of the difficulty." [83] In fact, the Supreme Council had several days before handled the question, but unforeseen factors made any discussion of the question by the Peace Conference impossible and led to a settlement along the lines Mr. Fullerton-Carnegie envisaged.

The Aland Islands Question and Finnish Recognition

Within two weeks after the Swedish note was written, the issue of Finland's frontiers was again a topic for discussion by the Su-

80. Miller, *18*, 159–62; League of Nations, *Official Journal*, spec. suppl. no. 1 (Aug. 1920), pp. 33–34; Sweden, Utrikesdepartementet, *Ålandsfrågan*, pp. 64–70.

81. Miller, *18*, 107.

82. Minute by [Fullerton-] Carnegie, May 7, 1919 (File 591/2/1 in FO/608/179, PRO).

83. [Sir] E[yre] C[rowe], May 7, 1919 (File 591/2/1 in FO/608/179, PRO).

preme Council. This important session of May 3 was provoked by a letter to President Wilson on April 26, 1919, from Herbert Hoover, the Director General of Relief, asking that the "recognition of the full independence of Finland" be expedited. Jules Laroche explained to his colleagues that this was no problem for France, who had already recognized Finland's independence. His country therefore supported the proposal made by the American delegation that Finland should be recognized. Lord Hardinge made it clear that England was also ready to recognize Finnish independence. However, two questions of some importance needed to be settled with the Finnish government. The first concerned Finland's borders in Petchenga, Eastern Kola, and the Aland Islands. Lord Hardinge observed there was no need to tackle this question immediately, but he thought it would be "very desirable that a stipulation should be made that the Finnish Government should agree to accept the decision of the Peace Conference in regard" to her frontiers—and, though he did not say so, thus give the Peace Conference carte blanche in solving the Aland question. The second question related to a Finnish grant of amnesty to Bolshevik Finns who had worked with the Allied armies in northern Russia. Since he was without instructions, the Japanese delegate, Baron Makino, pleaded he could not commit his government on this matter. Nevertheless, he personally believed that Finland should be recognized, and he agreed with Lord Hardinge that Finland should agree to abide by the Conference's decision on her frontiers. Pichon, however, voiced certain reservations. He noted that France's position was different from that of the other members of the Supreme Council, since she had already recognized Finland. France, therefore, could not add "new stipulations to the original terms of the recognition." She would be prepared in time, however, to instruct the French Legation in Helsingfors to act according to the lines developed by Lord Hardinge and Baron Makino.

Lansing disagreed with Lord Hardinge's proposal. He believed that a nation was entitled to its independence, and its government was also entitled to a recognition either de jure or de facto "as a matter of right, and it was not justifiable to put conditions on such recognition simply to serve some political purpose," a line of argument that had in no way influenced the United States government in its relations with Mexico a few short years before. Lansing appears to have forgotten that recognition had been used as a political weapon for the extraction of concessions many times in the past, as it was to be used many times in the future. When Lansing's line of argument was subsequently presented by the Swedes (in explaining why no reservation had been placed on their recognition of Finland in her possession of the Aland Islands) it generated little sympathy. Lansing believed recognition of Finland and its government had to be "without conditions." Like Pichon, however, he was ready in the future to join with other Council members "in making representations to the Finnish Government to urge it to accept the conditions mentioned by Lord Hardinge." In the end, all agreed to this approach, Lord Hardinge included.

Because of Lansing's and Pichon's opposition, it was agreed by the Council to recognize Finnish independence and the government in Helsingfors as the de facto government of Finland without conditions. Once this was done and diplomatic representation had been established, the American, British, and French governments would instruct "their representatives to urge the Finnish Government to accept the decisions of the Peace Conference in regard to the frontiers of Finland." The Finns would also be urged to grant an amnesty to the Red Finns who had fought with the Allied armies in northern Russia.[84]

Lord Hardinge had therefore failed in his attempt to give the Supreme Council exclusive control over deciding Finland's frontiers, in exchange for diplomatic recognition, which the Finns wanted so much. The failure to achieve collective action on the question through the Supreme Council, which is what Lord Hardinge's proposal really would have done, was a defeat for the Swedes. It made it possible, as we shall see, for members of the Council to avoid pressing the Finns and to handle the question not on a collective but on a unilateral basis. Handling it unilaterally, either to pressure or not to pressure the Finns, was in turn conditioned by the national interest of the state concerned, which in the Baltic was constantly changing, as the aftermath of the war

84. *PRFRUS 1919. PPC, 4,* 662–65, 667–68.

brought with it social revolution and political revolt and further wars.

Initially, the American reaction, at least on the part of Professor Morison, was to have the Finns pressured. Almost a month after this session of the Supreme Council, he recommended to Sheldon Whitehouse, the Counsellor of the American Embassy in Paris, that the State Department be cabled and, in line with the Supreme Council's decision of May 3, that Haynes in Helsingfors be instructed "to urge the Finnish Government to make a formal submission of its boundary questions, including the question of the Aland Islands, to the decision of the Peace Conference at Paris." [85] Several weeks later on June 19, a request to this effect was dispatched to the State Department by Whitehouse.[86]

Exchange of Notes between Finland and Sweden

While these events were unfolding the Finns made no move, waiting no doubt to see what would be the reaction in Paris to the Swedish note of April 22. However, during this period Sir Esme Howard—as a forewarning—let Ehrensvärd understand that it was doubtful whether the Peace Conference would take up the Aland question. His own proposal for a solution was for "some sort of Finno-Swedish condominium" over the islands—a proposal that the British would sponsor during subsequent discussions in the Peace Conference's Commission on Baltic Affairs and one that had been in the minds of Westman and Erich as early as 1918.[87] Finally, on June 5, the day following Professor Morison's memorandum to Whitehouse, Eugen Wolff, the Finnish chargé d'affaires in Stockholm, delivered his government's long-awaited reply. It began by referring to Westman's *démarche* of November 19 suggesting that the Aland question be decided by a plebiscite. The note expressed the great desire to see closer Finno-Swedish relations. It then went on to make the point that the Aland archipelago was joined to Finland geographically. Its

85. Morison to Whitehouse, June 4, 1919 (File 860D.01/49, Record Group 256, NA).

86. Whitehouse to the Department of State, June 19, 1919 (File 860D.01/25a, Record Group 256, NA).

87. Palmstierna, *Orostid*, 2, 327, 176, 277–79.

union with Sweden would be against the well-established principle demanding natural frontiers. The note argued that administratively the islands had always been considered part of Finland. It observed that the Alanders, who formed only a small portion of the Swedish minority in Finland, had during the preceding years shared the good as well as the bad fortunes of the Finnish people. It contended that the Alanders' desire to separate from Finland was due only to events emanating from the war.

The Alanders, the Finns maintained, enjoyed the "same political guarantees as the inhabitants of Finland in general." Their cultural needs had been provided for by the establishment of primary and secondary schools in which the language of instruction was Swedish. Finnish officials in the island group were in duty bound to use Swedish in their dealings with the population. Furthermore, the Alanders elected their own parish pastors, and the islands were merged from the administrative point of view into a single unit with its center at Mariehamn. The islanders had in no way been persecuted. On the contrary, they enjoyed the same political, cultural, and economic rights as the Finnish majority. The government, wishing to establish by constitutional arrangements greater guarantees in the future for the Swedish minority in Finland, had inserted into the projected Finnish constitution, to be examined by the Diet, arrangements that Finnish and Swedish be the two national languages of the country, that every Finnish citizen have the right before judicial and administrative authorities to use his maternal language whether Swedish or Finnish, that laws and administrative rules as well as the bills submitted by the government to the Diet and the replies, speeches, and other missives of the Diet to the government be in both languages, that in the establishment of administrative districts care would be taken to divide them, if possible, into Finnish and Swedish territorial units. Finally, army recruits would, as far as possible, be placed in military units composed of soldiers speaking their maternal tongue and would receive military instructions in that same language.

In the interim, the Finnish government had nominated a committee to work out projects aimed at the proper administrative measures to foster economic progress in the archipelago and to assist the Alanders in their cultural aspirations. This committee had commenced its work and had already submitted recommendations. Simultaneously, legislation being examined by the Finnish Diet would bestow on the Alanders a large amount of autonomy. Because of all this, the Finnish government could not consider the possibility of a plebiscite in the Aland Islands. The archipelago's separation from Finland would produce "great depression" in the Finnish as well as the Swedish areas of Finland. The unlimited right to self-determination would create "conséquences peu désirables," even "political absurdities."

Since Finland had had no control over her internal affairs until recently she had had no opportunity to demonstrate how she would treat her citizens. Separation of the Aland Islands from Finland against the wishes of Finland would only strain Finno-Swedish relations and make difficult any understanding between the two countries. From previous discussion of the Aland question Finland had the impression that Sweden's interests were primarily strategic. By consenting to the demolition of the Russian fortifications constructed on the islands during the war, Finland had proved its sincere desire to meet the interests of Sweden in this area. Thus, anxious of "confirming and maintaining the most friendly relations between the two countries," Finland was ready to consider "in a spirit of conciliation and sympathy" the actions which would "safeguard the military and political interests of Sweden" in the Aland question. To this end, it was ready to enter into negotiations with the Swedish government. Such direct negotiations, the Finns were convinced, would lead to a result satisfactory to both countries.

In ending, the note made clear that Finland was not interested in considering the Swedish note addressed to the Paris Peace Conference on April 22, a note which had caused an outburst of emotion in Finland, since the Swedish government in recognizing Finland had made no reservation on the matter of the Aland Islands.[88]

While this communication was being written and delivered to the Swedes, the Alanders were also furthering the question by

88. Sweden, Utrikesdepartementet, *Ålandsfrågan,* pp. 70–78; League of Nations, *Official Journal,* spec. suppl. no. 1 (Aug. 1920), pp. 35–37.

holding another plebiscite in the archipelago during the month of June. They were holding the plebiscite to convince all concerned that their desire for union with Sweden had not slackened. On the contrary, it had increased, having been nourished by the "aversion and lack of goodwill" of the government at Helsingfors and the Finnish Diet in assuring the Alanders on the matter of their language and culture. Of course, subsequent actions would mitigate this argument when the Finnish Diet, as the Finns had promised in their note to the Swedes, bestowed on the Alanders and Swedish-speaking Finns special rights and privileges. Nevertheless, at the time the lack of any such legislation appeared to strengthen the Alanders' position. In the vote that was taken, over 95 per cent of the Alanders voted for union with Sweden.[89] The fact, however, that only about one-third of those entitled to vote did so was lost sight of at the time. In spite of this fact, the extremely heavy vote made it obvious to all concerned "that a solid majority of the population of Aland was in favour of union with Sweden." [90]

As the votes were being tallied, the diplomatic exchange of notes between Finland and Sweden continued. On June 19, the very day Whitehouse was suggesting to the State Department that the Finns be pressured to submit their boundary questions to the Peace Conference, a lengthy Swedish note was handed to the Finnish Foreign Ministry in reply to its note of June 5.

In the note Westman pointed out that in delivering the proposal for a plebiscite in the Swedish *démarche* of November 19, 1918, he had also declared in the name of his government that a favorable reception of the proposal would contribute more than anything else to strengthening the ties between the two countries. It was with satisfaction, therefore, that his government had received a similar declaration from the Finnish government. However, to achieve this result the Swedish government was convinced that it was of the greatest importance that the question of the future regulation of the Aland archipelago be resolved by a

89. League of Nations, *Official Journal*, spec. suppl. no. 1 (Aug. 1920), pp. 42–43; Sweden, Utrikesdepartementet, *Ålandsfrågen*, pp. 92–96.

90. Herbert Tingsten, *The Debate on the Foreign Policy of Sweden 1918–1939*, trans. Joan Bulman (London, Oxford University Press, 1949), p. 309 n. 18.

plebiscite under the conditions stipulated in its note of November 19, 1918. The essential point for the Swedish government was the legitimate desire of the Alanders, founded on the right of national self-determination, to decide their own fate. This desire of the islanders had been expressed innumerable times and by an overwhelming majority. The note then recounted the numerous occasions on which this desire had been openly expressed. It denied that the Alanders' action had been inspired by the Swedish government. Stockholm did not believe that the Alanders' desire was born because of wartime events. The Swedish note then examined diverse factors, especially administrative, geographic, social, diplomatic, historical, demographic, and cartographic—many of which had been proffered in previous Finno-Swedish negotiations—justifying union of the islands with Sweden. The note denied the Finnish contention that the principle of natural frontiers made impossible the implementation of a plebiscite in the island group. As to Finland's special measures either proposed or actually taken to give greater guarantees to the Alanders, the Swedes observed that it was for the Alanders themselves to declare on these measures. The decision, however, recently taken by the Aland Diet—here the Swedish note was alluding to the plebiscite commenced by the Alanders that same month—appeared to indicate that the islanders did not feel that the new measures of the Finnish government were satisfactory. Continuing, the Swedes denied that a plebiscite would either separate an area long Finnish or weaken the position of the remaining Swedish-speaking Finns. Stockholm was convinced that the latter would gain nothing by preventing the Alanders from deciding their own fate.

Because of this the Swedish government could not associate itself in any way with the thoughts expressed in the Finnish note of June 5. Stockholm could not accept Helsingfors' offer of bilateral negotiations solely on the issue of the military interests that Sweden had in the Aland archipelago. Now that the Alanders wished to decide their own fate, Sweden's military interests in the archipelago were only of secondary importance. Sweden believed that if the islanders' right to decide their fate was not respected the Aland question would remain unresolved. It would have "grievous repercussions on the friendly cooperation between Sweden and Finland." This cooperation was counseled by their common history and civilization as well as by "their vital interests present and future."

The inability to arrive at a direct agreement had forced Sweden to appeal unilaterally to the Peace Conference. In concluding their long note the Swedes reiterated that a plebiscite and a solution to the question was the "necessary condition for the happy development of friendly relations between Sweden and Finland." If Finland believed it could not accept the solution proposed in the Swedish note of November 19, 1918, it was preferable to leave the decision to the Paris Conference. Sweden only hoped that public opinion in both countries would adjust to the Peace Conference's decision to intervene after making an impartial examination of the question "following the principles of right and the general interests of Europe." [91] Five days after the delivery of this note, Palmstierna noted in his diary that it had been "well received." [92]

Actually, of these two notes the conciliatory spirit and proposed laws proffered in the Finnish note—legislation that went beyond mere protection of the Alanders to encompass the whole Swedish minority in Finland—which were enacted into Finnish law in July of 1919,[93] could only have improved Helsingfors' position in Paris. Enckell's initial reaction upon his arrival in Paris, as he wrote to Donner in London, was that the anti-Finnish attitude at the Peace Conference was the same as that in London and perhaps more intense.[94] The later publication of the Swedish note of April 22, though it aroused the Finnish press, provoked "little interest" at the Conference. On the contrary, according to Enckell, the note's "menacing tone" and "degrading of Finland" as well as Stockholm's desire to take part in the discussions on the Aland question made an "unfavorable impression" and, what was even worse for the Swedes, "woke merriment among those

91. Sweden, Utrikesdepartementet, *Ålandsfrågan,* pp. 78–92; League of Nations, *Official Journal,* spec. suppl. no. 1 (Aug. 1920), pp. 37–41.

92. Palmstierna, *Orostid, 2,* 333.

93. League of Nations, *Official Journal,* spec. suppl. no. 1 (Aug. 1920), p. 12.

94. Donner, pp. 105–06.

knowledgeable." It was also presented at a most inopportune time—at least for the Swedes—for by this point the Allied powers were moving toward a recognition of the Russian counterrevolutionary movement under Admiral Alexander Kolchak and were not interested in increasing their difficulties in that quarter by handling the Aland question as desired by Sweden. The French, for one, were interested in restoring a strong Russia which would act as a counterweight against Germany and which would repay the tremendous sums France had lent her before the war. The French hope was that Finland, which had stopped the spread of Bolshevism in the north of Europe, would collaborate to bring about its downfall in St. Petersburg. This French approach to the Russian problem was supported by the Italians, while the British and American positions were uncertain. During the negotiations at Paris the Commission on Baltic Affairs was established ostensibly to deal with Scandinavian and Baltic problems and to keep in contact with Sazonov, now Foreign Minister of the Kolchak government. Sazonov, like other prominent Russian émigrés whom Palmstierna heartily detested, expressed himself as opposed to transferring the Aland Islands to Sweden, since Russia, even after Finland's freedom, was still a Baltic power, and any new military–political treaty dealing with the Aland Islands could not be concluded without Russian participation.[95] It was an objection that the Entente at this stage of the Paris negotiations could not ignore. All of these desires and conflicts were clearly mirrored in the deliberations of the Baltic Commission and the Supreme Council of the Paris Peace Conference. It is to these deliberations that we now turn.

95. Enckell, 2, 38–40; Palmstierna, *Orostid,* 2, 336–37. During the Mannerheim–Enckell visit to Stockholm in February, Clive reported that Enckell had informed him that Adolf Törngren, the Finnish delegate at the Paris Peace Conference, had had an interview with Sazonov. According to Törngren, the ex-Czarist Foreign Minister had stated "that it would always be essential for Russia to keep a military force in Finland but also in the Gulf of Bothnia and that there must be no question of ceding the Aland Islands to Sweden." Clive (Stockholf) to Curzon, No. 380, Feb. 20, 1919 (File 16086 in FO/371/3736, PRO).

CHAPTER 5

The Supreme Council

The Baltic Commission: First Phase

The first time the issue of the islands attracted the attention of the Baltic Commission was at its seventh séance on the late afternoon of June 13, one day after the Allied powers had officially recognized the Kolchak government and eight days after the Finnish note to Sweden. At this meeting, the first of seven on the issue, a communication by the British delegation on access to the Baltic tendered to the Commission that same day had specifically raised the question of the demilitarization of the Aland Islands. In the conversation that ensued, Sir Esme Howard, who was President of the Commission, admitted that he had been questioned by the Finnish minister in Paris as to whether the Commission was occupying itself with Finnish problems. Sir Esme had replied that the Commission was awaiting the termination of the Stockholm negotiations between Finland and Sweden. During this meeting no decision was taken, and the Commission soon turned to other tasks, the last comment on the issue being voiced by the French delegate, Albert Kammerer. He thought that the Finns and Swedes had to be allowed enough time to settle the issue between themselves. When they had arranged the question of the islands' sovereignty, he explained to his colleagues, the Commission would be able to arrange the question of the islands' 1856 servitude.[1] Kammerer's comments were thus in line with previous French advice to the Finns to delay submission of the question to the Paris Peace Conference as long as possible.

On June 16, three days after this meeting of the Baltic Commission but three days before the Swedish reply to the Finnish

1. *Procès-verbal* of the Commission on Baltic Affairs, Seventh Séance, June 13, 1919 (File 181.21901/23, *148*, 81–82, 87, Record Group 256, NA).

note of June 5, Count Wrangel called on Sir Esme Howard. He informed Sir Esme of the Finns' desire to commence discussions with Stockholm on protecting Sweden's military interests in the Aland archipelago. Though the Swedish reply had not yet been delivered, he revealed to Howard that his country could negotiate with the Finns only on the basis of the Alanders' expressed desires for union with Sweden. Because of this Wrangel "pressed" that the Aland question immediately be taken up by the Baltic Commission. To this Sir Esme agreed, promising to bring it up at the next session of the Commission.[2] However, he warned Wrangel that "he could not of course promise that [the] Commission would not decide to defer [the] question until [the] Finnish Government have sent a final reply."[3]

That the issue would not be compromised, as Kammerer and the French perhaps hoped, was made clear to the new Finnish Foreign Minister, Rudolf Holsti, during his visit to Stockholm on the day following Wrangel's interview with Sir Esme Howard. Holsti had stopped in Stockholm on his way back from Paris to sound out the Swedes on greater Finnish–Scandinavian collaboration in the Baltic as recommended by the British Foreign Office. On this question the Swedes felt that the Russian chaos might embroil the Finns, which would in turn compromise Sweden's policy of neutrality. As for the Aland question, the desire of the inhabitants for union with Sweden justified, Holsti was told, "the official Swedish expectation that Finland would cede to Sweden the sovereignty over these islands."[4] Hellner's desire for a prompt settlement of the question moved Holsti to remark that Finland, beset with financial difficulties and dangers, with a myriad of problems awaiting to be solved—a new constitution, the internal political situation, defense, the organization of imports and exports—found it impossible to give the "necessary attention" to a question which in comparison had to be "considered as [of] secondary importance." Therefore delay in handling the

2. Memorandum of conversation by Sir Esme Howard, June 16, 1919 (File 591/2/1 in FO/608/180, PRO).

3. Balfour (Paris) to Curzon, No. 1061, June 18, 1919 (File 591/2/1 in FO/608/180, PRO).

4. Rudolf Holsti, "Finland and the Baltic Region," *Proceedings of the Institute of World Affairs, 19* (Dec. 1941), 135.

question "had been inevitable." For example, he pointed out that during the last few months there had been three different Foreign Ministers (Stenroth, Enckell, and himself), and the present government was the second one within the year. Holsti believed that the moment chosen by the Alanders "to press their claim, has been most inopportune." He agreed with the Swedes that the question would not have been broached now had not the islanders pleaded self-determination and the desire for union with Sweden. Because of this he asked why there could not be an "amicable postponement of the question to a less awkward time, when all parties concerned had quieted down, and when [the] Aalanders had forgotten [the] Bolshevik element they had come into contact with, and were no longer impelled by fear." He reminded Hellner of all that Finland had done in stemming the Bolshevik tide. It was "necessary and only fair, that Finland should be given in return an opportunity to put her house in order, before being called upon to discuss [the] Aaland question." He therefore appealed to the Swedes not to embarrass his government "by further pressing the matter." In conversation with Sir Coleridge Kennard, the new British chargé d'affaires, Holsti repudiated any possible compromise based on compensation. Instead, he believed that if given the necessary time his government would be able "to woo [the] Alanders over from their present attitude." [5]

Receipt of this report in Paris moved Sir Esme Howard to note to Lord Hardinge that he was "inclined to agree" with the Finnish Foreign Minister that this was not the opportune moment for making a change in the islands' status. At any rate, Sir Esme warned, any decision to unite the islands with Sweden "would certainly cause a most violent reaction" of anti-Allied feeling in Finland. This question seemed to him to be one of those in which it was "best to temporize." [6]

The question was again posed for the Commission on June 19, the same day that the Swedish reply was delivered to the Finns. Sir Esme Howard observed to his colleagues that the Swedish

5. Kennard (Stockholm) to Curzon, No. 1029, June 18, 1919 (File 591/2/1 in FO/608/180, PRO).

6. Sir Esme Howard to Lord Hardinge, July 4, 1919 (File 591/2/1 in FO/608/180, PRO).

minister, Count Ehrensvärd, had impressed on him the urgency of the Aland question. He had replied to Ehrensvärd that the question would be submitted to the Commission, but the Commission would probably await the reply of the Finnish government before resolving the issue. He added that, though the Commission would be able to examine the question, it would be impossible for it to suggest to Ehrensvärd a "definitive solution" of the question as long as there was no Russian government to ratify the Commission's decision. Kammerer disclosed that he had spoken to Ehrensvärd in the "same sense." Sir Esme added his thought that, since England had recognized Finland's independence, the Aland question was primarily an affair between Finland and Sweden. This observation provoked no comments from his colleagues. Kammerer again turned the conversation to the question of Russia. He thought Russia had interests in the Aland question, not from the ethnographic point of view but from that of "military defense." The Italian delegate, the Marchese Pietro Tomasi della Torretta, also observed that the deciding point for Italy, at least for the moment, was the question of recognition; Italy had not yet recognized Finland's independence. This was an added reason for deferring any solution of the Aland question. Hoping to show that recognition of Finland did not necessarily commit one to the Finnish point of view on the Aland question, Kammerer observed that even though France had recognized Finland it had not guaranteed it territorially. Regarding Russia, Della Torretta added that her consent to any decision by the Commission was also necessary from the "practical point of view." For if this consent were not received, Russia would not uphold any decision by the Commission and would in fact "act in a contrary sense." Ending the discussion, Sir Esme Howard pointed out that the only thing the Commission could do would be to lay the groundwork. In the absence of any agreement with the Russian government the Aland question would have to be "entrusted to the League of Nations." It was agreed that Sir Esme in the name of the Commission would reply to Ehrensvärd in this sense.[7] The mention of the League of Nations by the British President of the Commission

7. *Procès-verbal* of the Commission on Baltic Affairs, Ninth Séance, June 19, 1919 (File 181.21901/23, *148*, 98, Record Group 256, NA).

was interesting, for it mirrored the thinking within the British delegation and was indicative of what future British policy would be in the Aland question and a clear indication that Stockholm could never really expect strong diplomatic support from London.

On the day following this meeting, Howard was given the opportunity to explain the Commission's attitude when Count Wrangel and Branting called on him. He explained that, since the Aland question concerned the former Russian Empire, it "could hardly be finally settled without the consent of a recognized Russian Government." Because of this the Baltic Commission thought they "could not do more at present than prepare the way for some final settlement," but with this reservation they were prepared to consider the question and perhaps make recommendations on the subject. Wrangel objected that this might delay settlement of the question for a considerable period. Sir Esme responded that the Commission was aware of this "drawback" but could not see their way to deal with it in any other way at present.[8]

This same day, Enckell, along with his colleague, Professor Yrjö Hirn, was also busy explaining and defending the Finnish case. Their host during this interview was Professor James Y. Simpson of the Political Intelligence Department of the British delegation dealing with Baltic questions. Both gentlemen appeared "a little disturbed" by information reaching them that the Aland question "was going to be dealt with more or less directly by the Baltic Commission at an early date as a result of pressure" by the Swedish delegation. In the conversation that ensued Enckell and Hirn maintained that Sweden was treating the entire question only as a "local affair" on the basis of President Wilson's concept of self-determination. Nevertheless, the Finnish government considered the question of the greatest importance for world peace, as shown by the interest in the island group in the past, especially by treaty arrangement. They insisted that Finland with the archipelago was of "far greater value to any country as an ally than Finland bereft of these Islands"—a

8. Memorandum of conversation by Sir Esme Howard, June 21, 1919 (File 591/2/1 in FO/608/179, PRO).

not-too-subtle hint to the Versailles victors. At the same time, they thought that there was a certain danger in having the question referred for a decision by the League at a future date, for if Germany were a member of the League by this point, she would have a voice in deciding the issue, and her influence would certainly be used to support the Swedish case. As Professor Simpson was not in a policy-making position, he remained silent before all these arguments. Therefore Enckell and Hirn expressed the desire to discuss the whole question with Sir Esme Howard as early as possible.[9]

Almost a week later Enckell again called on Professor Simpson and in the discussion that followed once more touched upon the Aland question. The tenor of this conversation showed that Enckell was quite aware of the Baltic Commission's initial decision to avoid handling the issue because of its involvement with the Russian question. He pointed out to Simpson a fact of which he was sure the Allied powers were aware: the Russian émigré group in Paris had strongly protested to his government "against any cession by Finland" of the Aland Islands to Sweden. Enckell feared that if the Baltic Commission, under Swedish pressure, attempted to solve the question for the Peace Conference, "they might make statements, even if no decision were reached and the matter referred to the League of Nations, which would be helpful to Swedish propaganda." [10]

In the interval between Enckell's two interviews with Professor Simpson the Swedes were also active. Seemingly thwarted in the Baltic Commission and undoubtedly hoping to acquire American support for the Swedish position, Branting, on the afternoon of June 21, called on Colonel House, one of President Wilson's closest advisers. In the discussion of the Aland question with House, Branting requested House's "good offices in getting a just and immediate settlement." [11] House's reply is unknown. It certainly could not have been an encouraging one, for at the

9. Simpson to Howard, June 21, 1919 (File 453 in FO/371/4380, PRO).

10. Memorandum of conversation by Professor James Y. Simpson, June 27, 1919 (File 453 in FO/371/4380, PRO).

11. Edward M. House, *The Intimate Papers of Colonel House,* ed. Charles Seymour (New York, Houghton Mifflin, 1928), *4,* 482.

next meeting of the Baltic Commission on July 2, which proved to be the most important meeting held by the Commission on the question, no American support for the Swedes was forthcoming. Indeed, with the possible exception of the plan offered by Sir Esme Howard, all comments and plans tendered during this meeting were hostile to the Swedish cause.

At this meeting Sir Esme noted that the exchange of notes between Finland and Sweden had led to no solution of the problem. In fact, the Alanders had by a plebiscite again registered their desire for union with Sweden. He then turned the attention of his colleagues to the memorandum presented to him by Vasili Maklakov, the Russian ambassador. This memorandum, which dealt almost exclusively with the strategic and military importance of the islands to both Russia and Finland, observed that possession of the islands by a state hostile to both powers was to be avoided. Sir Esme agreed with the Russian position to prevent the islands' use by a great power in any future war as a fortified base in the Baltic. He believed that this was the essential question.

A French memorandum, which had also been handed to Sir Esme Howard, was anti-Swedish and pro-Finnish in tone and clearly exposed France's orientation. Thus Kammerer remarked to his British colleague that the ethnographic argument—which was the central point in Sweden's case—was insignificant if compared with the important issue of defending the Gulf of Finland. He also agreed with Sir Esme that if the means could be found to prevent the islands' use by a great power the Commission would have solved the "principal difficulty." The Commission had to guarantee that no great power like Germany could land on the islands. He believed that it was bound to protect Russia "against this danger." Sir Esme did not completely agree to this last comment and observed that the Commission was also bound to Sweden. Though the Swedes based their claim at the moment on ethnographic grounds, there was no doubt in his mind that they also judged the question of the Aland Islands "as vital from the strategic point of view." Therefore, in his own memorandum to the Commission he had attempted to take into consideration the Swedish point of view. This memorandum by

Sir Esme Howard observed that any proposed settlement of the question would require Russian concurrence. On the other hand, acceptance of the Swedish and Alander thesis about the right of self-determination would thrust upon the Peace Conference the uninviting task of solving similar territorial transfers in more than one part of the world. Because of this the British delegation considered it preferable to leave any decision of this question to the League of Nations, should the League be asked to rule on the dispute. The memorandum went on to note the strategic importance of the islands to both the Swedes and Finns, stating that the islands should not fall into the hands of any great power. However, the question the British posed was whether denial of the islands to a great power would be better effected if they remained with Finland or were united with Sweden.

The general interest appeared to demand that the servitude of 1856 again be imposed on the archipelago and that the archipelago even be neutralized. Furthermore, to give satisfaction to both the Swedes and Finns the islands should be placed under the common protection of both countries. Under this condition, if a great power wanted the consent of one of the parties to a military occupation of the islands, the other party would be an obstacle to such an agreement. At the very least, common protection of the islands would render more difficult a military occupation. With the islands under this common protection, the Alanders in turn would be able to enjoy local autonomy under the protection of the League of Nations.

Della Torretta observed that, since Sweden had not suffered during the war because of the situation existing in the Aland Islands, he could not see why the question was being raised. He thought the ethnographic argument, which was the basis of the Swedish case, was unconvincing. Swedish anxieties on this question, he believed, did not justify the submission of the matter to the Peace Conference for a decision on a Baltic question not resulting from the war.

Kammerer observed that if the Commission had to "strive to assure justice for all the world," he "would prefer to favor Russia [rather] than Sweden." The latter country, according to Kammerer, had during the course of the war followed a policy "singularly dangerous" to the Allied cause. Sir Esme replied that the Swedes were very preoccupied with the Aland question. He feared that, if some sort of satisfaction were not given, it would only stir up in Sweden a great displeasure. This was to be avoided in order to have in the future a friendly Scandinavian bloc. This, Kammerer interjected, explained the British proposal for a "sort of condominium, under the guarantee of the League of Nations." He believed that, rather than accept this solution immediately, it would be preferable to proceed by examining all solutions envisaged, selecting the most acceptable one by a process of elimination. In the first place, they were all agreed that there would be no fortification of the Aland Islands as specified in the 1856 servitude. In the second place, as Della Torretta had pointed out, simply to give these islands to Sweden did not appear to be a satisfactory solution. Howard responded that the principal island (Aland) could perhaps be given to Sweden and the rest of the island group to Finland. The trouble with this solution, Kammerer observed, was that the rest of the archipelago was only a sprinkling of islands. Besides, the population became more and more Swedish as one approached the Finnish coast. In fact, the principal island represented 80 per cent of the island group. Could there be created, Sir Esme queried, "a free state, under the protection of the League of Nations"? It would be an unviable state, Kammerer responded, without "even enough resources for the maintenance of its lighthouses." All this, commented the American delegate, brought the Commission back to the British proposal for a condominium. Howard explained that the reason the British had proposed a condominium was to give Sweden the right to come to the assistance of the Alanders "if this was necessary."

What would be the objection, Kammerer asked, to keeping the islands Finnish? This solution, Kammerer continued, would have the advantage of maintaining the status quo and of not enmeshing the Allied powers in the question. He admitted that this was "not a good solution," but it was far better than allowing Sweden to intervene in an affair where she had no legal right. Both Swedish sentiment and that of the Alanders, Sir Esme answered, was "sharply hostile to Finland." He admitted that he was in favor of neutralizing the islands, maintaining at the same time the 1856 servitude on nonfortification. This stance was due to "purely political reasons derived from our situation in Sweden and in Scandinavia." On the other hand, England had no intention of allowing Russia a naval base in the archipelago. Thus, the only thing upon which agreement could be reached, Kammerer remarked, was neutralization of the islands. But neutralization in no way solved the territorial problem. Sir Esme thought that the Commission's note to the Supreme Council should state only the actual situation: that the Commission was agreed on the neutralization of the islands and the continuation of the 1856 servitude. No pronouncement would thus be made on the territorial question and that of the Alanders' nationality. These questions could be left to solution by the League of Nations, in case the islanders should appeal to the League. Nevertheless, Kammerer asked, were the Baltic Commission to make this statement to the Supreme Council, would not the Swedes be in a position to say: "Now the archipelago must return to us because it is entirely Swedish"? The British proposal for a condominium, Sir Esme replied, was intended to cover just such a situation. There was no urgency for the solution of this question, Della Torretta maintained. The situation as it stood was sufficient for the moment. Thus it was agreed that Sir Esme Howard, as president of the Commission, was to draw up a report expressing the Commission's desire for the neutralization of the archipelago and for the continuation of the 1856 servitude, avoiding the territorial and nationality questions. To this agreement the American delegate concurred. Regardless of what had been the advice to the American delegation by The Inquiry on the issue of the Aland Islands, French and Italian interests had prevailed.[12]

On the same day that this decision was made by the Baltic Commission, Donner in London was instructed by Enckell and Adolf Törngren, another member of the Finnish delegation, to depart immediately for Paris, though no reason was given for this request. Upon his arrival in the French capital, Donner was

12. *Procès-verbal* of the Commission on Baltic Affairs, Twelfth Séance, July 2, 1919 (File 181.21901/23, *148*, 117–20; for the Russian, French, and British memoranda, see *148*, 122–30, Record Group 256, NA).

informed that the Aland question appeared to be going badly and would most likely be settled in the near future to Finland's disadvantage. It was explained to Donner that everything had been done to prevent this, and, according to information that had come into the hands of the Finnish delegation, the Peace Conference had discussed the question at a special meeting, and it was believed that the issue would be settled immediately. It was added that there was no doubt that the Peace Conference had accepted the Swedish point of view and would declare that the island group should be joined to Sweden. Considering that the debates and the decision of the Baltic Commission had on the whole been favorable to the Finnish position and that Lord Hardinge in the May meeting of the Supreme Council had failed in his attempt to have the recognition of Finland tied to a Finnish acceptance of the Peace Conference's fixing of her frontiers, this fear and misinformation that was relayed to Donner spoke ill of Finnish sources of information and political intelligence at the Peace Conference.

As the conversation continued it was explained to Donner that Finland's last card was Donner's personal friendship with Sir Esme Howard, President of the Baltic Commission, to which the Conference had submitted the Aland question for study. It was hoped that at the last moment Donner might possibly change Finland's unfavorable position. The Finnish belief that an important but subordinate member of the British delegation would be swayed in a question such as this by a personal friendship is a sterling testimonial to Finnish naïveté and out of step with their prior and future actions. Wasting no time, Donner called on Sir Esme the following morning, July 4. The British delegate confirmed that in the Aland question Finland was in an unfavorable position because all members of the Conference had accepted the Swedish position. He explained that the principle of self-determination was extremely popular and that the Conference was ready to apply the principle not only to nations but also to groups and small areas where the population clearly announced its wishes. An Alander delegation, he pointed out, was at the moment in Paris describing the unanimous feeling for union with Sweden that existed in the archipelago. If the Aland question were soon to be taken up by the Conference he foresaw only an unfavorable decision for Finland. He noted that the Conference had given the question to the Baltic Commission for a report and the Commission had to report within a few days, after which the Conference intended to make its definitive decision. The prospects for Finland, Sir Esme Howard concluded, were very dark. Why Sir Esme was less than candid with his Finnish friend will shortly be made clear. Since Sir Esme was busy the rest of that day and the next, it was agreed that they would again meet on Sunday, July 6, to continue their discussion of the question.[13]

Later that same day Sir Esme presented for the approval of the Baltic Commission his draft letter to the Supreme Council. He first recounted the respective positions of Sweden, Finland, and Russia, observing that the Commission's recommendation to the Supreme Council, after "prolonged discussion," was that the servitude of 1856 imposed on Russia "should be maintained as against any power in possession of the islands, and further that the islands should be neutralized under the guarantee of the League of Nations." Regarding the actual possession of the archipelago, he admitted to a difference of opinion among the members of the Baltic Commission. The British and American delegations felt that the best solution to the question would be autonomy of the islands under a joint Finno-Swedish protectorate, while the French, Italians, and Japanese felt that because of the strategic importance of the islands no settlement could be achieved without the consent of Russia, which was at present unobtainable. In view of the Commission's decision, he was therefore unable to give the Supreme Council any recommendations beyond those mentioned. The only comment that the Commission was willing to make, Sir Esme added in his note, was that "if the question of any change of status in the islands were to be decided by an international body it had better be left to [a] decision by the League of Nations." [14]

When this memorandum was read by Sir Esme Howard to his

13. Ossian Donner, *Åtta år. Memoaranteckningar från åren 1918–1926* (Oxford, Eng., Oxford University Press, 1927), pp. 106–08. For Donner's friendship with Sir Esme Howard, see ibid., p. 31 ff., and also Sir Esme Howard, *Theatre of Life* (Boston, Little, Brown, 1936), *2*, 266.

14. Recommendation of [the] Commission on Baltic Affairs on the Aland Islands, Paris, July 4, 1919 (Political 1919: 11/468/468, LNA).

colleagues it was accepted by all the delegations. Kammerer observed that he had seen the Finns and had said to them that any solution of the Aland question appeared possible only in agreement with the Russians. They had replied to him that this conformed completely with Finnish interests. Therefore no Finnish objections would be raised to the declaration read by Sir Esme. It was then agreed that a communication explaining the Commission's decision in the name of the Conference should also be given to the Finns, Swedes, and Alanders, but to be forwarded to the parties only after the Supreme Council adopted the Commission's report. To this, all delegations gave their assent.[15]

This draft letter, drawn up by Sir Esme Howard the next day, July 5, and addressed to the Swedish and Alander delegations, began by stating that the Paris Peace Conference wished to see the Aland question settled in accordance with the wishes of the islanders. At the moment, however, the Conference felt it was very difficult for them to intervene directly in the sense suggested. Though the Allied powers had recognized the independence of Finland, the Conference felt it was impossible to ignore the great interest which Russia had in the settlement of a question on which the security of the Baltic largely depended. Hence, they were reluctant to arrive at any decision regulating the future possession of the islands at a time when there was no Russian government qualified to speak in the name of Russia on the question of the Aland Islands. At the same time there was another difficulty presented by the Aland question which was of a more general character. The Aland question, strictly speaking, did not arise out of the war and therefore did not properly fall under the competence of the Paris Peace Conference. Instead, the Allied powers believed that the best way in which the question could be settled would be by an amicable arrangement between the two governments, and they continued to hope that the two governments would make further efforts in this direction. If this proved impossible, they proposed that "in order to reach a settlement, recourse might be made to the good offices of the League of Nations." For the moment, the only formal opinion that the

15. *Procès-verbal* of the Commission on Baltic Affairs, Thirteenth Séance, July 4, 1919 (File 181.21901/23, *148*, 133–34, Record Group 256, NA).

Peace Conference felt itself competent to express was that the servitude of 1856 should continue and be imposed on whoever possessed the Aland Islands, and these islands should be neutralized under the guarantee of the League of Nations. On the latter issue, the Peace Conference would in due time communicate to the Secretary-General of the League of Nations a proposal covering this point.[16] While Howard was writing this draft letter, the Alanders were writing one to Howard informing him that over 96 per cent of the Alanders, in the recent plebiscite organized in the islands, had voted for union with Sweden. Their demand was for a plebiscite under impartial control whose result would be obligatory for Sweden and Finland.[17] Receipt of the Alander message in the British delegation prompted Professor Carr to observe that there was "no doubt as to the wishes of the Alanders for union with Sweden." They were "very honest and simple-minded people," and he was personally "sorry that nothing [could] apparently be done for them." [18] Though in the end Professor Carr was right, his remarks were premature, for the Swedish diplomatic counteroffensive was about to begin.

On July 6, as agreed, Sir Esme Howard, accompanied by Lady Howard, met Donner, and they spent the day together. Their visits to churches and museums were spaced with stops for lunch and tea, at which time the Aland question was discussed. Donner's first point was that legally the islands undoubtedly belonged to Finland, and any dissatisfaction with this situation had not been previously raised. He stressed that the archipelago was much more important to Finland than to Sweden, and its political importance was in no way balanced by the small population's temporary and unanimous desire for union with Sweden. Donner then got to the main point. He warned that all the work that had been done during the previous year in an attempt to estab-

16. *Procès-verbal* of the Commission on Baltic Affairs, Fourteenth Séance, July 7, 1919 (File 181.21901/23, *148*, 150, Record Group 256, NA); Draft Letter to be Addressed to the Swedish and Aland Islands Delegations, July 5, 1919 (Political 1919: 11/468/468, LNA).

17. Sweden, Utrikesdepartementet, *Ålandsfrågan inför Nationeras Förbund* (Stockholm, Norstedt & Söner, 1920), pp. 98–102.

18. Minute by E[dward] H[allett] Carr, July 8, 1919 (File 591/2/1 in FO/608/180, PRO).

lish closer relations between Finland and the Allied powers "would be completely wasted" if it could be rightly said that the Allies had taken the island group from Finland and given it to Sweden. The Allies' supporters in Finland would be defenseless before such an accusation. He maintained that the separation of the island group from Finland would make his country much weaker, which was contrary to London's interests, since Lord Curzon had repeated to him several times in the past Britain's "wish to create a strong Finland."

To these remarks, Sir Esme Howard declared that he saw only one way of solving the question to Finland's advantage, and that was to prevent it from being taken up by the Peace Conference, that is to say, by its directing organ, the Supreme Council. This could be done by delaying the decision, for, as he had already told him, immediate consideration of the issue before the Council could only lead to a solution against Finland's interests. According to Howard, it was necessary to find an excuse for adjourning discussion of the Aland question that would be accepted by the Peace Conference. The proposal that Sir Esme now offered was the decision that the Baltic Commission had already come to, namely, a declaration that Russia had "strategic interests" in the island group and because of this had to be heard from before any decision was taken. However, since Russia had no responsible government at the moment, its views could not now be heard, and so the Aland question would have to be adjourned. In this situation the Peace Conference would end up avoiding consideration of the Aland question, and probably in the end it would be transferred to the League of Nations. If this occurred, Sir Esme added "with a little smile," Finland would not have to worry, for the League would never detach a province from one state and give it to another. A Swedish victory in the question depended on an immediate decision by the Supreme Council.

But a number of questions posed themselves—at least in Donner's mind. Could he take responsibility for agreeing to Sir Esme's proposal? How would opinion in Finland, which had just gained its freedom from Russia, react if that country were brought back into the Aland question? Yet a decision had to be made quickly. Sir Esme said he was departing for London on July 9 and in doing so was relinquishing his post as President of the Baltic Commission. Therefore, either on the following day, Monday, July 7, or by the latest July 8, he had to give the report of the Baltic Commission to the Supreme Council. Under this pressure and with no time to consult the government in Helsingfors, Donner accepted Sir Esme's proposed declaration, which appeared to him the only alternative that could save Finland "from an immediate and disastrous decision by the Supreme Council."

On his part, Sir Esme promised to see that the Baltic Commission would finish its report within the next two days and pass it on to the Supreme Council. He further promised to see to it that the Commission would not mention anything about a future plebiscite. At the same time, he pointed out that the Alanders' demands for protection of their cultural interests should be covered by the Finnish government. Sir Esme's final comment was that by talking to Donner he had realized that for Finland the loss of the Aland Islands would cause far greater irritation than the disappointment that would arise in Sweden if Sweden's interests in this matter were not satisfied.[19] Thus, during these two discussions Sir Esme Howard had cleverly given Donner the impression that his personal intervention and Sir Esme's reaction to it had led to a formula which had saved the day for Finland. Actually, as we have seen, the decision to interject the issue of Russia into the Aland problem and to avoid coming to any decision had been made by the Baltic Commission prior to Donner's arrival in Paris. For England, at the very least, Sir Esme's act had gained Finland's good will, not to mention the gratitude of the Finnish minister in London.

The next morning Sir Esme Howard presented for the approval of the Baltic Commission his draft letter to the interested parties which he had composed on July 5. It was unanimously approved and without debate.[20] But word of what the Commission had decided was passed on to the Swedes the following day, July 8, when Branting called on Sir Esme. Pressured by Branting on when the Swedes were going to receive a reply to their note of

19. Donner, pp. 108–12.

20. *Procès-verbal* of the Commission on Baltic Affairs, Fourteenth Séance, July 7, 1919 (File 181.21901/23, *148*, 148 Record Group 256, NA).

April 22, Howard was forced to admit that a reply had been drafted by the Baltic Commission for the approval of the Supreme Council and it would probably be sent before long. If Sir Esme had been aware of the future difficulties that this admission would cause, he would probably have hesitated in making it. He explained to Branting that the Commission considered that no Baltic questions, the Aland one included, could be definitively settled without the agreement of a Russian government. Furthermore, the Aland question did not seem to be one for the Peace Conference to solve, since it had not really "arisen directly out of the war." The only recommendation it could give was to maintain the servitude of 1856 and possibly neutralize the islands. He emphasized to Branting that, because of Russian interests in any Baltic settlement, "to endeavour to come to a decision without arrangement with her would seem only to be laying up trouble for the future." Branting responded that "he fully understood this" and agreed with what Sir Esme had said. Howard "begged him to explain this to the Swedish Government when he returned [to Stockholm], which he promised to do." [21] However, the developing relationship between the Swedish government and the Supreme Council would prevent the dispatch of any communication to the interested parties as mentioned by Sir Esme Howard to Branting, and would in fact force the Commission to reconsider its decision on the Aland Islands.

The Baltic Commission: Second Phase

This new turn of events had begun as early as July 5, the day after Donner had first spoken to Sir Esme Howard. On this date the Swedish delegation requested an interview with Lord Balfour,[22] as well as one with Secretary of State Lansing,[23] so that the Swedish point of view could be presented. Though some within the British delegation thought it preferable that the Swedes first present their views in a note, Lord Balfour in the end personally

21. Memorandum of conversation by Sir Esme Howard, July 8, 1919 (File 591/2/1 in FO/608/180, PRO).

22. Note from the Swedish Legation in Paris requesting an interview with Lord Balfour, July 5, 1919 (File 591/2/1 in FO/608/180, PRO).

23. Ehrensvärd to Lansing, July 5, 1919 (Lansing Papers).

spoke to Count Ehrensvärd.[24] Lansing's interview was granted for July 9.[25] A similar approach was undertaken in London, where Crown Prince Gustaf was again visiting the British capital. On July 11, he discussed the whole question with Sir Ian J. Malcolm, Lord Balfour's private secretary, who promised to convey Gustaf's remarks to Balfour. In a letter written the following day Gustaf recapitulated his arguments. He denied that the agitation of the Alanders for union with Sweden was in any way instigated by the Swedish government. On the contrary, the Finnish claim to break away from Russia on the principle of self-determination naturally moved the Alanders, who were thoroughly Swedish, to claim the same right. They were unanimous in their desire to be united again with Sweden, with whom they had been united until 1809. Indeed, up to 1809 they had been regarded as separate from the Finns, and therefore it could not be said that they had always belonged to Finland. Because of the great irritation that the question had produced, and because Stockholm had been unsuccessful in coming to an agreement with Finland, it seemed to Gustaf "highly desirable that the matter be conclusively dealt with by the Peace Conference." The only thing Sweden desired was that the Alanders "be allowed to decide to which country they should belong in the future." Malcolm understood that this letter had "to be regarded as a strictly private 'aide-mémoire' and of course in no way an official document." [26] This comment was obviously meaningless, for in a constitutional monarchy like Sweden no crown prince would have engaged in a discussion or written a missive of this type except under Cabinet instructions. Maintaining this pretense, Balfour replied through Malcolm that he understood the private nature of Gustaf's communication, and his arguments were receiving Balfour's "most careful consideration." [27] The Swedish diplomatic offensive continued some days later when Branting and Count Ehrensvärd also called on

24. Minute by E[dward] H[allett] Carr, June 10, 1919? (File 591/2/1 in FO/608/180, PRO).

25. Kirk to Ehrensvärd, July 7, 1919 (Lansing Papers).

26. Crown Prince Gustaf to Sir Ian J. Malcolm, July 12, 1919 (Balfour Papers, *49750*, 10–12).

27. Sir Ian J. Malcolm to Crown Prince Gustaf, July 15, 1919 (Balfour Papers, *49750*, 13–14).

Clemenceau. The French Prime Minister, Branting explained after the interview, had displayed a great deal of sympathy for a solution of the Aland question according to the desires of the inhabitants but had also "insisted on the legitimate right of Russia to be heard" before any definitive solution could be obtained [28]—a now-familiar refrain.

All these Swedish endeavors appear to have had some effect on Robert H. Lord, head of the Russian Section of the American delegation. In a memorandum on July 17, two days before Ehrensvärd and Branting's call on Clemenceau, he pointed out to Joseph C. Grew, also of the American delegation, that the Aland question after Finland's recognition could no longer be "considered a question directly affecting Russia, [and] might be a subject where the Peace Conference could try to bring an immediate decision." However, Lord had one important qualification, namely, that since the question was a matter in which the British were far more concerned than the United States, he favored "leaving the initiative entirely to the British." [29] This point was accepted four days later when the American delegation informed the Department of State that, in their opinion, Haynes in Helsingfors should not commit the United States on the matter of Finland's frontiers until his British and French colleagues received "instructions to take similar action." It was thought that independent American pressure on the Finns was especially undesirable, as the Allied note to Admiral Kolchak on May 26 contemplated a settlement outside the Peace Conference by an agreement between Finland and Russia. If this were to fail, it then would be settled by League arbitration. On the additional questions of an amnesty for the Red Finns and the Aland Islands, both of which especially interested the British, it was the advice of the American delegation that they "should not be raised by our initiative." [30] This decision was the first breach in the Supreme Council's May agreement that after Finland was recognized the Allied missions in Helsingfors would urge the Finnish au-

28. *Bulletin périodique de la presse scandinave,* No. 72, p. 3.

29. Robert H. Lord to Joseph C. Grew, July 17, 1919 (File 760D.6115/4, Record Group 256, NA).

30. Ammission to the Department of State, July 21, 1919 (File 760D.6115/5, Record Group 256, NA).

thorities to accept the Peace Conference's decisions in regard to the frontiers of Finland.

In Helsingfors, the news that the Baltic Commission's report to the Supreme Council had interjected the issue of Russia was not well received. The Finnish government considered the Aland question to be an exclusive Finno-Swedish matter. Moreover, it was felt that, since Finland was free and independent, Russia had no interests in the question, and therefore the Baltic Commission was unjustified in speaking as it had of hearing Russia's views on the matter. To offset this Holsti agreed with Westman that there was no justification in including Russia in the Aland question, an issue that concerned only their respective countries. Therefore on July 21, the same day that the American delegation was advising the State Department not to raise the issue of Finland's frontiers, Holsti informed Donner in London, as well as Enckell and Törngren in Paris, that both Finland and Sweden would probably protest the Baltic Commission's decision that the Aland question could not be settled without Russia's participation. They were instructed to ascertain if the Peace Conference could be expected to change the decision of the Baltic Commission and to transfer the solution of the question to Finland and Sweden if the governments of these two states could reach a final agreement. The last information was that Finland would shortly hand Sweden a note on the Aland question.

Donner's immediate move was to confer with Sir Esme Howard, then in London. Initially Sir Esme was baffled at a protest being lodged, since no decision had been made by the Baltic Commission. It had only made a report which included a suggested decision to the Supreme Council. According to Sir Esme, a protest was unjustified, since the Commission's position was secret and he had only confidentially revealed it to Donner and Count Wrangel, his Swedish colleague, on the understanding that it would likewise in confidence be forwarded to their respective governments. Nothing in the meantime had changed the confidential nature of the Baltic Commission's proposition. It was still a proposition, and therefore it was impossible to contemplate protesting against it. On the question itself, Howard was very surprised that a protest from the Finnish side had even been considered, and that Finland would protest in conjunction with Sweden appeared to Sir Esme absolutely fantastic. He believed that if the Baltic Commission's proposition were to be accepted by the Peace Conference, Finland would have won a great victory and Sweden suffered a great defeat. Finland would win an adjournment of the question, which would put it past the present critical period. Conversely, Sweden would lose its most desired goal, a decision against which no appeal existed, to wit, a favorable decision by the Supreme Council. The Peace Conference, Howard observed, had only two choices: either to award the island group to Sweden or to adjourn the question. Because of the atmosphere pervading the Conference at this time no other solution was possible. Personally, Sir Esme was convinced that the Baltic Commission could obtain an adjournment by tendering the proposition that Russia had to be heard on the question. Any protest by Finland, either jointly or simultaneously with Sweden, would be a protest against the only solution devised by the Baltic Commission to Finland's advantage. If the Baltic Commission's plan was thwarted, it would mean eventual transfer of the islands to Sweden. Sir Esme believed that the idea of a joint Finno-Swedish protest had come from Westman, and he thought it a dangerous ruse aimed at having the question considered by the Peace Conference. Sir Esme added that any consideration of Russia's views in the future would in no way endanger Finland's possession of the island group. Actually it would lead to nothing more than a demand for a prohibition against fortification of the archipelago, a demand that both Finland and Sweden had already agreed to. He found it difficult to understand why the winner should protest with the loser. At the end, Howard repeated what he had stressed in the past: that the Peace Conference considered the best solution to be a Finno-Swedish agreement without the question's being submitted to any other party.[31]

Sir Esme soon forwarded the substance of what Donner had told him to Sir Eyre Crowe in Paris. It was Howard's opinion that Branting had probably communicated to Stockholm the information Howard had given him about the Baltic Commission's draft reply and Westman was "trying to make capital out of it

31. Donner, pp. 113–18.

and draw the Finnish Government into a protest." Provided the British delegation in Paris agreed, Sir Esme thought it would be advisable to contact Count Wrangel, who was in the French capital, and request him to contact Hellner. He was to point out to the Swedish Foreign Minister that while Britain had consistently held that a Finno-Swedish agreement would "be of material assistance in reaching a solution of [the] Aland question, any joint protest by the two countries against the view of the Baltic Commission could not fail to have an unfortunate effect in Allied countries and later in Russia so rendering an ultimate solution more difficult." To protect Donner he asked that his name not be mentioned and observed that perhaps Bell in Helsingfors might also be requested to speak to Holsti along these lines.[32]

Paris' reaction, however, was negative. Since the Baltic Commission's draft reply had not yet been considered by the Supreme Council, it could not "therefore be said to represent the policy of the [Peace] Conference." This incident, Balfour observed to Curzon in a slap at Howard, illustrated "the extreme inconvenience attending the premature communication to outside parties" of what passed at the Conference or its committees. He therefore could not recommend that action be taken along the lines suggested by Sir Esme until the Conference had made its decision on the question.[33]

This line of argument was also assumed by Finland's representatives at London and Paris. On July 24, Donner dispatched a cable to Helsingfors containing the substance of his talk with Howard, including the argument that no decision had been made on what was merely a proposal of the Baltic Commission. In Paris, Enckell and Törngren likewise communicated the opinion that Finland could not "officially protest against [a] secret proposition of a subordinate commission" of the Peace Conference. To begin with, the exact text of the report was not known. The only thing they knew that underlined Russian interests was in-

32. Curzon (London) to Balfour, No. 1026, July 26, 1919 (File 591/2/1 in FO/608/180, PRO).

33. Balfour (Paris) to Curzon, No. 1213, July 29, 1919 (File 591/2/1 in FO/608/180, PRO).

formation given to them by Professor Carr that the neutralization of the island group had been mentioned. This in itself did not justify any protest. Indeed, the Baltic Commission's actual project, in view of the present situation, was generally considered in Finland's favor. They warned that any joint Finno-Swedish protest to the Peace Conference would only be the prelude to a plebiscite in the archipelago. Therefore, like Donner and Sir Esme Howard, they too strongly recommended against any *démarche* to the Peace Conference. Instead they recommended that Helsingfors await the next decision of the Conference on the Aland question and Enckell's and Törngren's explanations before sending any new communication to Sweden.[34] Undoubtedly impressed by the objections that had been raised by their London and Paris missions as well as the words of Sir Esme, the Finns made no protest either alone or in conjunction with Sweden.

Because of the information that had been imparted by Sir Esme Howard to Branting and the knowledge that no real *démarche* in Paris was possible in concert with Finland, the Swedes were moved to turn to the Peace Conference on July 25, the very day Enckell and Törngren were sending their views to Helsingfors. In his note to Clemenceau as president of the Peace Conference, Ehrensvärd pointed out to him that the Alanders by a plebiscite made the previous month had again by an overwhelming majority expressed their sincere desire to have the island group reunited with Sweden. Cleverly skirting the issue of any protest over the report of the Baltic Commission, Ehrensvärd went on to observe that because of the importance of the new vote and the question itself, he desired to be "heard by the Peace Conference in order to explain to it the Swedish point of view regarding the problem of the Aland Islands, before a definitive decision is reached regarding it." An appearance before the Conference seemed to Ehrensvärd "all the more desirable because an opportunity was not given the [Swedish] Delegation to be heard before the Baltic Commission of the Conference."[35] This appeal by Ehrensvärd was presented to the Supreme Council six days later

34. Donner, pp. 117–18, 114.
35. *PRFRUS 1919*. PPC, 7, 448.

on July 31, and after a short discussion it was decided to give Ehrensvärd a hearing "regarding the Swedish views on the question of the Aland Islands." [36]

In London, on the day following Ehrensvärd's communication to Clemenceau, the newly established League of Nations, which was to play so crucial a role in this whole problem, took note of the Baltic Commission's decision. In a memorandum to his colleagues, the Secretary-General, Sir Eric Drummond, thought that when the Aland question came before the League Council the League Secretariat would have to be prepared with a plan providing for "temporary possession of the islands." Because of the conflicting Finno-Swedish claims, the Secretary-General was "not sure that government by a High Commission applied by the League in conjunction with local representation on the lines of the Danzig scheme may not prove the best solution." [37] For the moment, however, it was the Supreme Council sitting at Paris and not the League which was important.

In the agreed-upon Swedish presentation to the Supreme Council on August 4, Ehrensvärd recounted essentially the now-familiar Swedish case based on racial, linguistic, and historical grounds. Ehrensvärd's comments in the latter half of his presentation, however, revealed his knowledge of the proceedings and decisions of the Baltic Commission. He believed that the question of the neutralization of the islands under a League guarantee as recommended by the Baltic Commission and the question of the sovereignty of the islands could not be separated. He maintained that the whole question was a product of the war. Thus, the Paris Peace Conference, "called to decide all international questions having their origin in the war," was bound to take up the Aland question. Ehrensvärd dismissed the Baltic Commission's contention that no immediate solution of the problem was possible without the concurrence of Russia. If the delay over Russian concurrence lasted only a short time he thought no great harm

36. Ibid., p. 443.

37. Memorandum by the Secretary-General, Sir Eric Drummond, to Messrs. Monnet, Fosdick, Montaux and Colban, July 26, 1919 (Political 1919: 11/468/468, LNA).

would accrue. But a long delay appeared likely, and the Swedish government thought "serious inconveniences" would result from the indefinite postponement of the question. These inconveniences would in fact be "especially serious if the Conference were to place the solution in the hands of the League of Nations," for this would increase the delay. He warned the Supreme Council that "the possibility of an aggravation of the situation must be counted upon in the event of a decision too long postponed," and he denied that Russia could object to a plebiscite whose object was settlement of the Aland question between Sweden and Finland.

On the issue of the neutralization of the islands, Ehrensvärd was willing to admit that Russia as a Baltic power had great interests to safeguard. In the hands of any power the islands would cause apprehension to other Baltic states. Sweden, however, had no objection to their neutralization—especially because of their proximity to Stockholm—and its policy of strict neutrality stretching over a century made it better equipped than any other power to possess the islands and supervise their neutralization.[38]

After hearing Ehrensvärd the Supreme Council's decision, on a suggestion by Frank L. Polk of the American delegation, was that Swedish claims to the Aland Islands as reflected in Ehrensvärd's declaration be referred to the Conference's Baltic Commission for an examination and report.[39] The Swedes had been temporarily reprieved.

At the meeting of the Baltic Commission four days later on August 8, the issue was reconsidered. The absence of Sir Esme Howard had placed Della Torretta in the position of President. He recounted the action of the Supreme Council but noted to his colleagues that the Commission had already drawn up and unanimously adopted a report on the question. He proposed, therefore, that the Commission limit itself in replying to the Supreme Council, to the statement that it had already examined the question during the previous month, delivering to it the agreed report.

38. *PRFRUS 1919. PPC, 7,* 518–26; Sweden, Utrikesdepartementet, *Ålandsfrågan,* pp. 102–20; League of Nations, *Official Journal,* spec. suppl. no. 1 (Aug. 1920), pp. 45–51.

39. *PRFRUS 1919. PPC, 7,* 511.

No objections were raised and Della Torretta's proposed reply to the Supreme Council was accepted.[40]

It was not until the next meeting of the Commission on August 19 that the substance of the reply agreed upon in July was questioned. From Kammerer's remarks it was clear that the French had been influenced by Ehrensvärd's undisguised warnings to the Supreme Council that any delay in the solution of the Aland question would cause complications in the Baltic. Kammerer thought there was no reason to hurry solutions for problems when there was hope that subsequent events might solve them. If the Commission could not decide the Aland question without Russia because Russian interests were involved, neither could it leave in indefinite suspense the solution of the Aland question. What solution, he asked his colleagues, could the Commission give to the Aland question? He had already explained why he was not favorably inclined to the British proposal for a condominium. Though he was critical of the Swedish position during the war, he believed that the Aland Islands in the hands of the Swedes constituted less of a menace for the Russians than if the islands were in the hands of the Finns, provided, of course, the islands were neutralized and the servitude of 1856 continued. Della Torretta agreed with these sentiments. Unfortunately, he observed to Kammerer, the Russian situation did not show signs of being quickly resolved. He thought that there was an advantage in allowing questions like the Aland Islands to drag out, for at the worst, if the Peace Conference broke up before a solution was devised, this question, like so many other issues, would be left to the League of Nations. Regarding a definitive settlement, Della Torretta was unwilling to commit himself now. At the same time, he could not help but remark that no sooner was Finland recognized than the first gesture made was to "take from it a part of its territory." Though the majority of the Aland population was Swedish, it had to be remembered also that the whole Finnish population was of a mixed character. Finland was a country where everything was written in both Finnish and Swedish; the names of the streets, and the decisions of the courts were in both

40. *Procès-verbal* of the Commission on Baltic Affairs, Nineteenth Séance, Aug. 8, 1919 (File 181.21901/23, *148*, 189, Record Group 256, NA).

languages. There was "no ethnic unity." The League of Nations, which would have immense powers, would be able to "decide without hesitation" what he felt at the present moment.

After further discussion it was decided to tone down the anti-Swedish comments and to change the last three lines of the previously agreed-upon reply to the Supreme Council. The last lines of the note were now to read that if there were no immediate prospect of an early restoration of Russia, the Baltic Commission would be invited, before the breakup of the Peace Conference, to propose a "definitive solution" of the Aland question. As a concession to Swedish pressure the Commission omitted the letter to the Swedish and Alander delegations and in their new draft to the Supreme Council on August 25 removed all mention of the League of Nations, suggesting instead a definitive settlement by the Peace Conference. Thus the Swedes had won a partial victory and were once again in the picture.[41]

From Kammerer's and Della Torretta's comments during this meeting it was obvious that a split had occurred in the Franco-Italian position. The French, more sensitive than the Italians to possible complications in the Baltic, and thus to Swedish pressure, had to adjust their position. This French shift favoring a solution more in line with Swedish interests was explained privately by Kammerer to Professor Carr as a reaction by his country to the "failure of Finland to engage in military operations against" St. Petersburg which Paris during this period had been most interested in.[42]

Unknown to the Baltic Commission, but on the very day they were making this decision, the Finnish government presented a note to the Swedes expressing their willingness to consent to "extremely large concessions" to Sweden's point of view. The Finns expressed their readiness, provided their sovereignty over the islands was respected, to discuss measures that would bring about a satisfactory solution of the question for both sides. The Finns were inclined to consider further Swedish suggestions on military guarantees for Sweden; for example, the Finns had al-

41. *Procès-verbal* of the Commission on Baltic Affairs, Twentieth Séance, Aug. 19, 1919 (File 181.21901/23, *148*, 199–200, Record Group 256, NA); the note to the Supreme Council of August 25, 1919 (ibid., pp. 204–05).

42. Carr (Paris) to Gregory, Dec. 13, 1919 (File 591/2/1 in FO/608/180, PRO).

ready consented to the demolition of the Aland fortifications. Helsingfors wanted the question treated as a Finno-Swedish matter.[43] Since the Finns were offering only to discuss Sweden's strategic interests on condition that Finland's sovereignty over the islands be respected, it was obviously not in Sweden's interests to develop this Finnish proposal further. To have done so would have undercut her whole argument and would have jeopardized her position in Paris, which by August of 1919 she felt was extremely strong. To this Finnish proposal the Swedes gave no reply, except to ask that it be kept secret.

At the same time the Swedes were also apprehensive. A press statement by the British chargé d'affaires at Helsingfors recently transferred from Stockholm, Sir Coleridge Kennard, that the powers desired to see the Aland question amicably settled through direct Finno-Swedish negotiations brought Count Wrangel to the Foreign Office. He took exception to this statement, the Swedish minister informed Sir Ronald W. Graham, the Acting Permanent Under-Secretary. Sir Ronald was personally of the opinion that the view expressed by Kennard "was a harmless one, and that it probably represented both the views of the Peace Conference and the Allied Powers." Wrangel, however, was not impressed by this and retorted that he had been instructed by Stockholm "to declare that a very painful impression would be produced in Sweden" if the Peace Conference delegates were to show themselves "willing and able to settle the question of Spitzbergen, but were yet unwilling, or unable, to deal with the similar question of the Aland Islands."[44] Sir Esme Howard pointed out to Lord Curzon that he had made similar comments to Wrangel in the past and Kennard's remarks therefore could not have been new to the Swedish minister. What the latter was probably objecting to, Howard believed, was that these comments were made in Finland by the British diplomatic representative and might make the Finns more than ever insistent on the maintenance of the status quo in the Aland Islands. It seemed to Sir Esme that the more widely it was

43. Kennard (Helsingfors) to Curzon, No. 137, Oct. 6, 1919, and attached *note verbale* of the Finnish Ministry of Foreign Affairs, Oct. 2, 1919 (File 591/2/1 in FO/608/180, PRO).

44. Curzon (London) to an unknown addressee [Lord Balfour?], Sept. 8, 1919 (File 591/2/1 in FO/608/180, PRO).

known that this was the view of the Allied governments the more likely it was that both countries would "accept some compromise." Therefore he thought Kennard should be instructed to advise the Finns to reopen the negotiations with the Swedes "so as not to lay themselves open to the charge of procrastination." It was Sir Esme's impression that the Swedes were interested in finding "a way out of the present impasse and might be willing to modify their attitude as regards accepting a single plebiscite as the only solution of the question." [45]

Still uneasy several days after his interview with Graham, Wrangel wrote a private letter to Lord Balfour in Paris. He did not doubt, he wrote in reference to Kennard's statement, that his country, government, and fellow Swedes would be very contented if an agreement on the Aland question could be arrived at between Stockholm and Helsingfors without the interference of the Paris Peace Conference. Yet this seemed impossible to accomplish as long as Finland declined to negotiate or discuss the Aland question on the basis which in the opinion of Sweden was the center of the problem: the right and desires of the Alanders. Because of this Sweden continued to hope that the Paris Conference would settle the question. He allowed himself "quite informally and personally" to apply to Lord Balfour's "great impartiality" with the purpose of obtaining his support for a decision by the Supreme Council on the Aland question. Wrangel feared that it "would produce a very painful impression" in his country if the Peace Conference dealt with and decided the Spitzbergen question, which was in no way connected with the war, but simultaneously declined to settle the Aland one, which was a direct outgrowth of the war. He was leaving England for a few weeks and on his return would be passing through Paris, and he hoped Balfour would allow him to call and lay before him again and "de vive voix" the question which, as he knew, all Swedes considered of utmost importance for their country.[46]

45. Howard (Stockholm) to Curzon, No. 421, Sept. 19, 1919 (File 591/2/1 in FO/608/180, PRO).

46. Wrangel (London) to Balfour, Sept. 4, 1919 (File 591/2/1 in FO/608/180, PRO).

However, Swedish anxiety persisted, and to press the case Ehrensvärd called on Polk on September 8 and "asked that we take up the matter."[47] This was quickly followed by a letter to Polk in which Ehrensvärd elaborated the Swedish position. He began by observing that in their talk the previous day, Polk had touched upon the idea of letting the Aland question "rest until the League of Nations had been constituted in order to have it resolved by the organ of the League." Ehrensvärd had pointed out at that time the "inconveniences" involved in Polk's plan, "inconveniences" that he knew would bring objections from the Swedish government.

However, the Swedish minister felt that there were other points of general consideration that should also be raised. For example, he sincerely believed it very unwise to entrust the League from its very inception with a problem as delicate as the Aland question. This matter closely touched the "vital interests" of Swedes and Alanders. The Aland question would put the authority of the new organization to a difficult test in Scandinavia, and he thought it was in the "interests of the whole World to avoid in [bringing about] the downfall of this high authority."

By advancing this view Ehrensvärd thought he was in line with the American position. Here he referred to the Spitzbergen question which concerned a group of islands 400 miles north of Norway. Though the great majority of the islands' residents were Norwegian, the area was *terra nullius* and Norway wished to have her sovereignty over the island group recognized. He heard that the American delegate on the Spitzbergen Commission had rejected the proposal that the Spitzbergen question be resolved by a League mandate on the grounds that his government "did not think it wise to charge the League of Nations with the responsibility for the administration of the archipelago." Yet the responsibility that would be assumed by the League in the Spitzbergen question would be far less onerous than the one to be assumed in resolving the Aland question.

He then expanded on certain comments he had made to Polk the previous day on the political reaction in the North over both

47. Diary entry, Sept. 8, 1919 (Polk Papers).

questions. Ehrensvärd reminded Polk that he had agreed with him that it was a matter of the greatest importance to Finland that it come to an understanding with Sweden, and that the political future and independence of Finland depended on its relations with its Scandinavian neighbors. This was not true in the case of Sweden regardless of Finland's choice. He assured Polk, as he had the previous day, that Sweden could never have close relations with Finland if the Aland question were not resolved in a manner giving "satisfaction to the aspirations of the population of the archipelago." In the matter of the Spitzbergen question, he added that the solution envisaged—the recognition of Norwegian sovereignty over the islands—would probably provoke some bitterness in Sweden toward Norway, since the solution was not considered to give satisfaction to legitimate Swedish interests. Ehrensvärd was convinced that if the Aland question were resolved in conformity with the wishes of Swedish public opinion bitterness over the Spitzbergen question would disappear. But if Sweden were to be checked on both questions the agreement and close understanding between Denmark, Norway, and Sweden would be jeopardized.

These two questions—Aland and Spitzbergen—were intimately related with developments in the North. Close relations between the Scandinavian states had always been the aim of Swedish statesmen. Ehrensvärd noted that he had earnestly tried to realize closer understanding among Norwegians, Danes, and Swedes in order to make their countries form a phalanx "for the promotion of peace and neutrality" and in preventing outside influence from creating discord among them. It was because of this that he felt entitled to draw to Polk's attention the possible dangers that threatened, since these questions were of the greatest importance to his country.[48]

That Swedish overtures of a similar nature were made to the other Allied delegations is almost a certainty. We shall shortly see that their effect, as in the case of France, was matched and outweighed by Finnish counter-pressure conveyed especially through the person of General Mannerheim.

48. Ehrensvärd to Polk, Sept. 10, 1919 (File 860D.014/60, Record Group 256, NA).

The League of Nations Secretariat

Aside from the Baltic Commission, the Aland question was also a topic of discussion in the League Secretariat. On August 26, one day after the Baltic Commission's note was delivered to Paul Dutasta, the Secretary-General of the Peace Conference, a fifteen-page memorandum was written by Erik Colban, Director of the Minorities Section of the League Secretariat, thoroughly examining the whole question.

Though none of the problems touched upon in the memorandum were ever posed to the League, the role that Colban envisaged for the organization in the Aland question was interesting. Equally interesting was his awareness that, though the League was a super-association of states which could play an important role in international relations, its success was in the end dependent upon the support of the great powers, an awareness unfortunately lacking among some of the League's staunchest supporters. Colban's memorandum first cautioned that the Aland question was still a subject of discussion at the Peace Conference. Because it was a delicate question that had aroused feelings in both Sweden and Finland, the League should refrain from handling it as long as it was in the hands of the Peace Conference. Any scheme formulated by the League had to be postponed until the Peace Conference had come to a final decision. At the same time it was useful to be kept up to date on the negotiations and proceedings at Paris, especially since the good offices of the League had been mentioned by the Baltic Commission (Colban was of course unaware of the Baltic Commission's revised communication to the Supreme Council sent the previous day). He noted that the position of the Peace Conference toward the Baltic Commission's draft letters was unknown. It was therefore possible that the Commission's suggestion might not be adopted by the Peace Conference. Nevertheless, it seemed useful to submit suggestions on the Aland question for "preliminary consideration in order to be prepared against all eventualities."

First, he thought that the Conference's communication to the League's Secretary-General, as mentioned in the July draft letters, would be some type of recommendation. Colban noted that the

Commission's letters expressly stated that the question of the islands' possession did not fall within the competence of the Peace Conference. If this same view were adopted by the Peace Conference with regard to the suggested neutralization of the archipelago, it would mean that the Conference would take no decision but would leave the matter to the League of Nations, limiting itself to an expression of opinion as to "what should be decided under the auspices of the League." The recommendation from the Peace Conference would stipulate that the 1856 convention should be imposed upon any power in possession of the islands and that the archipelago be neutralized under the guarantee of the League of Nations. This latter proposal, it was thought, had in view an arrangement whereby the Aland archipelago would be demilitarized, unfortified, and excluded from military preparations or from serving as the base for such preparations, the examples cited being the Ionian Islands (under the treaty of November 14, 1863), the neutral zone between Sweden and Norway (convention of October 26, 1905), and to some extent the Saar Basin (paragraph 30 of the Saar Basin Annex to the Versailles Peace Treaty). The Conference's stipulation of neutralization would of course not alter the actual possession of the islands, which were Finland's, as the Conference intended neutralization to be realized while the islands still remained under Finnish sovereignty. It was obvious that neutralization of the islands would be meaningless if Finland were allowed to fortify the islands, use them as a military base, or impose on the Alanders military duties. It was not envisaged, however, that neutralization of the islands under a League guarantee would make it necessary to establish any special administration in the archipelago or to station a representative on the spot. League interference would come into play only when it was reported that the neutrality of the islands was being compromised. The only League involvement would be the appointment of a military commission to oversee the destruction of the fortifications constructed by the Russians during the war.

The question therefore posed was that of the position of the League toward any recommendation from the Peace Conference having to do with the neutralization of the islands under a League guarantee. The answer was that the League could not refuse to give the required guarantee. However, Colban continued, it was doubtful whether the Peace Conference's recommendation would of itself be sufficient for a decision to be taken by the League. If the Peace Conference did not feel authorized to settle the question as part of the general peace settlement, it seemed very doubtful whether the League would be entitled to settle the matter by its own authority. It was felt that Finland would be entitled to object to the neutralization of any of its territory by the League of Nations, and the taking of such territory under the League guarantee. As long as Finland did not adhere to the neutralization of the islands under a League guarantee, the plan could not be carried out. It was advisable, therefore, that the Peace Conference, simultaneous with its recommendation to the League, also secure the agreement of the Finnish government. As this was a political question, it was thought a solution could be effected in Paris without great difficulty. If no agreement were secured in Paris and the League received the recommendation from the Peace Conference, it would have to contact the Finnish government in order to obtain its consent. On the other hand, this might not have to be done as the whole Aland question might be presented in a "different shape and indicate other steps to be taken on the part of the League."

The neutralization of the islands was really the lesser problem to be faced. The most delicate problem was the desire of the Alanders, supported by the Swedish government, to be incorporated into the Swedish state. It was unknown whether the Swedes and Finns would follow the Baltic Commission's suggestion and come to an understanding by direct agreement. But if they did and this led to an understanding, the position of the League toward this understanding would depend entirely on the nature of the agreement. The League would have to consider any Finno-Swedish agreement on its merits. Thus any role for the League in the agreement could not be approved unless it was in "accordance with the principles of the League."

If the Finns and Swedes try to come to an understanding by a mutual agreement and fail, they might avail themselves of the further recommendation of the Baltic Commission and seek the good offices of the League in order to come to a settlement. This eventuality, Colban thought, did not make it at present either necessary or advisable for the League Secretariat to take steps. When the question did arise there would be ample time to consider it, and it would be easier to come to some definite conclusion when the League could freely ask the interested powers to give "available information." The position the League should assume and the proposals it should make to the Finns and Swedes in such an event could not be foreseen. It was possible that a mutual agreement between Finland and Sweden, with or without the League's good offices, would provide an international status for the Aland Islands analogous to that of the Free City of Danzig. If this were to be the final solution, it would be useful or perhaps even necessary for the League to appoint a Commissioner to help the local authorities to establish new conditions in the Aland archipelago.

The duties of such a League Commissioner would of course be dependent upon the nature of the agreement arrived at by the Finns and Swedes in which the assistance of the League is requested. The agreement would undoubtedly contain provisions with regard to the form in which the League guarantee was to be executed. Once the political and military questions were settled by the interested powers, the need for a League Commissioner would be limited to establishing a new order of things in the archipelago. His duties would include verification of the demolition of the Russian fortifications, and provision against the reestablishment of fortifications and against military arrangements in the islands. The Commissioner would make sure that the necessary constitutional rules are drawn up by the islands' duly appointed representatives, the analogy cited being that of the League Commissioner in Danzig. He would also represent the League of Nations in all other questions that may arise. Their number and character could not be determined, but it would in large measure depend upon the stipulation in the agreement between Finland and Sweden.

The next problem that Colban tackled was the question of the nationality of any prospective Commissioner. If the agreement did not spell out the nationality of the Commissioner, his nationality would depend upon the political picture at the time of his appointment. Because of the limited financial resources of the islands it was thought that a Commissioner from a neighboring Scandinavian state might involve the least financial strain.

Though Russia was considered by the Baltic Commission to be an important party to the Aland question, Colban did not believe that she would be entitled to object to neutralization of the archipelago under League guarantee while the islands were still under Finnish sovereignty. The Anglo-American proposal that the islands be placed under a joint Finno-Swedish protectorate appeared to be incompatible with any League protection or guarantee. If it were to be placed under a Finno-Swedish protectorate, it was thought the League would not be able to intervene directly but only through the two protecting states. Under Finno-Swedish protection, of course, no Commissioner would be appointed. It was difficult to express an opinion on whether a Finno-Swedish protectorate would solve the political problem of the Aland Islands. It was thought inadvisable, Colban's memorandum concluded, for the agreement to leave open a door for the protecting powers to interfere in the affairs of the island group. If one or both of the powers had special duties to exercise, this should be expressed in the agreement in order to avoid future disputes and difficulties. Where this division of duties was not spelled out, the Finns and Swedes should be entitled to act in concert.[49]

"An interesting survey of a difficult problem," minuted Sir Eric Drummond some days later. He agreed that the Aland question should not be placed before either the League Assembly or the League Council, except at the request of the Paris Peace Conference or a League member. However, sooner or later the question would come before the League. Meanwhile, Sir Eric disclosed, he would "write a discreet letter to Paris" reminding them of the Baltic Commission's report of July 4 and asking if further development had occurred, since it would be useful to the League to be kept up to date in view of its own obligations.[50]

49. Memorandum by E[rik] C[olban] on the Åland Islands, Aug. 26, 1919 (Political 1919: 11/468/468, LNA).

50. Minute by Sir Eric Drummond, Aug. 31, 1919 (Political 1919: 11/468/468, LNA).

As a former member of the British Foreign Office, Drummond was in a unique position to make an overture and ask for information. In his letter on September 1 to Sir George Clerk of the British delegation at the Peace Conference, he asked for information and justified his request by pointing out that there appeared to be a chance of the League being required "either to arrange, or to administer the settlement of the question." [51]

The reply of Professor Carr was to inform Sir Eric that the Baltic Commission's report of July 4 was never considered by the Supreme Council. Instead, after hearing Count Ehrensvärd on the subject they had referred the matter back to the Baltic Commission. Professor Carr enclosed the Commission's second report of August 25 and promised to keep Sir Eric informed of any further developments.[52] In examining the report, Frank P. Walters of the League Secretariat pointed out to the Secretary-General that the major change in the August 25 report was the closing recommendation that the Baltic Commission might be invited, before the Paris Peace Conference adjourned, to suggest a definitive solution to the Aland question. "A considerable difference," Drummond wrote. But he noted that once the League Council met, it would be for the Council, not the Peace Conference or its Baltic Commission "to solve these questions if raised by any interested state." [53] In this Sir Eric was quite right.

Clemenceau's Statement

Though the Aland question was for the moment dormant, King Gustaf, Edén, and Hellner were moved to discuss the matter at length with Sir Esme Howard when he called on them prior to his return to London and reassignment to Madrid. The first one who spoke to him on September 17 was Hellner. At this meeting the Swedish Foreign Minister maintained that the Alander desire for union with Sweden was spontaneous, but he saw no possibility of overcoming the present deadlock with the

51. Letter from Sir Eric Drummond to Sir George Clerk, Sept. 1, 1919 (Political 1919: 11/468/468, LNA).

52. Professor E. H. Carr to Sir Eric Drummond, Sept. 5, 1918 (Political 1919: 11/1072/468, LNA).

53. Memorandum by Frank P. Walters, Sept. 8, 1919, and Sir Eric Drummond's reply, Sept. 8, 1919 (Political 1919: 11/1072/468, LNA).

Finns who refused any plebiscite in the island group. He warned Sir Esme that the feeling in all Swedish political parties was strong for a decision on the question and "if the question were allowed to remain open, serious difficulties might arise between Finland and Sweden." For example, the Alanders might act unilaterally and declare their union with Sweden, which would move the Finns to use force, "and this would result in a violent agitation in Sweden to come to the assistance of the Alanders." His country, Hellner continued, was anxious to avoid a conflict and come to a friendly settlement of the matter, but to do this the Finns had to consent to the Alanders' demand for a plebiscite. He asked what was the Peace Conference's attitude toward Sweden's request that they decide the future of the archipelago. Sir Esme replied that he did not know what decision had been taken by the Supreme Council, and recounted the July decision of the Baltic Commission. He admitted that his own government thought an amicable settlement of the question between Finland and Sweden would be the best solution. Any agreement between them would of course be accepted by the Peace Conference. Howard explained that the Baltic Commission had felt it dangerous, in view of Finland's unsettled position, to impose on that country a solution which might weaken the government and lead to strong popular agitation in Finland. It was the general feeling that no Baltic question would be definitively solved "without [the] consent and approval of Russia, and it was further felt that the question was one which should better be submitted at a later date to the League of Nations than to the Peace Conference," since it could not be considered as a question that the Conference had been called on to deal with. Hellner responded that the government was pleased to accept nonfortification of islands, but he contested the view that the question was one for the League rather than the Peace Conference, arguing that it had arisen out of the war and the fragmentation of Russia. He observed that some time would elapse before the Council could handle the question, and it was dangerous to put off the problem. Howard then inquired if Sweden would compensate Finland for the islands. To this Hellner retorted that the Finns refused all compensation. He proposed that the Finns permit a plebiscite now, to be followed by a second one in two years' time—a proposal repeated many times by the Swedes in the past. Hellner thought that the Finns considered the Alanders' desire for union with Sweden a passing phase and that afterward the Alanders would be content to remain with Finland. This risk the Swedes were willing to assume. In ending his report to London, Sir Esme disclosed that both Wrangel and Swartz, the former Prime Minister, had spoken to him of Sweden's excitement on this question and earnestly hoped the Peace Conference would find a solution.[54]

Several days later, discussion on this question was continued when Sir Esme called on King Gustaf. During this meeting the King used the same language as his Foreign Minister and likewise emphasized the fact that all political parties in Sweden were united on the issue. He hoped that the Peace Conference would find a solution to the question which would quiet the agitation. Gustaf admitted to Howard that Sweden feared that Finland might once again be incorporated into the Russian state and that the Aland Islands, as in the past, would again be a menace to Sweden. The present opportunity seemed best for obtaining a solution which would be favorable to Swedish security. He believed that if the Peace Conference decided the Spitzbergen problem and left the Aland one unsolved, "this would make a very painful impression in Sweden." The King approved of the plebiscite proposal mentioned by Hellner which would require a second vote several years later. This formula, he thought, would "greatly relieve the tension on Sweden."

Sir Esme thought that there were grounds to the Swedish fear as regards the islands, were Russia once again to acquire Finland. Apart from the Alanders' desires, which were "worthy of consideration," there were perhaps distinct advantages in having the island group in Swedish hands, especially in case of a future Russo-German coalition. Sweden's natural fears of such a coalition and Russia's seizure of the area would draw Sweden "into the camp of any powers which were opposing such a coalition."

54. Howard (Stockholm) to Curzon, No. 418, Sept. 17, 1919 (File 591/2/1 in FO/608/180, PRO); Erik Kule Palmstierna, *Orostid; politiska dagboksanteckningar* (Stockholm, Tidens, 1953), 2, 356.

A world divided as in 1914 would probably move Sweden closer to Germany. Nevertheless, Howard could not help feeling that the future danger for Europe lay in a Russo-German coalition, since their rivalry in the Ottoman Empire, which was a major cause of their pre-1914 hostility, would probably disappear as a result of a peace settlement. On the whole the balance was in favor of Sweden having the islands. This appeared to him the best policy to support so far as it could be "done with discretion," and provided this solution could be "arrived at without causing serious disturbance in Finland, and further friction between Finland and Sweden, by means of an agreement accepted by the Finnish Government" on the lines suggested by Hellner.[55]

Two days later on September 24, it was Edén's turn to pressure the departing British minister. Again the same language used by Hellner and the King was repeated, and, like Hellner, Edén warned Howard that there was a real danger of the Alanders' acting unilaterally. Edén admitted that he had tried to dissuade them, since "he feared [it] would lead to serious complications." He was unsure how much he had influenced them. The Alanders appeared to think that to achieve their desires they had to make some move. It was the Swedish Prime Minister's belief that Finland's "future would be precarious" unless good relations existed between the two countries, "in which case Sweden would probably be willing to give Finland all the support she could in case her liberties were once more threatened by Russia." For example, Sweden could give Finland financial support if good relations were established. The Aland question could only be solved, Edén maintained, by the powers insisting on a solution and bringing pressure to bear on the Finns. Edén's attitude was negative. He dismissed Howard's argument that an unpopular decision against Finland on this question "might lead to the upsetting of the present Finnish Government, and possibly even to a second Red Revolution." Any delay, the Swede insisted, was dangerous. He also dismissed Howard's idea of a Finno-Swedish condominium over the islands, since he believed it would increase friction. He rejected border rectification on the grounds that the

55. Howard (Stockholm) to Curzon, No. 425, Sept. 22, 1919 (File 591/2/1 in FO/608/180, PRO); Howard, 2, 409–10.

northern population was loyally Swedish. The Swedes, Howard noted to London, felt that now was the opportune moment for a solution because of Finland's present difficulties, if only the powers "would take the matter in hand and bring pressure to bear on the Finnish Government in this direction." [56]

Sweden's desire that the Allies should bring pressure to bear on the Finns appeared on the road to fruition when, on the following day, September 25, the question was brought out into the open by Clemenceau, who declared in a statement before the French Chamber of Deputies—a statement subsequently described by Lord Curzon as "unauthorized and possibly unpremeditated" [57]—that Sweden, like Norway who had received Spitzbergen and like Denmark who had received Schleswig, would receive the Aland Islands.[58] Lord Curzon's appraisal, however, seems incorrect, for as early as July, Clemenceau appeared to have been—after reading a report by Pichon—in favor of the Swedish position. Later he was prevailed upon by Berthelot, because of Ehrensvärd's pressure, to give a promise to bring up the matter at the Peace Conference.[59] That the French position on this question was shifting had become obvious during the discussions in the Baltic Commission. But it was a change due not so much to Swedish pressure as to Finnish reluctance to "engage in military operations against" [60] St. Petersburg in which Paris had been interested during this period. Thus Clemenceau's statement was a trial balloon and the precursor of a new French position which became more obvious several days later in a note conveyed by the French delegation to the Peace Conference.

The note, with its substantive arguments, was a clear exposition of the Swedish case. The note began by rejecting the position of the Baltic Commission that the Aland question could not be considered by the Peace Conference since it was not a ques-

56. Howard (Stockholm) to Curzon, No. 432, Sept. 25, 1919 (File 591/2/1 in FO/608/180, PRO); Palmstierna, *Orostid, 2,* 359.

57. *DBrFP, 1919–1939,* 1st ser., *11,* 284.

58. France, Chambre des Députés, *Journal Officiel de la République Française,* Chambre des Députés, *Débats parlementaires,* Session ordinaire, septembre à octobre 1919, p. 4572.

59. Palmstierna, *Orostid, 2,* 339, 359.

60. Carr (Paris) to Gregory, Dec. 13, 1919 (File 591/2/1 in FO/608/180, PRO).

tion raised by the war. It pointed out that the Peace Conference had accepted on Norway's request the problem of settlement of the Spitzbergen question, which was even less connected with the war. The Aland question, the French note contended, "can and must fall within the general settlement which the Conference is making." The question concerned "in the highest degree the safety of the Baltic," and the note observed that it was part of the issue raised by Finland's independence and separation from Russia. Moreover, it was the direct concern of a number of states participating in the Peace Conference who were also signatories of the 1856 treaty which placed the Aland archipelago under servitude. Indeed, the situation of the island group had also to be considered because of the war. During the struggle the islands had been in the hands of Russia. It was important to decide their future fate. The present problem, however, existed only between Finland and Sweden because of the recognition of Finnish independence. It rejected the objection of the Baltic Commission that the question could not be discussed because of the absence of a Russian government by pointing out that this had not deterred the Allies from recognizing the legitimacy of Finland's independence. It was willing to admit that, to safeguard Russian military interests, neutralization of the islands under the League should be imposed upon whichever power possessed the island group.

The French believed that the Peace Conference would risk indisposing the Finns by taking up the Aland question. But the French could not see, however, "how Finland could refuse a solution based on the will of the inhabitants and where the security of Finland would be safeguarded by the neutralization clause." They also rejected the argument that no plebiscite could be allowed the Alanders, since they were a small minority of a larger Swedish-speaking community in Finland, on the ground that this was "a question of a well determined territory."

It was expected, of course, that the Finns would demand to be heard by the Peace Conference. Since it would be impossible to refuse them a hearing, the French proposed that the Conference take the initiative and invite them to present their views officially. The note, therefore, proposed that the Supreme Council inform Finland and Sweden officially that the Peace Conference was taking up the Aland question, invite Finland to make known to the Conference "without delay" her views on the matter, which would be examined by the competent commission of the Peace Conference, and, finally, invite this commission to present a project comprising, on the one hand, a plebiscite in the island group and, on the other, clauses for the neutralization of the area as well as any other provisions or guarantees that the commission felt obliged to suggest in consideration of Finnish and Russian points of view. In this arrangement the subsequent adhesion of Russia had to be provided for when a regular Russian government was recognized by the Allies.[61]

Though the Swedish public was unaware of France's decision to support Sweden's case, the arrival of the news in Stockholm of Clemenceau's statement was naturally received with the "greatest delight and satisfaction." It moved Branting to declare rightly that Clemenceau's words were "the first official promise in favor of the right of self-determination of the Aland population." He believed that the step was "in full accord" with what Sweden previously knew of Clemenceau's opinion and of "French opinion in general." [62] That it caused joy among the Alanders goes without saying.[63]

Helsingfors, however, was not amused. Kennard was quickly called to the Foreign Ministry and a protest lodged with him "against [any] settlement of [the] Aland Islands question on [the] lines foreshadowed in Clemenceau's speech." The British chargé's response was that he felt sure that Donner in London and Enckell in Paris would be kept fully informed of any proposals for dealing with the question which were contemplated in Paris. Personally, he had no information that any proposals were being considered except newspaper reports, which were so contradictory that they merited no attention.[64] During this interview

61. Note on the Aland Question by the French delegation [Sept. 29, 1919?] (File 860D.014/63, Record Group 256, NA).

62. Morris (Stockholm) to the Department of State, Sept. 27, 1919 (File 758.6114A1/43, Record Group 59, NA); Palmstierna, *Orostid, 2*, 359.

63. League of Nations, *Official Journal,* spec. suppl. no. 1 (Aug. 1920), p. 51; Sweden, Utrikesdepartementet, *Ålandsfrågan,* pp. 120–22.

64. Kennard (Helsingfors) to Curzon, Oct. 1, 1919 (File 591/2/1 in FO/608/180, PRO).

it was made quite clear to Kennard that "Finland would take up arms against Sweden rather than cede [the] Aland Islands." [65] As was to be expected, in the Finnish press Clemenceau's statement was "bitterly criticized." It was viewed as a tip to Sweden at the expense of Finland, a country that had suffered more than her Scandinavian neighbors. It was an action that would increase pro-German feeling in Finland, breed hatred of the Allies, and change Finnish foreign policy entirely. If this "seed of eternal bitterness" had to be sown, the American Commissioner, Haynes, reported, the least that could be done was to give Eastern Karelia and Petchenga to the Finns as an "anaesthetic before performing such a needlessly cruel and criminal operation." Even better would be a postponement of the decision until the passions and hatreds of the war had cooled. The Swedish government, since it was receiving and not losing territory, could well be patient in the Aland question.[66]

In the French Legation there was also discontent. Jean Fabre, the new French minister in Helsingfors, regretted the excitement that Clemenceau's statement had provoked, agreeing that any settlement of the Aland question should be postponed for some years, and advised Paris accordingly.[67] At about the same time Fabre was cabling the Quai d'Orsay, Carl Enckell called on Kammerer and asked for an explanation of Clemenceau's statement. Kammerer admitted that he was as surprised as Enckell was by Clemenceau's "improvisation," the effects of which the French Prime Minister himself had not been aware of. Kammerer disclosed that Clemenceau's pronouncement had no support in any decision of the Supreme Council. The latter had made the Schleswig decision in order to weaken Germany and the Spitzbergen decision because of Norway's continual pressure to have its sovereignty over these islands recognized. Kammerer said he knew nothing of the Supreme Council's attitude on the Aland question except that according to newspaper reports it would be treated on September 29. These words by Kam-

65. Kennard (Helsingfors) to Curzon, No. 512, Oct. 2, 1919 (File 591/2/1 in FO/608/180, PRO).

66. Haynes (Helsingfors) to the Department of State, Oct. 6, 1919 (File 758.6114A1/44, Record Group 59, NA); *PRFRUS, 1919, Russia,* pp. 721–22.

67. Haynes (Helsingfors) to the Department of State, Oct. 7, 1919 (File 758.6114A1/45, Record Group 59, NA).

merer only confirmed what Enckell had been told earlier that same day by Paul Dutasta, Secretary-General of the Conference. Questioned by Enckell as to whether the Aland question would be treated by the Supreme Council, though Finland as the possessor of the island group had filed no statement, Dutasta assured Enckell that Finland's position with regard to the Swedish demands was well known through the press. He did concede, however, that a statement addressed directly to the Peace Conference by the Finnish government would be desirable. Up to this point Enckell had avoided communicating with the Peace Conference, since he did not know whether the Supreme Council would handle a dispute between two neutral states. The likelihood that it would prompted him to ask Helsingfors for permission to submit a statement to the Peace Conference.[68] The four-page memorandum he handed in on October 2 merely affirmed that Finland had no objection to a neutralization of the archipelago, but the question of a plebiscite—and here was the crucial point—could not be admitted by the Finnish government.[69] In the interim, on September 30—before the French note which envisaged settlement of the Aland question in line with Swedish desires could even be considered—the Supreme Council decided, on a motion by Polk, to adjourn consideration of the Aland question pending an answer from Sweden on the subject of the Russian blockade.[70]

During this period Donner was also busy. On October 1, the day before Enckell's memorandum was delivered to the Peace Conference, he was informed that Helsingfors had approved of Enckell's request to present a memorandum. Donner was instructed immediately to depart for Paris to support Enckell's efforts, especially with the British. He was warned that the Finnish public—after Clemenceau's statement—was in a very excited state and that great hope was being placed on him to "save the situation."

The following day, as Enckell delivered the memorandum to the Peace Conference, Donner called on Lord Hardinge at

68. Carl Enckell, *Politiska minnen* (Helsingfors, Söderström, 1956), 2, 44–45.

69. Enckell's memorandum of October 2, 1919, was later also given to the League of Nations and can be found in League of Nations, *Official Journal,* spec. suppl. no. 1 (Aug. 1920), pp. 4–5.

70. *PRFRUS 1919. PPC, 8,* 464.

the Foreign Office. He had decided to make this call before his departure for Paris in order to prevail on the Foreign Office to oppose what appeared to be Clemenceau's desire for a solution of the question as indicated in his statement. Hardinge had in the past served as British ambassador to Russia so he well knew Finland and its problems. Donner, who had always found him "understanding and sympathetic" to Finland in the Aland question, now learned that Hardinge believed that the archipelago belonged to Finland and should continue in her possession.

When Donner questioned Lord Hardinge on Clemenceau's statement, Hardinge assured him that Clemenceau had no right to speak on behalf of the Allies. He insisted that no agreement had been reached between London and Paris on the Aland question that entitled the French Prime Minister to express himself in the way he had. Lord Hardinge personally thought that Clemenceau's statement had been nothing more than an ill-considered rhetorical device. Donner pressed Lord Hardinge for a firm assurance that the Aland question would not be decided quickly in Paris and without the knowledge of the British Foreign Office. He feared that there were forces at the Peace Conference which desired to present Finland with a fait accompli in the Aland question. In this long discussion it was agreed that Sir Eyre Crowe in Paris would be immediately instructed that, if the Aland question were to come up for discussion at the Supreme Council, he was to declare that he could not vote on the issue without first consulting his government. Consulted by Crowe, the British government would then object to any solution that gave the island group to Sweden.

This binding British promise was quickly cabled to Helsingfors, and, though the Finnish position now appeared secure, Donner continued on to Paris, not only because he had been ordered but also, most importantly, to check and see if the orders that Lord Hardinge said would be sent to Sir Eyre Crowe had really been dispatched. Donner and Enckell, unable to contact Crowe upon Donner's arrival in Paris, consulted Professor Carr, who had replaced Sir Esme Howard as the British representative on the Baltic Commission.

Professor Carr confirmed for them that instructions in this

sense had indeed been received from London, since the British government would under no circumstances agree to a separation of the archipelago from Finland.[71] Professor Carr's minuted opinion was that the French seemed determined to press the Aland question and support the plebiscitary solution, which he personally felt was the "only just one." He believed that the pretext given by the Baltic Commission in postponing a solution for the question "was quite irrelevant," and the Peace Conference could not bargain the island group against Sweden's cooperation in an unofficial blockade of Bolshevik Russia. It would be a good thing if the question could again be brought up for consideration.[72] Not so, replied Sir Eyre Crowe, who thought it should be dealt with by the League of Nations. He felt that the analogy that the Swedes continually drew with the Spitzbergen question was false. In the Spitzbergen question the Peace Conference knew that the agreement concluded would be acceptable to all the interested parties. This was not true in the Aland question, where "no agreement seems possible between Finland and Sweden." [73] In an attempt to explain Clemenceau's statement to Curzon, Crowe expanded his views on the whole question. He expressed the opinion that, keeping in mind the stage now reached in the Peace Conference's labors, it would probably be advantageous if the Aland question "were left to be taken up by the League of Nations," especially as any solution to this question did not promise to be as simple a matter as the Spitzbergen one. Indeed, in the Spitzbergen question, "a general agreement between all the interested parties was from the outset anticipated and soon realised." In the Aland question it is most "improbable that any agreement between Finland and Sweden can be arrived at, so that a settlement would have to be imposed which must give offence to one or the other if not to both parties." [74] Without British support the French plan was doomed to failure, for una-

71. Donner, pp. 119–24.

72. Minute by E[dward] H[allett] Carr, Oct. 10, 1919 (File 591/2/1 in FO/608/180, PRO).

73. Minute by [Sir] E[yre] C[rowe], Oct. 12, 1919 (File 591/2/1 in FO/608/180, PRO).

74. Crowe (Paris) to Curzon, No. 1957, Oct. 15, 1919 (File 591/2/1 in FO/608/180, PRO).

nimity was absolutely necessary in the Supreme Council, which was nothing more than the great powers sitting and deciding in concert the affairs of Europe.

The important move for the Finns, however, was to pressure Clemenceau directly. Chosen for this assignment was General Mannerheim, who, about a week after Enckell's and Donner's activities, took the opportunity on his way through Paris to ask questions and reiterate the Finnish position. Unlike Enckell and Donner, however, Mannerheim asked for and was received by Clemenceau himself. In his long interview with the "Tiger" of France, Mannerheim first thanked Clemenceau for France's previous support and especially for his country's diplomatic recognition. Knowing Clemenceau's anti-Bolshevik attitude, Mannerheim then briefly described the Finnish struggle for independence and its significance for Scandinavia and also the ingratitude that Finland had been shown. Mannerheim argued that if Finland had been entitled to support in her struggle for independence from anybody it surely should have come from Sweden. For six hundred years Finland had been Sweden's shield in the East. Indeed, Finns had shed their lives in Sweden's many wars on foreign soil. Instead, at the very height of the war Sweden "treacherously sought" to acquire the Aland Islands, which had been part of Finland for centuries. Mannerheim pointed out that his country recognized legitimate Swedish claims on the islands, but that Finland could not go beyond the offer—made during his Stockholm visit earlier in the year—for a joint organization of the islands' defenses. Was it right, he asked Clemenceau, to favor Sweden, which had stood neutral during the war, at the cost of Finland? "Could not Finland," he concluded, "seeing that she still fulfilled her historic mission as the bulwark of Western Europe against the East, lay claim to understanding, not merely from Scandinavia, but from the whole civilized world?" This comment with its allusion to Finland's possible role as the northernmost link in an anti-Bolshevik *cordon sanitaire* could not fail to impress Clemenceau. What Mannerheim was saying was that Finland, unlike Sweden, though it could be relied upon as a committed anti-Bolshevik ally, had vital interests that had to be understood and protected by France and the Allies especially in the Aland question. In concluding the discussion, Clemenceau with the greatest aplomb assured Mannerheim "that his statement to the Chamber of Deputies had been misinterpreted —he had never intended to promise Sweden the French Government's support." Clemenceau then informed the General that he would remove the misunderstanding to which his statement might have given rise.[75] Lacking British support for his envisaged settlement of the Aland question by the Peace Conference and under heavy pressure from the Finns who held out the promise of partaking in a *cordon sanitaire* against Bolshevik Russia, Clemenceau and the French had no real choice. They were once again firmly in the Finnish camp.

No Decision by the Conference

Though the French were now committed to the Finns, the same was not true of the Americans. Overtures by the Finnish minister in Washington, as well as reports from Sweden "conveying the impression" that the United States was in favor of Finland and opposed to the Swedish position, moved Secretary of State Robert Lansing, on November 8, to deny these reports. As far as the American government was concerned, the Secretary of State cabled the legations in Stockholm and Helsingfors, "the [Aland] question is still open," and the American government had not "felt called upon to take a position one way or the other." [76]

75. Carl Gustaf Mannerheim, *The Memoirs of Marshal Mannerheim,* trans. Eric Lewenhaupt (New York, E. P. Dutton, 1954), pp. 231–32; Carl Gustaf Mannerheim, *Minnen* (Stockholm, Norstedt & Söners, 1951), *1,* 365–66.

That the Mannerheim–Clemenceau understanding was based on Finland's Russian policy is clear if one can judge from the American reports at that time. Not long after this meeting Mannerheim had reported, it was learned from the American Legation in Stockholm, that Clemenceau had "intimated [that] Finland [could] keep [the] Aland [Islands] in compensation for [the] substantial services rendered [the] entente, that is to say participation in [the] war against Soviet Russia." Wheeler (Stockholm) to the Ammission (Paris), Oct. 31, 1919 (File 860D.00/105, Record Group 256, NA). From Helsingfors Haynes later reported that Mannerheim had been told by Clemenceau that the Aland Islands "would go to Finland if help was rendered [to the anti-Bolshevik General Nikolai N.] Yudenitch." *PRFRUS, 1919, Russia,* p. 735.

76. Lansing to the American Legations in Stockholm and Helsingfors, Nov. 8, 1919 (Attached to File 758.6114A1/59, Record Group 59, NA). See also the memorandum of a conversation with the Finnish Minister in Washington, D.C., by the

Three days after the dispatch of this cable, the Aland question was again posed to the Supreme Council. Clemenceau, however, was as good as his word. Berthelot, the Director of Political Affairs of the Quai d'Orsay, pointed out to his colleagues that the issue had already been submitted to the Council and that it had been decided to adjourn settlement of the question pending knowledge of Sweden's attitude toward the blockade of Russia. Clemenceau added that the Aland question might be dealt with by the Conference of Ambassadors set up by the Peace Conference to execute the peace treaty. He failed to explain, however, how the Aland question was connected to the treaty with Germany and thus within the purview of the Conference of Ambassadors.[77] The net result of the discussion was that no decision was reached by the Supreme Council on the Aland question during this meeting. This necessitated further delay, an action in keeping with earlier French advice to the Finns to defer the question at the Paris Peace Conference as long as possible.

On the same day that this decision was taken by the Supreme Council, Curzon was inquiring from Crowe whether it was true, as reported in the Swedish press, that the Supreme Council had decided that the Aland question should be treated separately from the Russian problem and that it was expected that Finland would submit the Aland question to it for a decision.[78] No such decision had been taken, Crowe quickly replied. In fact, he informed the Foreign Secretary, Curzon (Balfour had by now resigned), that at a recent meeting of the Supreme Council "the opinion was generally expressed that the settlement of the Aland Islands question as of all other formerly Russian territories, must be excluded from the programme." [79] The arrival of this news

Third Assistant Secretary of State, Aug. 9, 1919 (File 758.6114A1/46, Record Group 59, NA).

77. *PRFRUS 1919. PPC, 9,* 101–02. For a description and analysis of the Conference of Ambassadors see Gerhard P. Pink, *The Conference of Ambassadors (1920–1931),* (Geneva Studies, Vol. XII, Nos. 4–5, 1942; Geneva, Geneva Research Centre, 1942); and James Barros, *The Corfu Incident of 1923: Mussolini and the League of Nations* (Princeton, Princeton University Press, 1965), pp. 3–19.

78. Curzon (London) to Crowe, No. 1348, Nov. 11, 1919 (File 591/2/1 in FO/608/180, PRO).

79. Crowe (Paris) to Curzon, No. 1563, Nov. 13, 1919 (File 591/2/1 in FO/608/180, PRO).

at the League Secretariat from the Foreign Office some days later[80] prompted Erik Colban to write to Sir Harold Nicolson of the British delegation at Paris asking him for particulars. Colban was especially interested in the "exact wording of the decision of the Supreme Council, and the report upon which the decision may have been founded." [81] Colban minuted to Secretary-General Drummond that the "exact wording" of the Supreme Council's decision would be of interest to the Secretariat, and it was for this reason that he had ventured to write to Nicolson, provided Drummond had no objection to his note.[82] At first sight this leakage of information to the League Secretariat by the British Foreign Office appears unexplainable. However, since the British government, as we have seen, wished to have the Aland question handled by the League, and inevitably it was the British government that brought the question to the League, the imparting of this information was in no way out of the ordinary, but, on the contrary, directly in line with British policy.

At about the same time that this exchange was going on between the League Secretariat and the Foreign Office, Count Wrangel was busily writing to both Lord Hardinge and Sir Eyre Crowe in an attempt to further consideration of the question. In a confidential memorandum to Lord Hardinge on November 19, Wrangel maintained that, according to information from Paris, the French government appeared willing to take up the question for a decision. Accordingly he had been instructed by Stockholm to convey his government's "sincere desire" that the question be decided by the Peace Conference before its adjournment, expressing the hope that the British government would be good enough to instruct its delegates at Paris along these lines.[83] Hardinge's reply was that the Supreme Council's general opinion was that "settlement of the Aland question must be excluded from the list of questions still requiring treatment

80. Extract of Report No. 15 from the Foreign Office, Nov. 21, 1919 (Political 1919: 11/2137/468, LNA.)

81. E[rik] C[olban] (London) to Sir Harold Nicolson, Nov. 28, 1919 (Political 1919: 11/2137/468, LNA).

82. E[rik] C[olban] to the Secretary-General, Nov. 28, 1919 (Political 1919: 11/2137/468, LNA).

83. Wrangel to Hardinge, Nov. 19, 1919 (File 1259 in FO/371/4068, PRO).

by the present Conference before its adjournment." Because of the heavy labors that still faced the Conference he regretted that the British government did not "feel in a position to press the matter further." However, the suggestion had been made, with which the Foreign Office was "inclined to agree, that the dispute is a matter for consideration by the League of Nations." [84]

A letter to Sir Eyre Crowe in Paris soon followed. He was writing, Wrangel explained, to present Sweden's views if the question were to come before the Peace Conference. He went on to point out the justice of allowing the Alanders to decide their future through a plebiscite, which, if decided in favor of Sweden, would in the long run also be for the good of Finland. His plea was that this question receive Crowe's favorable consideration.[85] Crowe's response was that if the question did come before the Supreme Council for consideration and a decision, he would certainly keep in mind Wrangel's "views and arguments," whose "weight and importance" he fully recognized. He was not, however, very hopeful that the Supreme Council would feel justified in handling this question at the present stage of its deliberations. These were about to end, and there was "naturally some hesitation," as he had already explained, "to embark on so contentious a business, on which agreement between the directly interested parties is not apparently probable." [86]

The day before Crowe's reply was sent, November 25, words somewhat similar to Wrangel's were transmitted by the Swedes to the Peace Conference in an official note. The continual Alander desire for union with Sweden, the note observed, made the Swedish government "insist that a favorable solution concerning the desires of the inhabitants be made by the Peace Conference." It went on to point out that the archipelago's population had consistently demonstrated that its desires were "closely united with the spirit of nationality" and that the Aland question in particular was one which could not be left "unsolved without risking the provocation of serious consequences." [87] No reply by the

84. Hardinge to Wrangel, Dec. 8, 1919 (File 1259 in FO/371/4068, PRO); Palmstierna, *Orostid, 2,* 388.

85. Wrangel to Crowe, Nov. 23, 1919 (File 591/2/1 in FO/608/180, PRO).

86. Crowe to Wrangel, Nov. 26, 1919 (File 591/2/1 in FO/608/180, PRO).

87. Swedish note of Nov. 25, 1919 (File 860D.014/76, Record Group 256, NA).

Peace Conference was sent to this communication, but considering the information and intelligence that the Swedes had received on the Supreme Council's attitude on this question from official and unofficial channels, its refusal to answer the note should certainly have come as no surprise. Further pressure was attempted several days later, and the same type of reaction encountered, when the Alanders called at the Foreign Office and, after repeating their now-well-known desire for union with Sweden, also asked to see the Foreign Secretary, Lord Curzon.[88]

In Stockholm during this same period the Aland question was also a topic of discussion between the new British minister, Sir Colville Barclay, on one side, and Hellner and King Gustaf on the other. Though Barclay was calling on Hellner for the first time, a visit that one would assume to be merely pro forma, the Swedish Foreign Minister immediately launched into a discussion of the Aland question. He recapitulated everything that he had said to Sir Esme Howard and repeated the idea of a double plebiscite, stressing the principle of self-determination. Hellner divulged to Barclay that he had learned that the Aland question would be brought up at the Peace Conference by the Italian representative. Since Clemenceau had declared himself in favor of the island group's going to Sweden and since neither the United States nor Japan had any interests in this question, it seemed to him that Britain "was [the] only obstacle to a favourable decision on the part of the Supreme Council." He expressed the hope that the British government "would not stay in [the] way" of a settlement. Queried by Barclay, Hellner replied that he believed the Finnish government would be capable of handling any agitation without danger to the government and public order if the Paris Peace Conference were to decide on a plebiscite in the island group. On the other hand, he felt a "dangerous situation would probably arise in Finland if [the] Islands were handed now to Sweden, but this would be obviated by his proposal of two plebiscites which would give time for [the] execution of reforms prepared by [the] Finnish Government." If these reforms

88. Memorandum of conversation with the Alander delegation, Nov. 27, 1919 (File 1257 in FO/371/4068, PRO).

were satisfactory to the Alanders they would be satisfactory to the Swedish government. Hellner concluded the interview with the observation that while feelings were divided in Finland over the question they were unanimous in Sweden.[89] On the following morning, November 25, discussion of this question continued in an interview Barclay had with King Gustaf, who emphasized the importance of a decision being taken on the question before the Peace Conference adjourned. If the Peace Conference remained silent on the issue, there was a danger that the Alanders might proclaim their annexation to Sweden. This would of course strain Sweden's relations with Finland, and it was in everyone's interests to avoid this. King Gustaf then repeated his fear of Finland's falling once again into Russian hands and the island group's again becoming a menace to Sweden. In conclusion, like Hellner, he maintained that Great Britain was the only power who objected to a decision by the Supreme Council and asked London to "reconsider their point of view in a broad spirit for the future." [90] Barclay observed to the Foreign Office that the Aland question was "arousing considerable interest in Sweden" and, if the Peace Conference declared the question beyond its competence, there was the danger that the Alanders would proclaim "their annexation to Sweden." [91] In Helsingfors, Barclay's experience was duplicated when Lord Acton, the new British minister, made his first call on Holsti. Finland, the Finnish Foreign Minister maintained, clung to the island group for reason of "sentiment and strategy" and believed that the question could be settled by giving the Alanders "a large measure of autonomy." Holsti admitted that he was pleased after his conversations in London, where Finnish feelings on the subject were understood. To undercut the Swedish argument about the Alanders' right to self-determination, Holsti noted that it had been "flagrantly violated" in the case of the Austrians in the southern Tyrol,

89. Barclay (Stockholm) to Curzon, No. 1451, Nov. 24, 1919 (File 1259 in FO/371/4068, PRO).

90. Barclay (Stockholm) to Curzon, No. 1453, Nov. 24, 1919 (File 1259 in FO/371/4068, PRO).

91. Extract of Report No. 16 from the Foreign Office, Nov. 28, 1919 (Political 1919: 11/2224/468, LNA).

which had been ceded to Italy. His own sympathy, Acton informed the Foreign Office, was "with the political sentiments" expressed in this interview.[92]

The comment by Hellner, however, that the Italians at the Peace Conference would shortly raise the Aland question before the Supreme Council caused Lord Curzon to contact the British delegation at Paris. He presumed that this remark by Hellner was not to be taken seriously, and he proposed to inform Sir Colville Barclay and Lord Acton that the British government's view was "that the only course for the Alanders now is for them to lodge a claim before the League of Nations." [93] Sir Eyre Crowe's response was negative, as Lord Curzon had assumed. Crowe had no information to lead him to suppose that the Italian or any other delegation now proposed to bring the question before the Supreme Council. In fact, at all recent conversations in the Supreme Council regarding its work, it had "been explicitly or tacitly assumed by everyone that the Aland question will not be dealt with by the present Conference." [94] On December 12, the day this message was dispatched to London, Wrangel called at the Foreign Office and talked with Cecil Harmsworth, Curzon's Parliamentary Under-Secretary of State for Foreign Affairs. Wrangel "deprecated the probable reference" of the question to the League of Nations and complained of the delay that would occur, since he saw "little prospect . . . of the League coming into effective existence for a long time." The Alanders were uncertain as to their future, and dissension between Finland and Sweden would grow and the situation worsen unless the matter were quickly solved. Harmsworth assured Wrangel that he also looked upon the whole situation with "disquietude" and would make Wrangel's views known to the Foreign Secretary.[95]

In an obvious move to feel out the situation at the new world

92. Acton (Helsingfors) to Curzon, No. 698, Nov. 28, 1919 (File 1259 in FO/371/4068, PRO).

93. Curzon (London) to the British delegation at Paris, No. 1460, Dec. 11, 1919 (File 591/2/1 in FO/608/180, PRO).

94. C[rowe] (Paris) to Curzon, No. 1681, Dec. 12, 1919 (File 1259 in FO/371/4068, PRO).

95. Memorandum of conversation by Cecil Harmsworth, Dec. 12, 1919 (File 1259 in FO/371/4068, PRO).

organization, since the League now loomed on the horizon as the next court of appeal, the Alanders in the late afternoon of this same day approached its Secretary-General, Sir Eric Drummond. From the nature of the discussion it was obvious that they were aware that the Supreme Council's pending decision would be unfavorable and a blow to their desire for union with Sweden. It was explained to Sir Eric that they had "heard a rumour" that the Aland question would be transferred by the Peace Conference to the League of Nations. This decision they would receive "with regret," because it would mean a delay prejudicial to their wish to separate from Finland and unite with Sweden, which was supported by the large majority of the Alanders. They then brought to the Secretary-General's attention the plebiscite held on the islands in June, in which 96 per cent of the population voted in favor of union with Sweden, and expressed a willingness to hold another plebiscite should this prove necessary. Queried by Drummond as to whether they had considered an alternative policy such as the constitution of the island group as a free city like Danzig—here Drummond was reflecting, as we have seen, Secretariat thoughts on the matter—the Alander delegates answered that they had never considered such a possibility and were in no position to state "whether it would satisfy the aspiration of their people." Indeed, not even autonomy within the Finnish state would satisfy them, and they questioned whether the Aland Islands were strong enough to stand alone. They claimed the right of national self-determination, they explained to Drummond, not to achieve independence, but to achieve union with Sweden. Concluding the interview, they asked the Secretary-General whether, should the Aland question be transferred to the League Council, this would be for a decision or whether the League Council would require a restatement by the Alanders of their claim. If the League did have this duty, how long would be the delay?

In answer to the first question, Sir Eric said he imagined that the League Council in "considering any question would begin *de novo*." Therefore, he thought the Alanders should send him their statements, which he would transmit to the League Council. At the same time, they should ask to be heard personally by the

League Council, a request which Drummond was convinced the League Council would accede to. As to their second question, Sir Eric pointed out that it was difficult to say when the Supreme Council would take up the Aland question, either to settle it or to transfer it to the League. However, if it were transferred to the League Council he thought under normal conditions it would come up for discussion within a month after its submission.[96]

Though Drummond thought it would be difficult to predict when the Supreme Council would act, in actual fact the following day, December 13, the news that the Peace Conference would not handle the question was conveyed to Enckell in Paris by the Secretariat of the Supreme Council.[97] Some five days later King Gustaf again broached the issue with Barclay in Stockholm.[98] Hellner likewise had pressed him on the matter on December 8.[99]

In a last desperate attempt to ward off the blow that was coming, the Swedes almost instinctively turned to Washington, the citadel of idealism and the guardian of the concept of self-determination. Calling at the office of the Assistant Secretary of State, the Swedish minister wished to know if the United States had any objections to permitting submission of the Aland question either to the Supreme Council or to the Conference of Ambassadors. According to Ekengren, the Foreign Office in London "seemed to hesitate and gave the impression that they preferred to postpone action in the matter." His own thought was that possibly the United States "would be willing to approach" the British on the subject. The reply to this was that at this point, because of the Senate's rejection of the Versailles Treaty the previous month, the American ambassador in Paris, Hugh C.

96. Memorandum of conversation with the Aland delegates by E[ric] D[rummond], Dec. 12, 1919 (Political 1919: 11/2440/468, LNA). Unfortunately for the Alanders, not all their delegations were impressive. For an amusing account of the antics of an Alander delegation at the Foreign Office in London, see John D. Gregory, *On the Edge of Diplomacy; Rambles and Reflections, 1902–1928* (London, Hutchinson, 1929), pp. 191–92.

97. Enckell, 2, 47.

98. Barclay (Stockholm) to Curzon, No. 616, Dec. 18, 1919 (File 1259 in FO/371/4068, PRO).

99. Barclay (Stockholm) to Curzon, No. 598, Dec. 8, 1919 (File 1259 in FO/371/4068, PRO).

Wallace, had instructions merely to act as an observer. Thus, the United States could not discuss the Aland question in Paris, nor was it thought proper to make the inquiry suggested by Ekengren of the British. It was doubted whether the American government would ever take a stand on the Aland question one way or another. On the contrary, this appeared to be a Finno-Swedish problem, and the "United States was far from the scene." It was suggested to Ekengren that he make clear to the Swedish government that, because of the Senate's attitude toward the Versailles Treaty, it was impossible for the United States "to continue to carry on negotiations in Paris under the Treaty." [100] Stockholm's move to solicit Washington's support had been stymied.

In spite of the communications to both Wrangel and Enckell, the Aland question was again a topic of discussion at the Supreme Council on New Year's Eve. It was the last time that they would discuss the question, and, interestingly enough, it was raised by the Italian delegate, Giacomo de Martino. He thought that, because of the Alanders' heavy vote in favor of union with Sweden, the question presented no problems and should be settled before the Peace Conference broke up. This was opposed by Sir Eyre Crowe, who "was against raising this question *in extremis*." The Under-Secretary of the Foreign Office thought it was more a question for the League of Nations. In this he was supported by the French delegate, René Doynel de Saint-Quentin. Sir Eyre thought that any attempted settlement of the question by the Supreme Council meant dragging on the work of the Council indefinitely. He believed that a Commission would have to be formed, which, of course, would not arrive at any consensus, which in turn would force the Supreme Council to arbitrate. All this would take time. De Martino replied that the question appeared to him very clear and the formation of a Commission unnecessary. Crowe's rejoinder was that the fate of the archipelago interested Finland and was connected with the Russian question. "It was rather a delicate matter," he concluded. Added support for Crowe also came from Jules Cambon of the French delega-

100. Memorandum from the Office of the Assistant Secretary of State, Department of State, Dec. 20, 1919 (File 758.6114A1/54, Record Group 59, NA).

tion, who observed that there would be time enough to add the Aland question to the agenda when the necessity arose. Faced by a solid Anglo-French front on this question, De Martino decided not to press the matter and on this note the meeting adjourned.[101] Several days later the League Secretariat was informed by the Foreign Office that the British government wished the Aland question to be referred to the League of Nations not by Finland and Sweden but by the Alanders themselves.[102]

Thus, the Supreme Council in its autumn deliberations had ignored the Baltic Commission's second report of August 25—drafted under Swedish pressure—and its suggestion that a definitive solution of the Aland question be made by the Peace Conference. Instead, it had reverted to the Commission's initial draft report of July 4, which suggested that, if a change in the status of the island group were contemplated, it "be left to [a] decision of the League of Nations." The matter was "delicate," as Sir Eyre Crowe gently put it. Considering the intransigent position of the parties concerned, not to mention the question's relation to the Russian problem, this was the safest road to take.

Any solution offering less than what the parties were demanding would have antagonized either Finland or Sweden, states basically friendly to England and France. It goes without saying that the Russian émigré group headed by Sazonov also would have been antagonized. This was a situation neither England nor France could afford. The only way the Peace Conference could have handled the problem in a satisfactory manner was if Lord Hardinge's proposal had been accepted, conditioning the recognition of Finland on the understanding that she would accept the decisions of the Peace Conference regarding her frontiers. Lansing's objection, supported to some extent by the French, refused to admit that recognition was essentially a political act and that attaching conditions to it was in no way unjustified. Conditions to recognition had been attached many times in the past, as they were to be attached many times in the future, by the United States included. Even if the Finns had agreed to this

101. *PRFRUS 1919. PPC, 9,* 733.

102. Extract of Report 21 from the Foreign Office, Jan. 2, 1920 (Political 1920: 11/2660/468, LNA).

and attempts had been made at Paris to handle the question, there was no assurance that England and France would have held similar views on a solution. As it was, the British and French did diverge for a while in their approach to the question. Because of her interests in Scandinavia, England, after initially supporting the Swedish position in the Baltic Commission, decided to support the Finns—since unanimity in the Baltic Commission was shown to be impossible—in the sense that the Commission did not wish to have the question handled by the Peace Conference. Indeed, any decision by the Peace Conference giving the islands to the Swedes, even a unanimous one, would have greatly jeopardized the British position in Finland by drawing Britain into a situation where Finland would have had to be coerced into surrendering the archipelago to Sweden. France, interested in using Finland in the Baltic first against Germany and especially against Bolshevik Russia, finally decided to support the Finnish position despite Clemenceau's September decision, under pressure, to support the Swedish position. A *cordon sanitaire* starting with a committed Finland further to the East was better than one starting with an uncommitted and historically neutral Sweden further to the West. Only France's support of Finland in the Aland question made the former a certainty.

Since there was no overriding necessity for an immediate settlement of the question, referring the problem to the League of Nations, though a Fabian tactic, served a number of purposes. It avoided for the moment a definitive solution by the great powers and gave time to calm passions and cool tempers. By doing so, it helped England and France to maintain their positions in both countries, allowing them to act collectively as mediators and conciliators in an attempt to solve the problem in a manner satisfactory to all. Indeed, any solution arrived at through the League would be a solution associated with that organization and not with the great powers. The League therefore would serve as a useful if not indispensable facade behind which, and through which, Britain and France could exert their pressures and offer solutions to settle or compromise the Aland question.

CHAPTER 6

The League of Nations

King Gustaf's Visits to London and Paris

The action of the Supreme Council in avoiding a decision on the Aland question moved the Finnish government in February of 1920 to grant the Alanders, in an obvious attempt to undercut the separatist agitation, a measure of autonomy.[1] In writing the legislation the Finns had consulted the constitutions of the Channel Isles and the Isle of Man.[2] This concession of autonomy, however, was rejected by the Alanders[3]—a move in keeping with their previously expressed attitude in the autumn of 1919 that autonomy could be no substitute for union with Sweden.[4] If the Finns thought that this concession would improve their position in the eyes of world opinion they were wrong, for the Foreign Office, the American ambassador in London subsequently reported, believed that the grant of autonomy was "too limited in extent." [5]

In Sweden the fall of the Liberal–Socialist coalition government in early March of 1920, which had been in power since 1917, and Edén's inability to form a new government, forced King Gustaf to turn to Branting. If the Finns thought that the new government in Stockholm might be eager to settle the issue according to Finnish desires they were soon proven wrong, for the change of government in no way affected the resolve of the

1. League of Nations, *Official Journal,* spec. suppl. no. 1 (Aug. 1920), pp. 6–11.

2. Extract of Report 27 from the Foreign Office, Feb. 13, 1920 (Political 1920: 11/3066/468, LNA).

3. League of Nations, *Official Journal,* spec. suppl. no. 1 (Aug. 1920), pp. 54–57; Sweden, Utrikesdepartementet, *Ålandsfrågan inför Nationeras Förbund* (Stockholm, Norstedt & Söner, 1920), pp. 132–40.

4. League of Nations, *Official Journal,* spec. suppl. no. 1 (Aug. 1920), pp. 51–54; Sweden, Utrikesdepartementet, *Ålandsfrågan,* pp. 122–30.

5. Davis (London) to the Department of State, June 19, 1920 (File 758.6114A1/71, Record Group 59, NA).

Swedish government to press the Aland question. In fact, the all-new Social Democratic government led by Branting—held in high esteem in London and Paris—with Palmstierna, a person prone to push the Aland question, now Foreign Minister, presaged a more active Swedish policy in this matter. No sooner was Palmstierna in office than he made it quite clear that the new government would continue their predecessors' endeavors, with special prominence being given to the Aland question.[6]

The first move in this direction was the announced trip of King Gustaf to England and France. Palmstierna was personally pessimistic about the trip and feared that the King would "not find out very much in London." This was especially true since Sir Eric Drummond, the Secretary-General of the League, as well as the British minister in Stockholm, Barclay, had hinted that an independent Aland was a "possibility worth thinking of." Was this the English attitude? Palmstierna asked himself. If it was, then it was worse than a negative answer to Sweden's desires. For a free and independent Aland was more likely to become dependent on foreign powers and hence a greater menace to Sweden than the Aland Islands in Finnish hands.

Announcement of Gustaf's unofficial visit to England prompted Barclay to call on Palmstierna and ask what the King would do in London. Palmstierna directed the conversation to the Aland question and told Barclay that the only thing the Swedish government did not know for certain was the attitude of the British government on the matter. He claimed that Sweden's position had been approved by all the other powers and maintained that the London government had thwarted his approaches on the matter. This policy, the Foreign Minister feared, would contribute to an increasing anti-British opinion in Sweden. His feeling was that the British government was "opposed to the aspirations" of the Alanders. Barclay repeatedly denied this and contended that his government "had not given any expression of opinion as to [the] merits of the case," but on the contrary they had restricted themselves to the opinion that the Alanders, Finns, and Swedes should bring the matter to the League of Nations.

6. Erik Kule Palmstierna, *Dagjämning, 1920–1921; politiska dagboksanteckningar* (Stockholm, Tidens, 1954), p. 62.

Regardless of Barclay's comments, the attitude of the British government was compared—unfavorably of course—to Clemenceau's statement of September 25 of the previous year. Palmstierna was willing to admit that Scandinavians were a calm people, but events could develop very quickly—and there was some fear for this because of the present situation—and a violent mood break out. This interview caused Barclay to warn Curzon that King Gustaf would probably bring up the Aland question during his London and Paris visits. As for Palmstierna, his instructions to the King were that though Sweden maintained its position on the Aland question, if worse came to worst, it would agree to place the question before the League of Nations.[7]

This news led Sir Eyre Crowe on April 13, the same day King Gustaf was to stay at Windsor Castle, to contact Lord Stamfordham, King George V's private secretary, conveying to him Barclay's warning. Sir Eyre pointed out that it was the attitude of the government that the question should be settled by direct negotiations between the two parties or by appealing it to the League of Nations. He accentuated, in an obvious attempt to undercut any remarks that King Gustaf might make to King George, the opinion that the government had "shown no sort of hostility to the claims of the [Aland] Islanders." [8] In two conversations with King Gustaf on this same evening King George, "expressing his personal opinion"—a major qualification for a monarch in a constitutional democracy—made it clear that "he would be very glad if this difficult question could be settled by a plebiscite of the inhabitants of the islands." [9] This admission prompted Gustaf to cable Palmstierna that "he was satisfied" with his conversations with the British monarch concerning the Aland question.[10]

If Gustaf had been aware of the comments made to Holsti that same day at the Foreign Office, he would have been less contented. There it was explained to the Finnish Foreign Minister, who claimed that Gustaf had come to England for propa-

7. Barclay (Stockholm) to Curzon, No. 106, April 1920 (File 1259 in FO/371/4068, PRO); Palmstierna, *Dagjämning*, pp. 68–70.

8. Crowe to Stamfordham, April 13, 1920 (File 1259 in FO/371/4068, PRO).

9. *DBrFP, 1919–1939*, 1st ser., *II*, 283n.

10. Palmstierna, *Dagjämning*, p. 70.

ganda purposes, by John D. Gregory, Head of the Northern Department of the Foreign Office, that there was not the slightest chance that the Aland question would be dealt with by the Supreme Council and certainly not at the San Remo Conference which would shortly convene.[11] Certainly Gustaf's subsequent conversation with Lord Curzon several days later was less than pleasing. In this luncheon conversation, at which Count Wrangel was also present, Lord Curzon attempted to explain to the Swedish king the position of the British government on this complicated question. In reporting this interview to Barclay in Stockholm, Curzon noted that Gustaf seemed to be "under the impression" that the British government was opposed to a plebiscite on the island group, and that this hostile attitude during the Paris Peace Conference had thwarted settlement of the question according to Sweden's interests, since the other great powers had been in favor of the plebiscite. The King recapitulated for Lord Curzon the arguments about the Aland question, with which Curzon was of course familiar. But Gustaf appeared to be more concerned in discussing the attitude of the great powers at the present juncture than in discussing the question on its merits, as had been done so often in the past. He was especially interested in knowing why the case had been shelved by the Peace Conference. Why could it not be taken up at the San Remo Conference or elsewhere? Finally, he asked what would be the line the British government would adopt. Gustaf pleaded with Lord Curzon for the plebiscitary solution and warned that "if it were not adopted, a state of affairs might arise in which the islanders would declare their own incorporation with Sweden, thus presenting the latter with a *fait accompli* which might create a very difficult and embarrassing situation."

Lord Curzon rejected the contention that Great Britain "had at any time taken up an isolated position" on the Aland question, "still less a position which was hostile to Sweden." On the contrary, he rightly pointed out that when the question of Finland's independence had arisen in the deliberations of the Supreme Council, it was the British delegate who had proposed that Finland's recognition should be made dependent upon her ac-

11. *DBrFP, 1919–1939,* 1st ser., *11,* 298.

ceptance of the Peace Conference's decision on all questions pertaining to her frontiers. Curzon thought that, if this British proposal had been accepted, it would have allowed the Peace Conference to settle the Aland question. This British view, however, was not accepted by her allies. Instead, recognition of Finland had been made with no conditions attached. Thus, it was very difficult for the Allies, having recognized Finland's sovereignty—of which the Aland Islands were a part—to intervene subsequently and decree a separation of the island group from Finland. Curzon thought that the Allies had to a certain extent compromised themselves by this action. There was also another difficulty. Though the Aland question had been placed before the Peace Conference, had been discussed a number of times by the Supreme Council, and had been reported upon by the Baltic Commission, there had been during the past six months —leaving aside Clemenceau's statement in the French Chamber of Deputies—what seemed to Curzon "to be a tacit agreement that the case was one which could not really be decided by the Peace Conference at all." It could not be contended that the question arose out of the war or was connected with the treaties ending the war. If all this were so, King Gustaf queried, how did the Conference handle the question of Spitzbergen? Lord Curzon's answer was that the Supreme Council did not pronounce on the issue until the parties directly concerned had come to an agreement which the Supreme Council merely ratified. If similar conditions had existed in the Aland question, he felt sure the Peace Conference would not have hesitated in confirming it. Since there was absolutely no understanding between Sweden and Finland on the question, Curzon "thought that the Conference had realized that the case was not one in which they could any longer intervene with profit, and that some other solution must be found." In the Foreign Secretary's mind, there was only one solution that presented itself: that the Aland question be referred for settlement by the League of Nations.

Continuing, Lord Curzon pointed out to King Gustaf that the League's position was far different from what it had been six months before. The League now was in actual operation. The League Council, for example, had already met a number of times and had begun to exercise its functions and powers. In fact, several days before in Paris, it had been dealing with the Armenian problem. Thus, Curzon believed that reference to the League Council "now was no longer an abstract proposition or a theoretical suggestion, but an appeal to the one body, other than the Peace Conference, which was at all qualified to find a solution for international problems, and which by its constitutions and its powers might be expected to deal with a case such as this." He thought that the Supreme Council was unlikely to discuss the matter, and, if the Swedish case was as strong as King Gustaf had presented it—"and speaking personally and unofficially," Curzon admitted he had "always had a great deal of sympathy with it"—why hesitate in placing it before the League Council? The Finns, like the Swedes, would present their case, and the League Council, whether it dealt with the matter itself, gave it to a Commission of Inquiry, or transferred the question to the League Assembly, could advance a solution of the problem. In this way, public opinion would focus on the question and the desirability of a settlement, and the kind of development King Gustaf feared might be avoided. After these words Lord Curzon "earnestly counselled the King seriously to consider this suggestion and to examine with his Government whether, in the circumstances of the case, it was not the right step for them to take."

Since King Gustaf's instructions from Palmstierna were somewhat in line with Curzon's suggestion, Gustaf did not reject the Foreign Secretary's proposal outright. Indeed, Gustaf promised to examine it carefully. He had, however, two objections to this proposal. The first was that Sweden could not itself withdraw the Aland question after having unilaterally referred it to the Peace Conference. As far as the Swedish government was concerned, the Aland question was still being considered by the Supreme Council, and they were awaiting its decision. Then the King revealed that the Swedish government had received "private assurances" which made them "believe that France, Italy and Japan were in their favour and were prepared to agree to the plebiscitary solution." If this were the case, and assuming it was not England that stood in the way of such a solution, what obstacle was there to a decision by the Paris Peace Conference?

The King's second objection was that, assuming the Aland question was referred to the Council of the League of Nations, since any decision by that body according to the League Covenant had to be unanimous, there was nothing preventing an uninterested member of the Council from casting a veto.

In his reply to the first argument Lord Curzon admitted that this was his first intimation that the other great powers favored the Swedish position in the Aland question and had pronounced themselves in favor of the Swedish view. His own impression was that they had come to no definite decision on the matter. The Baltic Commission, according to Curzon, had recommended that the decision on the Aland question "had better be left to the League of Nations." He avoided mentioning, however, that the second report had talked of the Peace Conference itself. The Foreign Secretary thought there was nothing to prevent a great power from opening the question at any future meeting of the Peace Conference. But he did not think that at the San Remo Conference there would be much time for discussion of the Aland question. Curzon instead "ventured to hazard a prophecy that if it was so raised, the Supreme Council would be much more likely to endorse the suggestion of a reference to the League of Nations than they would be to pronounce definitely upon an issue that was so fiercely disputed."

King Gustaf asked Lord Curzon whether, were the Supreme Council to refer the question to the League of Nations, it would express its opinion to the League Council that a settlement of the question by a plebiscite "was the right way of dealing with the matter." Curzon's reply was that any opinion of this type by the Supreme Council to the League Council would "prejudge the matter" and that in referring the Aland question to the League Council "they would be much more likely to leave the latter an absolutely free hand."

As to the second argument, Curzon replied that the League Council was in a way on trial, and its decisions had to take note of world public opinion. Thus, it was hardly likely that any state, out of contumacy or for other reasons, would obstruct a decision to which the rest of the Council had concurred. These, however, were the conditions of reference to the League Council, and it appeared to argue, Lord Curzon observed, a certain lack of confidence in his own case if King Gustaf "refrained from recommending a reference solely on the ground that it might not be possible to secure a unanimous verdict."

The King then turned the conversation to the inconsistency of the Finnish government in claiming Eastern Karelia by invoking the principle of self-determination but denying the application of that same principle in the Aland Islands. Curzon reminded the King that the Karelian claim had not been admitted by the powers, for if this part of the Czarist empire were to be absorbed by Finland, it would be a source of trouble in the future between Finland and a resuscitated Russia.

Concluding the discussion, Lord Curzon assured the Swedish monarch that his government and country had only the friendliest feelings for Sweden and would take any opportunity to show this friendship. If the final solution were to transfer the islands to Sweden—as the great majority of the Alanders desired—no country would more warmly welcome this solution than the British government. But such a result could not, in Curzon's judgment, be arrived at by the procedure that King Gustaf seemed to have in mind, and he again earnestly pressed him to consider the more practicable and more expedient procedure that he had proposed: submission of the Aland question to the League of Nations.[12]

Lord Curzon's conversation with King Gustaf had made it quite clear to the Swedes, if it had ever been unclear in the past, that for the British government at least, no solution could ever be expected through the Supreme Council, nor could Sweden ever really expect assistance from any of the other great powers. Though Palmstierna was perhaps willing to go to the League—as we have seen—for an adjudication of the problem, to have appealed to it directly would have been extremely difficult for the new government. To do so would have been an admission that the great powers, or, to put it another way, the Supreme Council of the Paris Peace Conference, had refused to come to a decision on a question which on the surface at least was a clear case of national self-determination, a clarion call of the Peace

12. Ibid., pp. 283–87.

Conference itself. Such an action would have been an acknowledgment that Sweden had been checked at Paris and perhaps even an admission that in this question Sweden had few supporters. In sum, it would have been a serious blow to the prestige of Sweden and especially to the new government in power. In the end, the question would go to the League, but it would be Great Britain, not Sweden, whose appeal would take it there.

News of King Gustaf's intended visits to England and France naturally worried the Finnish government. To offset this move the Prime Minister, Erich, without consulting Foreign Minister Holsti, instructed the Finnish Legations in London, Paris, Rome, and Washington to present a note to the host government that Finland would very much appreciate its assurances and those of other states represented on the Supreme Council that extensive autonomy for the Aland Islands while the islands remained part of Finland would be the best way to solve the Aland question, and that neither the demands of the Swedish government nor those of the Alanders should cause consideration of the issue by the Supreme Council. Though Enckell delivered the note to the Quai d'Orsay, he protested to Helsingfors that it departed from Finland's prior policy of refusing any international consideration of the islands' sovereignty. When the note was delivered, Albert Geouffre de La Pradelle, Finland's legal advisor—and, interestingly enough, a legal expert for the French Foreign Ministry—became upset. Why had this been done? he asked Enckell. "Do you need a declaration by the powers that Finland has absolute sovereignty over Aland?" Enckell's reply that his government wished a declaration of disinterestedness caused De La Pradelle to observe that "according to the note an action is demanded, and it is against your interests to ask the Peace Conference to treat the question."

De La Pradelle's fears, however, were unfounded, for the French, like the British, had no intention of handling the issue through the Supreme Council. On April 16, on the very day of King Gustaf's arrival in Paris, an article, thought to have been inspired by the French Foreign Ministry, appeared in *L'Éclair* stating that France had no reason to favor Sweden at Finland's expense on the Aland question. Indicative that the French position would not be different from that of the British was a report of the Finnish press attaché that the Quai d'Orsay had issued orders to the press not to discuss the Aland question during King Gustaf's stay in Paris.[13] The arrival of the Swedish monarch, as one would have expected after the discussion he had had with Lord Curzon and the latter's explanation of the policy of the great powers on the Aland question, appears in no way to have influenced the French.[14] In fact, several weeks later on May 8, Palmstierna received no satisfying answer from the French minister, Delavaud, when he asked if Sweden could rely on France if the Alanders proclaimed their union with Sweden and presented the great powers with a fait accompli, an action that Palmstierna was willing to admit the Swedish government had been thinking about.[15]

Deteriorating Finno-Swedish Relations

The knowledge in Stockholm that no decision would be made by the great powers and that their desire was that the question should be handled by the League, preferably by the Swedes taking it there themselves, added to Swedish frustration and to the deterioration of Finno-Swedish relations. On May 13, a month after King Gustaf's London visit, Barclay in Stockholm reported to Lord Curzon the increasing Finno-Swedish tension. According to Barclay, Palmstierna had had a long conversation with Holsti, who was passing through Stockholm. Branting had also been present. Palmstierna first had assured Holsti that Sweden had only the friendliest feeling for Finland, and that his government supported the Finnish claims to Petchenga and Eastern Karelia. On the matter of the Aland Islands, however, the views of the Swedish government were different. The Alanders had openly stated they would not accept the autonomy that had recently been granted to them by the Finnish Diet. On the contrary, they were continuously appealing for union with Sweden, and these appeals had influenced the Swedish public. Because of this Palm-

13. Carl Enckell, *Politiska minnen* (Helsingfors, Söderström, 1956), 2, 55–58.

14. *Le Matin,* April 17, 1920, p. 1; *The Times* (London), April 17, 1920, p. 13; April 19, 1920, p. 11.

15. Palmstierna, *Dagjämning,* p. 75.

stierna suggested to Holsti that the best solution for this difficult problem would be for the Swedish and Finnish governments "to come to a friendly understanding on the matter." Palmstierna proposed to the Finnish Foreign Minister that, "as the principle of self-determination had been generally accepted by all the Powers" and applied in Schleswig and elsewhere, the two governments should apply the principle to the Aland Islands. The only thing he asked was "for the recognition of the principle." The details about how and when the plebiscite would take place could be settled later. Holsti categorically refused to accept Palmstierna's proposal. His rejection caused Palmstierna to draw Holsti's attention to the fact that this was the third time on which a Swedish government had made proposals to the Finnish government for a friendly understanding and that the latter on each occasion had flatly refused even to discuss the Aland question.

Palmstierna warned Barclay that the Aland question was now "entering a critical phase." The Alanders were determined to reject the autonomy granted to them by the Finnish Diet. The Swedish Foreign Minister felt that unless the Supreme Council took up the Aland question very shortly, the Alanders would probably bring matters to a head by declaring their union with Sweden. What then would be the attitude of the Finnish government, Palmstierna asked rhetorically. Military measures by the Finns against the Alanders would produce "a serious crisis," for Swedish public opinion was unanimous on the Aland question and "would not tolerate Finnish reprisals in Aland."

Barclay's recommendation was that, since Sweden and the Alanders were "on such good terms," the Swedish government not incite them but rather counsel moderation. Palmstierna replied that they would counsel moderation, but curbing national feeling once it was aroused was no easy task. "He insisted that the outlook was grave." Palmstierna admitted to Barclay that he had spoken to Delavaud in the same sense.

The next person to converse with Barclay on the Aland question was King Gustaf. He pointed out to the British minister that on his trip to London the previous month he had spoken to Lord Curzon of the "dangerous situation" that would come about if the Alanders were to act unilaterally and present the Supreme Council with a fait accompli. The King begged Barclay to warn Curzon that "such a situation appeared not improbable at a no[t] very distant date." The last person to talk with Barclay about the situation was Branting, who told how very concerned he was as to the "intractability of the Finnish Government, and as to the course events were taking."

Barclay was inclined to think that the Swedish government was "not over-exaggerating the likelihood of a crisis merely to ensure the question being dealt with by the Supreme Council." Rather, Barclay observed to Lord Curzon, the Swedes were sincerely afraid of being confronted with a situation which would threaten Finno-Swedish relations. Since the Alanders appeared intent on breaking their bonds with Finland and declaring their union with Sweden, Barclay asked if it would not be advisable for the British government to consider supporting the Alanders' claim. He felt the Aland question was "a far reaching one owing to the strategic position of the Islands," and well summed up in a prior report from Sir Esme Howard.[16]

The reports reaching the Foreign Office in London from George J. Kidston, the new British minister in Helsingfors, were also disquieting. Asked for his observations on the conversations held in Stockholm by Barclay, Kidston reported that though Holsti confirmed to him the general accuracy of the Stockholm conversations, he denied having refused Palmstierna's proposal for a plebiscite. He had instead promised to submit his proposal to the government in Helsingfors, making it clear to Palmstierna that he had little hope of its being accepted. Kidston understood that a formal refusal of the offer had now been addressed to Westman. When questioned by the British minister as to whether the Alanders would take immediate action themselves, Holsti was very vague. In fact, he appeared to be ignorant of the state of public opinion on the islands but promised Kidston to let him know as soon as he cabled and received information.

The British minister also reported that the Finns had no intention of coercing the Alanders to accept the autonomy recently given them. Instead, they hoped the autonomy law would in

16. *DBrFP, 1919–1939,* 1st ser., *II,* 314–16; Palmstierna, *Dagjämning,* pp. 79–80.

time attract the islanders and that within a few months they would see the value of accepting it. On the other hand, if they declared union with Sweden, Holsti "did not believe any Finnish Government could for a moment accept such a solution." Pressed by Kidston, Holsti refused to elaborate.

Kidston observed to Lord Curzon that it seemed impossible to find a Finn who would "give an unbiased opinion" on the question, and because of the remoteness of the island group, it was difficult to ascertain any independent opinion on what was occurring there.[17] More news from Kidston followed several days later on May 22. In this report the British minister disclosed to Lord Curzon that Prime Minister Erich had revealed to him the previous evening the information that the Governor of the Aland Islands had reported that the Aland Diet "might quite possibly in the near future declare [the] Islands' incorporation with Sweden." Such a decision, Erich commented, would never be recognized by the Finnish government, which "might have to take measures to enforce their authority." He begged Kidston that the great powers should as quickly as possible "issue a declaration of disinterestedness in [the] Aland question." The Prime Minister believed that the whole Swedish propaganda drive and the attitude of the Alanders were to a large degree based on the conviction that, if they agitated the Aland question long enough, the great powers would intervene in support of Sweden's claim.

Kidston suggested that the effect of such a declaration by the great powers might perhaps be contrary to what Erich anticipated. Sweden, once given a free hand, might capitalize on any Finnish difficulties in the peace negotiations with Russia and settle the Aland question unilaterally and in accordance with her own desires. Erich scoffed at the idea that Sweden would ever dream of going to war with Finland over the Aland question if she were convinced that there was no hope for any sympathy or assistance from the powers. Kidston responded that he had not yet had time to study the matter in detail, but it appeared to him that Erich might be greatly underestimating the pressure of Swedish public opinion on the Aland question. When Kidston asked who was to make the declaration that Erich desired, the

17. *DBrFP, 1919–1939,* 1st ser., *11,* 323.

latter replied that it should be made by the Supreme Council. Kidston pointed out that the Council had already made it clear that they could not handle the matter, and, even if they did pronounce on it, the League of Nations might still get involved in the question. Regardless of Kidston's observations, Erich persisted in his request for a formal declaration of disinterestedness by the great powers. Later that same evening Kidston met Holsti, who spoke to him in the same sense. To Holsti, Kidston replied that he could only report to Lord Curzon what had been said to him. He pointed out, however, that the Aland question concerned not only Great Britain but also France and Italy, and Erich and Holsti should speak to their ministers in Helsingfors. This Holsti promised to do.[18]

Three days after the receipt of Kidston's report at the Foreign Office, Donner called on Lord Hardinge. Donner had come to report to Lord Hardinge that Helsingfors "had heard that the Alanders were approaching the Great Powers direct to ask them whether, if they decide to break away from Finland and to join Sweden, they will be allowed to do so." Donner's request was that Great Britain should dissuade the Alanders from this action. Lord Hardinge replied that this was the first he had heard that the Alanders contemplated approaching the British government. However, he found it impossible to reply to Donner or even to discuss a hypothetical situation. With these comments Donner agreed. After reading the memorandum of this conversation Lord Curzon minuted that he was "sure that the Powers would Ask the League," and sarcastically added that "this would make Lord R[obert] Cecil [Chairman of the League of Nations Union] happy for 6 months." [19]

The Alander Declaration

Though decisions were being made in Stockholm and Mariehamn, they were not as far-reaching as Erich, Holsti, or Donner imagined them. Branting and Palmstierna must have been quite aware that allowing the Alanders to announce their union with Sweden would have placed them in a confrontation situation with Finland.

18. Ibid., pp. 324–25.
19. Ibid., p. 323n.

It would have been an action where the weaker of the two partners would have committed the stronger one while they lacked—as Curzon had made it clear to King Gustaf and Barclay to Palmstierna—great power sympathy and support.

In place of the Alanders' announcing their union with Sweden, and to reduce tension in the island group, Palmstierna arranged for a deputation of Alanders to visit the King—an idea that the Alanders had suggested themselves. Palmstierna justified the move to his colleagues on the grounds that the arrival of the deputation would provide a starting point for renewed action toward the great powers. To control the situation as much as possible Stockholm composed the declaration that the Alanders would make and then smuggled it over to them.[20] The effects of this action, however, were contrary to what Palmstierna had hoped. Indeed, the arrival of the deputation and their declaration to the King acted as a catalyst leading to a denouement of the whole situation.

In the period between the smuggling of the declaration to the Alanders and their arrival in Stockholm, Lord Curzon replied to Barclay's query on the advisability of the British government's supporting the Alanders' claim. The only action that the London government could take in this situation, the Foreign Secretary cabled, "would be to advise the Swedish Government to refer the Aland Islands question to [the] League of Nations." Would this advice, he asked Barclay, be acceptable to the Stockholm government at the present moment? [21] With the Alanders expected in Stockholm at any minute, it obviously was not.

The fairly short declaration of the Alanders to King Gustaf and to the Swedish people on May 31, several days after Lord Curzon's query to Barclay, began by recounting the actions and frustrations of the Alanders in realizing their desire for union with Sweden. Believing in the justice of their cause and spurning the autonomy recently given to them by the Finnish government, the Alanders reiterated that they would pursue their efforts to be allowed to determine their own future. The delay in realizing a solution to the problem according to the desires of the Alanders had "created a growing impatience" which would, if extended, or if the right given to other peoples and populations were denied

20. Palmstierna, *Dagjämning*, pp. 80–81.
21. *DBrFP, 1919–1939*, 1st ser., *II*, 337.

to them, give birth to the greatest apprehensions respecting their future. Because of this the population of the archipelago intended to convoke an assembly based on popular suffrage, in order to renew their determination for union with Sweden. They hoped that the Swedish government would succeed in making known the wish of the Alanders and in obtaining recognition of the desire which alone was capable of giving them satisfaction: union of the Aland Islands with Sweden.[22] The King's original reply to the Alanders, after being examined and rejected by Palmstierna, was rewritten by Palmstierna himself. "Am I allowed to say this? . . . I thought you and Branting wanted me to be more careful," the King telephoned. To this his Foreign Minister replied that they were "one heart and one soul in this issue." [23]

It was pointed out in the King's reply to the Alanders that all prior Swedish governments of whatever political complexion, along with the Riksdag, had attempted to implement a definitive plebiscitary solution. Though it was true that the Peace Conference had not yet resolved the issue, and direct negotiations with Finland had not proved fruitful, he asked the Alanders not to lose hope. He had learned "from leading political personalities," especially during his stays in London and Paris, that there was a "favorable disposition" toward their aspirations for union with Sweden. Gustaf was confident that the Alanders' long efforts would in the end be crowned with success.[24] In his own statement to the Alanders, Branting assured them that the Swedish government, supported by a unanimous public opinion, would not renounce its efforts to have the Alanders' right to self-determination recognized and to produce a solution which would give satisfaction to their wishes to be reunited with Sweden.[25] Late that same night Palmstierna informed the chiefs of all diplomatic missions in Stockholm that the Alanders' appeal could not fail to have a great effect on Swedish public opinion, and "if the matter was not settled without great delay he feared it would be very

22. League of Nations, *Official Journal*, spec. suppl. no. 1 (Aug. 1920), pp. 57–58; Sweden, Utrikesdepartementet, *Ålandsfrågan*, pp. 140–42.

23. Palmstierna, *Dagjämning*, p. 81.

24. League of Nations, *Official Journal*, spec. suppl. no. 1 (Aug. 1920), pp. 58–59; Sweden, Utrikesdepartementet, *Ålandsfrågan*, p. 144.

25. League of Nations, *Official Journal*, spec. suppl. no. 1 (Aug. 1920), pp. 59–60; Sweden, Utrikesdepartementet, *Ålandsfrågan*, pp. 146–48.

difficult to prevent an action from which there could be no withdrawal." [26]

What had been the purpose of the Alander deputation for the Swedish Foreign Minister? Palmstierna's belief was that no agreement could be arrived at with the Finns. He felt that any Finnish persecution of the Alander deputation would furnish Sweden with a new and good reason to appeal again to the great powers, arguing that Finnish repression was being undertaken when the issue was before the powers for settlement. The Alanders were to be martyrs to the cause of Swedish foreign policy. If the Aland question got even more urgent, it would automatically find its way into the League of Nations. He thought that this was what finally would happen.[27] On all these counts he was cynically correct.

The opinion of the Finnish minister in Stockholm, Werner Söderhjelm, reported the American chargé d'affaires, Post Wheeler, was that the situation was "very critical." Wheeler thought Söderhjelm feared that the Alanders' projected assembly was likely to lead to some Swedish action in the Aland question which Finland could not accept.[28] In his own conversation with Barclay, Palmstierna reiterated what he had told him several weeks before: "that the question was entering a critical stage." Indeed, the situation was so greatly aggravated that something had to be done quickly. He felt that the Supreme Council should make a decision on the Aland question. At this point Barclay read to Palmstierna excerpts from Lord Curzon's memorandum of his conversation with King Gustaf during the latter's visit to London in April, stressing in his reading those "paragraphs advocating reference to the League of Nations." Palmstierna responded that the issue was before the Supreme Council and should be handled by that body first. Reference to the League would only mean delay, and events were moving too quickly to allow this. Barclay urged "patience and moderation," observing that "hasty steps would only bring odium on those who had

26. Wheeler (Stockholm) to the Department of State, June 1, 1920 (File 758.6114A1/59, Record Group 59, NA).

27. Palmstierna, *Dagjämning,* pp. 81–82.

28. Wheeler (Stockholm) to the Department of State, June 1, 1920 (File 758.6114A1/59, Record Group 59, NA).

recourse to them." Palmstierna countered that the Swedish government was advising the Alanders in this sense, but that the latter, greatly impatient at the Supreme Council's inaction, might act unilaterally. At this point Barclay attempted to pin Palmstierna down as to what the Swedish government would do in an emergency. Would they, for example, he asked, dispatch troops to the island group? The only reply that Palmstierna would give was that Swedish public opinion would not tolerate Finnish reprisals in the Aland Islands. He begged Barclay to inform Lord Curzon of the latest Alander declaration. He hoped that the Supreme Council, realizing the gravity of the situation, would pronounce themselves on the question and come to the only acceptable decision: recognition of the Alanders' right to self-determination. Palmstierna admitted that he had spoken in the same sense to Barclay's American, French, Italian, and Japanese colleagues. He had also called on the Finnish minister, Söderhjelm, with whom he had first consulted, and they had agreed that they were in the "presence of a grave crisis" where something had to be done as quickly as possible, since "delays only aggravated the already serious state of tension existing between the two countries."

The next morning, June 1, Barclay called on Söderhjelm himself and asked the Finnish minister for his observations on the latest developments. Söderhjelm admitted that the "situation was grave," and it was imperative to have a settlement of the Aland question in the "near future if serious trouble was to be avoided." He had no suggestions to make and the whole matter appeared to him to have reached an impasse. On the one hand, the Alanders wanted to be united with Sweden, and, on the other, the Finnish government was determined to prevent it. After some discussion Söderhjelm said he thought it might be possible to find a formula calming the present excitement. If the Supreme Council were to declare that they were examining the just claims of both countries, such an action would have a "quieting effect and prevent the Alanders from taking any drastic step, the consequences of which would be fraught with the greatest dangers."

Late that same afternoon, Barclay received three of the most important members of the Alander deputation, Carl Björkman, Johannes Eriksson, and August Karlsson. The last two had spoken to Sir Eric Drummond in December of the previous year. Barclay, who had foreseen that the Alander deputation would wish to call on the diplomatic missions of the great powers in Stockholm, had told Palmstierna that he did not think that the missions should receive them. Palmstierna's reply was that it would be a great mistake if Sir Colville refused to see the Alanders, for some of his diplomatic colleagues had already promised to do so. Sir Colville's refusal would be interpreted as a sign that Great Britain was an obstacle to the Alanders' aspirations. Faced with this argument, Barclay accordingly agreed with Palmstierna that a small delegation of the Alanders could call at the various diplomatic missions.

During his conversation with the Alanders at the British Legation, Sir Colville was handed a petition written in English. He was begged to forward it to Lord Curzon with the request that it be transmitted to the Peace Conference. In reading the petition Barclay was struck by the sentence: "We Alanders are determined not to shrink from even the most desperate steps in order to gain our purpose though we are still hoping for a peaceable solution of our question by the assistance of the Great Powers." He asked the Alanders what they meant by it. Did it mean that the assembly proposed by them would declare the islands united with Sweden? This they emphatically denied. The only thing the proposed assembly would do would be to "reiterate the firm and irrevocable determination" of the Alanders to be united with Sweden, and to persist until they had attained this goal. They assured Barclay that no hasty steps would be taken, but they hoped the great powers would settle the question for the Alanders in the only manner that would be acceptable to them: recognition of their right of self-determination. They warned Barclay that if the great powers took no action the Alanders would in the end have to act, but in that situation no one could predict what might occur. Finland, they felt, would bow to a decision dictated by the great powers, but she would resist forcibly any other decision, and the "good relations between Sweden and Finland would be jeopardized for many years to come." Barclay in replying strongly impressed upon his callers the "absolute necessity for patience and moderation, and pointed out to them that any precipitate or drastic action on their part would only turn public opinion against them." The Alanders repeated that no hasty steps would be taken by them.

During their stay in Stockholm the Alanders also visited the leaders of all Swedish political parties, who without exception gave their support to the Alanders' claim, expressing confidence in a solution favorable to the Alanders. This reaction, Barclay thought, confirmed King Gustaf's statement concerning the unanimity of Swedish public opinion. That the Aland question was the chief topic of discussion in the Swedish press goes without saying.

In his observations to Lord Curzon, Barclay wrote that he believed the latest Alander declaration had aggravated the situation a great deal, and it would be aggravated even more when the projected Alander assembly made its pronouncement. Even at this moment it had reached a danger point, and eventualities would have to be faced. Barclay felt that the Alanders up to that moment had skillfully conducted their campaign. They had resorted only to legal methods. Initially they had endeavored to have the question settled by direct negotiations between Finland and Sweden. When this failed they had appealed to the Peace Conference, invoking the right of self-determination, and were now awaiting the decision of the Supreme Council. He did not presume to anticipate Supreme Council decisions, but the main lines that could be followed in a settlement of the Aland question were not numerous. First, the Supreme Council could recognize the Alanders' appeal, and details as to how and when the plebiscite would take place would be settled later. In line with the Supreme Council's decision Finland would give way. The decision would produce on Finland's part a great deal of recrimination, and Sir Colville felt "she may throw in her lot openly with Germany." The Supreme Council might perhaps decide that the Aland question was one for the League of Nations. This move, in Palmstierna's opinion, would be impractical because of the delays it would cause and the increasing impatience of the Alanders, who wanted the question settled at least in principle.

Another possible solution would be for the Supreme Council to declare that it was considering the claims of both parties and was prepared to hear their respective cases. Barclay thought that the advantage here would be a calming down of the present agitation in Finland and a preparation of public opinion there for the inevitable loss of the island group. This, however, could be but a temporary decision. The Supreme Council could, of course, declare the question outside its competence. The danger here was that the Alanders might change their tactics and declare their union with Sweden. It was impossible to predict what would follow from such a declaration. Finland might attempt to prevent the union. The Alanders would appeal to the Swedes, and, with public opinion in Sweden unanimous on the subject, a clash with Finland would be inevitable. In this way a permanent irritant in Finno-Swedish relations would result. That there was in power in Stockholm a socialist government, which had firmly supported the Alanders in their cause, accentuated the danger. The last possibility was for the Supreme Council to abstain from making any decision. This, Barclay feared, would be the same as if the Supreme Council declared the Aland question outside its competence.

There was one thing, Barclay observed to Lord Curzon, that he was sure of, and that was that the Alanders desired union with Sweden. He believed that means had to be found to "have this union effected in the most peaceful manner, and in such a way as will least affect future neighbourly relations between Finland and Sweden." Finland had made the mistake of underestimating the Alanders' desire for union with Sweden. She was realizing it now. Previously, Finland had refused to entertain any monetary or other compensation for the Aland Islands. However, Barclay thought Helsingfors might change its mind when it realized that the loss of the archipelago was inevitable.[29]

29. *DBrFP, 1919–1939,* 1st ser., *11,* 340–43. Barclay's observation that Finland "may throw in her lot openly with Germany" was not as far fetched as it appears. On May 14 and May 22, 1920, the Finnish minister in Washington called on Frank L. Polk to press the Finnish case. He admitted to Polk in his first call on May 14 that if the islands were taken away from his country, it would be necessary for the Finns to "throw in their lot with Germany." When Polk noted that Sweden had made a similar threat, the Finnish minister agreed this was

During this period the French minister, Delavaud, was also busy. In an interview with Söderhjelm he pointed out the long-run difficulty in postponing a decision on the Aland question and stated that a majority of the Supreme Council approved of the Swedish position. His own proposal was that the Supreme Council act as a "mediator in the dispute." Informed of this conversation, Enckell in Paris immediately called on Emmanuel Peretti de la Rocca, Director of the Political Department of the Quai d'Orsay. The latter assuaged Enckell's anxieties by making it clear that Delavaud's comments about the Supreme Council's attitude were incorrect. He also informed Enckell that Delavaud had acted without instructions and therefore his comments were to be ignored. Peretti confirmed the fact that neither the Supreme Council nor the Conference of Ambassadors was interested in the question. Even if the Supreme Council did handle the Aland question, there was no assurance that it would recognize the Wilsonian concept of national self-determination. Enckell hoped that with Finland's admission to the League of Nations the Supreme Council would stand by its decision not to handle the question. As a League member Finland would submit itself to the Covenant, and, therefore, any Alander complaints about suppression would be obviated. In his opinion the Aland question was chiefly a matter of whether Sweden would be able to strengthen its power position in the Baltic at Finland's expense, which according to the Swedes would be executed through a plebiscite on the island group. In his report to Helsingfors Enckell recommended that the government strongly resist the Swedish propaganda campaign, which at the most would result in an appeal to the great powers. He concluded with the observation that the latest actions in Stockholm had again pushed the Aland question to the fore, but he thought Sweden's position in the whole matter had not improved.[30]

---

so, but noted that the Swedes in the past "had been pro-German." Polk suggested that the same charge had been leveled against the Finns. He agreed to this, too. The Finnish minister then informed Polk that his government had been assured by the British that "they would not grant . . . these Islands to Sweden." Diary entries, May 14 and May 22, 1920 (Polk Papers).

30. Enckell, 2, 59–60.

Arrest of the Alanders

The reaction that Palmstierna thought would be produced in Finland by the Alanders' declaration and their deputation to Stockholm was not long in coming. On the afternoon of June 3, Wheeler, the American chargé d'affaires in Stockholm, reported to the State Department that Finnish minister Söderhjelm had received a note of protest from the Finnish Foreign Ministry for delivery to the Swedish government. Söderhjelm, however, had asked for permission to delay delivery of the note until tensions had relaxed a bit. He disclosed to Wheeler that he feared that unless Sweden's reply was "most conciliatory a rupture of relations will follow."[31] The only delay allowed by the Finnish Foreign Ministry was twenty-four hours, and on the following day, June 4, Söderhjelm delivered the note to the Swedes.[32] Upon receipt of the note Palmstierna suggested to Söderhjelm "that the note be kept secret so as not to [inflame] public opinion." Söderhjelm referred this suggestion back to Helsingfors, which replied that matters had gotten to such a point that they preferred to have the note published.[33] The note presented to Palmstierna by Söderhjelm protested against the action of the Swedish government in becoming—without regard to Finland's rights and interests—spokemen for a portion of the Alanders who illegitimately claimed separation of the archipelago from Finland. Thus Sweden was assisting this group in its intrigues. It called attention to the fact that Finland had sovereignty over the island group, a sovereignty that Sweden had recognized without reservation. Because of this Finland delared that it would resist any proposition incompatible with her sovereignty in the Aland Islands.[34]

The same day Söderhjelm delivered this note to the Swedish Foreign Ministry, his associate in London, Ossian Donner, called

31. Wheeler (Stockholm) to the Department of State, June 3, 1920 (File 758.6114A1/60, Record Group 59, NA).

32. League of Nations, *Official Journal,* spec. suppl. no. 1 (Aug. 1920), p. 20; Sweden, Utrikesdepartementet, *Ålandsfrågan,* p. 22. Barclay reported to Lord Curzon that the Finnish note was not delivered to the Swedes until June 5. *DBrFP, 1919–1939,* 1st ser., *11,* 344.

33. *DBrFP, 1919–1939,* 1st ser., *11,* 344.

34. League of Nations, *Official Journal,* spec. suppl. no. 1 (Aug. 1920), p. 60; Sweden, Utrikesdepartementet, *Ålandsfrågan,* p. 150.

on the Secretary-General of the League, Sir Eric Drummond. Ostensibly, Donner had come to inquire about Finland's application for membership to the League of Nations. Sir Eric explained to the Finnish minister that Finland could not become a member of the world organization until after the meeting of the League Assembly, which was set for the autumn. Donner pointed out that this was somewhat unfortunate, as a problem had arisen which might involve a League member and Finland. He explained to Drummond that he wished to talk to him confidentially on the matter, though he admitted "he had no authorization from his government to raise the question." He then referred to the Aland problem. Donner began the discussion by noting that his government had extended to the Alanders a large measure of autonomy, hoping that their agitation for union with Sweden would thus cease. Unfortunately, this step had failed and the Alanders had dispatched a deputation to Stockholm to request the Swedish government for "immediate action." He had heard, Donner continued, that Sweden was likely to proclaim that Swedish protection extended to the Alanders. This proclamation, the Finnish minister warned, "would raise the dispute in acute form," as his country could never admit that the archipelago could be taken away from her by this method. Donner explained that though Finland realized that a majority of the Alanders desired union with Sweden, the population of the island group was so small that his government believed that the desires of the islanders could not be the controlling factor. On the contrary, the territorial and military considerations involved in the question made it impossible for his country to give way. Indeed, Donner made it clear that Finland "would be prepared to fight to the last on the point."

He then asked Sir Eric if any article of the Covenant applied in this situation. The Secretary-General replied that he could not give him a considered opinion but he reminded Donner of Articles 11 and 15, and especially paragraph 8 of the latter article. Drummond added that, as far as he could see, since both countries believed that they had an excellent case, the Aland question was one which might be offered for Council arbitration. This comment by Drummond elicited no reply.

If Donner's visit had been to sound out the Secretary-General and perhaps impress him with Finland's intransigence on the Aland question, he had been more than successful. For it was Sir Eric's impression after his talk with Donner "that the Finns considered the matter as domestic, and would with difficulty brook interference by any outside body, no matter how impartial the latter might be." [35]

That same day matters came to a head in the Aland Islands. Finnish Prime Minister Erich, accompanied by the Ministers of War and Commerce, had landed at Mariehamn "to remonstrate with [the] local leaders and dissuade [them] . . . from further action tending to embarrass [the Finnish] Government." [36] He then explained to the Alanders the provisions of the recently passed autonomy law. Speaking for his fellow islanders, Julius Sundblom declared that they "could not be led, either by threats or promises," to renounce their rightful demand for a plebiscite, and he added that they had no intention of assisting implementation of the autonomy law. Sundblom reminded Erich that Finland had obtained its freedom through the right of self-determination, and she should allow the Alanders that same right. The reply of the Finnish authorities was to arrest Sundblom and Carl Björkman the next day, June 5, for high treason and to rush troops to the archipelago.[37] Arrival of the news in Stockholm moved the Swedish government to instruct Westman to address a note to the Finnish government inquiring whether the arrest of the Alander leaders, Sundblom and Björkman, "was due to their appeal to Sweden, [the] Peace Conference, and the Great Powers for recognition of their right to determine their national Status by means of [the] Plebiscite-appeals made in 1918 and 1919 and now once more renewed." [38] Westman's instructions were an obvious attempt to acquire greater details, since an immediate Swedish protest without adequate information had its

35. Record of conversation E[ric] D[rummond], June 4, 1920 (Political 1920: 11/4639/468, LNA).

36. Magruder (Helsingfors) to the Department of State, June 4, 1920 (File 758.6114A1/61, Record Group 59, NA).

37. League of Nations, *Official Journal,* spec. suppl. no. 1 (Aug. 1920), p. 21; Sweden, Utrikesdepartementet, *Ålandsfrågan,* pp. 20–22.

38. *DBrFP, 1919–1939,* 1st ser., *II,* 344.

risks. The day following the arrest of the Alanders, King Gustaf summoned Barclay and his French colleague, Delavaud, to express his agitation at the arrest of Sundblom and Björkman on their return to the islands. He hoped that both England and France "would give [counsels] of moderation" to Finland. He warned that if the Aland leaders were severely dealt with by the Finns there would be no answering for the reaction of Swedish public opinion and the consequences that would follow. The Swedish monarch requested Barclay to urge upon Lord Curzon "once more the necessity for [the] Supreme Council pronouncing themselves one way or another." [39] In the meantime, from Paris Ehrensvärd pleaded that the Alanders declare their independence, and once this was done Sweden should appeal to the great powers to prevent the dispatch of Finnish troops to the islands. He thought the powers' reaction to such a request would be favorable. The trouble with this advice, Palmstierna noted, was that Finnish troops were already quartered in the islands. The Swedish Foreign Minister felt that in the end the issue would be presented to the League.[40] The question of who would submit the matter was one he avoided answering.

The same day King Gustaf was receiving Barclay and Delavaud, June 6, the Swedish ministers in London and Paris submitted a note suggesting that the Aland question be offered "to the decision of the Supreme Council." As the French Foreign Ministry subsequently admitted to the American Embassy, the British government, "arguing that the Supreme Council held but infrequent meetings and would find it difficult to give time to the examination of the problem of the Aland Islands, proposed to place the matter before the League of Nations." France, it went on to explain, willingly agreed to this proposed procedure, which seems to be in perfect accord with the sole desire it entertained in regard to this question—that "it should be treated with impartiality and settled with equity." [41]

The following day a Swedish note was also delivered to the

39. Ibid.

40. Palmstierna, *Dagjämning*, p. 85.

41. French Foreign Ministry to the American Embassy, July 4, 1920 (Attached to File 758.6114A1/86, Record Group 59, NA).

State Department in Washington. In this communication it was pointed out that as late as April 18 the Swedish government had asked the Peace Conference to consider the Alanders' wish that a plebiscite be held in the island group. Because of the number and importance of other questions being considered by the Peace Conference, its directing organ, the Supreme Council, did not think it could devise a solution on this matter, which was of the "highest importance for the maintenance of tranquillity in the Baltic." The note went on to explain that even prior to its overtures to the Peace Conference, the Swedish government had attempted to negotiate the problem directly with Finland on the basis of a plebiscite which would offer guarantees and would be binding on both countries. Though these efforts had failed Sweden wished to hold direct negotiations with Finland. In line with this approach Sweden, as late as the middle of May, again attempted to come to a direct understanding with Finland on this question but without success. The Finnish Diet had instead granted to the Alanders a limited autonomy. According to the note, the autonomy offered was inadequate and the law had been repudiated by the islanders.

During this whole period the Alanders had waited patiently and with confidence for the Conference's decision. The long delay in solving the question, however, had aggravated the Alanders. This had led to the sending of a delegation to Stockholm that reiterated not only their wish for a plebiscite but also their fears for the future if the right of self-determination were not accorded to them. The Alanders' intention of convoking an assembly to affirm their desire for union with Sweden had not failed to make a deep impression on Sweden and produce the warmest sympathy in the Swedish people. Under these circumstances the Swedish government, viewing with "disquiet the growing agitation in the archipelago" and fearing that "regrettable events" could arise, believed that it should once again address itself to the great powers, asking them as quickly as possible to take the Aland question under consideration. The Swedes were of the opinion that the Aland question was an outgrowth of the war, and it was natural that a definitive solution of this matter also be devised by the Conference. If the Supreme

Council, overburdened by other tasks of great importance, found it could not treat the question, the Swedes suggested that the Council could perhaps bring about a useful exchange of views between the governments of Washington, Paris, London, Tokyo, and Rome. In closing, the note reiterated the great importance that Sweden attached to the question, which, as it was threatening to take a disquieting turn, needed to be solved "with the least possible delay." [42]

From the tenor of the note it was obvious that it had been sent to the Swedish Legation in Washington before the arrest of the Alander leaders had become known. In a sense it was a naive note. For to ask for an exchange of views among the great powers outside the Supreme Council was to blind oneself to the fact that the Supreme Council was nothing more than the great powers acting in concert. If the exchange of views among the world capitals and its inclusion of Washington was meant to bring the United States in on the Swedish side, on the assumption that self-determination was the idea of the American chief of state, the Swedes would be disappointed. In a memorandum to the Secretary of State some days after receipt of this note, Oscar L. Milmore, who had served in Stockholm during the war and who in the end played an important role in settling the Aland question, pointed out that it did not seem practicable for the American government to express any opinion on the ultimate fate of the Aland archipelago. On the other hand, he thought "it might be useful for the Secretary [of State] to point out to the Swedish and Finnish Ministers the serious consequences of a disturbance of the peace of the Baltic. Open hostility between Sweden and Finland at this time would encourage the Bolsheviks and endanger law and order in the whole of Europe." [43]

On the same day that this Swedish note was communicated to the State Department, the British minister in Helsingfors, Kidston, who was also unaware of the arrest of the Alander leaders,

42. Note by the Legation of Sweden at Washington, D.C., June 7, 1920 (File 758.6114A1/63, Record Group 59, NA).

43. Memorandum on the Aland Islands situation for the attention of the Secretary [of State] by O[scar] L[ongfellow] M[ilmore], June 12, 1920 (Wilson Papers, ser. VI, File No. 3129).

reported to Lord Curzon his thoughts and impressions on the Aland question. He noted that if self-determination were to be the determining factor in this matter, then the archipelago should be given to Sweden. However, upon a geographical, administrative, and historical examination the Aland question assumed a different aspect. The islands from the Finnish side were connected to the mainland by a continuous chain of large and small islands, rocks, and rocky skerries. From the Swedish coast it took two hours across an open body of water to reach the westernmost islands. To draw an effective boundary through this maze of islands and rocks would be difficult, and the great powers, if they undertook consideration of the question, would be expected to take a hand in this task. The difficulty of exercising any control in this labyrinth of islands was exemplified by the large-scale smuggling that was being carried on, especially in the matter of spirits, which virtually nullified the Finnish prohibition law. Needless to say, any frontier line drawn across these islands would aggravate the situation and greatly handicap the administration of justice.

Kidston thought he should point out this practical consideration, and, though a plebiscite would lead to the union of the islands with Sweden, he could not but think that this would be the beginning of a whole series of practical problems that could be solved neither by Finland nor Sweden alone and might necessitate extended and troublesome interference by the powers. This was important, for Kidston understood that in other areas plebiscites had not in every instance brought a final solution of the problems at issue and that this seemingly simple method of handling nationality questions had even been found to bring about unexpected difficulties.

Aside from the practical difficulty of actually fixing the frontier, there was the larger question of whether it was advisable to create a precedent whereby a minority in one state could, because it was a majority in a given area, claim that this area should be unified with another state to which its inhabitants belonged ethnographically. He did not know whether the doctrine of self-determination on these lines would be accepted as a ruling principle in the peaceful times that were yet to come, but it seemed to Kidston that awkward analogies with the Aland case might be found, and that Cyprus suggested itself, though there were undoubtedly others that could be cited.

Kidston believed that the Finns had damaged their own case by their attitude on the question of Eastern Karelia. They contended that being at war with Bolshevik Russia put Eastern Karelia in a different position from the Aland Islands. They argued that subjects of one's enemy could legitimately claim to be annexed to oneself, but one's own subjects, as in the case of the Alanders, had no right to annex themselves to one's friends. The British minister thought this argument was "a specious one," though he was willing to admit that there was "an element of commonsense underlying it."

Kidston then turned to the Finnish desire for a declaration of disinterestedness by the powers in the Aland question. They had been so sanguine in anticipating that a declaration would reduce the agitation both in the archipelago and Sweden that he had to warn them that, in his opinion, they were underestimating the pressure of public opinion both in the islands and in Sweden. Before Erich's departure for the Aland Islands his confidence appeared to have been dampened, Kidston wrote, but, nevertheless, the Finnish Prime Minister still insisted that a declaration of disinterestedness "was the only thing that could save the situation."

Kidston assured Curzon that in all his conversations with the Finns he had "counselled moderation" and had called their attention to the danger of trouble with Sweden in the West at the very moment they were about to engage in peace negotiations with the Bolsheviks in the East. In his last conversation with Erich before the latter's departure for the island group, he had urged the Finnish Prime Minister to make to the Alanders every concession that he possibly could and suggested that they might be placated by widening even more the autonomy which the Finnish government had granted them. Erich had admitted that because of Finnish party politics certain concessions had been withheld, but he would see what could be done in the direction Kidston had suggested.

Kidston then disclosed to Lord Curzon that his Norwegian colleague, Andreas Urbye, who was well informed on Finnish political questions, was very disturbed by the situation. Though he appreciated Sweden's difficult position, he assured Kidston at the same time that there was not a single Swedish- or Finnish-speaking Finn who would consent to the Aland Islands' being ceded to Sweden. Any government in Helsingfors that even thought of the idea would quickly collapse. Finnish- and Swedish-speaking Finns might disagree on how the Alanders shall be treated, but they were united in the belief that the islands should be retained by Finland. These observations by Urbye, he felt, were correct based on his own sources of information, the attitude of the newspapers, and on what he had gleaned from conversations and from personal observations since his arrival in Finland.

Urbye had also warned that if the Alanders faced the Finnish government with a fait accompli, he feared the Finns would be bound to use force. Since the Finns "did not have a light hand in such matters"—witness their suppression of the Finnish Reds—Urbye was uneasy.

As to his French colleague, Fabre was recommending that the Quai d'Orsay abstain from interfering in the question, not because of the difficulties in which interference might involve the powers but for what Kidston called "a reason more characteristic of Latin diplomacy, namely, that any solution that the Powers might be able to devise would almost certainly be unsatisfactory, while the present situation gives the opportunity of playing off Finland and Sweden against one another and keeping them both on their good behaviour in anticipation of what the verdict may be." Kidston rightly observed that, if the Aland deputation in Stockholm correctly represented the attitude of the islanders, Erich's mission to the islands was likely to be unproductive, though he thought that—and here he was wrong—Erich's arrival and that of the other ministers might have a sobering effect on the Alander leaders after their Stockholm visit.

In closing, Kidston had one other possibility to add to the ones offered by Barclay on how the Aland question might be handled by the powers. He asked if it would not be possible for the Supreme Council to announce that the Aland question was one in which they were not convinced of their own competence without an investigation on the spot. They would then propose to Finland and Sweden the dispatch of an impartial observer to decide, not the merits of the dispute itself, but whether the Aland question was a matter in which the powers should be asked to adjudicate at all. He admitted that this was perhaps a weak and impractical suggestion, but it was the only one which occurred to him aside from those already proffered by Barclay.

To be prepared for all eventualities, on the following day, June 8, Kidston cabled to suggest that "expert naval opinion be taken on [the] possibility of drawing up [a] workable frontier between [the] islands and the Finnish mainland," provided this had not already been done.[44] While this note was being communicated to London, Wrangel called on Curzon at the Foreign Office. Naturally he had come to discuss the Aland question, now complicated by the Alanders' declaration at Stockholm and their subsequent arrest. Lord Curzon reminded the Swedish minister of his conversation with King Gustaf in April, at which time the Swedish monarch had maintained that the question should be brought up by members of the Supreme Council at the San Remo Conference. At that time Curzon had prophesied that it would not be brought up, and if it were the Conference would be in no position to deal with it. The only time the matter even appeared at the Conference, he explained to Wrangel, was during a particular "boring interlude of the Conference" when he had seen the French Prime Minister, Alexander Millerand, "closely studying a book the title of which was 'The Aland Islands.' " He had inferred from this that the issue would be soon raised by Millerand, but it was not. Since the issue had not been raised at San Remo, it did not appear to the Foreign Secretary any more likely to be raised at the forthcoming meeting of the Supreme Council at Spa or anywhere else. Wrangel had to realize, Lord Curzon insisted, that the Supreme Council did not wish at this stage of its deliberations to assume the settlement of any problems aside from those it already had. His repeated opinion, which he had expressed to King Gustaf, was that if Sweden's friends were to raise the issue at a future meeting of the Supreme Coun-

44. *DBrFP, 1919–1939,* 1st ser., *11,* 347–50 and n.

cil, it would more likely refer the question to the League of Nations than take any action itself.

"Indeed," Lord Curzon asked the Swedish minister, "how could the Supreme Council decide the matter? If its decision were in favour of the Swedes, how could it eject the Finns, who were already in possession? Was it to declare a blockade of Finland, or even to make war on Finland? Or was it to land forces on the Aaland Islands and turn out the agents of the Finnish Government? It was inconceivable that the Supreme Council should take any such course." However, on the other hand, the League was in existence and functioning. The question at hand was of the type intended to be referred to that organization. Sweden was a member and, though Finland was not, it was allowed under the League Covenant to participate in any deliberations dealing with the matter. If his country desired a prompt solution of the question—and indeed it appeared to Lord Curzon desirable not to delay longer—and her case was as strong as she said it was, why did she not appeal to the League immediately and ask for an early hearing of the question and a quick decision? If Sweden believed that Finland would not accept or abide by a League decision, Curzon could point out in reply that, assuming the League's decision was unanimous and supported if necessary by the Assembly, the opinion not of two or three powers but of the civilized world, it seemed impossible to Curzon that Finland could indefinitely resist this kind of pressure. He urged Wrangel to press his government to take this step.[45]

Though not yet officially burdened with the Aland question, the League Secretariat cautiously continued to watch it, and across the city of London at Sunderland House, where they were temporarily housed, this situation appeared to them "very black."[46] This attitude was obviously also held by the British Cabinet, which discussed the question on June 11, several days after Lord Curzon's interview with Count Wrangel.[47]

45. Curzon (London) to Barclay, No. 173, June 8, 1920 (File 1259 in FO/371/4068, PRO).

46. Minutes of a directors' meeting, June 9, 1920 (General 1920: 40/4793/854, LNA).

47. Minutes of a meeting of the British Cabinet, June 11, 1920 (CAB/23/21, PRO).

Curzon Submits the Dispute to the League

As these events took place in London, an exchange of notes between Finland and Sweden about this same time helped to widen the Finno-Swedish breach. A Swedish note on June 7, in reply to the Finnish note of June 3, pointed out that from the time the Alanders had first made their desires known, Sweden had never hidden from the Finnish government its belief that the Alanders' claims, based on the right of self-determination, were "entirely legitimate." On the other hand, the Swedish government had attempted to resolve the Aland question in concert with Finland through a plebiscite. It felt that neither Sweden's attitude nor the position of the question at the Paris Peace Conference justified the note that had been communicated to it by the Finnish government. It went on to say that in its note of June 19, 1919, the Swedish government had related in a detailed manner its views on the different aspects of the Aland question. Sweden still maintained the views expressed in this note and had "no reason for adding here anything whatever." [48]

The terse Finnish reply on June 8 was calculated to remove the whole question from the realm of interstate relations. Writing in the third person, Holsti observed that a "certain number of Finnish citizens belonging to the Aland population" had—even after the entry into force of the autonomy law for the Aland Islands passed by the Finnish Diet—"openly and without reservations manifested their aspirations of obtaining with the support of a foreign power and under its protection the separation of Aland from Finland." By reason of this act the persons in question were under Finnish law guilty of criminal acts obliging the Finnish state to intervene. The judicial inquiry that would follow would ascertain their degree of culpability. The issue was removed from all future discussion, according to the Finnish Foreign Minister, since the whole affair was considered by the government of the Republic as an "internal Finnish question." [49]

In reply two days later, the Swedes noted that the persons

48. League of Nations, *Official Journal,* spec. suppl. no. 1 (Aug. 1920), p. 61; Sweden, Utrikesdepartementet, *Ålandsfrågan,* pp. 150–52.

49. League of Nations, *Official Journal,* spec. suppl. no. 1 (Aug. 1920), p. 61; Sweden, Utrikesdepartementet, *Ålandsfrågan,* pp. 152–54.

arrested for voicing the islanders' views on their right to self-determination had only repeated and stressed demands which the Alanders had addressed previously, especially to the Paris Peace Conference where the Aland question was still being deliberated. It then went on to deny that putting into force the autonomy law for the islands—promulgated over the protests of the Alanders—constituted a new situation that could in itself justify the measures taken, measures provocative not only to the Alanders but to others as well.

The most telling point in the note was the analogy between the Aland situation and the one in Eastern Karelia. It began by noting that the principle of self-determination claimed by the Alanders had also been invoked by the Finns in their liberation struggle. Indeed, the Finnish government several times, and most recently in a communication to the Russian Foreign Ministry on May 20, 1920, had invoked this same principle as an argument for the union of Eastern Karelia, a province inhabited by Finns, with the Finnish state. It went on to remark that the Finnish government had received deputations from Karelia and that it had also supported Karelian aspirations with the great powers—obvious allusions to the Aland deputation to Stockholm in May and to the support rendered them by the Swedish government. The note warned that, if Finland desired to maintain good relations with Sweden, as so often declared in Finland and equally desired by Sweden, Helsingfors had to consider the fact that Swedish public opinion was unanimous in its sentiment that the arrests constituted a "violation of an inalienable right." With a view to future Finno-Swedish relations, Sweden thought itself called upon to insist that the Finnish government seriously consider the Swedish position as developed in the note.[50]

Holsti's reply on June 12 alluded to Sweden's actions and to those of the Alanders as an attempt to present Finland with a fait accompli. He doubted that in an analogous situation Sweden would have acted otherwise than had Finland. The note dismissed as "erroneous and untenable" the Swedish comparison of the Aland situation to the one in Eastern Karelia on the grounds

50. League of Nations, *Official Journal,* spec. suppl. no. 1 (Aug. 1920), p. 62; Sweden, Utrikesdepartementet, *Ålandsfrågan,* pp. 154–56.

that the Karelians were being persecuted and badly treated at the hands of the Bolsheviks—implying that the Alanders were not. It then turned to the opinion of the Swedish public that the arrests ordered by the Finnish authorities were a "violation of an inalienable right." Holsti contended that judicially no Finnish citizen had the right to enter into negotiations with a foreign state directed against the powers and the territory of Finland. He did not believe that legal opinion in Sweden admitted this right to any Swedish citizen. Therefore it was impossible to see what inalienable right was violated on the part of the Finnish authorities in taking against its own citizens steps founded in Finnish law, even though the Swedish government disapproved of these steps and described them in its note as provocative not merely with regard to the Alanders. Holsti maintained, as previously declared, that the government of the Finnish republic considered the question as an "internal Finnish affair." In conclusion, Holsti greeted with satisfaction the Swedish declaration on the importance of keeping good relations between the two countries. This, he felt, demonstrated that the fundamental conceptions of the Swedish and Finnish governments were essentially identical in these matters.[51]

In an interview that same day with the correspondent of *The Times* of London, Palmstierna observed that the Aland question "was creating a situation of dangerous irritation." He also believed that it was "high time that the Supreme Council should intervene," and insisted that the arrested Alanders be released. Donner's response in London was that "Sweden's possession of the [Aland] Islands would place Finland at the mercy of any Power which held, or was allied with a Power holding, the Islands." If this statement annoyed the Swedes, his concluding remark that the Alanders' demands for union with Sweden "would be carrying the principle of self-determination to a point of absurdity" could only have infuriated them.[52]

On the day following the Holsti note, Sunday evening, June 13, Palmstierna called on Barclay. He warned the British min-

51. League of Nations, *Official Journal,* spec. suppl. no. 1 (Aug. 1920), p. 63; Sweden, Utrikesdepartementet, *Ålandsfrågan,* pp. 156–58.

52. *The Times* (London), June 14, 1920, p. 13.

ister that the present government would fall and that it was possible that Swedish public opinion might turn against England if nothing was done to resolve the Aland question. The issue, he maintained, had to be taken up one way or another. He then indicated that Barclay might suggest to London that the League be given the problem. Impressed by their talk, Barclay on the following day returned the call and showed Palmstierna the cable that he intended to dispatch to Lord Curzon. According to the Swedish Foreign Minister, the cable was so badly phrased that he had to redictate it.[53] Whether this was the cable finally sent to Curzon is unclear. However, that Palmstierna in his talks had influenced the British minister is quite clear from the report received in London.

Barclay's report commenced with the assertion that the Aland question had "reached a critical point." Though Sweden was displaying moderation and appealing to Britain and France, Finland was displaying a very independent attitude and was perhaps being supported by Germany. He pointed out that the present leaders of the Social Democratic government, Branting and Palmstierna, had "always been friends of England." During their short tenure in office they had succeeded in turning Swedish public opinion westwards. Barclay warned—and here Palmstierna's comments to him were obvious—that there was an "imminent danger" of the Branting–Palmstierna government's collapsing, if they failed in the Aland question, and their being succeeded by a government less favorably inclined to the Western powers. At the moment Swedish public opinion was unanimously supporting the government, but if they were unsuccessful it would turn against them, charging that their pro-Western policy was a failure. This had to be avoided. It seemed to him that it could be avoided only if the Supreme Council gave an early decision in the question. If this were "precluded for superior reasons," would it not be possible, he asked, for the Supreme Council to declare the Aland question beyond its competence and refer it to the League organization? At the same time, the Supreme Council would enjoin both countries to take no warlike steps and to cease writing diplomatic notes to each other. Only a

53. Palmstierna, *Dagjämning,* p. 87.

declaration from the Supreme Council would satisfy the Swedes. He thought that unless that was done the British government would "have to bear alone the odium of refusing to have the question even entertained by the Supreme Council." Britain, he observed, was in an increasingly strong position in Stockholm, owing to the Swedish government's policy. If they were to fail, Britain would be the loser. Barclay apologized for troubling Curzon personally, but he considered the question of "primary importance, both from the point of view of peace in the Baltic and of British interests in Sweden." [54]

To keep the initiative they now had and to impress upon the powers the urgency of the situation, the Stockholm government made several moves to increase the pressure. Wrangel, for one, called on Sir Eyre Crowe to complain of Finnish troop movements in the Aland Islands over which his government was "seriously perturbed." The Swedish minister maintained that the servitude of 1856 was looked upon "as one of the fundamental conditions for peace in the Baltic," and that Finnish troops in the island group were contrary, if not to the words, at least to the spirit of the 1856 convention. Wrangel hoped that the British would "find it possible to advise the Finnish Government, as soon as possible, to re-establish the military 'status quo ante' in [the] Aland" Islands.[55] After some discussion among King Gustaf, Branting, and Palmstierna, they instructed Westman in Helsingfors to return to Stockholm to report his views on the situation that had arisen.[56] This action was offset somewhat when the Finns made no similar move; Söderhjelm remained in Stockholm. At about the same time King Gustaf cabled King George reminding him of their April conversation in regard to the Aland question.[57]

54. *DBrFP, 1919–1939,* 1st ser., *11,* 355–56.

55. Verbal statement by Wrangel to Crowe, June 14, 1920 (File 1259 in FO/371/4068, PRO). It had been reported the previous day from Helsingfors that according to Holsti "only one extra battalion has been sent to Aland and that it is hoped shortly to withdraw [the] battalion which was already there." Kidston (Helsingfors) to Curzon, No. 500, June 13, 1920 (File 1259 in FO/371/4068, PRO).

56. Palmstierna, *Dagjämning,* pp. 88–89; League of Nations, *Official Journal,* spec. suppl. no. 1 (Aug. 1920), p. 21; Sweden, Utrikesdepartementet, *Ålandsfrågan,* p. 26.

57. Palmstierna, *Dagjämning,* p. 90.

King George's reply on June 16 assured King Gustaf that he had not forgotten their conversation about the island group. Indeed, it had been "carefully and sympathetically considered" by his government, who were of the opinion that "if it were again brought before the Supreme Council it would inevitably be referred by them to the League of Nations." Since the date on which the Supreme Council itself would convene was uncertain, there was the "danger of prolonged delay." Under these circumstances his government "strongly advised" that the Aland question be referred to the League as quickly as possible. Inasmuch as the Swedish government felt that they had a strong case, it was recommended that Stockholm itself submit the Aland question to the League Council. If they did not someone else would "undoubtedly take the initiatory step." King George admitted Gustaf's "plea for urgency" but believed that the course his ministers suggested would be in the "end the most expeditious." [58] For Palmstierna the only gratifying part of this message was the admission that England on her own, not Sweden, might appeal the Aland question to the League if Stockholm failed to act. If this were done the situation would again be fluid, but with the added attraction that it would be London, not Stockholm, that appealed the issue to the League. In this way the government's prestige in the world at large and in Sweden especially would be unharmed and its position secure.

Information was not long in coming that the British on their own had decided to bring the Aland question to the attention of the League. On the following day Barclay was instructed by Lord Curzon to repudiate quickly and firmly Palmstierna's imputation that the British government was the "only power to stand aloof," while the French, Italian, and Japanese governments were favorably disposed to the Swedish contention that the Aland question be dealt with by the Supreme Council. This charge, which was completely unfounded, he had not been able to dislodge from the Swedish mind, in spite of his repeated explanations to King Gustaf and the Swedish minister in London, Count Wrangel. Curzon maintained that the British government had never objected to having the question raised at the Supreme

58. *DBrFP, 1919–1939,* 1st ser., *11,* 357.

Council. Indeed, he noted sarcastically, it had waited for the day "when it would be mooted by one of Sweden's numerous friends." Opportunities had been many, but they had not been taken advantage of in meetings of the Supreme Council at London, Paris, and at San Remo in Italy. Nor was there any reason to believe that, if there was a meeting of the Supreme Council at Spa, Belgium, in July, they would introduce the Aland question at that time. If they did, it was more than likely that there would be no time to discuss it and almost certain that it would be transferred to the League, whose intervention in a question like the Aland Islands was expressly covered by the League Covenant and could not be "indefinitely postponed."

Because of this he had consistently given the Swedish government the same advice: refer the matter to the League of Nations. Sweden's refusal to do so, and her friends' reluctance to raise it in some other form had brought matters to a head that was "fraught with danger to [the] peace." In fact, if quick action was not taken, it would render the whole situation "almost insoluble save by force."

Under these circumstances, Curzon continued, and in order to ascertain French views quoted by the Swedes as opposed to referring the Aland question to the League, he had informed the French Embassy in London that, if the Aland question was not referred to the world organization by Sweden, he thought that it would be his duty to refer the question under Article 11 of the Covenant. The reply of the French Prime Minister, Millerand, was one of approval. Therefore, the previous evening, June 16, Curzon had called Count Wrangel and informed the Swedish minister of Millerand's reply and of Britain's proposed appeal to the League. Wrangel, he informed Barclay, "did not exhibit any surprise," his only comment being that he would immediately inform Stockholm. This information Barclay was also to communicate to the Swedish government. Lord Curzon understood that when a reference of this type was made to the League, the Secretary-General invited both countries as quickly as possible to submit statements of their case, and an early meeting of the League Council was convened to consider the matter. By referring the question to the League he expected quicker and more effective action than would be obtained by waiting for a meeting of the Supreme Council, which was often postponed from day to day, or was unable to deal with the Aland question, even when it was held.[59]

Curzon's objections were immediately conveyed to Palmstierna by Barclay, who assured Curzon that in all conversations with King Gustaf and Palmstierna he also had repudiated the imputations on the attitude of the British government. During their conversation Palmstierna had disclosed to Barclay that he had already heard through Count Wrangel in London of Lord Curzon's decision to refer the Aland question to the League Council. He asked Barclay to inform Curzon that Sweden regretted that it could not withdraw its appeal from the Paris Peace Conference, but it had no objection to the British government's referring the whole question, including the arrest of the Alander leaders, to the League. His only recommendation was that the Swedish government found it "desirable, in [the] interests of peace and order on [the Aland] Islands," for London to suggest to the League Council "that they should demand Finnish restoration of [the] military *status quo ante* on [the] Islands." Palmstierna's other worry was about the arrested Alanders. He had heard that the preliminary judicial proceedings had been completed and that their case would soon be handed over to the Procurator General, at which point it would be more difficult to obtain their release, because of Finnish judicial procedure. His suggestion was that the British government might hint to Finland that it delay handing the case to the Procurator General. Barclay's closing observation was that Palmstierna appeared very relieved at the way events were moving and was "hopeful of a speedy solution as [a] result of [the] action" of the British government.[60]

Indeed, the Swedish Foreign Minister felt contented. He believed that the whole question had been resuscitated from the static state into which it had fallen, and events had forced the powers to consult with each other over the question. Their re-

59. Ibid., pp. 357–58. It was explained to Enckell in Paris on June 23 that Millerand had not wanted to oppose Curzon's proposal of referring the Aland question to the League, but neither had he wished to take the initiative. Enckell, *2*, 63.

60. *DBrFP, 1919–1939*, 1st ser., *11*, 358–59.

ferral of the matter—at least in Palmstierna's mind—to the League was a disavowal of the Finnish argument that the whole question was "an internal affair." If Sweden had submitted the question it would have been interpreted as a sign of weakness. Moreover, in the present situation Finland, because of the arrest of the Alanders, was appearing before the League in a less favorable light. Palmstierna's main preoccupation was to restore the military status quo ante and to get the arrested Alander leaders mentioned in Curzon's submission of the conflict to the League Council.[61] On both of these points Palmstierna would be disappointed. Curzon's referral of the dispute on June 19 to Sir Eric Drummond, the League's Secretary-General, avoided both questions. Instead he invoked the right conferred under Article 11 of the Covenant to bring to the Council's attention the Aland question, "as a matter affecting international relations, which unfortunately threatens to disturb the good understanding between nations upon which peace depends." [62] This appeal by Curzon caused Holsti to inquire of Kidston whether this meant that the British government "were convinced of [the] justice of [the] Swedish claim." The British minister assured him that Curzon "had

61. Palmstierna, *Dagjämning*, p. 90. That the issue of the arrested Alanders influenced the Swedish government, there is no doubt. On July 1, Count Wrangel called on Lord Hardinge and asked him whether the British government might find it possible "to give a hint to the Finnish Government to cease the prosecution" of the two arrested Alander leaders. Lord Hardinge replied that it appeared to him that the Swedish minister was proposing that the London government "should take a very serious step in interfering with [the] judicial and internal affairs of Finland." The Permanent Under-Secretary thought a distinction should be drawn between the arrest of the leaders and consideration of the Aland question by the League. The Swedish minister had to realize, Hardinge went on, that the British government disliked "interfering in the internal affairs of a foreign country," especially as in the present situation it might be imputed that the British government was "departing from an attitude of complete impartiality upon the question at issue." Therefore he held no hope of intervention on the part of the London government as requested by Wrangel. It would be a different matter, he added, if the League Council at their forthcoming meeting made the proposal to the Finnish government to delay the proceedings until a solution of the question had been found. *DBrFP, 1919–1939,* 1st ser., *11,* 374. As for the French, Enckell in Paris had been admonished as early as June 11 that Finland would gain nothing by making Sundblom and Björkman political martyrs, and Enckell cabled to Helsingfors in this sense. Enckell, *2,* 61–62.

62. League of Nations, Council, *Minutes of the Seventh Session of the Council of the League of Nations Held in London, July 9–12, 1920,* pp. 34–35.

acted in a spirit of absolute impartiality and without any preconceived ideas as to respective merits of conflicting claims." To his response Holsti made no further comment. It was Kidston's understanding that the Finns in their answer to the League were likely to invoke Articles 10 and 15 of the Covenant and especially paragraph 8 of the latter article.[63]

Palmstierna, of course, could not have been completely satisfied with Curzon's message to Sir Eric Drummond. The Foreign Secretary had in his message to the Secretary-General kept the question to be presented to the League narrow in scope rather than broad as desired by Palmstierna. But Curzon's decision to refer it to the world organization was in keeping with the British interpretation of the role that the League could play in world affairs. To London, the League was "a co-operative association of independent states" where nations could air their grievances.[64] It was looked upon by most British governments as another tool supplementing traditional diplomatic methods. In fact, Article 11 of the Covenant, which Lord Curzon had cited in his message to the Secretary-General, declared "any war or threat of war" in any part of the world to be "a matter of concern to the whole League." This declaration was an opening for the British, as in the Aland question, to interfere legally. It furnished her with a valuable basis "for using her mediatory and conciliatory influences whenever she wished to do so," two diplomatic tools that had by long practice and tradition come to distinguish British diplomacy.[65]

For the French, the decision by the British to refer the question to the League produced no hardship. In Paris, the League was looked upon as not so much a tool for mediation and conciliation as one to be used along with France's other postwar security arrangements as a protection against German aggression. Her interest in the League would lapse only if its initial attempt at mediation and conciliation in the Aland question failed and

63. Kidston (Helsingfors) to Curzon, No. 509, June 21, 1920 (File 1259 in FO/371/4069, PRO).

64. Alfred Zimmern, *The League of Nations and the Rule of Law, 1918–1935* (2d ed. rev. London, Macmillan, 1939), p. 346.

65. Arnold Wolfers, *Britain and France between Two Wars* (New York, Harcourt, Brace, 1940), pp. 321–25.

measures of a coercive nature were envisaged. For the French, the League's coercive machinery was to be used only against Germany.[66]

Since tension in the Baltic between Finland and Sweden over the Aland Islands was in the long run as detrimental to British as it was to French interests, both continued their endeavors but collectivized their actions through the League. Their influence over both Finland and Sweden on a bilateral basis had proved ineffective, and, because they were unwilling to impose a decision either on one side or the other, referral to the League, where the process of mediation and conciliation could continue, supplemented their diplomatic efforts. It helped to keep the parties apart and cool tempers, and it furnished valuable time during which some sort of a solution might be devised.

Thoughts in the League Secretariat and British Foreign Office

The realization that the Aland question would sooner or later be referred to the League of Nations moved the Secretariat to examine the whole subject on June 18, the day before Lord Curzon submitted the question to the world organization. According to a short memorandum written by Dr. Eelco Nicolaas van Kleffens of the Legal Section and read by its Director, Dr. Joost Adrian van Hamel, the recognition of Finland did not mean that the territory it claimed as Finnish had been recognized by the powers. Indeed, those powers which had been represented at the Paris Peace Conference had avoided giving a definite opinion on the matter. They had especially left unanswered the question of Finland's sovereignty over the Aland Islands. This question had been left for decision by bilateral negotiations between Finland and Sweden. Kleffens noted parenthetically that at the same time the powers had never declared that in the end they would not feel obliged to interfere in the Aland question themselves.

Thus, if Finland, after its admission to the League, became involved in a dispute with Sweden over the Aland Islands and invoked the "League's protection to preserve her territorial integrity against external aggression under Article 10 of the Covenant," the other party to the dispute would be able to question

66. Ibid., pp. 153–55.

Finland's claim to the island group. Indirectly, therefore, the League organ, which would have to deal with the problem, would be placed in the position of declaring "whether Finland has sovereignty over the Aland Islands or not." [67]

Four days later, on June 22, Donner was informed by Sir Eric Drummond of Lord Curzon's note invoking a meeting of the League Council on the Aland question. On the following day in Paris, Enckell called on Peretti de la Rocca, Director of the Political Department of the Quai d'Orsay, to ascertain the French position. Peretti's advice was that Helsingfors should allow the Aland question to run its course and that everything was working to Finland's advantage. He assured Enckell that as far as he was concerned he was on the side of justice, that is to say, completely on the Finnish side. In his report to Helsingfors, Enckell wrote that the League would probably handle the matter calmly, delaying the question to allow passions on both sides to cool. He thought that this was in the League's own interests, for it could make no decision which would provoke violent discontent and turn opinion against the League itself. Therefore, Finland had no reason to fear League intervention if it maintained its rights and avoided actions that provided material for sensational propaganda. Enckell did advise, however, that the government make arrangements to combat the Swedish press campaign, which had reached considerable proportions.[68]

On this same day, June 23, as Enckell conversed with Peretti de la Rocca, Donner in London called on the Secretary-General, Sir Eric Drummond. Donner, who was in a "perturbed frame of mind," thought that Curzon's action invoking a League meeting was "somewhat unfriendly towards Finland." Sir Eric assured the Finnish minister that this was not true, and that the British action was "solely in accordance with the terms of the Covenant." Furthermore, unless the Covenant was to be regarded as a useless instrument, the action of the British government was quite justified, and Drummond was sure that it was not inspired by any hostile feelings toward Finland. Donner explained to the Secre-

67. Recognition of the territory of Finland by E. N. van Kleffens, June 18, 1920 (Political 1920: 11/4639/468, LNA).

68. Enckell, 2, 63–64.

tary-General that he feared that Finland, in any hearing of the question by the League, would be at a disadvantage, since she was not a member of the organization as was Sweden. Sir Eric gave his formal assurances that the League Council would want full equality of treatment for the two countries, and that he would use any influence he had in this direction. He believed that, if questions of this character could not be dealt with in an impartial manner by the League Council, the organization as such would become, to his mind, "a harmful body, whose disappearance ought to take place."

The conversation then turned to a discussion of when and where the Council would meet. Drummond thought the Council would convene in London, Paris, or Brussels, and promised to inform Donner quickly when anything definite was decided. He also promised to inform him privately as to how the members of the Council would be represented.

At this point Donner asked for Sir Eric's advice on the attitude Finland should assume in this matter. Sir Eric responded that though this question put him in a "very awkward position," he was prepared to tell Donner personally that he thought it "would be a mistake" for his country "absolutely to refuse discussion" of the Aland question in the League Council, "on the ground that it was a purely domestic matter," and thus solely within Finnish competence. This claim, the Secretary-General noted, would of course be advanced by Finland, but it should be presented in such a manner that, if the League Council rejected it, "Finland would be ready for the question to be discussed and dealt with by the Council." [69]

To Curzon, however, on the previous day, Drummond had proposed that the League Council submit the question to arbitration.[70] After his interview with Donner ended he called a meeting of the Secretariat's section directors where he proffered this line of approach, but the reception it received was far from

69. Record of [a] Conversation by E[ric] D[rummond], June 23, 1920 (Political 1920: 11/5024/468, LNA).

70. An unsigned memorandum entitled "Procedure to be Adopted by the League" [June 30, 1920?] (File 1259 in FO/371/4069, PRO); Hardinge to Drummond, July 7, 1920 (Political 1920: 11/5526/468, LNA).

friendly. Before discussing what should be the League's approach in this difficult question, Sir Eric first disclosed that he had had discussions about the matter with both Finnish and Swedish representatives and repeated Donner's fears and his own assurances that Finland "would receive absolutely equal and impartial treatment" by the League Council. It was Drummond's own opinion that the best time to convene the Council would be in London on July 5, 6, or 7, provided Léon Bourgeois, the prior French president of the Council, would consent to come to the British capital. An alternative solution would be for a meeting in Brussels attended by the British Prime Minister, David Lloyd George, but he considered this alternative undesirable as it would make the Council meeting "appear a side-show" to the convening of the Supreme Council at Spa. It was agreed by all present that this was the proper approach, and that the Finns and Swedes would find Lord Balfour more acceptable than any other British representative.

Sir Eric then turned the conversation to the problem of how the Aland question should be handled by the League. His own thoughts, as he had written to Lord Curzon the previous day, were that the League Council should propose to Finland and Sweden that they accept a commission to inquire on the question, the parties promising in advance to accept the commission's findings—a polite way of suggesting compulsory arbitration. He thought the commission's members would then be selected from nationals of three impartial states, for example, Czechoslovakia, Spain, and Switzerland. If, however, Stockholm and Helsingfors refused to accept this solution, the League Council as an alternative should propose that the commission of inquiry report at a later date with recommendations to the League Council. Drummond observed that, in either instance, "the Commission would endeavour to settle the matter by mediation, and to secure agreement between the parties."

His first proposal was not to the liking of any of his colleagues. For one, Erik Colban, the Director of the Administrative and Minority Sections, did not think that Finland and Sweden were likely to accept it, unless the commission was given "very strict instructions" on matters like the military use of the island group.

Objections to the first plan were also voiced by Dr. van Hamel, the Director of the Legal Section. He thought it meant that the League would have to impose a "complete system of Government" including treaties on the protection of minorities, etc. It was Dr. van Hamel's opinion that it would be far better to attempt to secure an agreement by means of mediation between Finland and Sweden as proposed in the Secretary-General's second plan. As he was aware of the political import of the question, he did not believe the dispute would be "settled by reference to existing principles of law, or even of justice." To Dr. van Hamel it was not, strictly speaking, either a juridical or an arbitral dispute. Colban reiterated his initial reaction that both parties would refuse the Secretary-General's first plan. Because of this he thought it would be far better merely to appoint a commission of inquiry with instructions to report to the League Council, leaving the Council to devise a settlement at a later meeting. Under threat of a Council decision Colban continued, the Finns and the Swedes might reach an agreement. In the end, this is exactly what happened.

Sir Eric, in spite of the reservations and comments of his colleagues, still maintained his original position: "that it would be wiser to endeavour to induce the parties to accept a Commission whose decisions should be binding." However, he was willing to admit that, if difficulties presented themselves in initiating this plan, the second plan could still be executed "without prejudicing its chances of success." [71] Regardless of his concluding observations, this meeting caused the Secretary-General to reconsider what he had written Lord Curzon the previous day. In a new message penned to Curzon that same day, June 23, he proposed instead that the League Council appoint from three impartial countries a commission of inquiry which would proceed to the islands.[72]

This proposition was viewed in the British Foreign Office as

71. Minutes of a directors' meeting, June 23, 1920 (General 1920: 40/5039/854, LNA).

72. An unsigned memorandum entitled "Procedure to be Adopted by the League" [June 30, 1920?] (File 1259 in FO/371/4069, PRO); Hardinge to Drummond, July 7, 1920 (Political 1920: 11/5526/468, LNA).

a "reasonable and unobjectionable course," and it was suggested that the British representative at the League Council be given instructions to support it. It was considered far wiser than the suggestion Drummond had originally offered to Lord Curzon, since it did not require prior Finnish or Swedish consent to the commission's findings, something neither party would have agreed to.

It was therefore suggested that Lord Balfour be instructed to advocate the dispatch to the island group of an impartial commission of inquiry whose report would be considered at a subsequent meeting of the League Council. The commission was to be given every facility by the parties. To ease tensions, the measures taken by the Finns against the Alanders were to be suspended, the arrested leaders allowed to return to the islands, and Finnish troops to be withdrawn. On the other hand, one of the things that the commission had to investigate was the charge of Swedish propaganda in the island group. If the Council consented to this approach, as seemed likely, the British government could await the findings of the commission. Under this arrangement the British government would not have to take a stand on the question until the disposition of the islands was actually discussed by the League Council, a discussion that might not have to take place "if as is to be hoped, the decision of the Commission of Enquiry is accepted by the disputants." [73] The feeling that Drummond's second plan—to dispatch an impartial commission of inquiry to the islands—was preferable to his first was conveyed by Lord Hardinge to the Secretary-General on July 7. The Permanent Under-Secretary observed that Finland and Sweden would "certainly expect a decision by the League itself." [74]

The same day this letter was written, the British Foreign Office's point of view was developed in greater detail in an unsigned memorandum which was circulated within the British government. According to this position paper, for that is what it essentially was, the Foreign Office reiterated—though it did not

73. An unsigned memorandum entitled "Procedure to be Adopted by the League" [June 30, 1920?] (File 1259 in FO/371/4069, PRO).

74. Hardinge to Drummond, July 7, 1920 (Political 1920: 11/5526/468, LNA).

identify it as Drummond's proposal—that the "best procedure to ensure an impartial and equitable solution of the question would be for the Council of the League to appoint a Commission to proceed to the Islands in order to conduct an enquiry there and report to the Council the solution which it recommends." The commission's report then might be discussed at a later session of the League Council at which the Finns and Swedes would be present. The memorandum went on to suggest that the commission's members should be appointed from states in no way involved in the dispute. At the same time, from the Finnish and Swedish governments the "fullest facilities" were to be obtained for the conduct of the inquiry.

The memorandum then suggested that the League Council, to reduce tension, might request the Finnish government to suspend its judicial proceedings against the Alander leaders and allow them to return immediately to the island group, a procedure that Lord Hardinge thought possible and one to which he had alluded in his conversation with Count Wrangel some days before. The memorandum repeated, however, the Foreign Office's view that no useful purpose would be served by attempting to obtain from the Finns and Swedes "their unconditional assent to the findings of the Commission, whatever they may be." To strengthen the commission's position it was advisable to stipulate unanimity in any report they might make and the semblance of any divergency of opinion among the commission members was to be carefully avoided. The Foreign Office was particularly interested in having the commission instructed to investigate closely Helsingfors' allegations that the Alanders' attitude was the result of Swedish propaganda. If this could be proven, Sweden's most powerful argument would collapse, and, though the memorandum did not say so, so would Sweden's case.

The memorandum then turned to Russia's interest in the islands, which it felt the League Council would not lose sight of. Because of the unsettled nature of Finno-Russian relations, the Foreign Office thought it may be considered necessary to add to the commission's recommendations some words anticipating Russian complaints that they had not been consulted in the matter, especially since the Russians had complained on June 28 that the question had been submitted to the League without their consent.

For the moment the author of the memorandum thought it unnecessary "to sketch the views of His Majesty's Government as to the proper solution of this difficult question." If the League Council decided to dispatch a commission of inquiry to make a report, any opinion expressed would be premature pending receipt of the commission's report. It was hoped that the commission's conclusions would be accepted by the parties, and in that case it would be unnecessary for the British government to develop its own views on the question.

However, there was one consideration which appeared to the Foreign Office to be of the greatest importance, and that was the demilitarization and, if possible, the neutralization of the island group. Naval or military forces, and fortifications or guns should be prohibited on the islands, and the archipelago should not be used as a naval or military base for offensive or defensive operations. It was suggested that the commission might be informed that the League Council considered this condition as absolutely necessary in any solution of the Aland question.[75]

In the meeting of the League Council that commenced two days after this memorandum was written these considerations were uppermost in the minds of the British delegation. But not so in Finnish minds. Their attitude, as Enckell and Donner explained to Drummond, was that while the military position of the island group was "admittedly an International question its Political Status was purely a domestic question and as such not within the competence of the Council." Sir Eric's Secretariat colleagues, on the other hand, maintained that the "whole Aland question was essentially one question" and the Council's task at the inception of the discussions was "to consider whether or not the whole question was of domestic or international concern." Once this problem was settled they could then handle and perhaps perma-

75. *DBrFP, 1919–1939,* 1st *ser., II,* 372–73. For the Russian note of June 28, 1920, complaining that the Aland question had been submitted to the League without its consent, see Jane Degras, ed., *Soviet Documents on Foreign Policy* (London, Oxford University Press, 1951), *I,* 190.

nently solve the problem of demilitarizing the islands. However, Colban warned that the Aland question "was extremely complicated." [76]

Since, in the Council debates of July 9–12, the Finnish attitude and position was of paramount importance, its objections to the Council's competence were for the moment successful in delaying the establishment of any commission of inquiry as envisaged by Drummond and the British Foreign Office. At the end of these July debates a commission was appointed, but its task was to investigate a problem entirely different from the one posed in the Foreign Office's memorandum.

76. Minutes of a directors' meeting, July 7, 1920 (General 1920: 40/5369/854, LNA).

CHAPTER 7

The League's Two Commissions

League Council Discussions in London

Word that Lord Balfour would be the British representative on the League Council moved Donner to contact the former Foreign Secretary to explain to him the Finnish position. This approach was rebuffed by Balfour on the grounds that he did not consider it proper to meet delegates from either of the two countries prior to the Council meeting. Thwarted in this direction, Donner then turned to Lord Bryce, who, though not a member of the government, was nevertheless a close friend of Balfour's and thus in a position to learn and hence reflect official British thinking on the Aland question. The reaction from Lord Bryce was encouraging, to say the least, for Bryce, the Finnish minister soon learned, was as partial to the Finnish cause as Donner himself. He succinctly pointed out to Donner that anyone, like himself, who had traveled by ship from Finland to Sweden—an allusion that the island group was a continuation of the Finnish mainland—could solve the Aland question in a matter of minutes. The Aland Islands, he commented, belonged to Finland. Period.

Continuing his soundings of British opinion, Donner, on July 7, two days before the League Council convened, called on Lord Northcliffe, press magnate and owner of *The Times* of London. Considering the fact that *The Times* often reflects official British opinion, a favorable reception here would have augured well for Finland. Donner was not to be disappointed. In his conversation with Lord Northcliffe, Donner observed that, with the League Council soon to convene, *The Times* was being offered an excellent opportunity editorially to warn it against making any precipitate decision which could in the future cause complications. To prove his point he showed how a rash decision by the League Council could cause unpleasant precedents for the British Empire in Ireland, the Channel Islands of Jersey and Guernsey, Gibraltar,

Malta, Cyprus, and in other overseas possessions. If the League Council were to decide that the desire of a population, though small in numbers, was enough justification to transfer a somewhat isolated area of one country to another, there would in the future be no end of surprises. It was, for obvious reasons, in Britain's interests to see to it that no such precedent was established by the League Council in the Aland question. Donner also noted that *The Times* had in the past been friendly to his country, as when it supported Finland against the Russification policy of the former Czarist government.

Lord Northcliffe's reply showed that Donner had made his point. *The Times,* Northcliffe agreed, had indeed always been Finland's friend in the past and wished to be so in the future. He also was of the opinion that an editorial should be published along the lines suggested by Donner. Northcliffe then summoned Hugh McGregor, the foreign news editor of *The Times,* after Donner stressed that the projected editorial should treat the Aland question exclusively from the British viewpoint, inasmuch as an editorial either for one side or the other would defeat the purpose for which the editorial was intended. After explaining to McGregor what Donner wanted, Northcliffe directed him to see to it that the projected editorial appeared in *The Times* of July 9, the day that the League Council actually convened. He then asked McGregor to take Donner to his office where the Finnish minister could explain to him in detail what he wanted the projected editorial to contain. When Donner and McGregor started to leave, Northcliffe repeated to them once again what he had stated previously: that they should remember that in the Aland question *The Times* was on Finland's side. The next night Donner phoned McGregor, who reassured him that the projected editorial was ready and would appear as scheduled the following day, July 9. But when Donner opened *The Times* on the morning of July 9 the agreed-upon editorial was missing.[1] By this point, however, the League Council had convened, and Donner had to curb his curiosity as to what had happened until the morning session of the Council had adjourned.

1. Ossian Donner, *Åtta år. Memoaranteckningar från åren 1918–1926* (Oxford, Eng., Oxford University Press, 1927), pp. 129–32.

This private meeting of the Council, the first meeting of many on the Aland question, was held in St. James' Palace. Lord Balfour's proposal that he be rapporteur and that France's Léon Bourgeois preside as president of the Council was quickly adopted. Also adopted was Bourgeois' proposal that the Swedish and Finnish representatives be allowed to attend the Council deliberations even though Finland was not a League member. His explanation was that, though the Finns had not yet been admitted to the League, they had nevertheless made an application for admission to the organization which would be dealt with when the League Assembly convened.

With these details out of the way, Branting read to the Council members the now-well-known views of the Swedish government on the matter of the Aland Islands. In reply, Enckell, who represented Finland along with Donner and Karl Gustaf Idman, the Finnish minister in Denmark, repeated the views of the Finnish government and observed that, if the Alanders' right to secede from Finland were granted, this same right might then be claimed by other Finns of Swedish origin—a hint that other people and minority groups might make the same demand. This warning was the same that Donner had made to Lord Northcliffe. Enckell noted that the recognition of Finland by Britain—and he could have added by other states—had been unconditional. This comment prompted Lord Balfour to ask Branting if Sweden's recognition had also been unconditional, whereupon the Council agreed that Branting would prepare for the Council a note on the interpretation Sweden wished to put on her recognition of Finland.

At this point Enckell introduced the argument that his country considered the Aland question "as one of domestic concern," noting that the Alanders had been given the largest measure of autonomy that any minority group had ever obtained anywhere in the world. For the moment this important objection was sidetracked when Branting observed that an Alander delegation was in London, and that the Council could ascertain the islanders' sentiments directly by asking them to testify. Bourgeois asked if the Finns had any objections to the Alander delegation's being heard. Enckell's evasive reply was that he was not sure how the delegation was elected and could express no opinion on the subject. He believed that it was a question for the Council to decide. Documentation presented by Branting covering this point increased the pressure. Enckell now objected that the Alanders represented but a small minority of the Swedish population of Finland. He considered himself a member of that Swedish population in Finland which protested strongly against the Alanders' actions. As far as Bourgeois and the Italian delegate, the Marchese Imperiali di Francavilla, were concerned, this was no answer to the question posed. Did Enckell agree or did he refuse to hear the Alanders? Bourgeois remarked that the Council did not wish to assume responsibility for deciding this matter without Finnish concurrence. Further pressure was applied by Lord Balfour, who maintained that, if the Council refused to hear the Alanders, world public opinion would feel that, though the Council had been convened to handle the question, it had refused to hear one of the parties most deeply involved. He thought that the Alanders would probably say nothing which the Council had not already heard, and to invite them to the Council "would in no way prejudice the result." He asked Enckell directly if the value of the Council decision, whether favorable or unfavorable, would not diminish if it refused to allow the Alanders to testify. Under this pressure the Finns could not maintain their resistance, and Donner, speaking for his colleagues, made it clear that they did not refuse permission to have the Alanders testify. But it was to be understood that the Alanders' views "were not conclusive." In fact, the Alanders' "views were unimportant as compared with the political importance of the Islands to Finland." With this essentially procedural question out of the way, the Council turned to a matter more substantive in nature.

Bourgeois began by asking if the Finnish and Swedish delegations had any observations to make on the application of the League Covenant to the question before the Council. Did they have any statement to submit on the legal aspect of the Aland question and the procedure that should be followed? Since the Finns had made no secret of their argument that the whole question was a matter of domestic concern, these comments by Bourgeois were an open and not-too-disguised invitation to the Finns to broach the question. Bourgeois went on to add that the Council was in a somewhat difficult position, for neither Finland nor Sweden had submitted statements or indicated the procedure which they wished to have followed in the question before the Council.

Branting's reply was that the attitude of his government was presented in the memorandum he had read at the beginning of the meeting. Sweden was asking for an immediate plebiscite in the Aland Islands to decide whether they should remain under Finland's sovereignty or whether they should be united with Sweden. His country maintained that the procedure of the Council in this question should be governed by Articles 15 and 17 of the Covenant, or in the end by Article 11. Sweden, however, was making no formal demand to the Council on this issue.

Enckell's explanation was that Finland had offered no opinion to the procedure the Council should follow, since she was not a member of the League. This dispute had been brought to the League by Great Britain. His country maintained that there was no danger of war, that the dispute between the Alanders and his government "was a question of internal politics," and that the desire of Sweden to intervene had in no way transformed the "question into one of an international character." Branting expressed the opinion that the question ceased to be internal as soon as Great Britain brought it to the notice of the world organization. Enckell insisted that there "was no danger of war," and that the "solution of the problem was still a matter of domestic concern." If it was a matter of interpreting the Covenant, he drew the Council's attention to paragraph 8 of Article 15: "If the dispute between the parties is claimed by one of them, and is found by the Council, to arise out of a matter which by international law is solely within the domestic jurisdiction of that party, the Council shall so report, and shall make no recommendation as to its settlement." Bourgeois observed that this meant that Finland was claiming that the Aland question was covered by paragraph 8 of Article 15 and was therefore denying the Council's competence in dealing with the question. Enckell agreed that this was a correct interpretation of his remarks and the Finnish position. On these words the meeting adjourned.[2]

On this same day a memorandum embodying the Finnish objection was drawn up and forwarded to the Council. According to the Finns, while they wished to respect the Council's authority, they could not in the present question admit that the dispute could be dealt with by the Council because of Britain's request. They denied that any war or threat of war existed, points covered under Article 11 of the Covenant, which had been invoked in Lord Curzon's note to Sir Eric Drummond. Indeed, the situation between the Alanders and the Finnish government was not an international crisis but one of "domestic nature." The annexationist interpretation of this situation by a neighboring state—Sweden was not mentioned directly by name—anxious to aggrandize itself at Finland's expense, could not transform the situation into an "international question." If world peace were disturbed over this question, it would not be Finland's fault. She only asked the maintenance of the status quo. The large measure of autonomy bestowed on the Alanders made it difficult for the Finns to understand how, in this question, there could be a threat of war. Nor could they understand how an internal minority question could, by the intervention of a third party, be turned into a question of international importance. As in the Council discussions earlier that day, they invoked paragraph 8 of Article 15 of the Covenant, stating that this "dispute arises out of a matter which by international law is solely within the domestic jurisdiction" of the Finnish state.[3]

Branting on this day was also busy communicating with the Council by way of the Secretary-General, Sir Eric Drummond. As had been requested he attempted to explain his country's point of view with regard to its recognition of Finland in early January of 1918. He noted that, though this "declaration was unconditional," it was obvious that a declaration of this nature only implied the "recognition of a lawful and constitutional [Finnish] Government, and [had] nothing whatever to do with

2. League of Nations, Council, *Minutes of the Seventh Session of the Council of the League of Nations Held in London, July 9–12, 1920,* pp. 1–9, 36–41.

3. Ibid., pp. 46–47.

the definition of the frontier lines of this State." Frontier conflicts between states were a common occurrence, and the Swedes found it difficult to understand how the unconditional recognition of a state could in the future protect it from frontier difficulties. Branting went on to explain that at the time Finland was unconditionally recognized, Sweden was interested in assisting Finland during a "particularly critical situation"—an allusion to the Bolshevik insurrection from within and attack from without—and at a time when she had not yet been recognized by any other state.

On the matter of how the question should be handled, he repeated what he had stated in the Council debate: that the Alanders be allowed immediately to decide by plebiscite whether the island group should remain under Finland's sovereignty or be united with Sweden. He also drew the Council's attention to the fact that the prosecution of the arrested Alander leaders and the garrisoning of Finnish troops in the islands, aside from the main question at issue, "must necessarily jeopardise the good feelings between [the] two neighbouring nations." [4]

The adjournment of the meeting allowed Donner to question McGregor at *The Times* about why the promised editorial had not appeared. McGregor's lame excuse was that there had been no room for it in that day's edition. Donner displayed surprise that an editorial Lord Northcliffe had personally wanted had been deleted because of space. He hoped that McGregor would see to it that the editorial would appear the following day, perhaps at the expense of something else. McGregor then promised that the editorial would appear the following day, Saturday, July 10. When it appeared, according to Donner, it "attracted great attention." [5] That the editorial was friendly to Finland and subtle in its attack of the Swedish position was obvious to all. It noted that the Aland Islands were really a continuation of the granite reef which bordered Finland's southwest coast. To undercut the Alanders' position, it inferred that their desire for union with Sweden was the result of the anarchy that had gripped the islands

4. Ibid., pp. 48–51; League of Nations, *Official Journal,* spec. suppl. no. 1 (Aug. 1920), pp. 65–66.

5. Donner, pp. 132–33.

following the Russian Revolution and the excesses of the Russian garrison and the Finnish Communists. Because the Aland question was complex it expressed the hope that the League Council would "come to no hasty decision," especially since it was the world organization's first case in no way a direct outgrowth of the Versailles Treaty. The Council had to consider not only the present situation "but the permanent interests of all concerned." It cautioned that these interests were "much wider than those of the Aaland islanders themselves." To present the Finns in the best light possible it observed that the Alanders had been given a wide measure of autonomy and reminded its readers that President Wilson himself had stated that there were "obvious limits to the right of self-determination." Finland was worried that the islands under Swedish control might again be fortified. It was the duty of those states who had given Finland her independence—a clear hint to the British and the French—to see "that this independence shall not be menaced, even theoretically, by any territorial adjustment they may make or sanction." This was one of the difficulties, *The Times* concluded, that the League Council had to "solve in a broad spirit." [6]

To Donner, McGregor's explanation of the delay in publishing the promised editorial was unsatisfactory. Lord Northcliffe was known for his authoritative manner, and it appeared strange to the Finnish minister that an editorial Northcliffe had ordered had been omitted for a lack of space and, of course, contrary to his orders. Donner decided to investigate. He soon ascertained that after his visit to *The Times* offices on July 7, Lord Northcliffe had been worried about what would be the Foreign Office's reaction to the contemplated editorial. He therefore decided to find out from his younger brother, Cecil Harmsworth, the Parliamentary Under-Secretary of State for Foreign Affairs. Though the inquiries made showed the government to be well disposed toward the promised editorial, the delay incurred made it too late for the July 9 edition of *The Times*. That the editorial had made an impact was evident almost immediately. At a luncheon given by the British government for the League Council and the Finnish and Swedish delegations following the Council's

6. *The Times* (London), July 10, 1920, p. 13.

morning session of July 10, Lord Robert Cecil, Chairman of the League of Nations Union, asked Donner if he had read that day's editorial in *The Times* dealing with the Aland question. It was, Lord Cecil observed, an editorial worth great consideration.[7]

During that morning session of the League Council, the impression was strong that the sympathies of the Council were with Finland. The first to be heard from during the Council's second day of private discussion were the Alander delegates, who repeated their desire for union with Sweden. They denied, when questioned by Branting, that their wish to separate from Finland had been due to Swedish propaganda. When the Alanders left, Bourgeois drew to the attention of his colleagues the Finnish note expanding on their argument that the Aland question was one of a domestic nature, as well as the two letters from Branting explaining Sweden's recognition of Finland and suggesting the way the question should be handled by the Council. Finally, he produced a memorandum presented by the Secretary-General concerning the procedure to be followed by the League Council in the present question. After all this, Bourgeois asked his colleagues "whether the sovereign rights of Finland were in question."

Branting argued that Finland's right to exercise her sovereignty could not be questioned, but he insisted that Finland's action in the Aland question was of a "character likely to disturb the good understanding between the two countries." Bourgeois asked whether Finland, in coming to the Council to explain her position, had only intended to decline the Council's competence, or whether Finland considered the Council competent to examine the question in the "interests of peace." For the purpose of soliciting and setting the stage for a Finnish answer a more perfect question could not have been posed. Enckell's response was that his country in its negotiations with Sweden had insisted that the actions of the Finnish government in the island group "were questions of internal policy," and hence Sweden had no right to interfere. He had in the meantime been instructed by his government to assume the same position before the League Council,

7. Donner, pp. 133–34.

to wit, "that the dispute between the Islanders and the Government of Finland was a question of internal policy."

Bourgeois, in reply, read to the Council the third paragraph of the Secretary-General's memorandum. This paragraph contended that whether the decision on the Finnish claim of domestic jurisdiction was negative or positive, it nevertheless was the duty of the Council, under paragraph 3 of Article 15 of the Covenant, to endeavor to bring about a friendly settlement of the dispute between Finland and Sweden. He reminded Enckell that Finland had been admitted to the Council on the same footing as any member of the world organization. Bourgeois drew attention to paragraph 4 of Article 15 of the Covenant, which stipulated that if the Council was unsuccessful in an endeavor it could publish a report on the facts of the dispute with any recommendations that it thought just and proper. The question, the French representative noted, had been submitted by Great Britain, but could the Council adjourn "without having suggested a solution"? Enckell retorted that the Council could in no way interfere with the judicial process now unfolding in Finland involving the arrested Alander leaders. He raised two other points. The first, over who had sovereignty over the islands, had been settled by the recognition of Finland as an independent state. The second was the strategic and military question of the islands, which had been suspended because of doubts whether the 1856 treaty demilitarizing them was still operative. He thought that the Council might call for an agreement on the islands' military and strategic status, but this question in no way involved the problem of who had sovereignty over the island group.

For the moment Bourgeois asked the Council to reserve discussion on these points on which there was no agreement, and to examine the question of the 1856 treaty which had been raised by Enckell. He asked whether the 1856 treaty was still operative. If the treaty was still operative, had it been respected? Enckell responded "Yes" to the second question, pointing out that the Russian fortifications constructed during the war had been demolished by a commission under Swedish control. The situation in the islands was therefore in conformity with the requirements of the 1856 treaty. Branting noted that this had occurred only because of Swedish insistence. In answer to a question posed by Bourgeois, Enckell observed that the stationing of troops on the islands—which was what Finland was doing at that very moment—was not contrary to the 1856 treaty. Since no one raised any objection to this interpretation of the 1856 treaty, Branting included, Bourgeois remarked that both Finland and Sweden considered the 1856 treaty operative, and that Sweden did not consider the dispatch of Finnish troops to the islands as contrary to the treaty.

The discussion then reverted to the Finnish objection that there was no threat to the peace. Bourgeois recalled that in any dispute, regardless of the sovereign acts executed by a state within its borders, the League Council might, where these acts caused agitation in a neighboring country, "consider whether it was not bound to intervene in the interests of peace, basing its intervention not on the ground of right but on that of the general duty of the League to secure the peace of the world." He asked if it was reasonable to fear that the dispute would continue, and that the passions aroused in both countries by the Alanders' actions would be a cause of tension between the two countries.

Branting replied that his government and Swedish public opinion wished to maintain the peace, but it was necessary to assuage the feelings raised in Sweden and to give satisfaction to what everyone there, regardless of party affiliation, "considered fair and reasonable." If the tension was prolonged, he thought that "unfortunate incidents were bound to occur." His appeal therefore was for the Council not to suspend the question. Enckell denied that there was any danger to the peace. On the contrary, the attitude of the Swedish government toward the Alanders' claims was connected with the difficulties that now faced the Council. The autonomy bestowed by his government on the island group was meant to satisfy the Alanders. He explained that the Alander leaders had been arrested, because it had been rumored that, if the Finnish government failed to intervene, the Alanders "would convoke a national assembly to proclaim the separation of the Islands from Finland, and would appeal for the support of the Swedish Government."

Branting replied that Enckell was "unduly optimistic" in believing that there was no danger to the peace. He maintained that his government had in its actions with the Alanders confined itself to expressions of sympathy and to bringing the Aland question to the Paris Peace Conference. The movement originated with the desires of the islanders. It was impossible to deny that the Alanders desired union with Sweden, and this situation would continue in spite of the autonomy granted them by the Finnish government. At this point Enckell explained to the Council the autonomy granted by his government to the Alanders. Queried by Lord Balfour, Branting replied that even if the autonomy law were further enlarged, the Alanders would not accept this as a solution of the question.

The discussion then turned to a consideration of Russian interests in the island group. Enckell explained that his government held that the Aland archipelago was a part of the autonomous Finland which had proclaimed its independence in late 1917. The recognition of Finland by Russia and by other states implied the recognition of this territorial position. Indeed, the Russian government had not denied that the islands formed a part of his country before the separatist movement had arisen in the archipelago and before Sweden had shown interest in the matter and presented it to the Paris Peace Conference. Paul Mantoux, Director of the Political Section of the League Secretariat, then read to the Council two messages of the Russian government, the first dated October 3, 1919, and the second dated July 1, 1920. The October message denied the Peace Conference's right to intervene in the Aland question. It observed that there was no treaty between Russia and Finland fixing the latter's borders, and in the absence of such a treaty the islands could not be transferred to Sweden without Russia's consent. Because of the geographic location of the islands Russian interests "were intimately bound with their disposal" and therefore the Russian government could not recognize any agreement disposing of the islands made without its consent. The July message was in large measure a repetition of the October one. After further exchanges among Lord Balfour, Bourgeois, and Enckell, the Finnish representative concluded the meeting by assuring the Council that his country was ready to agree to the military neutralization of the islands.[8]

The discussion continued at a private meeting of the Council late that afternoon. Branting began the proceedings by reading a statement protesting the Finnish contention that the Council was not competent to handle the Aland question. The situation, he maintained, was critical, and if the Finns persisted in their attitude and failed to withdraw their troops from the Aland Islands "a conflict was likely to arise." Lord Balfour remarked that Branting's statement brought to the fore the most difficult problem with which the Council had to deal, namely, whether the Aland question was one of "domestic jurisdiction" and hence excluded from the League's competence. Branting retorted that even if it were an internal question, "it had an external repercussion which brought it within the competence of the League." The League's duty was to conciliate all disputes threatening the peace but to refrain under the Covenant from interfering in the internal questions of a state. This was an unusual situation.

To handle this matter the Council proposed to establish a commission of jurists to advise them on the Finnish contention that this question was one of "domestic jurisdiction." Since the Permanent Court of International Justice had not yet been established, the Council would have to appoint a special commission to deal with this question. Inasmuch as this procedure would entail some delay, the Council was apprehensive because of Branting's words, and they hoped that both countries would try to "smooth down matters and calm the populations concerned." Their feelings on this matter were directed to both delegations. The Council regretted that this procedure would entail a delay, but they thought it essential to gain from competent authorities an opinion on the Finnish objection that this was a question of "domestic jurisdiction." If they found that it was, the League could not then be liable for any evils that might develop. It was also proposed that the Commission of Jurists be asked to advise on the exact status of the 1856 treaty and the 1908 convention dealing with the Baltic. It was understood that by referring the question to the Commission of Jurists no formal begin-

8. League of Nations, Council, *Minutes of the Seventh Session of the Council of the League of Nations Held in London, July 9–12, 1920,* pp. 10–19, 52–55.

ning of a process had begun under Article 15 of the Covenant. Summing up, Bourgeois noted that both parties accepted the Commission of Jurists. The jurists would be chosen by the Council from among men of the "highest impartiality." The Commission, composed of three members, would be nominated by the President of the Council. These conclusions by the Council were then adopted.[9]

The last meeting on the Aland question at this seventh session of the League Council took place on Monday, July 12. It was the first public meeting on the matter. Lord Balfour began the meeting by reading his report summarizing the Council's deliberations. After Branting and Enckell promised in behalf of their governments to maintain the peace, the Council's resolution was adopted establishing a commission of three international jurists to give an advisory opinion to the Council as quickly as possible on the questions: First, does the Swedish case, as presented to the League Council on the Aland question, arise out of a matter which by international law was solely within Finland's jurisdiction, under the meaning of paragraph 8 of Article 15 of the Covenant? Second, what was the present state of the international obligations, i.e. the 1856 treaty and the 1908 convention, regarding the demilitarization of the Aland Islands? [10]

The impression gained by the Finns during these London meetings and in subsequent confidential discussions was that the League Council was favorably disposed toward them. The League Council, it appeared, wished to avoid its responsibility and Swedish criticism in this matter and believed that it could do so by submitting the question of the Council's competence to a commission of jurists. The Greek representative, Demetrios Caclamanos, had frankly admitted this. Indeed, Joost Adrian van Hamel, the Director of the Legal Section of the League Secretariat, later divulged to Donner that Lord Balfour had hoped, when the question was submitted to the Commission of Jurists, that they would reach the conclusion that the Council was not

9. Ibid., pp. 22–25, 56–57; League of Nations, *Official Journal,* spec. suppl. no. 1 (Aug. 1920), pp. 66–67.

10. League of Nations, Council, *Minutes of the Seventh Session of the Council of the League of Nations Held in London, July 9–12, 1920,* pp. 30–31, 58–63.

competent to treat the Aland question on the grounds that it was an internal Finnish problem. The Council could then have easily unshouldered the burden by declaring its noncompetence, an action for which they could never have been criticized. At any rate, the London meetings put the Finnish representatives in an optimistic and generous frame of mind, and their reports to Helsingfors—particularly those of Donner and Idman—reflected this, especially in their compliments of Enckell's defense of the Finnish position.[11] Even if the tactic of submitting the question of the Council's competence to a commission of jurists failed as far as the Finns were concerned, it nevertheless further delayed consideration of the Aland question, allowing tempers and passions to cool, and was thus to Finland's advantage.

The Commission of Jurists

It was the Secretary-General's opinion that the decision reached by the Council on the question "was better than could have been hoped." Developing Russo-Polish relations seemed to be moving toward a general conference on Baltic questions, as well as on Russian and German boundary problems. If this were to occur, the question of the status of the Aland archipelago was sure to arise, and if the Council had definitely committed itself on the matter, there would have been difficulties in broaching the question with Russia as a party to the discussions. Therefore he thought a commission of jurists had "turned out to be a wise plan," and Drummond "rather hoped that the Commission's Report would not come in too soon." [12]

The problem that now posed itself to the League Council was the composition of the Commission of Jurists that had been agreed upon. In reporting to the State Department from London,

11. Donner, pp. 134–35, 140; Carl Enckell, *Politiska minnen* (Helsingfors, Söderström, 1956), 2, 67–68. Dr. van Hamel's information to Donner about Lord Balfour's attitude was on firm ground. A few days before the League Council convened, Balfour had admitted to Lord Hardinge that he was "under the impression that the Finns [were] in a strong position under Article 10 of the Covenant" and that the League of Nations had "no grounds for interference in an internal affair affecting the boundaries of Finland." Minute by [Lord] H[ardinge], July 7, 1920? (File 1259 in FO/371/4069, PRO). On this point see also Enckell, 2, 80.

12. Minutes of a directors' meeting, July 14, 1920 (General 1920: 40/5547/854, LNA).

Ambassador John W. Davis pointed out that recourse to the Commission was necessitated by the fact that the Permanent Court of International Justice was not yet established. He then disclosed that he had been asked whether he "would consent to act as one of the members of this Commission." Davis had replied that this depended on his government's permission. He noted that two eminent authorities in the field of international law, the Swiss, Max Huber, and the Dutchman, Antonius Struycken, were being considered for appointments to the Commission. Though Davis' own desire was not to serve unless there were some good reasons to the contrary, he thought that "it would be helpful if America could be represented on this Commission by some person of repute not in Government service." [13]

As he received no reply, Davis again contacted Washington a week later on July 21. He assumed that Washington's silence denoted that the State Department did not want him to sit on the Aland Commission, and he had accordingly rejected the invitation that had been proffered. The Finns and Swedes, he reported, were "pressing [the] League to appoint [a] commission without delay," and he thought that "unofficial American participation would be helpful to [the] cause of [the] League with American [public] opinion." [14] President Wilson, Davis was informed that same day, deferred to his desire not to serve on the Aland Commission. He proposed instead the veteran diplomat Henry White, former member of the American peace delegation at Paris, and Davis was instructed to convey to the League Council the President's suggested choice.[15] American participation, at least during this phase of the Aland question, was to go no further, for Davis immediately informed the State Department on the following day, July 22, that White had informed him that if he were selected for the Aland Commission he would be unable to serve.[16]

On July 30, in San Sebastian, at the next session of the League Council, its eighth, it was announced that Max Huber and An-

13. *PRFRUS, 1920, 1,* 32–33.
14. Ibid., p. 33.
15. Ibid.
16. Ibid.

tonius Struycken had been appointed to the Commission of Jurists along with Professor Ferdinand Larnaude, Dean of the Faculty of Law at Paris, who was to preside as president, while Georges Kaeckenbeeck, of the Legal Section of the League Secretariat, was selected as the Commission's secretary.[17] The Commission held its first meeting in Paris on August 3 and completed its task on September 5. At the invitation of the Commission, both the Finns and the Swedes tendered their views upon the questions submitted by the Council.

The Finnish case was initially presented to the Commission by Enckell on July 23. It was essentially a restatement of Finland's position.[18] Sweden's case was presented to the Commission of Jurists several days later by Count Wrangel. Wisely Wrangel based his case, more so than did Enckell in that which he offered for Finland, on legal arguments, and dwelt in particular upon the nature, scope, and purpose of the League Covenant. Since the Finnish case rested largely on the argument that paragraph 8 of Article 15 applied, and therefore the Aland question was an internal matter, Wrangel maintained that the provisions of paragraph 8 of Article 15 were "quite vague" and could in many cases give rise to an uncertain interpretation. It was known, for example, that paragraph 8 did not appear in the draft covenant drawn up by the Paris Peace Conference in February of 1919. Indeed, the motives which had caused its inclusion in the final draft of the Covenant were not very clear, and it appeared that reasons totally different in nature from those which interested the Commission had dictated its insertion into the Covenant. The demand for greater autonomy within a state or the demand of a particular area of a state to break away and become totally independent were matters that were perhaps covered by the Finnish argument. In the Aland question, however, another state, i.e. Sweden, desired a modification of the border, to which Finland objected. This was a dispute between two states which was covered by Article 15. Clearly the League of Nations, in order to

17. League of Nations, Council, *Minutes of the Eighth Session of the Council of the League of Nations Held in San Sebastian, July 30–August 5,* 1920, pp. 6–7, 92–93.

18. Finland, Ministeriet för Utrikesärendena, *La question des îles d'Aland (Octobre 1920)* (Helsingfors, Imprimerie du Gouvernement, 1920), pp. 23–30.

fulfill its mission of keeping peace and good relations between nations, could not relinquish its right to intervene in order to settle such a dispute.

Turning to the argument that Article 10 of the Covenant had perpetually stabilized all borders, and thus also the borders of Finland, Wrangel observed that this article really aimed at the prevention of territorial conquests and did not exclude the possibility of border rectifications that circumstances might require under the organs of the new world organization. To prove his point, he quoted the British commentary on the League Covenant, which stated that Article 10 had to be read in conjunction with Articles 11 and 19, which made it obvious that the League Covenant was not "intended to stamp the new territorial settlement as sacred and unalterable for all times, but, on the contrary, to provide machinery for the progressive regulation of international affairs in accordance with the needs of the future." It was the absence of such machinery, the British commentary recalled, and the survival of outdated treaties that had led to countless quarrels in the past. Thus these articles were a new step in international relations which would do away with, as far as possible, one of the main causes of war in the past. Count Wrangel also cited Lord Robert Cecil, who, as a member of the British delegation at Paris, had had a most important role in drafting the Covenant. According to Lord Cecil at a speech given in London in mid-June of 1919, Article 10 merely protected League members from external aggression directed against their territorial integrity. It did not mean that frontiers could not be changed. Indeed, Cecil believed that one of the most frequent causes of international disputes and wars was the permanent freezing of state frontiers through treaties. He believed that the raison d'être of the Covenant was to avoid resort to force when a change of frontiers was thought necessary and to bring about settlement of the matter by discussion and debate. Provisions similar in nature, Wrangel added, had been included in the draft covenants tendered by the governments of a number of countries, including his own, as well as Switzerland and Holland.

It was evident, therefore, from Articles 11 and 19 that, at the time the Covenant was drafted, the possibility of League intervention in settling border questions between neighboring states was envisaged. By giving to any member of the League under Article 11 the right to call to the organization's attention any situation likely to disturb interstate relations, it envisaged disputes similar to the Aland question. It was also obvious that the League's intervention was not to be limited simply to urging states in a dispute to settle their differences, but that it could bring about, if need be, a definitive settlement of the problem. Continuing, Wrangel noted that Article 19 permitted the examination of those "international conditions whose continuance might endanger the peace of the world." Here again it seemed manifest that League intervention should be coercive in nature, and if this were not the case the organization would lose any authority it had in such questions. It appeared illogical that, in a border dispute brought to the League Council under Article 15, one of the parties to the dispute could paralyze Council action by asserting that the question was purely a domestic matter. This objection was all the more inadmissible since the Council had been entrusted with the question under Articles 11 and 15. In such a case the League Council must neither refuse to examine the matter nor limit itself merely to mediation. The latter procedure could never bring about the desired settlement, especially in a question as delicate as the Aland one.

At this point Wrangel turned to the actions and fears of the Alanders. Their desire for union with Sweden, he maintained, was no moment's fancy. It sprang from their fear of being denationalized by Finnish immigration to the islands. This fear of the Alanders appeared justified, since mainland experience demonstrated the propensity of the Finns to expand at the expense of the Swedes. If the League Council were unable to settle this question, Wrangel warned, it would lead to a crisis which might become critical due to an incident for which neither state could be held responsible. Neither the Swedish government nor the Swedish people entertained any idea of annexing the islands, which is what the Finns had charged in the Council discussions. But, like any civilized nation, it was impossible for them to remain indifferent to the fact that people of Swedish stock in a neighboring territory had manifested firmly and consistently their wish to be reunited with Sweden. To these legal and other generalizations, Wrangel now added the historical facts heard so often before and related the events which had occurred in the island group during and immediately after the war. It was felt that these would prove that Article 15, paragraph 8, did not apply in the case of the Aland Islands question.

As to the second question posed to the Commission, namely, the present status of the international obligations concerning the demilitarization of the Aland Islands, Wrangel again wisely leaned heavily on legal arguments buttressed by historical facts. Essentially his contention was that the convention of 1856 had not lost its applicability because of the World War which in the end included all of its signatory powers. Wrangel thought that the 1856 convention should be replaced by a "new and more precise agreement" to which his own country and Finland would be parties. His own country was favorably disposed to a complete neutralization of the islands, but he saw no reason to go into details on this question at the present time. Wrangel had finished his presentation of the Swedish case.[19]

Enckell's second presentation to the Commission of Jurists on August 10 was mostly taken up with supplying explanations of an historical nature concerning the presence of foreign troops on the island group during the last years of the war, a question that had been previously posed to him by the Commission.[20]

The Swedish reply was not long in coming, and it was delivered to the Commission by Count Ehrensvärd on the following day, August 11. The Swedish minister noted that the League Secretariat had sent to his government Enckell's memorandum, presented to the Commission on July 23. Though Sweden considered that it had already refuted all the essential arguments in this memorandum, it did not wish to allow the opportunity to pass of taking them up once again, point by point. At the same time it hoped that the Alanders themselves would be allowed to appear before the Commission and comment on the Finnish declarations,

19. Sweden, Utrikesdepartementet, *Ålandsfrågan inför Nationernas Förbund* (Stockholm, Norstedt & Söner, 1920), pp. 166–92.

20. Finland, Ministeriet för Utrikesärendena, *La question des îles d'Aland*, pp. 52–57.

especially on the question of the origins of the Alanders' desire for union with Sweden. Ehrensvärd then attempted to deal with all the points that the Finns had raised and especially with Sweden's recognition of Finland without reservations. Annexed to Ehrensvärd's memorandum was a twenty-two-point factual refutation of statements and evidence that Enckell had presented in his communications to the Jurists.[21] The Finnish and Swedish presentations had terminated.

By comparison, the Swedish arguments were far more legal in nature, an approach that could not help but impress a jurists' commission established to deal with legal questions. The report of the Jurists on September 5 was a complete vindication of the Swedish position. It concluded that the dispute between Finland and Sweden did not refer to a question which under international law was to be left to Finland's domestic jurisdiction. Because of this the League Council was therefore competent to make any recommendations it deemed "just and proper" under Article 15, paragraph 4, of the Covenant. As to the 1856 convention, the Commission decided that it was "still in force" and was instituted "in European interests." The convention, according to the Commission, made it possible for every interested state to insist upon the execution of its provisions, and it followed from this that its restrictions were also obligatory and binding upon any state in possession of the archipelago.

The Jurists had arrived at the first of these decisions in a most novel manner. The Commission believed that Article 15 paragraph 8 was an attempt to protect a state's domestic sovereignty, and rejected very early in its deliberations the belief that bringing a dispute to the League Council was sufficient to label it as an international problem and therefore subject to the League's jurisdiction. According to the Commission, a question either was international in nature or was under a state's domestic jurisdiction, "according to its intrinsic and special characteristics." It was therefore necessary to consider the "intrinsic and special characteristics" raised by the Finns and the Swedes over the Aland question in order to decide whether the question was international in scope and therefore within the jurisdiction of the League Council.

21. Sweden, Utrikesdepartementet, *Ålansfrågan*, pp. 194–232.

Turning first to an examination of the principle of self-determination, the Commission postulated that the right to dispose of national territory was essentially an attribute of state sovereignty. However, positive international law did not recognize the right of national groups, as such, to separate themselves from the state of which they were a part by the simple expression of a wish, any more than it recognized the right of other states to claim such a separation. A dispute of this nature between two states, under normal conditions, was a question which international law left entirely to the domestic jurisdiction of one of the states directly concerned. Any other solution would be an infringement of a state's sovereign rights and would produce difficulties and instability which was a denial of the very idea of the state, and would also place in danger the interests of the international community. All this, however, generally applied to a nation already definitively established as a sovereign state which was an independent member of the international community. But from the point of view of international and domestic law the metamorphosis of states, their formation, transformation, dismemberment resulting from wars, and revolutions, created "situations of fact which, to a large extent cannot be met by the application of the normal rules of positive [international] law." Thus the lack of territorial sovereignty, either because the state is not fully formed or because it is undergoing transformation or dissolution, produces an obscure and uncertain legal situation which will not crystallize until the developmental period is completed and a new situation in respect to territorial sovereignty is established. It was in this situation that the principle of self-determination came into play. Aspirations of certain sections of a nation, based on tradition or a common language, may come to the fore and produce effects which have to be taken into account in the interests of the internal and external peace of nations. Self-determination could be applied in a number of ways like the formation of an independent nation or the choice of joining one of two states. This principle, however, like that of the protection of minorities, had a common object—an assurance to some national group of the maintenance and development of its social, ethnic, and religious characteristics. At the same time, the Commission observed that geographical, economic, and other similar considerations might put obstacles in the way of the realization of self-determination. In that type of situation extensive concessions to the minority involved might be necessary and may even be dictated in the interests of peace.

Because of all this the Commission had to decide whether, from the standpoint of territorial sovereignty, the situation in the Aland archipelago in the independent Finnish state was "of a definite and normal character," or whether it was a "transitory and not fully developed situation." To answer this question the historical background "marking the development of the political and legal position" of Finland and of the Aland Islands had to be examined. In this investigation the Commission looked at the autonomy granted Finland and the Aland Islands by Czar Alexander I in 1809, the effects that the Russian Revolution had in Finland, diplomatic recognition extended to Finland by various countries after its proclamation of independence which the Jurists dismissed as having no value during wartime especially when given by belligerent powers, the internal situation in Finland and the anarchy following independence, especially the disorganization of political and social life which made it difficult to say exactly when Finland, "in the legal sense of the term, actually became a definitely constituted sovereign State," the resistance of the Alanders to the Russians in 1809 which ended with Finland's being made a part of the Russian empire before the Aland Islands were annexed to the empire, the purport of the Finnish declaration of independence, which the Jurists denied made it possible for Finland, at the very moment of its separation from Czarist Russia and thus "outside the domain of positive law [to] invoke the principle of this law in order to force upon a national group a political status which the latter refuses to accept." All these considerations, as well as the situation in the archipelago after the Russian Revolution, the attitude of the Alanders themselves, the attitudes of Sweden and Finland, the comparison of Finnish and Alander objectives, the former interested in independence, the latter in union with Sweden, and the military events in the island group in the winter of 1918, brought the Commission of Jurists to the conclusion that the position of the Aland Islands was "not yet clearly defined." This conclusion forced the Commission to decide—in line with its theory of "intrinsic and special characteristics"—that the question was international in scope and thus within the competence of the League Council, since it arose at a time when "Finland had not yet acquired the character of a definitely constituted State."

On the question of the 1856 convention, the Commission's decision was less novel. The Jurists noted that the 1856 convention and its attachment to the Treaty of Paris was in no way affected by the Baltic Declaration of April 23, 1908, signed by Germany, Denmark, Russia, and Sweden, which merely confirmed the territorial status quo of the contracting powers. Indeed, this declaration could in no way have affected the 1856 convention, since the signatory states were not the same—England and France were not parties to the 1908 declaration. As to the argument that the 1856 convention had been affected by the war, the Commission pointed out that the three signatories were allies during the 1914–19 period, and the Treaty of Paris could not be considered as having been abolished by the war, since most of the signatories to that treaty, including Russia, had not been at war with each other. Moreover, the Russian fortifications constructed on the islands during the war in no way affected the convention, regardless of the fact that no protests were lodged by England and France, the other signatories to the convention. It could not be admitted, the Jurists maintained, that "acts committed by one contracting party and tolerated by the others, though contrary to a convention, can result in the abolition of the convention; it would be still more inadmissible to allow a provision solemnly incorporated in a great European Treaty to be abolished by such acts." An examination of the political conditions during 1856 showed that the Aland convention had "in reality a much wider bearing." This was mirrored in the actions of all the powers during the Paris negotiations; Lord Clarendon's remarks in the House of Lords were cited to show that the convention was meant to be a rule of law for Europe in general and for the Baltic in particular.

Thus the admission that the 1856 convention had the "character of a settlement regulating European interests" made it obvious that such a settlement could not "be abolished or modified by the acts of one particular Power." Nor could it be abolished by agreements between some of the 1856 signatories. Russia was bound by the convention as long as she controlled the islands, and her recognition of Finland in no way relieved the latter of the same responsibility. Finland could not "escape from the obligations imposed upon it by such a settlement of European interests." As to Sweden, she could, like Russia, as an interested power "insist upon compliance with the provisions of this Treaty." This was something that Sweden had always done in the past anyway, and it was never questioned by the 1856 signatories. Possession of the islands by Sweden would of course reverse the obligation, and Finland as an interested power would be able to invoke this same right. All this had forced the Commission to its decision that the 1856 convention was still operative and that any interested state could insist on its compliance, with the state in possession of the archipelago also being bound.[22]

Enckell has subsequently complained that the Commission in great secrecy obtained information from the Swedes and Alanders which it never bothered to check with him. Whether this is the complaint of a rejected suppliant is hard to say. Considering the nature and composition of the Jurists' Commission and especially the men who composed it—men eminent in their chosen profession and with a world-wide reputation—it is difficult to accept this charge. Enckell has also charged that the Legal Section of the Secretariat did not pass on to the Commission materials which he had given it. If this is true it appears that the Finns neither officially nor unofficially lodged any protests which would have helped discredit the Commission, its report, and especially its decisions. Lastly, Enckell has charged that Kaeckenbeeck was influenced by his colleague in the Legal Section of the League Secretariat, Åke Hammarskjöld, the son of Sweden's wartime prime minister and the older brother of Dag Hammarskjöld, future Secretary-General of the United Nations.[23] It is hard to understand, however, how this could have in turn affected the Commission's decisions, since Kaeckenbeeck, as secretary of the Commission, had no vote.

22. League of Nations, *Official Journal,* spec. suppl. no. 3 (Oct. 1920), pp. 1–19. For a further discussion of the report, see Philip Marshall Brown, "The Aaland Islands Question," *The American Journal of International Law, 15* (1921), 268–72.

23. Enckell, *2,* 70, 73, 78.

In September, however, these points in no way monopolized the thoughts or the attention of the League Council scheduled to convene in Paris. The Commission's decision that the League Council was competent in the question of the Aland Islands gave the Council no choice and forced it to accept the unappetizing task of attempting to solve the Aland question. For the Council to have denied its competence after the Jurists' had publicly proclaimed it was absolutely out of the question.

League Council Discussions in Paris

That the news of the Jurists' report was received with joy by the Swedes[24] and with dismay by the Finns[25] goes without saying. In the Finnish delegation, Idman, the minister in Denmark, proposed that they should refuse to take part in any Council discussions on the matter by referring to the fact that the Jurists' report was founded on Swedish and Alander information which they had not been given the opportunity to refute. Enckell thought that from the tactical point of view this approach was inadvisable, since it would provoke a Finnish conflict with the League. In this he was supported by the government in Helsingfors.[26] To the delegations assembling at Paris, however, and especially to the British and French delegations, was posed the important question of how the Council was to proceed. An answer to this question was soon offered by the French. In an interview with Léon Bourgeois soon after his arrival in Paris, the new British representative, Herbert A. L. Fisher, former Oxford don and Minister of Education in the British Cabinet, discovered that in this question the French, like the British, wished to see the appointment of a Commission of Inquiry. The only divergence in approach was that Bourgeois wanted the Commission to make a "statut provisoire" granting the Aland Islands "temporary autonomy till the matter could be definitely settled with Russia." [27]

This same approach was still in the mind of the League's Secretary-General. About the middle of August, while the Com-

24. Erik Kule Palmstierna, *Dagjämning, 1920–1921; politiska dagboksanteckningar* (Stockholm, Tidens, 1954), pp. 121–23.

25. Donner, pp. 134–35; Enckell, *2*, 70–71.

26. Enckell, *2*, 72.

27. Diary entry, Sept. 16, 1920 (Fisher Papers).

mission of Jurists was still sitting, Drummond expressed to his associates—obviously aware that the Commission's report would be favorable to the Swedish thesis—that after the Jurists' report he thought that the League Council "would probably not do more than appoint a Committee to try and help on an amicable settlement of the difficulties between Sweden and Finland." [28] At the same time, however, the Russian aspect of this problem also weighed heavily on his mind. He admitted to the Spanish ambassador in Paris, José Martin Quiñones de Léon, who was also Spain's Council representative, that he was anxious for the Council to confine itself, in any discussion of the Jurists' report, to the "legal points involved in the Report, and not even discuss the political aspects of the question itself or even those arising out of the Report." He hardly thought that the question could be definitively settled until the situation in Russia was more stable. Russia, Drummond felt, still had a claim to the islands and, if not consulted, would challenge any decision arrived at. Consultation with Russia at present was of course impractical, but that might not be the case in the immediate future. He understood from Paul Mantoux, Director of the League's Political Section, that Quiñones de Léon entirely agreed to this approach, as did Bourgeois.[29] The Council discussions that followed and its decisions were largely governed by these prior agreements.

Thus this Paris session of the League Council was to spend little time on the question and most of that in a discussion of its legal aspects as previously agreed. At the first meeting, which was a private one, on the morning of September 16, Fisher listened, as he wrote in his diary, to a "tedious and irate" [30] Finn express his country's case. The "tedious and irate" Finn was, of course, Enckell, who observed that the Jurists' report contained "several incorrect statements of fact," which he then discussed at some length. The discussion went no further, and it was decided to resume examination of the question the following day

28. Minutes of a directors' meeting, Aug. 18, 1920 (General 1920: 40/6195/854, LNA).

29. Drummond to Quiñones de Léon, Aug. 28, 1920 (Political 1920: 11/6427/468, LNA). See also Mantoux to Drummond, Aug. 27, 1920 (Political 1920: 11/6427/468, LNA).

30. Diary entry, Sept. 16, 1920 (Fisher Papers).

after Enckell's memorandum had been distributed to the Council members.[31]

On the following day, however, Fisher held a private meeting with Bourgeois in which Kaeckenbeeck replied to the criticisms raised by Enckell. Then they discussed the report which Fisher was to make to the Council, and it was agreed that the report should state that the Council was competent to handle this question as claimed by the Jurists, and that it should name members of a commission of inquiry.[32]

Because of this meeting it was not until September 18, at another private session, that the question was again examined by the Council. As on the previous day, "preliminary discussions" took place between Fisher and Bourgeois at the latter's room.[33] The initial remarks between Branting and Ehrensvärd on one side and Enckell on the other reexamined the old arguments about the meaning to be attached to Sweden's unconditional recognition of Finland. When this ended Fisher read his report on the question and the resolution asserting the Council's competence which he had drawn up with Bourgeois the previous day. Bourgeois reminded both the Finns and the Swedes that, under Article 15 of the Covenant, Fisher's report and his resolution would be considered as adopted unanimously even without their concurrence. When no objections were raised, Fisher's report and resolution on the competence of the Council in the Aland question were adopted. At this point Fisher read the resolution also agreed on by Bourgeois the previous day as to what the Council's procedure in the Aland question should be. According to Fisher, the Commission of Inquiry was to "present to the Council the necessary factors on which it might base a recommendation for a settlement of the dispute." Were this resolution to be adopted, he hoped that both governments would do all they could to assist the Commission. No objections were raised and the resolution

31. League of Nations, Council, *Minutes of the Ninth Session of the Council of the League of Nations Held in Paris, September 16–20, 1920*, pp. 2–5. The full text of Enckell's preliminary observations on the report of the Jurists' Commission can be found in League of Nations, *Official Journal, 2* (Jan.–Feb. 1921), 66–75.

32. Diary entry, Sept. 17, 1920 (Fisher Papers).

33. Diary entry, Sept. 18, 1920 (Fisher Papers).

was adopted.[34] So far everything had gone according to plan. It appeared to Fisher that the Finns accepted these resolutions, much to everyone's "relief with a good grace." Branting thanked him, which Fisher thought was "wrong," and after that day's session discussed with him at some length the Finns' despotic behavior which he felt had to be quickly checked. "The Swedes," Fisher noted, "are clearly delighted with the report." [35]

On Monday, September 20, things did not go according to plan, thanks chiefly to the actions of Enckell. At this public meeting the activities and decisions of the previous Council meeting were reenacted. Fisher's report was read, as were his two resolutions, which were of course adopted. On the first resolution, however, dealing with the Council's competence, the Finns and the Swedes abstained, while the second, establishing the Commission of Inquiry, was adopted unanimously by the Council, the Finns and Swedes included.[36]

With this out of the way, Enckell requested the floor. Bourgeois hesitated. The Director of the Secretariat's Legal Section, Dr. van Hamel, to whom Enckell had confided his intentions before the meeting, approached Bourgeois and whispered to him that Enckell's speech would contain nothing dangerous.[37] This assurance was not completely correct. In the statement Enckell now read he observed that the Council had declared itself competent to examine the Aland question though the Finns and Swedes had abstained in the voting. He noted that according to the terms used by Bourgeois, the Council's President, and the rapporteur, Fisher, the Council's declaration did "not pre-judge in any way the fundamental question at issue." He declared that his government could not "accept any other interpretation" of Bourgeois' words than that the Council, in declaring itself competent, did not "intend to pre-judge in any way the statements contained in the Report of the Jurists," which he had contested

34. League of Nations, Council, *Minutes of the Ninth Session of the Council of the League of Nations Held in Paris, September 16–20, 1920,* pp. 16–19, 72–77. For the full text of Enckell's supplementary statement to the Council see League of Nations, *Official Journal, 2* (Jan.–Feb. 1921), 75–77.

35. Diary entry, Sept. 18, 1920 (Fisher Papers).

36. League of Nations, Council, *Minutes of the Ninth Session of the Council of the League of Nations Held in Paris, September 16–20, 1920,* pp. 30–31.

37. Enckell, 2, 73.

a number of times. His acquiescence in the procedure that the Council was about to undertake was therefore "accompanied by an express stipulation" that his government reserved to itself the right, in prosecuting the case, to uphold the position that it had maintained from the beginning, to wit, "that the legitimate interests of Finland are bound up with its right of sovereignty over the Aland Islands, and that consequently Finland alone is entitled to take a decision on the subject of a plebiscite."

When Enckell had finished Bourgeois asked Branting if he had any observations to make concerning Enckell's declaration. Branting's reply was that it had in no way modified the situation.[38] Bourgeois' own attitude, as well as that of certain Secretariat officials, appeared to be one of displeasure. According to Enckell's statement, unless a clear statement was forthcoming at that time, the Alanders would get the impression that the Council had approved of the Jurists' argument that the Alanders had by their separatist movement acquired rights which would be violated if the Finns now attempted to annul them.[39] Some days later Enckell received instructions from Helsingfors to confirm in writing the reservations that he had made. In the note which was drawn up on September 29, it was further declared that the Finnish government was "unable to consider at any time whatsoever a recommendation of the Council of the League of Nations, the direct or indirect result of which would be to deprive Finland of its right of sovereignty over the Aland Islands." [40] Drummond objected. Enckell replied that though this statement could be interpreted to mean that the Council could not ignore Finland's sovereignty over the island group, his country was convinced that the Council, after a complete and fair examination of the question, would come to respect Finland's sovereignty over the archipelago. The note, to Enckell, was an attempt to open the eyes of public opinion led astray by Sweden's propaganda compaign.[41] Finland, by Enckell's Council statement and its note of September 29, had thrown down the gauntlet. Unless a com-

38. League of Nations, Council, *Minutes of the Ninth Session of the Council of the League of Nations Held in Paris, September 16–20, 1920,* pp. 30–33.

39. Enckell, *2,* 74–75.

40. League of Nations, *Official Journal, 2* (Jan.–Feb. 1921), 78.

41. Enckell, *2,* 75–76.

promise could be devised recognizing her sovereignty over the islands, Finland was in a collision course with the League Council.

In a Foreign Office memorandum on the Aland question for the guidance of the British representative at the League Council, this problem was closely examined. The unknown author of this paper felt that there was little to be added to the Foreign Office's memorandum of July 7. However, in the light of recent developments it was thought that the League Council "would be well advised to explore most carefully the merits of some form of internationalisation of the islands under Finnish protection, guaranteed by the Allied Powers." He felt that there were three arguments for a compromise of this nature: one, it had become increasingly clear during the weeks that had passed that a solution of the question along these lines "would not be unacceptable to the more sober-minded and far-seeing elements both in Sweden and Aland." Though the Finns were "evidently determined not to lose all control over the islands," which became attached to the mainland when the surrounding waters froze in the winter, their attitude "would probably be considerably modified if a solution were proposed" which would save them from any future conflict with a resuscitated Russia and would simultaneously ensure for them "some semblance of control over the islands." Second, any Council decision unacceptable to either of the two countries "might well be attended by disastrous consequences," affording Russia an opportunity to press her claims on the area. Lastly, the fact that, though Russia was deeply concerned in the ultimate fate of the archipelago, she had not been consulted in the matter "would inevitably weaken the moral authority of the League in dealing with a refusal by either party to accept any decision taken by the League." [42]

In the end, the proposal tendered in this paper never came to fruition, but the obstinacy of the Finns in general (a trait that Sir William Tyrrell had warned about during the Peace Conference negotiations) and of Enckell in particular had clearly had its

42. An unsigned memorandum entitled "Memorandum of Foreign Office views, for the guidance of the British representative on the League of Nations, on the Aland question" [Nov. 3, 1920?] (File 62 in FO/371/5452, PRO).

effect on the British. Aside from Enckell's statement to the Council and the subsequent Finnish note, Holsti in Helsingfors was also doing his bit to make it clear to London that in this matter there was a united and inflexible Finnish attitude. Immediately after the Council session had ended, but before the dispatch of the Finnish note, he informed the British minister, Kidston, that his countrymen "were bitterly disappointed" that the Council had accepted the Jurists' report. Indeed, it had been hoped that Fisher would support the Finnish position. He thought that the whole procedure had been unfair. Though Finland had been requested to present the Finnish case, she was never given the opportunity to refute subsequent Swedish arguments. He noted that the text of the Jurists' report reached Helsingfors only on September 20, several days after it had been accepted by the League Council. Thus the opportunity had never been given to his government to instruct Enckell and the Finnish delegation at Paris on raising objections to the report. He feared that the new commission might repeat this procedure and give a decision without allowing Finland to refute the arguments advanced by Sweden. He believed that the new commission should examine the question by an on-the-spot investigation.[43]

Following Enckell's statement a note of caution was immediately voiced by Fisher on the matter of the new commission. In a statement to the press, he observed that, whatever the Council's decision would be after the Commission of Inquiry had reported, it would in no way be binding for the parties concerned. Finland would have complete freedom of action after the Council had made its decision. On his return to London on September 24 from the League Council meetings in Paris, Donner called on John D. Gregory, Head of the Northern Department of the Foreign Office, seeking confirmation of Fisher's remark to the press. He was assured by Gregory that it was correct. Gregory also noted that Kidston in Helsingfors had reported that the Finnish government was upset by the way the question had been handled at the recent Paris meetings of the League Council, but he felt there was no reason for fearing anything. His government was in

43. Kidston (Helsingfors) to Curzon, No. 607, Sept. 21, 1920 (File 1259 in FO/371/4070, PRO).

no position to make an official statement, but he confirmed to Donner that the League Council would under no condition make any proposal for changing the present situation unless it was acceptable to both sides. Somewhat similar assurances were given to Donner a week later by Dr. van Hamel of the League's Secretariat, namely, that the Council would make no proposal that was not acceptable to both sides. Because of this Dr. van Hamel regretted that the Finnish government had already approved the autonomy law for the Aland Islands. He thought that little could be added to it, but an autonomy law for the island group would have been a convenient starting point for a Council proposal on the question.[44]

And what was Fisher's attitude toward all this? He thought the whole question would be "very difficult," though he admitted to his old friend, the classicist Gilbert Murray, that progress had been made. It had been the first occasion in which the League Council had "actively interfered to prevent hostilities," while its intervention had "achieved a moratorium" in the Aland question.[45] As events were to develop, the moratorium was to last for about nine months.

The Commission of Inquiry

Establishing the membership of the Commission of Inquiry, because of the political nature of the Commission's proposed work, proved to be, unlike the task of choosing the Commission of Jurists, exceedingly difficult. France, Paul Mantoux informed Commander Dionizo Anzilotti, Under Secretary-General of the League, did not wish to be represented on this commission. Because of the sensitive nature of the Commission's work, this French desire to refrain from being enmeshed in it was understandable. Any decision that the Commission would arrive at was sure to alienate one side or the other in this dispute. For these same reasons Fisher had informed Bourgeois that England also would refuse to serve on the Commission. As substitutes Bourgeois was disposed to nominate a Belgian, a Swiss—here he was thinking of Professor William Rappard, Director of the

44. Donner, pp. 139–40.
45. Fisher to Murray, Sept. 21, 1920 (Fisher Papers).

League's Mandates Section—and an Italian.[46] In forwarding Mantoux's information to the Secretary-General it was proposed that Anzilotti go to Paris if Drummond thought it desirable for him to see Bourgeois while Major Anthony Buxton of the Secretariat was seeing Fisher.[47]

The day after this cable was sent, September 24, Mantoux again contacted the League Secretariat to inform them that Bourgeois was firm in his desire to avoid French and British representation on the Commission. However, since the previous day his thoughts on the problem had further crystallized, and it was his desire that the presidency of the Commission be in the hands of a Belgian, who would probably be Baron Eugène Beyens, Belgium's former Foreign Minister, with Italian and Swiss representation, Rappard to represent the latter.[48] On this same day Fisher, cabling to Bourgeois through Mantoux, reiterated that he and Lord Balfour were agreed that it was inadvisable to have English representation on the Commission. On the other hand, they asked Bourgeois if he would agree to substitute an eminent American in place of the Italian. It was Balfour's suggestion that Elihu Root, the former American Secretary of State, be considered, or the American ambassador in London, John W. Davis. They thought it "more important to secure a very prominent man even if some delay is necessitated." [49] In Drummond's opinion it was very important that the Commission's report "should carry the greatest possible weight." This could be ensured by appointing British and French representatives with excellent reputations as he had suggested. Of course he would agree to whatever proposals met Bourgeois' and Fisher's approval, but he hoped that the French objection would not be maintained.[50]

Fisher's proposal that an American be considered had its effect, and Bourgeois' reply was that he would contact the American ambassador in Paris. As for the other two members of the Com-

46. Mantoux (Paris) to Anzilotti, Sept. 23, 1920 (Political 1920: 11/7065/468, LNA).

47. Howard to Drummond, Sept. 23, 1920? (Political 1920: 11/7065/468, LNA).

48. Mantoux (Paris) to Walters, Sept. 24, 1920 (Political 1920: 11/7065/468, LNA).

49. Fisher (London) to Mantoux for Bourgeois, Sept. 24, 1920 (Political 1920: 11/7065/468, LNA).

50. Drummond to Howard, Sept. 24, 1920 (Political 1920: 11/7065/468, LNA).

mission, Bourgeois was still partial to Baron Beyens, but in the meantime, on the matter of Swiss representation, Felix Calonder, former President of the Swiss Republic, had been recommended to him by the Swiss minister in Paris as being more important than Rappard.[51] Meanwhile, any hopes that Drummond may have held that Bourgeois would consent to French representation, which would move the English also to be represented on the Commission, was squashed by Bourgeois himself. He insisted that the Commission should have neither British nor French representation for a number of reasons: Lord Curzon, for example, had brought the dispute to the attention of the League; France had furnished the president of the Commission of Jurists, Professor Larnaude; and both England and France were signatories of the 1856 convention.[52] However, Drummond was persistent. He was still of the opinion that a Commission composed of Britain's former wartime Prime Minister, Herbert Asquith, and France's former Colonial Minister, Étienne Clémentel, together with a Swiss—and here he agreed that Calonder would be a better choice than Rappard—"would make the best Commission." He feared that an American could not be appointed without a great delay because of the approaching American elections.[53] To press this type of arrangement Drummond on September 28 called on Lord Balfour. His reception was encouraging, for Balfour also attached "great importance to [the] appointment to [the] commission of men of wide reputation." Because of the practical difficulties of quickly getting a first-class American, Balfour was willing to take the matter up with the government and promised to contact Drummond accordingly.[54]

A few days later, on September 30, a Cabinet discussion of the question took place, but Drummond was rebuffed. The Cabinet consensus was that it would be better if Britain were "not

51. Mantoux (Paris) to Buxton, Sept. 27, 1920 (Political 1920: 11/7065/468, LNA).

52. Mantoux (Paris) to Drummond, Sept. 29, 1920 (Political 1920: 11/7152/468, LNA).

53. Minute by E[ric] D[rummond], Sept. 27, 1920 (Political 1920: 11/7065/468, LNA).

54. Drummond (London) to Denis, Sept. 28, 1920 (Political 1920: 11/7140/468, LNA).

mixed up in this high[ly] contentious matter." The responsibility that Great Britain had already "incurred by urging that the question should be referred to the League of Nations would be increased if a leading part on the proposed Commission was taken by a British representative." The Cabinet's view was that efforts should be made to acquire for the Commission the services of an American, and they "were not in favour of an English representative unless a French representative of equal distinction were also appointed." [55] In conveying this information to Drummond, Sir Maurice Hankey, the secretary to the Cabinet, pointed out that, if an American could not be found, the Cabinet's attitude was that Lord Buckmaster, the former Lord Chancellor, might be a more suitable British representative than Asquith.[56]

The decision that the British Cabinet desired an American, "even at [the] cost of some delay," was immediately communicated by Drummond to Bourgeois in Paris. The Secretary-General also explained that, if no American were available, London was willing to agree to a "distinguished British subject if [a] French citizen of equal distinction [were] allowed to serve." [57] To avoid this situation Bourgeois now began to search in earnest for a prospective American candidate. His approach to the American ambassador in Paris was made indirectly and informally through Mantoux. In reporting this contact to Washington, Ambassador Hugh C. Wallace pointed out that Beyens had accepted, Italy's Council representative, Maggiorino Ferraris, was willing to serve but had not yet received Rome's consent, while Calonder had not yet responded, though the Swiss government was willing to see him serve on the Commission. Mantoux informed Wallace that both Bourgeois and Balfour were very anxious to have an American representative as the fourth member of the Commission. If the three above-mentioned men were finally appointed it was hoped that they could commence their preliminary work in Paris in ten days. They would in turn constitute the Commission if no American were appointed. The work of the Com-

55. Minutes of a meeting of the British Cabinet, Sept. 30, 1920 (CAB/23/22, PRO).

56. Hankey to Drummond, Sept. 30, 1920 (File 1259 in FO/371/4070, PRO).

57. Drummond to Mantoux, Sept. 30, 1920 (Political 1920: 11/7152/468, LNA).

mission, Mantoux observed, would "not be confined to considerations of law or theory." The Commission was to attempt to find in the Aland Islands question "an acceptable compromise based on considerations of *common sense and political expediency.*" It was desired that the American nominated should have these qualifications and likewise be someone with an international reputation. The work would take several months and require visits to the area. Wallace's request was for instructions.[58]

Receipt of this information in Washington caused the Acting Secretary of State, Norman W. Davis, to write immediately to President Wilson. He pointed out that the Aland Islands question was "of an exceedingly vexing character" and one that threatened the peace of the Baltic area. It seemed therefore "eminently desirable" that the invitation to have an American sit on the Commission be accepted. He believed that an American sitting on the Commission "would serve, furthermore, to render explicit America's deep interest in the welfare of the world through the instrumentality of the League of Nations." His "personal conviction" was that it would be desirable to appoint an American fitted to represent the United States in this task.[59] Considering the fact that the other major powers, England and France, were making every attempt to avoid serving on the Commission, Davis' message stands as a classic example of the myopic idealism that has often pervaded American foreign policy in the past and especially during the Wilson administration. After Davis' message Wilson's response could be predicted. Thus Washington's reply to Paris was that Wallace should informally advise Mantoux that President Wilson "would consider favorably" a request to nominate an American representative for appointment to the Commission.[60] Within four days after dispatch of this message Bourgeois officially and orally requested the nomination of an American.[61] Fortuitously, almost six months before, Abram I. Elkus, former American ambassador to the Ottoman Empire and a member of the Court of Appeals of New York State, the highest tri-

58. Italics added. *PRFRUS, 1920, 1,* 34.

59. Davis to President Wilson, Oct. 7, 1920 (Attached to File 758.6114A1/135, Record Group 59, NA).

60. *PRFRUS, 1920, 1,* 35.

61. Ibid.

bunal in the Empire State, had written to Wilson offering his services and help "in the solution of the Near Eastern or any of the European questions." He trusted that the President would call upon him, and he was sure that he could arrange to be at the President's disposal.[62] It was Elkus' name that was put in nomination.[63] To the Secretary-General this was "very good news."[64] Not so to the American missions in Helsingfors and Stockholm, which raised objections to any American participation on the Commission.[65] Their objections, however, fell on deaf ears in Washington, and Elkus hurried to meet his Commission colleagues in Stockholm.[66] But the appointment of Elkus did not establish a four-man Commission, for it was soon followed by the report that Ferraris had "resigned for private reasons."[67] Rome was obviously no more interested in getting involved in this "vexing" problem than either London or Paris. The group that now began studying the Aland Islands question was composed of Beyens as president, Calonder, and Elkus, with Emil Nielsen of the League Secretariat as secretary to the Commission. Of the original grouping of Beyens, Calonder, and Ferraris the Swedes had gotten two of the men they had hoped for on the Commission. Who the two preferred men were is unclear.[68]

While these arrangements were being made to constitute the Commission of Inquiry the Finnish position hardened further, and the Swedes, because of internal Swedish politics, found themselves in a weaker position. On October 13, Idman wrote a letter to the Secretary-General enclosing an account of an interview that he had had with a correspondent of a Finnish newspaper, in

62. Elkus to President Wilson, April 21, 1920 (Wilson Papers, ser. VI, File No. 1323).

63. *PRFRUS, 1920, I,* 35.

64. Minutes of a directors' meeting, Oct. 15, 1920 (General 1920: 40/7602/854, LNA).

65. Morris (Stockholm) to the Department of State, Oct. 19, 1920 (File 758.6114A1/103, Record Group 59, NA); Morris (Stockholm) to the Department of State, Oct. 19, 1920 (File 758.6114A1/104, Record Group 59, NA); Murphy (Stockholm) to the Department of State, Oct. 23, 1920 (File 758.6114A1/107, Record Group 59, NA); Ira Nelson Morris, *From an American Legation* (New York, Alfred A. Knopf, 1923), p. 266.

66. *PRFRUS, 1920, I,* 36.

67. *The Times* (London), Nov. 10, 1920, p. 11.

68. Palmstierna, *Dagjämning,* p. 141.

which he denied that the Council by its September decision had approved the idea advocated by the Swedes that his country did not possess sovereignty over the Aland Islands. He had given this interview, he explained to Drummond, because of the general concern in Finland caused by the Council's decision that, on the basis of the Jurists' report, it was competent to make recommendations for a solution of the problem. Idman had believed that it was his duty, as a member of the Finnish delegation, to seek to calm public opinion in his country, which could easily turn against the League Council. The interpretation of the Council's decision expressed in this interview, he explained, was his "personal conviction" though, after Enckell's statement to the Council in the name of their government, several League Secretariat officials had assured the Finns that the Council did not wish to contest Finnish sovereignty over the islands.[69]

This same day, at the urging of Mantoux, his old University of London colleague, the philosopher and anthropologist Edward Westermarck, a member of the Swedish community in Finland who had been attached to the Finnish delegation during the Council's September meetings, called on Commission members Beyens and Calonder in Paris. He was the first Finn to be received by them and his interview lasted almost an hour. Hurrying to the Finnish Legation, he informed Enckell that his visit with the Commission members had impressed him "most favourably." [70]

In the Aland Islands, the League Council's decision to accept the Jurists' report caused the Alanders to assume that this decision recommended the extension to them of the right of self-determination. The text of the Alanders' communication to the League Council on October 15 was kept secret by the French Foreign Ministry, undoubtedly in an attempt not to arouse passions. At the same time the Alanders were urging, on Palmstierna's advice, that the Finnish troops and governor be removed from the islands. Because of this Enckell and Idman, on October 20, called on Drummond at Brussels, where the League Council was having

69. Idman to Drummond, Oct. 13, 1920 (Political 1920: 11/7545/468, LNA).

70. Edward Westermarck, *Memoires of My Life*, trans. Anna Barwell (London, Allen & Unwin, 1929), p. 286.

its tenth session. Whatever fears that they might have had about unilateral moves by the Alanders was justified, for during this period gun-running to the islands from the Swedish mainland was in progress, and, though it was being done without the support of the Swedish government, it was certainly being done with their knowledge. Enckell pointed out to the Secretary-General that the type of declaration that he had urged in September had to be given now in order to avoid complications. Realizing that the Finnish request was justified, Drummond and Mantoux, with the assistance of Enckell and Idman, drew up a pertinent reply.[71] It was presented for the Council's approval at a private meeting on October 23 by Lord Balfour, who explained that the Secretary-General "thought it advisable to draft a letter . . . informing the Islanders of the true position." It was approved without debate, with the Council expressing the hope that both governments "would do their best to prevent any popular outbreak pending enquiry by the Commission and the decision of the League." [72] The letter to the Alanders, sent by the Belgian Council President, Paul Hymans, warned that the Council in its September decision had not pronounced "an opinion as to the whole matter or as to the validity of the right of self-determination of peoples in the case of the Aaland Islands." The political side of the question would be examined by the Commission of Inquiry with the purpose of assisting the Council to arrive at a decision. Until that decision was made, the duty of all parties concerned was to "refrain from any action which might create new difficulties." It reminded the Alanders that up to the present moment no change had been made in the islands' status.[73]

With this problem covered by Drummond's and the Council's quick action, Enckell took advantage of his presence in Brussels and called on Baron Beyens. In his interview with the president of the Commission of Inquiry, which lasted for several hours, Enckell gave him a complete picture of the Finnish position on the Aland question. His impression of Beyens after this first

71. Enckell, *2*, 76; Palmstierna, *Dagjämning*, p. 135.

72. League of Nations, Council, *Minutes of the Tenth Session of the Council of the League of Nations Held in Brussels, October 20–28, 1920*, pp. 16–17.

73. Ibid., pp. 158–59. On this point see also ibid., pp. 58–59, 154–57.

meeting was favorable. Further meetings with Beyens and Calonder took place subsequently in Paris, where Enckell, with the support of Idman, gave oral and written replies to various questions posed by the Commission and explained in some detail the events of 1917–19.[74]

In Sweden, the results of the September general elections had been favorable to the Farmers' League and especially to the Conservative party. Correspondingly, the Liberal party and particularly the Social Democratic party lost seats.[75] The increase in Conservative party strength made impossible the continuance in office of Branting's Social Democratic government. At the same time, the lack of a parliamentary majority by any party prevented the formation of a stable Cabinet. The stalemate created was not broken until some weeks later, when the King asked Baron Louis De Geer to form a non-party Cabinet of civil servants. De Geer's choice for Foreign Minister was his old friend in London, Count Wrangel, while the vacancy in London was to be filled by Palmstierna. The new prime minister was certainly less committed to pressing the Aland question than the previous government. When offered the post De Geer had hesitated to take it, since he feared that a war with Finland over the Aland question was possible, a war which he also thought would be as sheerly lunacy as going to war with Norway would have been in 1905 when the latter broke up the union of the two countries. Under no circumstances did he want this responsibility.[76] Therefore it has been correctly observed that under his government "interest in the Aaland question seems to have fallen off considerably." [77] The imminent arrival of the Commission of Inquiry, however, required that Branting and especially Palmstierna be present to deal with them, since it was largely due to their endeavors that the Aland question had been brought to the League

74. Enckell, 2, 77–78.

75. *The Times* (London), Sept. 23, 1920, p. 7.

76. Louis De Geer, *Politiska hågkomster från åren 1901–1921* (Stockholm, Norstedt & Söner, 1926), pp. 99–105. On the question of De Geer's policy toward the Aland problem, see also Palmstierna, *Dagjämning*, pp. 155, 157–58, 161–62, 164–65.

77. Herbert Tingsten, *The Debate on the Foreign Policy of Sweden 1918–1939*, trans. Joan Bulman (London, Oxford University Press, 1949), p. 109.

Council. No sooner was De Geer installed in office than, on November 6, the Commission of Inquiry arrived in Stockholm.

On the very day of their arrival Beyens and Calonder (Elkus and his secretary, Oscar L. Milmore, who had served in Sweden during the war, did not arrive until November 15) dined with King Gustaf. The Swedes' impression of them was favorable.[78] At this dinner, however, and at all subsequent informal meetings De Geer scrupulously avoided discussing the matter which had brought both of these gentlemen to Stockholm. It was his feeling that only in the most official manner was information to be given to them on the Aland question. The only occasion on which he actually discussed the Aland issue was when Calonder remarked that the question ought to be arranged in a way which would avoid war, a comment with which De Geer, because of his own attitude, readily agreed.[79] This approach was, of course, entirely different from that of Palmstierna, who used every occasion to press the Swedish point of view. In the days that followed, the discussions with Beyens and Calonder swept the whole range of topics having to do with the Aland question.[80] At one point Beyens asked—a query which would assume greater future import—the "interesting . . . [and] very delicate question" of why the Swedes had refused to support the Finns in 1918. Since Palmstierna had been Minister of Marine during that period, he was chosen to answer the question.[81]

The arrival of Elkus on November 15, however, appeared to shatter the rapport that the Swedes thought they had developed with the Commission. The Swedes very quickly developed an intense dislike for Elkus. Palmstierna thought that Elkus was against them and did not take his assignment seriously, while Calonder, he felt, was apparently on their side.[82] As will be shortly seen, Palmstierna was wrong on both counts.

On November 23, with its work in Stockholm finished, the Commission departed for Helsingfors. A heavy fog, however, delayed them, and they did not complete their passage until sev-

78. Palmstierna, *Dagjämning,* p. 168.

79. De Geer, p. 105.

80. Palmstierna, *Dagjämning,* pp. 167–75.

81. Ibid., p. 167.

82. Ibid., pp. 174–76.

eral days later, passing the Aland archipelago in the daytime.[83] Their investigation in Finland was as complete as the one they had made in Sweden. During their stay in Finland, which lasted until December 8, they had interviews with President Stahlberg, Prime Minister Erich, Foreign Minister Holsti, Gripenberg, Hjelt, Stenroth, Idman, Mannerheim, the Chief of the Finnish General Staff, a deputation from the Swedish community in Finland, the ministers of commerce and justice, as well as with assorted ethnologic, linguistic, and historical experts.[84] By the end of the Finnish visit, however, and before the Commission visited the Aland Islands from December 9 to 12, where they interviewed the governor, Sundblom, Björkman, and other prominent leaders of the Alander community,[85] Baron Beyens had made up his mind.

Primarily, Beyens informed British minister Kidston, he was "impressed by the violence of feeling" which the Aland question aroused in Finland. After passing through the island group, he was "no longer in any doubt as to their belonging geographically to Finland." In Beyens' opinion, the problem was "to find the practical solution which will best guarantee future peace in the Baltic, treating the question on broad lines without paying too much attention to theoretical considerations." In this approach he believed that he had the "full support" of Calonder but was "not quite so sure" of Elkus, who he thought "may be swayed by American notions and be inclined to regard the question from the ideal rather than the practical point of view." [86]

Beyens might have added, though he did not, that the principle of unfettered national self-determination was no more attractive to a Belgian like himself than it was to a Swiss like Calonder. Its implications were dangerous for a small country like his own,

83. Nielsen (Helsingfors) to Drummond, Dec. 5, 1920 (Political 1920: 11/9484/468, LNA). Palmstierna's belief that the fog delayed the Commission and caused them to pass the Aland Islands at night is incorrect, as Nielsen's report to the Secretary-General clearly shows. Palmstierna, *Dagjämning,* p. 175.

84. Nielsen (Paris) to Drummond, Dec. 22, 1920 (Political 1920: 11/9863/468, LNA).

85. Nielsen (Paris) to Drummond, Dec. 22, 1920 (Political 1920: 11/9863/468, LNA).

86. Kidston (Helsingfors) to Curzon, No. 410, Dec. 7, 1920 (File 62 in FO/371/5452, PRO).

racked by rising linguistic tensions between Walloons on one side and Flemings on the other, tensions which are polarizing Belgium's politics today. And Calonder? Would a Swiss, a citizen of a country composed of three nationalities and four linguistic groupings, if one includes here Romansh, assume an attitude different from that of Beyens? Most unlikely. Then there is another consideration that has to be kept in mind. Finland in defeating the Bolsheviks during her independence struggle had shown courage, steadfastness, and determination against this social and political disease which threatened Europe and the world, a disease which, for men of two supremely bourgeois societies, Belgium and Switzerland, was the ultimate anathema. On this issue Sweden was no Finland—an attitude that Beyens had explored in Stockholm when he asked why no Swedish help was given to the Finns in 1918. Certainly of the two countries Finland was more committed to the idea of a *cordon sanitaire* than was Sweden. Even if the islands were to be taken away from Finland, how was this to be done? It would be difficult and would perhaps produce more problems than it would solve. In the end, antagonizing Finland held more risks than antagonizing Sweden.

But the problem that now faced these two gentlemen was how to convince Elkus that Finnish possession of the archipelago had to be viewed from the "practical" rather than the "ideal" point of view. Here they encountered no major obstacle, for Elkus subsequently admitted that, after all the hearings were concluded and the Commission met to come to a decision, a procedure which lasted a week or so, they found that they were "unanimous about the result." A skeletal outline of the report was made, which was then discussed for several days. Beyens then drafted the report, which Elkus felt "was written with rare fidelity to the skeleton and . . . not only followed the letter . . . but the spirit." [87] President Wilson, to whom Elkus wrote explaining the report, "expressed himself as pleased with the decision." [88] For President Wilson this was easy, because he had already compromised the self-determination principle during the Paris negotiations, when, as Sir Harold Nicolson reminds us, the southern Tyrol, contain-

87. Elkus to Drummond, May 9, 1921 (Political 1921: 11/12363/468, LNA).
88. Elkus to Drummond, June 10, 1921 (Political 1921: 11/11550/468, LNA).

ing the Brenner Pass and a German-speaking population, was given to Italy seemingly for strategic considerations.[89] But how was Elkus converted to Beyens' and Calonder's point of view? What made a Wilsonian like Elkus agree to a decision that was contrary to the whole principle of national self-determination and caused him subsequently to talk disparagingly of the whole Aland question,[90] talk which brought down on him the wrath of the Swedish press? [91] Again, like Wilson at Paris, a far more important strategic consideration was presented to Elkus which overruled the application of self-determination. What was the consideration offered? It was that Finland in the north of Europe, more so than Sweden, was an obstacle to the spread of Bolshevism. "I am of the opinion," Elkus wrote to Secretary of State Charles Evans Hughes in a discussion of the Aland report, "that Finland should be encouraged as much as possible, both because the Finns are an active, energetic and industrious people and because *they act as a barrier to the spread of those doctrines which emanate from Russia.*" [92] Thus practicality, not idealism, as Baron Beyens desired, and "common sense and expediency," as Mantoux desired, had won out in the end.

The report Beyens drew up, which was approved by Calonder and Elkus, was a detailed exposition of the whole question. Its initial observation—and here Beyens' influence was obvious—that the archipelago's eastern side appeared to be a continuation of the Finnish mainland and was connected to it during the winter when the surrounding waters froze, while on the western side it was separated from Sweden by a deep channel was a clear warning to any Swedish reader of the arguments and the thoughts that were to follow. Moreover, the report observed that the sheet of water, "the Skiftet" with its numerous rocks and islets, which separated the islands from the Finnish mainland "would be a bad frontier between two States, extremely arbitrary from the geographical point of view." This geographic situation and the freezing of the Skiftet in the winter that connected the

89. Sir Harold Nicolson, *Peacemaking 1919* (London, Constable, 1933), pp. 169–70.

90. *New York Times,* May 15, 1921, Section 7, p. 2.

91. *Bulletin périodique de la presse scandinave,* No. 113, pp. 4–5.

92. Italics added. Elkus to Hughes, April 14, 1921 (File 758.6114A1/167, Record Group 59, NA).

islands to the Finnish mainland would place Finland in serious danger, or at least weaken her defensive position, if the archipelago were in foreign hands. Conversely, Sweden was protected from this type of problem by the open and narrow Aland Sea. In the concluding section of the report's first part there was also an examination of the archipelago's population, agriculture, industry, merchant marine, emigration, and commerce—which incomplete records seemed to show was probably as much with Finland as it was with Sweden.

In the second part of the report Beyens examined the political history of the Aland Islands from the earliest times. He dismissed, however, the contending arguments of both the Swedes and Finns about the importance of the earlier history of the island group. In the opinion of the Commission, it was the more recent events, beginning with the year 1808, which above all had to be taken into account "because they have created a new situation, altogether different from that of the past, on the shores of the Baltic and have contributed to the determination of the political and legal status of Finland for more than a century." Indeed, it was by studying this situation and this status closely that it seemed convenient in the Commission's opinion to consider the solution of the problem provoked by the Alanders' claim. Nevertheless, an examination of the earlier history of the Aland Islands appeared to show that under the 1634 constitution the archipelago "was definitely joined" to the administration of the provinces of the Finnish mainland and not to those west of the Bothnian Gulf in what was Sweden. Why was this done, the Commission asked. It was done, they thought, because the archipelago was geographically connected to the Finnish mainland.

The historical summary of the period after 1808, though impartial in tone, was rich in detail, which—and this is perhaps reading into the summary—by recounting Finland's trials and tribulations under the Czar could not help but invoke the reader's sympathy. On the important question of the Finnish civil war—and here again Beyens' attitude was exposed—the report pregnantly noted that there had existed in Sweden at that period a strong opposition to any intervention in the struggle, since many viewed Finland's turmoil as a "class struggle rather than a battle to death between legal order and communist anarchy." The historical summary, however, was merely an introduction to the third part of the report, which was the most important.

The third part of the report began by stating that in this problem the Commission believed that the primary question at issue was a legal one, namely, Finland's right of sovereignty over the Aland archipelago. Here they wished to discuss whether Finland was a sovereign state after its union with Czarist Russia had been dissolved and whether her sovereignty extended to the archipelago as it did to other parts of Finland. Skirting the whole issue of whether Finland had really been sovereign as a Grand Duchy under Czarist Russia, they were of the opinion that Finland's birth as a sovereign state commenced and could be dated from the moment it declared its independence from Russia in early December of 1917 and not in May of 1918 as decided by the Commission of Jurists. Their analogy was that the United States dated its independence and therefore really its sovereignty as of July 4, 1776, which is contradicted by no one, and not from the Versailles Treaty of 1783. Receiving military assistance as did the Finns (German) or the Americans (French) in winning independence in no way detracted from their sovereignty. Indeed, this had occurred many times in the past and states in no way lost sovereignty merely because they received outside assistance to reestablish their authority. Nor would the Commission admit that it followed that, because the Finnish government had been dispersed by the Finnish civil war, it had lost its sovereignty. Though it took refuge outside of Helsingfors it continued to function, it raised an army, and it reconquered provinces, all acts of sovereignty.

Turning to the second question, whether Finland's sovereignty also extended to the Aland Islands, the Commission noted that independent Finland in 1917 had included the island group. Its subsequent recognition by other states admitted her into the community of nations, since she had fulfilled one of the most important necessary conditions, which is the possession of sufficiently determined frontiers. The Commission was thus not moved by the Swedish argument that recognition of a state did not necessarily mean recognition of her frontiers. The Swedish recognition note had contained no reservations, and it appeared difficult for the Commission "to admit that a diplomatic document of this kind [could] contain a restriction which does not figure in the text." The Finnish government, when it received the Swedish communication, "was justified in believing that this recognition implied no reserve relative to her frontiers and consequently with regard to the Aaland Islands." Moreover, under the Treaty of Fredrikshamn Sweden "had renounced the possession of the Archipelago for ever." It would appear that Sweden in early 1918 viewed the Finnish state as still in "process of formation," but according to the Commission this entity had had clearly defined frontiers for over a hundred years.

Whatever reservations were implied by the Swedes or stated and withdrawn as in the case of the British were overshadowed in the Commission's mind by the primary question of sovereignty over the islands. The principal argument against the Finns' right of sovereignty was based on the military events which took place in the archipelago during the winter of 1918. In the Commission's opinion an attempt to expel the Russian forces was made by the Finns. They insisted that, under principles of international law, the fact that the area was occupied for a time by the enemy did not mean that the state temporarily lost its "right of sovereignty over the invaded portions of its territory." In fact, before the Swedish expedition had even left the islands, the Finns dispatched a military governor to the area. It performed further acts of authority in withdrawing the exequatur of the Swedish Vice-Consul and in expelling from the islands a Swedish journalist. In neither action was a protest lodged by the Swedes. Indeed, Stockholm requested a new exequatur for another consular agent, a request considered in Helsingfors as an implicit recognition of Finnish rights in the island group. This examination brought the Commission to the decision that Finnish sovereignty over the Aland Islands was "incontestable" and that legally they formed a part of the Finnish state.

Fear of being swamped by the Finns and the activities of the Finnish Socialists, who allied themselves with the Bolsheviks, were undoubtedly, the Commission believed, what drove the Alanders to desire union with Sweden. Once started, the movement gained momentum and it was the Commission's belief that a plebiscite, if held, would be overwhelmingly for union with Sweden. But was it possible to acknowledge as an absolute rule that a minority in a state had "the right of separating itself from her in order to be incorporated in another State or to declare its independence?" To concede to either linguistic or religious minorities or to any "fractions of a population the right of withdrawing from the community to which they belong, because it is their wish or their good pleasure, would be to destroy order and stability within States and to inaugurate anarchy in international life; it would be to uphold a theory incompatible with the very idea of the State as a territorial and political unity." Justice and liberty, which were embodied in the self-determination formula, had to be applied in a "reasonable manner" in the relations between the minority and the state. The separation of a minority from a state and its attachment to another state could only be considered as an exceptional solution, "a last resort when the State lacks either the will or the power to enact and apply just and effective guarantees." What were the guarantees? They were guarantees of religious, linguistic, and social freedom. In the case of the Alanders the protection of their language was important. However, to accomplish this it was not necessary for the Alanders to be incorporated into the Swedish state. Separation could be avoided. A more conservative approach was possible. The Commission believed that Finland was ready to grant to the islanders "satisfactory guarantees and faithfully to observe the engagements which it will enter into with them": of this the commission had no doubt. To take the archipelago away from the Finns while they were willing to give guarantees appeared to the Commission unjust from the historical, geographical, and political points of view. All arguments militated in favor of the status quo.

Historically, especially since 1809, the islands were a part of Finland. Geographically the islands were a continuation of the Finnish mainland, which made it impossible to draw a practical frontier line. Even if a frontier line were drawn it would be difficult to curb smuggling, especially during the winter when the islands are connected to the mainland. Moreover, a separation of the islands from Finland would compromise the position of the

Swedish community in Finland, and would be an "irreparable blow" to that community. It would irritate the Finnish majority to such an extent that it "might perhaps drive the Republic into political combinations and alliances directed against Sweden." From a strategic point of view the islands in Finnish possession were no threat to Sweden, and the reverse was equally true. Thus the Commission saw no reason why Swedish interests should take precedence over Finnish interests. It dismissed the fear that the two countries would go to war over the issue. Their mutual fear was having the islands fall into the hands of any great power. Politically, Finland's services to herself and to others in repulsing the Bolsheviks after a bloody struggle could not be forgotten. Had she failed, the gate to revolutionary expansion would have been opened, and Scandinavia would, without question, have been the first menaced. It would be extraordinary gratitude toward Finland, the Commission believed, to take territory from her to which she attached the greatest importance, more so since she was a new state which had the "pride and susceptibility of youth." She would be alienated from her Scandinavian neighbors, who needed her as she needed them. Russia was sure to rise again. Therefore it was in the general interest to hasten the consolidation of the states which had once been part of the Czarist Empire. To contribute to this situation, the Commission felt, would be important. To dispel any apprehensions that the Alanders might have, however, the Commission proposed a number of guarantees to be demanded of Finland in favor of the Alanders.

Before enumerating its proposals the Commission rejected the suggestion that the Aland Islands be given their independence. Even assuming that Finland would agree, the Commission felt that the islands did not have the necessary financial resources to be an independent state. It also rejected the suggestion that matters should stand as they were and after a period of time a plebiscite should be held to ascertain the Alanders' feelings. The belief was that a waiting period would allow passions to cool, a belief the Commission denied, noting that it was a suggestion to the liking of neither the Alanders nor the Finns.

The proposals recommended by the Commission to guarantee

the Alanders minority status within the Finnish state were four in number. First, they recommended that in the province of Aland exclusively, primary schools and technical schools should give instruction only in Swedish, to the "obligatory exclusion of Finnish, confirmed by law," that the Alanders be accorded the right of preemption on every occasion when offers to purchase land are made by outsiders, that newly arrived settlers in the islands be granted the franchise only after a stay of five years, and finally, that the Alanders be allowed to present a list of three candidates to the government at Helsingfors for the position of governor, who was to be chosen only from this list. To force the acceptance of these proposals the Commission recommended that, if the Finnish government refused to grant these guarantees, a plebiscite then be held to ascertain the Alanders' wishes. If the League Council were to share the Commission's views and recommend adoption of these proposals by Helsingfors, they believed that "certain amendments to the law of autonomy would be sufficient to give a legal force to the new guarantees granted to Aaland which would thus assume an international character." If any difficulties were to arise in the application of these guarantees, it would be the duty of the League Council to intervene. The Finnish government, also, should grant to the Alanders "the right of direct recourse" to the League Council's good offices. Instead of authorizing the Alanders to approach the Council directly if differences concerning the application of the guarantees were to arise, the Commission thought that this right might be reserved to Sweden or to the other Scandinavian states. The Commission in fact envisaged even recourse to the Permanent Court of International Justice at The Hague by either party if their differences could not be ironed out in any disagreement over the guarantees.

On the demilitarization of the island group, the Commission noted that the Jurists' report considered the clauses of the 1856 convention as still in force. Its only suggestion was that stricter clauses could be suggested and greater guarantees might be adopted so that actions like Russia's during the war might not be repeated. It looked kindly upon the neutralization of the islands in a treaty to which the great powers and all the states bordering the Baltic would be signatories.[93] The fact that the Commission's report on a number of points contradicted the Jurists' report was to be Sweden's only strong arguing point. The situation had reversed itself, much to the relief of London and Paris, and Sweden now found herself in the unenviable position Finland had occupied when the Jurists' report had been released.

League Council Discussions in Geneva

Publication in the Swedish press of résumés and extracts from what was purported to be the report of the Commission of Inquiry moved Ehrensvärd to call on Drummond on the afternoon of April 22, 1921. He asked the Secretary-General if he might have a copy of the report, or at least examine it. Drummond replied that he had not yet seen the report himself, and that only one copy of it existed. He admitted that it had reached the League Secretariat and that it had been forwarded to the printers who had it then. Therefore he did not see how he could assist Ehrensvärd in his request. Ehrensvärd persisted, however, and asked whether anyone in the Secretariat could furnish him with information on certain points in the report about which his government had contacted him. Drummond explained that this request put him into a rather difficult position, as he could hardly feel justified in supplying information to one side which was not supplied to the other. He hoped that the Commission's report would be in the hands of the Swedes by the end of the following week at the latest. Ehrensvärd pressed his request and assured Drummond that the information received would be kept in absolute confidence by his government and in no way disclosed. Under these conditions Drummond agreed and summoned Emil Nielsen, the secretary of the Commission. The interview that took place between Nielsen and Ehrensvärd was in Drummond's presence. Nielsen answered all the questions put to him. The interview over, Ehrensvärd thanked Sir Eric for the courtesy that had

93. League of Nations, *The Aaland Islands Question; report submitted to the Council of the League of Nations by the Commission of Rapporteurs* (Document du Conseil B 7. 21/68/106, Genève, le 16 avril 1921) (Genève, Imprimerie Kundig, 1921). For a further examination of the Commission's report see Charles Noble Gregory, "The Neutralization of the Aaland Islands," *The American Journal of International Law, 17* (1923), 64–72.

been shown him, though he appeared "somewhat unhappy." [94] On the following day Drummond wrote to Enckell informing him of Ehrensvärd's visit. He recounted the Swede's request and explained that this information had been given to him orally. In line with his desire to remain impartial in this affair he then divulged to Enckell the substance of the Commission's report. This information, the Secretary-General observed, was to be treated by Enckell in the same manner as it was when communicated to Ehrensvärd.[95]

On May 10, Enckell was invited to the French Foreign Ministry for a talk with Jean Gout, who handled League affairs for the Quai d'Orsay. Gout hoped, he told Enckell, that in Finland the Commission's report would be received in a dignified manner and without exultation which might hurt Swedish feelings and make League mediation difficult.[96] The next day in Stockholm the first official Swedish reaction was reported by Barclay, who informed Lord Curzon that Count Wrangel, the Foreign Minister, considered the Commission's "recommendations unfair and very unsatisfactory." It was Wrangel's opinion that the premises on which they were based were "distinctly weak." He could not understand why Finland's defeat of the Bolsheviks "should be grounds for attributing [the] islands to her." His country, Wrangel noted, would make the strongest protest against the Commission's findings.[97] The same day Barclay sent this communication, Palmstierna called on Lord Curzon at the Foreign Office to discuss the Commission's report. He proceeded "to debate the whole case *ab initio*," Curzon informed Barclay, and to recapitulate all the arguments heard so often in the past. Curzon doubted, as he remarked to Palmstierna, that the League Council would discredit a unanimous report by its own Commission "by reopening [the] case, or declining to accept the advice which was given them." Supporters and friends of the League of Nations would

94. Record of [an] interview by E[ric] D[rummond], April 22, 1921 (Political 1921: 11/12295/468, LNA).

95. Drummond (Geneva) to Enckell, April 23, 1921 (Political 1921: 11/12295/468, LNA); Enckell, 2, 82.

96. Enckell, 2, 82.

97. Barclay (Stockholm) to Curzon, No. 85, May 11, 1921 (File 85 in FO/371/6948, PRO).

not wish to see any blow given to its prestige by the League Council, its own executive body. Curzon's own urgent advice was for the Swedish government "to yield to the situation, to accept perhaps with reluctance, but to carry out with loyalty, the decision of the Council, should it be of the character anticipated." At the moment, "the only wise course for the Swedish Government to take, was to accept the decision, to which they had been willing to refer, and to suppress any mortification or resentment which they might be disposed to feel." Palmstierna promised to communicate Curzon's advice to Stockholm.[98] Some time later Palmstierna called on Fisher "to say in advance" that his government would decline to accept the Commission's report on the Aland Islands. This, Fisher replied, would be "so much the worse for Sweden." [99] From these interviews it was obvious, assuming that Sweden had entertained any hopes, that after the Commission's report great-power support for Sweden would be lacking. In Helsingfors, the reaction in May 1921 was the reverse of what it had been in September of 1920 following the report of the Commission of Jurists. Holsti "expressed satisfaction at [the] general terms" of the Commission's report. His initial reservation was on the Commission's recommendation that the Finnish government should grant the Alanders the right of direct recourse to the League Council, which he feared might "give rise to frequent vexatious appeals." [100]

Reservations on this point were also in the mind of the Foreign Office. It felt that allowing the Alanders to appeal directly to the League in the event of any dispute with the Finns "would go beyond the sphere of the Covenant." If the League Council adopted the Commission's report and passed a resolution embodying the recommendations made by it, this resolution would not be binding on Finland. It was therefore proposed that Finland be invited to accept certain provisions found in the minorities

98. Curzon (London) to Barclay, No. 137, May 11, 1921 (File 85 in FO/371/6948, PRO).

99. Diary entry, June 1, 1921 (Fisher Papers). For the cold reception given Count Wrangel on a trip to London when he came to plead the Swedish case during this period see Palmstierna, *Dagjämning,* p. 183.

100. Russell (Helsingfors) to Curzon, No. 94, May 17, 1921 (File 85 in FO/371/6948, PRO).

treaties whereby a breach of the Alanders' rights could be brought to the Council's attention by any League member. Finland would have to accept the obligation to appear and to answer any charges made, or be forced to do so by a Council resolution with which she would have to comply.[101] It was not until June 8, however, that Curzon conveyed to the secretary of the Cabinet the knowledge that he favored adoption of the Commission's conclusions. In doing so he voiced exception to the recommendation that the Alanders be granted the right of direct access to the Council. He was strongly opposed to this on two grounds: one, if this right were given it would go beyond the Covenant's sphere and be in contravention of the definitely established principle found in the minorities treaties that appeals to the Council should come only from governments; two, by encouraging the islanders "to make groundless appeals, with the primary object of irritating the Finns," there would tend to be either an increase or a preservation of the "existing state of friction in lieu of allowing it to be smoothed away by the passage of time"[102]—a clear indication that Curzon and the Foreign Office had been influenced by Holsti's observation. Almost a week later the secretary of the Cabinet was again contacted. This communication contained observations that Donner had made at the Foreign Office on June 6. The Finnish minister intimated that his government was on the whole satisfied with the Commission's report and was willing to accept its recommendations for safeguarding the Swedish language and for granting the Alanders the right of preemption of land. He inquired, however, whether the teaching of Swedish to the obligatory exclusion of Finnish precluded the establishment of private Finnish schools for the purpose of giving instruction to the small Finnish element in the Aland Islands. On the matter of the appointment of a governor for the island group he was of the opinion that a clause be added that the holder of this appointment should enjoy the Finnish government's confidence as well as that of the Alanders. This

101. An unsigned and undated minute (May 26, 1921?) on certain legal points raised by the report of the Commission of Inquiry (File 85 in FO/371/6948, PRO).

102. The Under-Secretary of State for Foreign Affairs to the Secretary of the Cabinet, June 8, 1921 (File 85 in FO/371/6949, PRO).

would give his government the right of rejecting all candidates proposed and beginning a new panel. Donner also pointed out that if Finland included the Commission's recommendations in the autonomy law of the Aland Islands, international guarantees would be superfluous, since the Aland Islands autonomy law could not be altered without the consent of the Alanders.[103] By June 16, one day before the League Council was to convene in Geneva, Holsti expressed his willingness to accept the Commission's recommendations dealing with: the exclusive use of Swedish in the Aland schools; denial of the franchise for five years to recent Aland immigrants; and preemption of land purchase by the Alanders. He refused to accept the recommendations that the governor could only be selected from a list of three candidates proposed by the Alanders and that the Alanders shall have the right to appeal directly to the League Council in any difficulties that might arise between themselves and the Finnish government.[104] That the Commission's report would be accepted by the League Council went without saying. The task of the League Council was to reconcile the recommendations of the Commission with what the British and the Finns would be willing to accept. On one of their objections the Finns were supported by the British—that to the Alanders' right to appeal directly to the Council in any dispute with the Finnish authorities. Thus it was on the question of the selection of candidates for governor that difficulties would arise. On the Commission's alternate suggestion, that the Alanders be given the right to appeal directly to the Permanent Court of International Justice at The Hague, no problem was posed, for the League Secretariat's Legal Section pointed out that under the statute of The Hague Court only states could appear before the Court. This automatically disqualified the Alanders.[105]

The plan of the Swedish delegation was to have Branting speak to Fisher, to Viscount Kikujiro Ishii, the Japanese Presi-

103. The Under-Secretary of State for Foreign Affairs to the Secretary of the Cabinet, June 14, 1921 (File 85 in FO/371/6949, PRO).

104. Rennie (Helsingfors) to Curzon, No. 182, June 16, 1921 (File 85 in FO/371/6949, PRO).

105. Enckell, 2, 83.

dent of the Council, and also to Gabriel Hanotaux, the French representative who was substituting for the ill Bourgeois, requesting that Professor Larnaude, the president of the Commission of Jurists, be summoned. At the same time, Palmstierna would approach the Chinese delegate, Wellington Koo, asking him to talk with the Alanders.[106] Branting's interview with Fisher on June 18 did not go well,[107] for Fisher felt that Branting was "rather intransigent." [108] His success with Viscount Ishii appears to have been no greater, for the President of the Council considered the Commission of Jurists dissolved and was unwilling to summon Larnaude, though he did promise to discuss with his colleagues Branting's request.[109] Palmstierna, on the other hand, was successful with Koo, but the impression made by the Alanders hindered rather than helped the Swedish case.[110] As these Swedish endeavors were grinding away, Fisher, in a private meeting of the League Council on the afternoon of June 18, proposed, and his colleagues agreed, that the first meeting on the Aland question for Monday, June 20, be public.[111] Since previous Council discussions of the Aland question had always been private, with the public meeting being held only after an agreement had been reached, Enckell thought that this move was a Swedish attempt to influence the Council members and create for Sweden a favorable opinion by the very fact that the first meeting would be public. He nevertheless accepted.[112] Conversely, the Swedes initially refused.[113] On closer examination Fisher's proposal appears as a shrewd move to expose the Swedes—who obviously were going to be the intransigent party in this meeting—to the uncomfortable light of day, which would make any Swedish protest against the Commission's report extremely difficult.

106. Palmstierna, *Dagjämning,* p. 185.

107. Ibid., p. 186.

108. Diary entry, June 18, 1921 (Fisher Papers).

109. Palmstierna, *Dagjämning,* p. 185.

110. Ibid.

111. League of Nations, Council, *Minutes of the Thirteenth Session of the Council of the League of Nations Held in Geneva, June 17–28, 1921,* p. 14.

112. Enckell, 2, 84.

113. Palmstierna, *Dagjämning,* p. 187.

At the Council's Monday meeting Enckell's statement, of course, approved of the Commission's conclusions. His government was willing to accept its recommendations on the exclusive use of Swedish for public instruction, the Alanders' right of preemption on immovable property, and the restriction of the franchise for five years to island immigrants. As Holsti had made clear before, Enckell expressed reservations on the question of how the governor was to be selected and on the right of the Alanders to appeal directly to the Council in any dispute between themselves and the Finnish authorities.

Branting's statement, which had been written for him by Ehrensvärd, began with the observation that the time "was not yet ripe for a final solution" of the Aland question. He believed that the Commission's report did not contain the basis of a "solution or even of a tolerable compromise." To discredit the Commission he alluded to Elkus' statement to the *New York Times* which had incensed the Swedes, and to the fact that the Commission had answered only the question of sovereignty but had avoided committing themselves on the second question, that of the neutralization of the archipelago. His request was that the Commission of Jurists be heard on the differences that obviously existed between their report and the one made by the Commission of Inquiry. To oppose the Alanders' desires, Branting warned, would "give rise to perpetual unrest and be a continued source of fresh disputes." The Council must therefore "not impose an unnatural solution, which would effect nothing and would only give rise to fresh conflicts." What would be the effect, he observed, if the Council's first political settlement should result in a population's being bound against its will to a country with which they were not united legally and to which they were strongly opposed. In his remarks on Enckell's statement Branting noted that there was a considerable difference between the guarantees recommended by the Commission and those which, according to Enckell, his government was willing to accept. This was especially true on the selection of the governor and the Alanders' right of direct appeal to the Council. In closing this meeting, Viscount Ishii remarked that the Council's September 1920 resolution was still valid, as far as its competence was concerned, under Article 15 paragraph 8 of the Covenant. It "had full liberty" to deal with the basic question and to "recommend any solution" which appeared to it to be "most conducive" to maintaining the peace, taking into consideration the legitimate interests of all parties involved. In order to devise a solution the Commission of Inquiry had been asked to furnish the Council with a report by study and direct observation of the facts. This task had been well performed. The Council was now at liberty, conforming with its duties under the Covenant, to make use of the material that had been collected, together with that to be furnished in the coming deliberations.[114] That evening at a dinner at Drummond's home, Fisher, Jean Monnet, the League Deputy Secretary-General, and Hanotaux "discuss[ed] at length the procedure to be followed in . . . [the] Aland isles . . . and we reach[ed] agreement." [115]

On the following afternoon a private conference was held in Drummond's room to discuss again the procedure to be followed in the Aland question. Here also there was complete agreement. The decision was that Fisher and Hanotaux were to meet Branting and inform him that the Council would accept the Commission's report and that they would insist on the neutralization of the island group.[116] The next day, June 22, at 3 P.M., Branting was invited to a "useful talk" with Fisher and Hanotaux.[117] At this meeting Branting had "put before him [the] basis of a settlement." [118] At 5 P.M. Enckell appeared, on an invitation from Fisher, who asked him not to use the front entrance of his hotel. The discussion began by Fisher's pointing out to Enckell that Sweden had a very strong case. The proposition offered the Finnish representative was that recognition of Finland's sovereignty over the islands, which would be a denial of self-determination, had to be counterbalanced by concessions on the Finnish side. The concessions that Fisher and Hanotaux desired were

114. League of Nations, Council, *Minutes of the Thirteenth Session of the Council of the League of Nations Held in Geneva, June 17–28, 1921,* annexes 198 and 198a, pp. 2–5 and 16–17.

115. Diary entry, June 20, 1921 (Fisher Papers).

116. Diary entry, June 21, 1921 (Fisher Papers).

117. Palmstierna, *Dagjämning,* p. 188.

118. Diary entry, June 22, 1921 (Fisher Papers).

neutralization of the islands and guarantees for the Alanders. Fisher observed that he would have to answer his Liberal party friends in London on what grounds he had refused the self-determination principle in the Aland question. He felt it was unfortunate that the autonomy law had already been enacted, for it would have served as sufficient compensation to the Swedes, but because it did exist, newer concessions would have to be added. Hanotaux openly admitted that he was less interested in the Alanders than in a disappearance of the question based on a compromise which would estop Sweden in the future from interfering in the fate of the archipelago again. The Council resolution proposed by Fisher and Hanotaux would recognize Finnish sovereignty over the islands, its agreement to neutralize the area, and its agreement to supplement the autonomy law of the Aland Islands with added guarantees. Before this resolution was proposed to the Council they wanted to know whether Enckell's government agreed and whether he would cooperate. Enckell replied that without the slightest doubt his government would accept the proposal offered.[119] Enckell "is ready to make all the necessary concessions" Fisher wrote in his diary[120] after the interview and undoubtedly with a certain amount of satisfaction.

The next day's private meeting of the Council dealing with the Aland question was in the afternoon. Since the consultations of the previous days had produced a consensus especially between the British and the French, with only minor details to be ironed out with the Finns, it proved to be, mainly for the Swedes, an arduous and frustrating afternoon. It began with Ishii's rejection of the Swedish request to call the Commission of Jurists to comment on the report of the Commission of Inquiry. Fisher thought that there were "grave objections to opposing the opinions of two Commissions appointed by the Council." The Council agreed. Branting objected, and requested that his formal protest be indicated in the Council's minutes. To trip up the Finns, and in the hope that they would invoke their September 1920 reservation, Branting then asked Enckell if his government would accept the Council's decision. Yes, Enckell replied, well aware

119. Enckell, 2, 86–88.
120. Diary entry, June 22, 1921 (Fisher Papers).

after his discussion with Fisher and Hanotaux what the Council's decision was going to be. And Sweden? Ishii asked. It is "prepared loyally to attribute to the decision of the Council its full value under the Covenant," Branting retorted. However, he continued, "future events may take place independently of the will of the Swedish Government, creating a new situation in the islands, which it may be impossible to consider as covered by the decision of the Council." Fisher was surprised by the declaration and hoped that Sweden "would withdraw it." To lessen the tension that now gripped the chamber, Ishii called "an intermission for tea." What was meant, Ehrensvärd tried to explain when the Council reconvened, was that if future conflict were to arise in the island group his government reserved the right to have recourse again to the League's good offices. Fisher accepted this explanation. At this point in the proceedings the Alanders were heard. They were subjected to extensive questioning. When this was over, Fisher moved that the question be settled, since all the necessary information had been collected. There were three points to be considered: it had to be recognized that the islands should remain under Finnish sovereignty and that the existing guarantees enjoyed by the Alanders had to be strengthened to preserve their language, to secure their property, and to protect their franchise by placing restrictions on new immigrants to the islands, and to see that governors would be appointed who enjoyed the Alanders' confidence. He thought that the best way to handle the question of guarantee would be by direct Finno-Swedish consultations assisted by Council representatives. If this failed the Council would be called upon to define the guarantees. Third, military neutralization of the islands must be assured so that no danger to Sweden could ever arise from the archipelago. For this to be accomplished the 1856 convention would have to be replaced by a more comprehensive treaty following the lines of a Swedish draft previously submitted to the League Council. Hanotaux concurred. The Swedes were frantic. A real settlement, Branting sparkled, "could only be reached by taking into account the wishes of those who were most nearly concerned." In Fisher's proposed solution "there was no place for the sentiments of the Islanders, who had declared that there would be no peace in a solution of this character." In spite of the further guarantees to be given to the Alanders, "discontent would remain and would probably provoke incidents which would imperil them." His country could not abandon the Alanders in exchange for a neutralization of the islands. The latter advantage "could not be purchased at the cost of Swedish honour." [121]

Branting's last-minute objections, however, meant nothing. Sweden had already, along with Finland, committed herself to an acceptance of the Council's decision. Thus Fisher and Hanotaux had outmaneuvered Branting, who had hoped that the Finns would invoke their reservation of September 1920, which in turn would have made it possible for Sweden to present a similar reservation and thus take the issue out of the Council and return it to where it was when brought there by Lord Curzon in June of 1920.

The Alanders during the Council meeting, Fisher diaried, had made "an excellent impression but it is clear they have no grievances." [122] During dinner that night at Drummond's home Branting had sat next to him, Fisher wrote to his wife, and was "in the depths of gloom because I have given the Aland island case to Finland." The Swedes were "furious—vanquished by [a] quick point maneuver on the part of Hanotaux and [my]self." But not everyone could be satisfied, "and we went as far as we could to satisfy the Swedes." [123]

A private Council discussion on the question continued on the following morning, June 24. It commenced with a long speech by Ehrensvärd somewhat sentimental in nature, recounting the ties between Alander and Swede. He dwelt on the weaknesses of the guarantees, the differences between the two reports, the fears of the Alanders of being denationalized, and the dangers of putting the islanders under a regime they did not want. He asked consideration for a provisional regime on the island group and a subsequent plebiscite. Enckell observed that the Swedish proposal involved delay, and the Swedes had in the past counselled

121. League of Nations, Council, *Minutes of the Thirteenth Session of the Council of the League of Nations Held in Geneva, June 17–28, 1921,* pp. 34–37; Enckell, *2,* 88–92.

122. Diary entry, June 23, 1921 (Fisher Papers).

123. Fisher to his wife, June 24, 1921 (Fisher Papers).

against any delay in settlement of the question. Branting again returned to the question of consulting the Commission of Jurists. After some discussion, and undoubtedly to appear reasonable on this issue, it was agreed that the Commission of Jurists could be asked if the Commission of Inquiry had "adduced new facts calculated to modify" their opinion concerning Finland's sovereignty over the island group in 1917. In an attack led by Paul Hymans, the Belgian representative, Branting's second question was rejected on the grounds that it was asking the Jurists for their opinion on the Commission of Inquiry's report, which was not admissible. Branting reserved his right to protest against this decision. The Jurists' opinion it was agreed, was to be in writing and ready for the Council's afternoon session. As this meeting ended Fisher asked whether the Finns and Swedes wished to negotiate between themselves with or without the Council's assistance, or whether they desired the Council itself to settle the question of the guarantees. The decision reached was that the parties would furnish an answer to Fisher's question by the afternoon session.[124]

At the afternoon session the Jurists' answer, signed by Larnaude and Struycken, Huber being absent from Geneva, was "no" to the question that had been posed. But the Council was not moved, and nothing developed for the Swedes in this direction. To Fisher's query, posed at the end of the morning session, Branting replied that the Swedes were ready to partake in consultations with the Finns regarding guarantees for the Alanders, though he had serious doubts on the possibility of finding effective guarantees for the preservation of the Alanders' Swedish culture and nationality. On Fisher's initiative Hymans, the Belgian, was nominated and agreed to assist these Finno-Swedish consultations. Ishii then asked Fisher to draw up a definitive resolution to be presented to the Council when it reconvened later that night.

The resolution offered by Fisher to the Council at 7 P.M. encompassed all the points raised during the previous days' deliberations. It recognized Finnish sovereignty over the islands and the need for further guarantees for the Alanders as well as neutralization of the archipelago. The guarantees were to be inserted into

124. League of Nations, Council, *Minutes of the Thirteenth Session of the Council of the League of Nations Held in Geneva, June 17–28, 1921*, pp. 38–39.

the autonomy law and were to include protection of language, property, franchise, and the appointment of the islands' governor. These guarantees, the Council recognized, would best be achieved through bilateral talks with Council assistance if necessary. In accordance with the Council's desire the Finns and Swedes had decided to seek an agreement. Should they fail, the Council would undertake to fix the guarantees. The enforcement of these guarantees would be undertaken by the League. The 1856 convention was to be replaced by a broader agreement, conforming largely to one already drafted by Sweden, so that the archipelago would never be a menace to Sweden. Fisher's resolution was adopted. Branting raised no objection but read a long, emotional statement which ended with the observation that his country would "not abandon the hope that the day will come when the idea of justice shall have so permeated the conscience of the peoples, that the claims inspired by such noble motives and a national feeling as deep as that of the population of the Aaland Isles will be triumphantly vindicated. Thus it will make its voice heard, and will at last have justice done to it." He believed that after what had occurred in the Council there was little possibility that the meeting with the Finns under Hymans' presidency would be productive. Because of this the Council would have to pronounce on the matter of the guarantees.[125] Diplomatically isolated, incapable of acting unilaterally, supported by a weak government at home (De Geer had resigned in February and was succeeded by another nonparty cabinet of civil servants under Oscar von Sydow), and faced by the negative attitude of the Council and especially the British and French, the Swedes could do nothing but capitulate. Fisher's interpretation of the Council's decision, however, was entirely different from Branting's. "I really think," he wrote to his wife, "we have averted war between Finland and Sweden." [126]

Branting, however, proved wrong in his prediction that nothing fruitful would come out of the bilateral discussions presided over by Hymans. The first question that faced the parties was how the Alanders were to appeal to the Council in any dispute be-

125. Ibid., pp. 40–43.

126. Fisher to his wife, June 26, 1921 (Fisher Papers).

tween themselves and the Finns. The Swedes wanted to have the right to bring any Alander complaint directly to the Council themselves. The compromise finally devised was that Finland would pass on to the Council any Alander complaint along with its own observations. The biggest stumbling block was the question of how the islands' governor was to be selected. Here the Finns wished to prevent anyone who had been a leader in the Alanders' separatist movement from being nominated and opposed any procedure which might make this possible. Wishing to discuss this issue, Enckell visited Fisher on Sunday morning—again using the back stairs of the hotel. Though Fisher thought Enckell's views "to be reasonable" he asked him to return that evening when Hanotaux could also be present. Hanotaux, unlike Fisher, was less understanding and charged that Enckell's intransigent attitude on this question was counterproductive. The formula that Enckell finally hit upon was that any candidate nominated for the governor's position would have to show prior administrative experience. None of the separatist leaders could qualify under this stipulation. Hymans' proposal was that he advance this compromise scheme, since he thought Branting would be more likely to accept it if it appeared that it was Hymans' idea. This was done, and, as Hymans predicted, Branting approved.[127] The week-end negotiations completed, Hymans presented the agreement to the Council on Monday morning, June 27. It was stipulated that the guarantees would be inserted into the Alands autonomy law and were to include the following: The Alanders would not be required to support any schools other than those where Swedish was the language, and all state schools would give instruction in Swedish. Finnish was not to be taught in state schools in the islands except with the consent of the islanders—a stipulation allowing privately supported instruction to the Finnish minority. The Alanders were allowed preemption on land purchases. Immigrants to the islands would have their franchise restricted for five years. The governor would be nominated by the Finnish President in agreement with the President of the Aland Diet. If no agreement could be reached,

127. Enckell, 2, 94–96; Diary entry, June 26, 1921 (Fisher Papers); Fisher to his wife, June 26, 1921 (Fisher Papers).

the President of the Republic would choose the governor from a list of five candidates nominated by the Aland Diet, the candidates "possessing qualifications necessary for the good administration of the Islands and the security of the State." The Alanders would have the right to use for their needs 50 per cent of the land tax revenue aside from other revenues mentioned in the autonomy law. These guarantees would be watched over by the League of Nations. Finland would forward to the Council with its observations any petitions or claims of the Aland Diet in connection with the application of these guarantees. In any case of a juridical character, the Council would consult The Hague Court. This agreement was accepted and annexed to the Council's resolution of the 24th.[128]

The Swedes did not wish "to be complemented. 'Ni fleurs, ni couronnes.' So the final act of the drama," Fisher diaried, was "accomplished very quietly in the middle of a session devoted to the minor work of the Council." [129] And he was pleased. "We have reached a settlement, not without difficulty," he wrote to Gilbert Murray, "for both the Swedes and the Finns were very obstructive, of the Aland islands question and the settlement is so intrinsically just and fair and is so obviously framed in the interests of European peace, that I have little doubt but that it will stand. Branting fought very hard for the Swedes and was much downcast at the decision though in private he did not deny its Justice. . . .

"We succeeded, however, in extracting from the Finns a considerable enlargement of the law of autonomy, which delights the Alanders and it is significant that the Finnish Gov't would never have made these concessions to the Swedes, though they were prepared, after a little steady pressure, to make them to the Council of the League. Indeed it is clear to me now *that the dispute could never have been settled by the ordinary methods of diplomacy*." [130]

128. League of Nations, Council, *Minutes of the Thirteenth Session of the Council of the League of Nations Held in Geneva, June 17–28, 1921*, pp. 52–53.

129. Diary entry, June 27, 1921 (Fisher Papers).

130. Italics added. Fisher to Murray, June 27, 1921 (Fisher Papers).

Conclusions

It has been the collective security feature or the sanctionist feature of international organization that has held the greatest attraction for the greatest number. The hope and belief that international security and retribution for the peace-breaker could be achieved through the medium of an international organization has twice in this century led to the establishment of just such an organ. The underlying assumption was that the combined strength of the international community and the execution of disinterested foreign policies by all states—especially the great powers—for the benefit of the community rather than for any selfish power considerations would force the establishment of behavioral patterns that would in time solidify into universal norms to be obeyed by all the members of the community. Realistically, and keeping in step with past historical experience, the organizations established have always delegated to the more powerful members of the community greater responsibility in maintaining the peace. In the League Council, for example, which was the executive organ of that body, as well as in the Security Council of the United Nations, which has primary responsibility for maintaining the peace, permanent great power representation was stipulated and the great power veto was included at their inception. However, it must be pointed out that in the League Council a negative vote cast by any state was sufficient to impede action by that body.

In actual practice, though states have acknowledged the value and possibilities of cooperation through international organization and have attempted to fuse international organization whenever possible into their foreign policy goals, they have never done this at the cost of what they have considered to be their vital national interests. Feelings of a world community, though seemingly stronger under the United Nations, which is a more nearly universal organization than the League ever was, have still been too abstract to warrant or inspire sacrifices, at least in the minds of policy-makers, for nations either close by or far away unless vital national interests were being threatened or jeopardized.

However, when great power cooperation is not forthcoming, decisive action against any aggressor has proved impossible. The collective security feature of international organization pivots on the willingness of the great powers to act in concert for the benefit of the international community. Naturally, political tension or competition between or among the states in this grouping, either within or without the organization, is reflected in their ability or inability to cooperate for the universal goals for which the organization is striving and in which their unique position in the gallery of states has given them a privileged role. Thus, by its very nature the collective security system, with its privileged role for the great powers, was never meant to be and can never be directed against an erring great power, at least through the medium of the organization. Only by combinations outside the organization comprising power greater than its own can a great power be thwarted. Because of this the collective security feature of international organization has proved to be less effective than its staunchest supporters would have wished. The experiences of the League and the United Nations therefore reflect a dismal series of failures whenever international coercion was attempted against a great power: Italy during the Corfu incident of 1923, Japan in Manchuria, and Italy in Ethiopia. The only times it has worked was when smaller powers not allied with any great power were involved. It was this unique combination of factors that explains the League's major success in 1925 against the Greeks after their foray into Bulgaria.[1] As to the U.N., the organization's assistance to South Korea, which was really more a case of collective defense than collective security, was not taken under the Security Council's security provisions but was based on a recommendation of the Council to the member states—a recommendation in no way obligatory—made possible by the fortuitous absence of the Russian representative. The U.N.'s ad hoc peacekeeping operations, not envisaged in the Charter, have been

1. James Barros, "The Greek–Bulgarian Incident of 1925: The League of Nations and the Great Powers," *Proceedings of the American Philosophical Society, 106* (Aug. 27, 1964), 354–85.

developed in an attempt to handle situations which are not questions of security and the maintenance of territorial integrity but which would nevertheless be dangerous if allowed to fester or continue uncontrolled (Sinai, Congo, Cyprus, and one might wish to include also the role played by observer groups in Israel, Lebanon, Kashmir, and Yemen). Even here the question of financing these operations, basically a political and not a legal question, has limited their future range and effectiveness. Indeed, it would appear that the sanctionist feature of international organization has been nothing more than a great myth which has often mesmerized policy-maker and public alike. It had more dedicated supporters outside the organization than inside. It appears that Sir Eric Drummond, who was to serve longer as Secretary-General than any of his successors, was wary of coercion through international organization.[2] He viewed the purpose of the organization in more conservative terms. Drummond believed that the role of international organization was to build up "a system of international cooperation," and by so doing "permanently to maintain the peace of the world." It was not merely peaceful settlement that was important but having the organization do everything possible "to build up a tradition and a practice that will prevent dangerous disputes from developing in the future." [3] In its settlement of the Aland question the League fulfilled both of these purposes.

But recourse to international organization's peaceful procedures also serves a number of other important political functions. Rather than have a complainant state immediately resort to force after conventional bilateral negotiations have failed, it offers to the state another means of continuing the struggle. It increases the number of options for the policy-maker, an important consideration if the complainant state's options have been exhausted or if it is locked in conflict with a much more powerful state, and the ultimate alternative is resort to force. Certainly this was true in the Aland question in the sense that the next logical step, after the collapse of Finno-Swedish negotiations in the early summer of 1920, appeared to be a resort to force by the Swedes—an awesome

2. See Drummond's attitude on the question of sanctions in ibid., p. 385.

3. Appendix C in James Barros, *The Corfu Incident of 1923: Mussolini and the League of Nations* (Princeton, Princeton University Press, 1965), p. 317.

decision for a country that had painfully acquired a reputation for neutrality in world affairs generally and in Europe particularly. Palmstierna's actions, as we have seen, were therefore geared to forcing the English and the French to bring the issue to the League themselves. For Palmstierna to have submitted the question would have perhaps jeopardized the government's position with the electorate and with the Riksdag, and would also have been a blow to Sweden's prestige—all of which was avoided by Lord Curzon's appeal.

The struggle that then commences within the organization becomes one of words and procedure. It concentrates on influencing important personalities and delegations, and a war of maneuver between the contesting parties continues unceasingly. Moreover, recourse to the organization makes it possible for the complainant government to mend its political fences at home. It answers the charges of its critics by pointing out to the electorate that the struggle has not ceased, that it has not accepted the negative reply of the other party, and has indeed appealed the dispute to a higher authority.

The organization also offers a convenient option for other powers who, during the inconclusive bilateral negotiations, attempted to mediate or conciliate the dispute. It allows them a forum through which their activities can continue apace, as it did for the British and French in the Aland question. It also becomes a convenient escape mechanism which they can invoke when they are pressed by either one side or the other for political support. The reply, "Why not take it to the League or to the United Nations"? is conveniently offered when states are pressed for a definite commitment—an approach used by Lord Curzon and the British unendingly from the Versailles negotiations until the Aland question was appealed to the League in the summer of 1920.

Once the dispute is taken to the organization there is nothing to keep it from being taken there again and again. Peaceful settlement through international organization depends primarily upon the willingness of the parties to settle the dispute, since a solution for peaceful settlement was, under the League, as it is under the United Nations, merely a recommendation with no binding force.

The fact that the League Council solved the Aland question was, as we have seen, made possible by a unique combination of factors not likely to be often repeated. For the Swedish delegation at Geneva in 1921, diplomatically isolated, supported by a weak government at home, and incapable of acting unilaterally, the alternatives posed were the choice between the desirable and the possible. The desirable was Swedish acquisition of the Aland Islands. But this was not possible following the Commission of Inquiry's report, which the League Council and especially the British and the French were willing to support. To have continued the struggle, ignoring the compromise solution offered, raised the question whether the attention of the Swedish public, whose interest in the question was flagging, could or would be continually focused on the issue for years to come. And even if it could be done, would it be worth it? In the long run it would have made no sense considering the strained relations that would develop with Finland, a country with whom the Swedes were tied by history and religion, and who from a geopolitical point of view was Sweden's buffer and shield against the menace from the East. On the other hand, the compromise offered was possible and went a long way toward satisfying some of Sweden's legitimate demands: neutralization of the island group and extensive guarantees to the Alanders, who received the most far-reaching minority rights enjoyed by any group in Europe. Thus Swedish security would be protected, as well as Swedish culture and nationality in the Aland archipelago, and a normalization of relations with Finland would be made possible—a normalization deeply desired by both sides.

In practice, most disputes of this nature which have reached the League or the United Nations have come to no definitive settlement. But the mere fact that they reached the organization, essentially for reasons already mentioned, has often led to a release in tension which, if allowed to accumulate, could have led to an impulsive action to be regretted by all. In a sense the endless debates in the League over Danzig, minority treatment, Polish–Lithuanian affairs, etc., and those in the United Nations over Kashmir, decolonization, Southern Africa, Israeli–Arab border problems, Cyprus, etc., fill a psychological need to explode, and fortunately the very existence of the organ allows the explosion to be verbal rather than military. In fact, the delay caused by recourse to the organization has often gained the valuable time needed to quiet tempers and enable the slow wheels of diplomacy to attain some control over the situation, as in the Aland question, to pick an example from an earlier period, or as in the case of the Turkish bombings in Cyprus in the summer of 1964. International relations, like life, are never static, and a problem insolvable today may with time not only be solvable but even disappear as an irritant in the international community, as witness again the Aland question, or the questions of Trieste and the Greek civil war.

Therefore, the role the organization plays, not only for the accused state and the complainant state but also for the neutral state and the states interested in continuing their mediatory and conciliatory actions through the organization, must be examined within a total international and domestic political process. The organization becomes an instrument of state whose principles can be appealed to, manipulated, or invoked, all for the purpose of serving the policy goals of the state or states in question. On the other hand, during the last seven decades international organization has also developed as another actor with an important role to play in the international community. Its very presence acts as a buffer, allowing it to play the role of the impartial third party, or as a sounding board, allowing the struggle to continue in a peaceful fashion.

In particular its chief officer, the Secretary-General, has assumed greater initiative and responsibility and has become more politically active, than was, let us say, Sir Eric Drummond. Though Drummond interpreted his office conservatively, viewing it essentially as an administrative position, it would appear from recent evidence[4] and from his actions during the Aland question, especially on the problem of what type of men and what men in particular were going to comprise the Commission of Inquiry, that Drummond was more forceful and active behind the scenes than most people have thought or than prior writers have given

4. Barros, "The Greek–Bulgarian Incident of 1925: The League of Nations and the Great Powers," 362–63.

him credit for. The greater role of the Secretary-General in the United Nations is, of course, partly due to his stronger position under the Charter, but the bipolar world and the growth of Afro-Asian membership in the organization has also led to a greater delegation of responsibility to the Secretary-General by the constituent parts of the organ, especially in peace-keeping operations, and it has seemingly given him a power base on which he can depend for support if his activities irritate a member state and especially a great power. Relaxation in East–West tensions, however, might reverse this trend. For in the end, no Secretary-General can survive if placed in confrontation with a great power, as Trygve Lie quickly learned during the Korean experience and as Dag Hammarskjöld also learned when he was attacked by the Russians over his handling of the Congo operation. Drummond, of course, avoided this situation by staying out of the limelight and acting behind the scenes. However, it has to be kept in mind that the period between wars in which he operated was still a classic balance-of-power world in which the Secretary-General had little room for maneuver and with nothing akin to an Afro-Asian block to depend on for support.

Both of the international organizations established during this century were based on the experience of their drafters. The people at Paris in 1919 wove into the League Covenant all the experiences and ad hoc institutions that European history and practice had produced, stretching from the Peace of Westphalia and even before. And the drafters of the United Nations Charter? They, too, built on previous foundations, and these were the League's interwar experiences. An actual examination would show that the similarities between the League and the United Nations are far greater than their differences. The basic building blocks in both of these institutions, however, have been the sovereign nation states, which, rather than diminishing in importance, have in fact grown, demanding from their citizens, regardless of constitutional structure or form of government, the highest political loyalty. Thus both institutions have been constructed by political entities, all of whom in theory are legally equal and all of whom, correspondingly, are free agents in an organization to which they have surrendered not a fraction of their sovereignty. The anarchy that therefore often manifests itself within the organization is only a reflection of the anarchy that pervades the international community. The lack of success mirrored by the organ in collective security matters or in its failures to bring about peaceful settlement even when only minor powers are involved, though discouraging, is only an indication of a deeper problem. The problem is not only the uncompromising nationalism of our day but the fact that, even after two terrible wars which have racked the world to its foundations, power and only power is still the deciding factor in interstate relations. No peaceful settlement yet devised by an international organization has ever been accepted by the parties for altruistic reasons. It was power considerations that decided the Aland question, and it is power considerations that decide all questions in the international community, regardless of whether or not they are submitted to an international organ. Modern international organization has never been established with the purpose of inevitably being a substitute for the nation-state system. Instead, it was established to work within that system as best it could by taking into account the power realities that move it. Its successes, therefore, are the successes of the states who are willing to use it, and its failures a reflection of the power factor, which could not be dislodged or compromised. Acceptance of the fact that international organization works within an anarchic power system is the first step toward an understanding of its limitations and possibilities and makes possible greater toleration toward its failures and shortcomings in the field of peaceful settlement. Indeed, to blind oneself to this fact is to be myopic to one of the basic realities of the international community. Until the members of this community are moved by some higher goals or values, which does not appear to be in the offing for the immediate future, the process of peaceful settlement will continue to operate, whether for good or for evil, within this context and Hobbes' observation that "*potestas non veritas facit legem*" (power not truth makes law) will still be the order of the day.

APPENDICES

Appendix A

January 8, 1915

Le Gouvernement Impérial me charge de faire à Votre Excellence la communication suivante: Le Gouvernement Russe croit savoir que la flotte allemande profitant de la prochaine congélation du skärgord d'Aland aurait l'intention d'occuper l'archepel d'Aland afin de s'en servir comme base d'opérations contre les côtes du Golfe Finois et aussi pour empêcher tout trafic maritime entre la Russie et la Suède. Dans le but de contrecarrer ce projet d'attaque et pour assurer autant que possible la navigation commerciale entre la Russie et la Suède dans le Golfe Bothnique, les autorites russes prennent des mesures particulières pour la défense de l'archipel d'Aland. Le Gouvernement Impérial croit de son devoir d'en prévenir le Gouvernement Royal d'une façon strictement confidentielle, en appuyant sur le fait que toutes ces mesures ont un caractère exclusivement défensif et pour le temps de la guerre. Le Gouvernement Impérial espère que si, malgré le strict secret dans lequel sont prises ces mesures elles étaient quand même ébruitées, le Gouvernement Royal s'emploirerait à calmer l'opinion publique suédoise au sujet du caractère des mesures précitées et des intentions exclusivement défensives du Gouvernement Russe.

Appendix B

Les Ministeres de France et d'Angleterre sont autorisés à confirmer les assurances antérieurement données au Gouvernement Royal par le Ministre de Russie et à déclarer que leurs Gouvernements respectifs ont également reçu du Gouvernement Impérial l'assurance que les mesures aux quelles la Russie a dû recourir dans les îles d'Aland ont un caractère exclusivement défensif et n'ont été prises que pour la durée de la guerre.

Bibliography

Unpublished Sources

Balfour, Lord, Personal papers and letters, Department of Manuscripts, The British Museum, London.

Holsti, Rudolf, Memoirs and recollections of Rudolf Holsti: Abridgment of the author's memoirs, MS, Hoover Library, Stanford University.

Fisher, Herbert A. L., Diary, personal papers and letters, Bodleian Library, Oxford University.

Lansing, Robert, Diary, personal papers and letters, Manuscripts Division, Library of Congress, Washington, D.C.

League of Nations, Aland Islands Dossiers, in Archives Division, United Nations Library, Palais des Nations, Geneva, Switzerland.

National Archives of the United States, Foreign Affairs Division, Washington, D. C., *Procès-verbaux* of the Commission on Baltic Affairs of the Paris Peace Conference 1919, Record Group 256.

———, Foreign Affairs Division, Washington, D.C., Reports and papers of the American commission to negotiate peace at Paris, 1918–1919, Record Group 256.

———, Foreign Affairs Division, Washington, D. C., Reports and papers of American diplomatic missions overseas, 1914–1921, Record Group 59.

Polk, Frank L., Diary, personal papers and letters, Sterling Library, Yale University.

Public Record Office, London, Minutes of the meetings of the British Cabinets, 1920–1921, Cabinet Record Group 21.

———, Reports and papers of the British delegation at the Paris Peace Conference, 1919, Foreign Office Record Group 608.

———, Reports and papers of British diplomatic missions overseas, 1914–1921, Foreign Office Record Group 371.

White, Henry, Personal papers and letters, Manuscripts Division, Library of Congress, Washington, D.C.

Wilson, Woodrow, Personal papers and letters, Manuscripts Division, Library of Congress, Washington, D.C.

Official Documentation

Dnevnik Ministerstva Inostrannykh del za 1915–1916 gg (The journal of the Ministry of Foreign Affairs for 1915–1916) [The journal of

Baron Mavriky Fabianovich von Shilling], *Krasnyi arkhiv* (Red archives), *32* (1929), 3–87.

L'expédition suédoise de secours aux îles d'Aland en 1918. Exposé rédigé d'après les documents officiels en réponse aux observations du gouvernement finlandais et M. W. van der Vlugt, professeur de droit à l'université de Leyde, Stockholm, 1921.

Finland, Ministeriet för Utrikesärendena, *La garde civique de Nystad à Aland et l'expédition suédoise à Aland en 1918,* Helsinki, Imprimerie du Gouvernement, 1921.

———, Ministeriet för Utrikesärendena, *La question des îles d'Aland (Octobre 1920),* Helsingfors, Imprimerie du Gouvernement, 1920.

France, Chambre des députés, *Journal Officiel de la Republique Française,* Chambre des députés, *Débats parlementaires.*

———, Ministère des Affaires Étrangères, Commission de publication des documents relatifs aux origines de la guerre de 1914, *Documents diplomatiques français,* Paris, Imprimerie Nationale, 1929–1936, 3d ser., 11 vols.

Germany, Auswärtiges Amt, *Die grosse Politik der europäischen Kabinette, 1871–1914,* ed. Johannes Lepsius, Albrecht M. Bartholdy, and Friedrich Thimme, Berlin, Deutsche Verlagsgesellschaft für Politik, 1922–1927, 40 vols.

Great Britain, *Hansard's Parliamentary Debates,* 3d ser.

———, *Parliamentary Debates,* 4th ser.

———, Foreign Office, *British and Foreign State Papers,* London, Ridgway, and subsequently H. M. Stationery Office, 1841—, 162 vols.

———, Foreign Office, *British Documents on the Origins of the War, 1898–1914,* ed. G. P. Gooch and Harold Temperley, London, H. M. Stationery Office, 1926–1938, 11 vols.

———, Foreign Office, *Documents on British Foreign Policy, 1919–1939,* ed. E. L. Woodward, Rohan Butler, and J. P. T. Bury, London, H. M. Stationery Office, 1947—, 1st ser., 13 vols.

———, Foreign Office Historical Section Handbooks, *The Åland Islands,* London, H. M. Stationery Office, 1920.

Italy, Ministero degli Affari Esteri, Commissione per la Pubblicazione dei Documenti Diplomatici, *I documenti diplomatici italiani,* Roma, Libreria dello Stato, 1956—, 6th ser., 1 vol.

League of Nations, *The Aaland Islands Question; report submitted to the Council of the League of Nations by the Commission of Rapporteurs* (Document du Conseil B 7. 21/68/106, Genève, le 16 avril 1921), Genève, Imprimerie Kundig, 1921.

———, *Official Journal* (1921).
———, *Official Journal,* spec. suppl. no. 1 (Aug. 1920).
———, *Official Journal,* spec. suppl. no. 3 (Oct. 1920).
———, Council, *Minutes of the Seventh Session of the Council of the League of Nations Held in London, July 9–12, 1920.*
———, Council, *Minutes of the Eighth Session of the Council of the League of Nations Held in San Sebastian, July 30–August 5, 1920.*
———, Council, *Minutes of the Ninth Session of the Council of the League of Nations Held in Paris, September 16–20, 1920.*
———, Council, *Minutes of the Tenth Session of the Council of the League of Nations Held in Brussels, October 20–28, 1920.*
———, Council, *Minutes of the Thirteenth Session of the Council of the League of Nations Held in Geneva, June 17–June 28, 1921.*
Russia, Komissiia po Izdaniiu Diplomaticheskikh Dokumentov, *Dokumenty vneshnei politiki SSSR,* Moscow, State Publishing House, 1957–, 10 vols.
———, Komissiia po Izdaniiu Dokumentov Epokhi Imperializma, *Die internationalen Beziehungen im Zeitalter des Imperialismus; Dokumente aus den Archiven der zarischen und der provisorischen Regierung,* ed. Otto Hoetzsch, Berlin, R. Hobbing, 1931–1943, 1st ser., 5 vols.; 2d ser., 3 vols.; 3rd ser., 4 vols.
Sweden, Sjöförsvarsdepartementet, *Ålandsuppgörelsen,* Stockholm, Norstedt & Söner, 1918.
———, Utrikesdepartementet, *Ålandsfrågan inför Nationernas Förbund,* Stockholm, Norstedt & Söner, 1920.
U. S., Department of State, *Papers Relating to the Foreign Relations of the United States, 1918, Russia,* Washington, D.C., Government Printing Office, 1931–1932, 3 vols.
———, *Papers Relating to the Foreign Relations of the United States, 1919, Russia,* Washington, D.C., Government Printing Office, 1937.
———, *Papers Relating to the Foreign Relations of the United States, 1919. The Paris Peace Conference,* Washington, D.C., Government Printing Office, 1942–1947, 13 vols.
———, *Papers Relating to the Foreign Relations of the United States, 1920,* Washington, D.C., Government Printing Office, 1935–1936, 3 vols.
———, *Proceedings of the Brest-Litovsk Peace Conference,* Washington, D.C., Government Printing Office, 1918.
———, *Texts of the Finland "Peace,"* Washington, D.C., Government Printing Office, 1918.

Unofficial Documentation

Degras, Jane, ed., *Soviet Documents on Foreign Policy,* London, Oxford University Press, 1951–1953, 3 vols.

Dumont, Jean, *Corps universel diplomatique,* Amsterdam, 1726–1731, 8 vols.

Hertslet, Edward, *The Map of Europe by Treaty,* London, Butterworths, 1875–1891, 4 vols.

Magnes, Judah L., ed., *Russia and Germany at Brest-Litovsk,* New York, The Rand School of Social Science, 1919.

Marchand, René, ed., *Un livre noir, diplomatie d'avant-guerre d'après les documents des archives russes,* Paris, Librairie du Travail, 1922–1934, 3 vols.

Martens, G. F. de, *Nouveau recueil de traités,* Gottingue, Librairie de Dieterich, 1817–1841, 16 vols.

———, *Nouveau recueil général de traités,* Gottingue, Librairie de Dieterich, 1843–1875, 20 vols.

Miller, David Hunter, *My Diary at the Conference of Paris,* New York, Appeal Co., 1924, 21 vols.

Stieve, Friedrich, ed., *Iswolski im Weltkriege; der diplomatische Schriftwechsel Iswolskis aus den Jahren 1914–1917; neue Dokumente aus den Geheimakten der russischen Staatsarchiven,* Berlin, Deutsche Verlagsgesellschaft für Politik und Geschichte m.b.h., 1925.

Wegerer, Alfred von, ed., *Das russische Orangebuch von 1914,* Berlin, Deutsche Verlagsgesellschaft für Politik und Geschichte m.b.h., 1925.

Primary Sources

Alströmer, Jonas M., *Diplomatminnen från tio huvudstäder, 1908–1933,* Stockholm, Hökerbergs, 1951.

Andersson, Otto, *Les origines de la question d'Aland; l'Aland en 1917–1918,* Helsingfors, Imprimerie du Gouvernement, 1920.

De Geer, Louis, *Politiska hågkomster från åren 1901–1921,* Stockholm, Norstedt & Söner, 1926.

Donner, Ossian, *Åtta år. Memoaranteckningar från åren 1918–1926,* Oxford, Eng., Oxford University Press, 1927.

Enckell, Carl, *Politiska minnen,* Helsingfors, Söderström, 1956, 2 vols.

Gregory, John D., *On the Edge of Diplomacy; Rambles and Reflections, 1902–1928,* London, Hutchinson, 1929.

Grey, Sir Edward, *Twenty-five Years, 1892–1916,* New York, Frederick A. Stokes, 1925, 2 vols.

Gummerus, Herman, *Sverige och Finland 1917–1918*, Stockholm, Holger Schildt, 1936.

Hellner, Johannes, *Memorandum rörande sveriges politik i förhållande till Finland under tiden från Finlands självständighetsförklaring till det finska inbördeskrigets slut*, Stockholm, Norstedt & Söner, 1936.

———, *Minnen och dagböcker*, Stockholm, Norstedt & Söners, 1960.

Hjelt, Edvard, *Från händelserika år. Upplevelser och minnen*, Helsingfors, Söderström, 1920, 2 vols.

House, Edward M., *The Intimate Papers of Colonel House*, ed. Charles Seymour, New York, Houghton Mifflin, 1926–1928, 4 vols.

Howard, Sir Esme, *Theatre of Life*, Boston, Little, Brown, 1935–1936, 2 vols.

Hübner, Joseph Alexander von, *Neuf ans de souvenirs d'un ambassadeur d'Autriche à Paris sous le second empire 1851–1859*, Paris, Plon-Nourrit, 1904, 2 vols.

Léouzon le Duc, *Les îles d'Aland*, Paris, Hachette, 1854.

Mannerheim, Carl Gustaf, *The Memoirs of Marshal Mannerheim*, trans. Eric Lewenhaupt, New York, E. P. Dutton, 1954.

———, *Minnen*, Stockholm, Norstedt & Söners, 1951–1952, 2 vols.

Morris, Ira Nelson, *From an American Legation*, New York, Alfred A. Knopf, 1923.

Napier, Elers, *The Life and Correspondence of Admiral Sir Charles Napier*, London, Hurst & Blackett, 1862, 2 vols.

Nekludoff, Anatole, *Diplomatic Reminiscences*, trans. Alexandra Paget, London, John Murray, 1920.

Palmstierna, Erik Kule, *Dagjämning, 1920–1921; politiska dagboksanteckningar*, Stockholm, Tidens, 1954.

———, *Orostid; politiska dagboksanteckningar*, Stockholm, Tidens, 1952–1953, 2 vols.

Räikkönen, Erkki, *Svinhufvud the Builder of Finland: An Adventure in Statecraft*, London, Alan Wilmer, 1938.

Reutersward, Pontus, *Generallöjtnanten och envoyén Edvard Brändström svenskt sändebud i Ryssland 1906–1920*, Stockholm, Norstedt & Söners, 1947.

Sazonov, Serge, *Fateful Years 1909–1916*, London, Jonathan Cape, 1928.

Stenroth, Otto, *Ett halvt år som Finlands första utrikesminister*, Helsingfors, Söderström, 1931.

Westermarck, Edward, *Memoires of My Life*, trans. Anna Barwell, London, Allen & Unwin, 1929.

Williams, H. Noel, *The Life and Letters of Admiral Sir Charles Napier,* London, Hutchinson, 1917.

Secondary Sources

Albertini, Luigi, *The Origins of the War of 1914,* trans. and ed. Isabella M. Massey, London, Oxford University Press, 1952–1957, 3 vols.

Albion, Robert G., *Forests and Sea Power,* Harvard Economic Studies, 29, Cambridge, Mass., Harvard University Press, 1926.

Barros, James, *The Corfu Incident of 1923: Mussolini and the League of Nations,* Princeton, Princeton University Press, 1965.

Cullberg, Albin, *La politique du roi Oscar I pendant la guerre de Crimée,* Stockholm, Författarens, 1912–1926, 2 vols.

Danielson-Kalmari, Johan R., *La question des îles d'Aland de 1914 à 1920,* Helsinki, Imprimerie du Gouvernement, 1921.

Gelfand, Lawrence E., *The Inquiry: American Preparations for Peace, 1917–1919,* New Haven, Yale University Press, 1963.

Hallendorff, Carl, and Schück, Adolf, *History of Sweden,* trans. Lajla Yapp, London, Cassell, 1929.

Jackson, J. Hampden, *Finland,* New York, Macmillan, 1940.

Hannula, Joose O., *Finland's War of Independence,* London, Faber & Faber, 1939.

Nicolson, Sir Harold, *Peacemaking 1919,* London, Constable, 1933.

Pink, Gerhard P., *The Conference of Ambassadors (1920–1931),* Geneva Studies, Vol. XII, Nos. 4–5, 1942, Geneva, Geneva Research Centre, 1942.

Reid, Helen D., *International Servitudes in Law and Practice,* Chicago, University of Chicago Press, 1932.

Scott, Franklin D., *The United States and Scandinavia,* Cambridge, Mass., Harvard University Press, 1960.

Sjoestedt, Erik, *La question des îles d'Aland,* Paris, Grasset, 1919.

Smith, Clarence J., *Finland and the Russian Revolution 1917–1922,* Athens, University of Georgia Press, 1958.

Söderhjelm, J. O., *Démilitarisation et neutralisation des îles d'Aland en 1856 et 1921,* Helsingfors, 1928.

Tingsten, Herbert, *The Debate on the Foreign Policy of Sweden 1918–1939,* trans. Joan Bulman, London, Oxford University Press, 1949.

Váli, Ferenc A., *Servitudes of International Law,* 2d ed. London, Stevens, 1958.

Vlugt, Willem van der, *La question des îles d'Aland considérations suggérées par le rapport des juristes,* Paris, Dumoulin, 1920.

———, *Réponse au livre bleu du gouvernement de Suède,* Leyde, E. J. Brill, 1921.

Ward, A. W., and Gooch, G. P., eds., *The Cambridge History of British Foreign Policy, 1783–1919,* Cambridge, Eng., The University Press, 1922–1923, 3 vols.

Wolfers, Arnold, *Britain and France between Two Wars,* New York, Harcourt, Brace, 1940.

Wuorinen, John H., *A History of Finland,* New York, Columbia University Press, 1965.

Zimmern, Alfred, *The League of Nations and the Rule of Law, 1918–1935,* 2d ed. rev. London, Macmillan, 1939.

Articles

Barros, James, "The Greek-Bulgarian Incident of 1925: The League of Nations and the Great Powers," *Proceedings of the American Philosophical Society, 106* (Aug. 27, 1964), 354–85.

Brown, Philip Marshall, "The Aaland Islands Question," *The American Journal of International Law, 15* (1921), 268–72.

Gregory, Charles Noble, "The Neutralization of the Aaland Islands," *The American Journal of International Law, 17* (1923), 64–76.

Holsti, Rudolf, "Finland and the Baltic Region," *Proceedings of the Institute of World Affairs, 19* (Dec. 1941), 134–43.

Ramm, Agatha, "The Crimean War," in J. P. T. Bury, ed., *The New Cambridge Modern History,* Cambridge, Eng., The University Press, 1960, *10,* 468–92.

Tarlé, E., "La diplomatie pendant la guerre de Crimée et le congrès de Paris (1853–1856)," in Vladimir P. Potemkin, ed., *Histoire de la diplomatie,* trans. Xenia Pamphilova and Michel Eristov, Paris, Librairie de Médicis, 1946, *1,* 435–58.

Vallentin, Hugo, "Sweden and the Åland Islands," *The New Europe, 6* (21 Feb. 1918), 184–88.

Newspapers

Le Figaro

Isvestia

Le Matin

New York Times

Pravda

Le Temps

The Times (London)

France, Ministère des Affaires Étrangères, *Bulletin périodique de la presse scandinave*

Index